EXTREME SURVIVORS

EXTREME SURVIVORS

60 of the World's Most Extreme Survival Stories

EXTREME SURVIVORS

Collins
An imprint of HarperCollins Publishers
Westerhill Road, Bishopbriggs, Glasgow G64 2QT

Paperback Edition 2012

Printed in Hong Kong

British Library Cataloguing in Publication Data
A catalogue record for this book is available from the British Library

ISBN 978 0 00 748277 1
Imp 001

All mapping in this publication is generated from Collins Bartholomew digital databases.
Collins Bartholomew, the UK's leading independent geographical information supplier, can provide
a digital, custom, and premium mapping service to a variety of markets.
For further information:
Tel: +44 (0) 141 306 3606
e-mail: **collinsbartholomew@harpercollins.co.uk**
or visit our website at: **www.collinsbartholomew.com**

If you would like to comment on any aspect of this book, please write to:
Collins Maps, HarperCollins Publishers, Westerhill Road, Bishopbriggs, Glasgow G64 2QT
e-mail: **collinsmaps@harpercollins.co.uk**
or visit our website at: **www.collinsmaps.com**
twitter.com/CollinsMaps

CONTENTS

SHIPWRECKS

HOSTAGES

FOREWORD

Having spent my life in so many dangerous and at times unforgiving terrains, I have learnt that to come out the other side alive you have to find the spirit to keep going, whatever the cost. Each of the stories in this book tells of that same spirit in those who endured. As individuals we can not conquer a mountain or a storm, but we can learn to harness nature's elements, and our own limitations, to see almost any ordeal through.

Appropriate preparation and experience are essential for any expedition, but they are no guarantee of safety. Even the wariest of adventurers can fall foul to difficult conditions, faulty equipment or lapses in concentration. Only by keeping calm and finding confidence in their own abilities will they stand a chance of passing through the constant threats thrown up by nature. Within this book are stories of those who ventured out with an awareness and appreciation of the danger ahead, but who faltered, rallied and survived: Joe Simpson's horrific fall on Siula Grande in 1985; Aron Ralston, trapped by rocks and forced to amputate his arm; Ernest Shackleton's epic South Georgia expedition and his determination to return his stranded men alive.

Alongside these, are the stories of great difficulty and suffering, but endured by those who survived without that experience and equipment. These are the horror stories that defy the statistics. Tales of plane crashes, kidnappings and prison escapes, the stories of 'everyday' people unprepared for the hardest conditions: good samaritan Ricky Megee, who survived an astonishing seventy-one days by consuming lizards, leeches and frogs after being left for dead; Cambodian journalist Dith Pran's four years of starvation and torture under the Khmer Rouge, and his desperate escape when the regime was overthrown; the three young Australian girls who walked for 1,600 km through the desert to find salvation.

There are so many compelling character traits to admire in all the survivors featured in this book, even in the 'bad-guys' – the bank robbers and prisoners who escaped or the hijacker who vanished into legend. These people, too, show the enduring spirit for survival, adventure and for freedom. They were motivated to escape whatever it was that restrained them. It is the same motivation felt by many adventurers to avoid the nine-to-five, the desk job and the pension scheme. Fear of injury and death must be ever-present during a daring escape, just as on a dangerous climb, but the fear of the mundane, of accepting the humdrum, can be far more terrifying. And, of course, there is a price to pay for high adventure – in unending sweat, fear, discomfort and pain.

But no one ever said it would be easy.

BEAR GRYLLS

BEAR GRYLLS

Soviet submarine *K-19* 208

Hugo Grotiu[s]
'Bonnie Prince Charlie' 118 92
Mary, Queen of Scots
Gunther Plüschow 126
Antonio Ferrara 112
Operation Frankton 138 12
Leo Bretholtz
Richard Charrington

Mt St. Helens eruption 40
Dan Cooper 106
Aron Ralston
Albert & Rita Chretien 88 58
Storm King Mountain fire 50

Jasper Schuringa 250

Flight 1549 Hudson crash 54 76

9/11 terrorist attacks

Escape from Alcatraz 102

Apollo 13 30

Captain James Riley 182

Steven Callahan 218

Robert Tapscott & 200
Roy Widdicombe

Íngrid Betancourt 240

Henri 'Papillon' Charrière 98

Maurice & Maralyn Bailey 212

Juliane Köpcke 32

Joe Simpson 44

Poon Lim 202

Whale ship *Essex* 188

Chilean miners rescue 80

Flight 571 Andes crash 34

Commodore George Anson 174

Ernest Shackleton 192

SURVIVAL 14
PRISON 92
WAR 118
SHIPWRECKS 174
HOSTAGES 230

10

Robert Bartlett
16

156 Cornelius Rost

an Baalsrud
142

The Great Escape
46

34 Natascha Kampusch

28 Gary Powers

Captain Anthony Farrar-Hockley
162

Tōkyō earthquake
20

Terry Anderson
230

246 Roy Hallums

William Brydon

122   24

236

Wilco van Rooijen
68

Climbing Haramosh

150

ben van Assouw

Naheeda Bi

Heinrich Harrer

USS *Indianapolis*
204

Dith Pran
168

252

Freddy Spencer Chapman

134

Freighter *Maersk Alabama*

Bahia Bakari
74

Mutiny on the *Bounty*
62   178

William Shotton

Ricky Megee

196   198

Cargo steamer *Trevessa*

Aboriginal relocation   22

14 Douglas Mawson

11

SURVIVAL

Another Antarctic Winter

EXPLORER DOUGLAS MAWSON WAS STRANDED ON THE ANTARCTIC ICE WHEN HIS COLLEAGUE FELL INTO A CREVASSE. WITH FEW PROVISIONS HE WAS FORCED TO EAT HIS HUSKIES TO SURVIVE. HE TREKKED 480 KM (300 MILES) BACK TO BASE ONLY TO MISS HIS SUPPLY SHIP BY HOURS, FORCING HIM TO ENDURE ANOTHER WINTER OF BRUTAL CONDITIONS.

DATE:
1912–13

SITUATION:
ANTARCTIC EXPLORATION

CONDITION OF CONFINEMENT:
STRANDED ON THE ICE

DURATION OF CONFINEMENT:
SEVERAL WEEKS

MEANS OF ESCAPE:
TREKKING, EATING HUSKIES

NO. OF ESCAPEES:
1

DANGERS:
FREEZING TO DEATH, STARVATION, FALLING INTO A CREVASSE, VITAMIN A POISONING

EQUIPMENT:
HUSKIES, SLEDGE, SOME PROVISIONS

ABOVE RIGHT
Australian geologist and Antarctic explorer Douglas Mawson (1882–1958).

Way down south

The average wind speed at Cape Denison was 80 km/h (50 mph). It regularly gusted at 320 km/h (200 mph). But Douglas Mawson and his colleagues would have to get used to it. For the next two years this was going to be their home.

Mawson was born in Yorkshire in 1882 but grew up in Australia. A geologist by education, he had been bitten early by the exploring bug. He was the principal geologist on an expedition to the New Hebrides (now Vanuatu), and he wrote one of the first major geological studies on the area. He was just 21 at the time.

The early twentieth century was the age of the great Antarctic explorers. In 1910 Mawson had turned down an invitation from Robert Falcon Scott to join his ill-fated Terra Nova Expedition.

Instead, Mawson organized his own adventure, the Australian Antarctic Expedition. This would carry out geographical exploration and scientific studies of King George V Land and Adelie Land, the part of the Antarctic continent directly south of Australia. At the time this region was almost entirely unexplored. Mawson also wanted to include a visit to the South Magnetic Pole.

The Australian Antarctic Expedition

Mawson and his team departed from Hobart on 2 December 1911, on board the SY *Aurora*. They landed at the wind-buffeted Cape Denison on Commonwealth Bay on 8 January 1912, where they built the hut that would serve as their Main Base for the expedition. They also established a Western camp on the ice shelf in Queen Mary Land.

Mawson had initially wanted to explore the area by air and had brought the first aircraft to Antarctica, a Vickers monoplane. But it suffered damage and the engine struggled in the cold. All their exploring would have to be done on foot, with dogs and sledges. However, by the time they had fully established their camp, the weather was worsening and it was soon too severe to travel in. The men stayed in the hut to see out the long, dark months of an Antarctic winter.

Sledging to disaster

By November 1912, the nearly constant blizzards had eased and the exploration program could begin. Mawson divided the men into seven parties: five would operate from the Main Base and two from the Western camp.

Mawson himself would lead a three-man sledging team along

with Xavier Mertz and Lieutenant Belgrave Ninnis. They set out east on 10 November 1912, to survey King George V Land. For five weeks all went smoothly. They mapped the coastline and collected many fine geological samples. Then, as they were crossing what was to become the Ninnis Glacier, disaster struck.

Mawson was driving the sledge, which spread his weight evenly over the ice, and Mertz was skiing. But Ninnis was on foot and his weight breached the surface. He plunged into a snow-covered crevasse, taking the tent, most of their rations, and the six best dogs with him. Mertz and Mawson could see one dead and one injured dog on a ledge 50 m (160 ft) down the massive crevasse, but Ninnis was gone.

A long way from home

Mawson and Mertz said a brief service for their colleague and then turned back. They had a primus stove and fuel but only one week's provisions and no food for the dogs. They were separated from home by 480 km (300 miles) of the most brutal terrain on earth.

Their first goal was to get to a spare tent cover that they had stashed behind them on their journey. To reach this they sledged continuously for twenty-seven hours. They rigged up a frame for this outer shell of canvas from skis and a theodolite.

***

Mawson's teams had explored large areas of the Antarctic coast and discovered much about its geology, biology and meteorology. They had also accurately determined the location of the South Magnetic Pole.

***

The trek back was slow going and they soon ran out of food. They had no choice but to kill their huskies one by one and eat them. There was hardly any meat on the animals, and even though they mixed it with a little of their tinned food, the men were almost constantly hungry. The bones, guts and sinew that they could not digest they gave to the remaining dogs.

Poisoned

Mawson and Mertz were so desperately hungry that they ate the huskies' livers. Unfortunately, these contain a toxic concentration of Vitamin A. Although Vitamin A was only identified in 1917, Inuit peoples had long known about the poisonous nature of these organs. The livers of polar bears, seals and walrus are similarly dangerous.

The two men got very ill very quickly on their journey back. They were racked with sickness, diarrhoea, abdominal pain, dizziness and became irrational. Their skin turned yellow and began to peel from their muscles. Their hair and nails fell out.

Mertz ate more liver than Mawson because he found the dog's tough muscles too hard to eat and he suffered the worst. As well as the physical deterioration, he became gripped with madness. He would lie curled up in his sleeping bag refusing to move, or would rage violently. At one point Mawson had to sit on Mertz's chest and seize his arms to stop him wrecking their tent. He even bit off the tip of his own frostbitten little finger. After several major seizures, Mertz finally fell into a coma and died on 8 January 1913.

Walking home alone

That left Douglas Mawson to trek the last 160 km (100 miles) alone. At one point he tumbled into a deep crevasse. He was only saved from plummeting to certain death by his sledge, which jammed itself into the ice above him. He then hauled himself back up the slender rope that attached him to the sledge.

***

In 1916, the American Geographical Society awarded Mawson the David Livingstone Centenary Medal. He was later awarded the OBE and was also knighted.

***

Mawson finally made it back to Cape Denison in February, but further misfortune awaited him. The *Aurora* had sailed away just a few hours before. Mawson and the six men who had stayed behind to look for him were forced to spend a second winter in the brutal arms of Cape Denison until they were finally rescued in December 1913.

Douglas Mawson peering over the edge of the crevasse into which his comrade Lt. Ninnis has fallen along with his sledge, dogs and supplies.

Death in the Unknown North

IN 1913 A SCIENTIFIC VOYAGE TO THE UNEXPLORED HIGH ARCTIC BECAME TRAPPED IN THE ICE. AFTER A LONG DRIFT ACROSS THE BEAUFORT AND CHUKCHI SEAS THE SHIP WAS CRUSHED AND SUNK. THE CREW AND SCIENTIFIC STAFF WERE FORCED TO SURVIVE ON THE ICE AND THEN ON THE SHORES OF DESOLATE WRANGEL ISLAND.

DATE:
1913

SITUATION:
SHIPWRECK

CONDITION OF CONFINEMENT:
TRAPPED IN ARCTIC ICE, STRANDED ON A BARREN ISLAND

DURATION OF CONFINEMENT:
1 YEAR

MEANS OF ESCAPE:
TREKKING ACROSS ICE FLOES, LIVING WILD, RESCUE

NO. OF ESCAPEES:
20

DANGERS:
HYPOTHERMIA, HUNGER, EXHAUSTION, POLAR BEARS, MURDER

EQUIPMENT:
CAMP EQUIPMENT, RIFLES, SLEDGES, DOGS

ABOVE RIGHT
The vast Arctic landscape from the edge of the Arctic Ocean.

Held fast in a frozen sea

HMCS *Karluk* had been stuck fast in the Arctic ice for more than a month and now expedition leader Vilhjalmur Stefansson knew they would be there all winter. That meant they needed food. So Stefansson made a bold decision – he would leave the ship to command a small hunting party to track and kill caribou. Meanwhile the ship's captain, Robert Bartlett, would look after the scientists, crew and Inuit hunters on board.

It might have been a good idea, had currents in the ice not pushed the ship away as soon as Stefansson was gone. The two parties would never see each other again and for the team on the *Karluk* it was the beginning of a tortuous, year-long struggle for survival.

A million square miles

Vilhjalmur Stefansson was a Canadian-born anthropologist of Icelandic origin who had spent nearly six years studying the Copper Inuit in the icy wilds of Arctic Canada. He returned home in 1912 with an even more adventurous plan: to explore the 'area of a million or so square miles that is represented by white patches on our map, lying between Alaska and the North Pole'.

This area, known as the 'High Arctic', was subject to competing sovereignty claims by Norway, the United States and Canada. Stefansson didn't have too much trouble persuading Canadian Prime Minister Robert Borden to back him financially; the expedition would strengthen Canada's claim to any new islands discovered in the Beaufort Sea. There was only one condition: Stefansson had to depart by June 1913, a tight schedule.

The hasty adventurers

The expedition would head to Herschel Island off the north Yukon coast and there divide into two parties. A Northern Party would sail the converted brigantine *Karluk* further north until it either found land to explore or was stopped by ice. Meanwhile, a Southern Party would carry out surveys and anthropological studies in the Mackenzie River delta.

On board were many expert scientists, but only two of them had polar experience: Alistair Mackay, the medical officer, and James Murray, an oceanographer. Other personnel included William McKinlay, a 24-year-old Glasgow science teacher and Bjarn Mamen, a 20-year-old Norwegian skiing champion.

The *Karluk's* captain, 36-year-old Newfoundland-born Robert Bartlett, had commanded Robert Peary's ship on his 1909 expedition. Bartlett worried that *Karluk* wouldn't be able to withstand sustained ice pressure, and lacked the power to force a passage through the ice. Furthermore, the June deadline meant that Bartlett had to hastily assemble a crew in Esquimault, British Columbia.

Towards Herschel Island

Karluk left Esquimault on 17 June 1913 and by 2 August had rounded Point Barrow, the northernmost point of Alaska. Here the ship first encountered polar ice. She was soon trapped, and drifted slowly eastward for three days before once again reaching open water at Cape Smythe where they picked up two Inuit hunters, Keraluk and Kataktovik, together with Keraluk's wife Keruk and two young daughters Helen and 3-year-old Mugpi.

> 6 Heaven help us all if
> we failed to reach
> Herschel Island. 9
> **William McKinlay**

Brass plates on the ship's bow were damaged by thick ice and soon she struggled to make headway. On 13 August they were 235 miles (378 km) east of Point Barrow, and still had a similar distance to travel to Herschel Island. They were seized by the ice and began to drift slowly westward;

by 10 September *Karluk* had retreated nearly 100 miles (160 km) towards Point Barrow.

The slow-closing vice

With *Karluk* ice-bound, Stefansson made his big decision. He would lead a six-man party to hunt caribou near the Colville River. He expected to be gone for about ten days and left on 20 September.

But on 23 September the ice floe in which *Karluk* was trapped began to move, and soon the ship was travelling up to 60 miles (97 km) a day to the west. There was no way that Stefansson's party would be able to find their way back to the ship.

Blinding snow and thick mist made it difficult for Bartlett to calculate *Karluk's* position. He also knew that the thickening ice would soon crush and sink the vessel. Bartlett ordered supplies and equipment to be transferred on to the ice. The men spent their time hunting seals and polar bear to boost their supplies.

By mid-November, *Karluk* had started moving southwest, towards the Siberian coast. Within another month they were about 140 miles (230 km) from Wrangel Island. Bartlett led a remarkably positive Christmas celebration, but the optimism was short lived: with the New Year came ominous twanging and drumming sounds from the ice.

On 10 January 1914 there was a loud bang. Bartlett hurried to the engine room and saw water gushing through a 10 feet (3.0 m) gash. He gave the order to abandon ship. The crew rescued as much of the rations as they could before the splintered ship sank. Stranded on the ice were 22 men, one woman, two children, 16 dogs and a cat.

Shipwreck camp

This ragtag group built a snow igloo with a canvas roof and another shelter from packing cases. They had a small kitchen with a stove and enough food for several months. But they were still on a moving ice floe. They would

have to attempt the march to Wrangel Island as soon as the lengthening days brought enough light.

> 6 One was a confirmed drug
> addict ... another suffered
> from venereal disease; and in
> spite of orders that no liquor
> was to be carried, at least two
> smuggled supplies on board. 9
> **McKinlay on the crew of the Karluk**

However, Bartlett was persuaded to let a four-man advance party head out. They left on 21 January and were never seen again.

Another group began to get restless, and on 5 February they, too, departed for Wrangel after demanding a share of supplies from Bartlett. They also gave him a letter absolving him of any responsibility in their initiative. A single scarf was the only evidence of them that was ever found.

For two more weeks the survivors scraped an existence in their snow-bound home. Then Bartlett decided the days were long enough to attempt the trek to Wrangel, which he calculated was 40 miles (64 km) away. In fact it was twice as far.

Bartlett laid supply depots on the route to help his inexperienced colleagues cope with the hazards of ice travel. When he felt they were ready for the main journey he divided them into four teams and sent the first two away on 19 February. Bartlett himself led the last two groups from the camp on 24 February, leaving a note of the party's location in a copper drum in case the camp should drift into an inhabited area.

The ice surface was very broken up and the parties were soon slowed by a series of jagged ridges up to 100 feet (30 m) high. Forced to hack a pathway through these towers of ice, they advanced only 3 miles (5 km) in a week. Exhausted and with many suffering from frostbite, they finally reached land on 12 March, a long, barren spit of sand on the northern shore of Wrangel Island.

ARCTIC OCEAN

Beaufort Sea

4 SHIPWRECK CAMP
The ship drifts west, northwest and then southwest before finally being crushed and sunk 80 miles (128 km) off Wrangel Island.

3 TRAPPED IN THE ICE
The *Karluk* drifts with moving ice, making it impossible for the hunting party to find the vessel.

2 HUNTING PARTY
Stefansson leads a party of six on a caribou hunt on 20 September.

Herschel Island

Wrangel Island

Herald Island

Point Barrow

Prudhoe Bay

5 WRANGEL ISLAND
Two four-man parties are lost marching towards Wrangel, before Bartlett successfully leads the survivors there on 12 March 1914.

Cape Jakan

1 TOWARDS HERSCHEL ISLAND
The *Karluk* rounds Alaska and passes Point Barrow on 2 August 1913. By mid-August it is icebound, 235 miles (378 km) short of Herschel Island.

Point Hope

Chukchi Sea

ALASKA

RUSSIAN FEDERATION

East Cape

Kotzebue Sound

Bering Strait

Chukotskiy Poluostrov

Seward Peninsula

Yukon

Port Clarence

Nome

U. S. A.

6 BARTLETT'S JOURNEY
Bartlett and Kataktovik then make an epic 700 mile (1,100 km) march in awful conditions to Emma Town (near East Cape), to get aid.

St Lawrence Island

St Michael

7 RESCUED AT LAST!
After picking up a lift back to Alaska, Bartlett is finally able to get a ship to rescue the survivors on Wrangel.

Bering Sea

St Matthew Island

Nunivak Island

KILOMETRES	0	100	200	300
MILES	0		100	200

No rest for the captain

Bartlett had planned for the group to just rest on Wrangel Island before moving on to Siberia. However, three men – Mamen, Malloch and Maurer – were injured, and others were so weak and frostbitten that he decided they could not be moved. He and Kataktovik would journey alone: as a pair they could move more quickly, but the fate of the entire party lay on their shoulders.

They left on 18 March, with seven dogs and provisions for 48 days (30 days for the dogs), on the arduous trek towards Siberia. They were in almost constant danger: the ice would often shift and break up around them leaving patches of open water. When they rested, drifting snow would cover their provisions forcing them to waste precious energy digging out their supplies.

On 4 April the pair finally reached land near Cape Jakan on the northern Siberian coast and were amazed to see sledge marks which they followed to a small village of Chukchi indigenous people. The Chukchi received them hospitably, giving the weary travellers shelter and food. On 7 April they set out for East Cape and the villages on the Bering Sea coast. The next three weeks saw the worst weather Bartlett had ever experienced: relentless blizzards, hurricane force winds, and temperatures often below -50 °C (-58 °F). They finally reached Emma Town, a settlement a few miles west of East Cape, on 24 April.

In the 37 days since leaving Wrangel Island, Bartlett and Kataktovik had travelled 700 miles (1,100 km), and all but the last stage of this on foot. Bartlett hitched a lift with a Russian vessel and reached Nome in Alaska on 24 May.

Violence on Wrangel Island

No sooner had Bartlett and Kataktovik left the Wrangel party than arguments broke out over the sharing of food. There were grave shortages of biscuit, pemmican (a compound of dried meat, fat and sugar) and dog food.

> **'The misery and desperation of our situation multiplied every weakness, every quirk of personality, every flaw in character, a thousandfold.'**
> **McKinlay on Wrangel Island**

Frostbite was crippling several of the party and a number of people also suffered from a hideous form of nephritis brought on by badly made pemmican. Malloch died on 17 May, but his tent-mate Mamen was too ill to see to his burial; the body lay beside him for several days, creating a 'frightful smell'. Mamen died ten days later.

The supply of seal meat dwindled and the party was reduced to eating rotten flippers and hide. When summer finally brought birds, men lied about the numbers of eggs they found. On 25 June a gunshot was heard and fireman George Breddy was found dead in his tent. The true cause was never determined, but he was suspected of being the biggest food-thief, and perhaps a cruel justice was delivered.

As August came and the weather turned cold, the miserable souls on Wrangel began to prepare to endure an Arctic winter.

The unlikely rescue

Bartlett, meanwhile, had persuaded the master of a cutter, *Bear*, to help him rescue the stranded party. Unfortunately, *Bear* had several essential stops to make on the way up the Alaskan coast. It was also forced to double back to pick up more coal, and was stopped by ice just 20 miles (32 km) from the island. These delays were heartbreaking for Bartlett, but he managed to persuade the captain of another vessel, *King and Winge*, to head for Wrangel Island and look for the survivors.

The morning of 7 September was wintry and the spirits of the 14 survivors on Wrangel were hopelessly

Mugpi, a 3-year-old girl, was the youngest survivor of the *Karluk* voyage.

low. When the proud salute of a ship's whistle reached their ears and they turned to see *King and Winge* lying a quarter of a mile offshore, many dropped to their knees and wept.

Aftermath

Bartlett was acclaimed as a hero by press and public and was honoured for 'outstanding bravery' by the Royal Geographical Society. However, an admiralty commission censured him for taking *Karluk* into the ice, and for allowing the second party to leave the main group, despite the letter of absolution.

Stefansson's impromptu caribou hunt led to an extended exploration. He finally returned in 1918 after four years' absence, reporting the discovery of land previously unknown even to the Inuit.

He was honoured by the National Geographical Society and was made president of the Explorers Club of New York. In Canada his reception was cooler.

The family of Inuit hunters returned to their former life at Point Barrow. Mugpi, the 3-year-old girl, was the very last survivor of the *Karluk* voyage; she passed away in 2008 after a full life, aged 97.

The Day the World Shook

THE OCEAN LINER *EMPRESS OF AUSTRALIA* WAS LEAVING YOKOHAMA HARBOUR WHEN ONE OF THE MOST DEVASTATING EARTHQUAKES IN HISTORY LEVELLED TŌKYŌ AND THE SURROUNDING AREA. MORE THAN 100,000 PEOPLE DIED IN THE SHOCKS AND THE FIRESTORMS THAT FOLLOWED, BUT THE SHIP'S CREW STAYED TO HELP THOUSANDS MORE SURVIVE THE DISASTER.

DATE:
1923

SITUATION:
EARTHQUAKE

CONDITION OF CONFINEMENT:
ON BOARD AN OCEAN LINER IN A BURNING PORT

DURATION OF CONFINEMENT:
12 DAYS

MEANS OF ESCAPE:
CAPTAIN'S PROFESSIONALISM, INDIVIDUAL COURAGE

NO. OF ESCAPEES:
2,000 PLUS MANY OTHER REFUGEES

DANGERS:
TREMORS, FIRE, DROWNING

EQUIPMENT:
SHIP'S EQUIPMENT

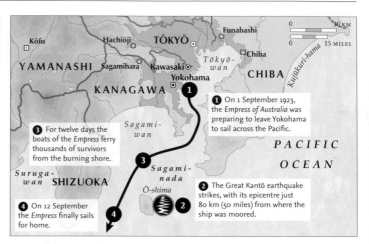

1 On 1 September 1923, the *Empress of Australia* was preparing to leave Yokohama to sail across the Pacific.

2 The Great Kantō earthquake strikes, with its epicentre just 80 km (50 miles) from where the ship was moored.

3 For twelve days the boats of the *Empress* ferry thousands of survivors from the burning shore.

4 On 12 September the *Empress* finally sails for home.

A world turned upside down

The scene could have been taken from a romantic movie: a beautiful ocean liner snug against a wharf, cheering passengers lining her rails, streamers and confetti falling like coloured rain on the hundreds of well-wishers on the dockside.

Seconds later the movie would become a tragedy as one of the most devastating earthquakes in history shattered the scene.

Thousands would die in the initial shocks and the catastrophic fires that followed. But thanks to the cool leadership of the liner's captain and the selfless actions of her crew and passengers, many thousands more would survive.

Disaster on an unprecedented scale

It was 11.55 a.m. on Saturday, 1 September 1923 and the *Empress of Australia* was making ready to depart from her berth at Yokohama, Japan.

Then, without warning, the entire dock moved several feet up in the air. Suddenly it plunged back down again, cracking into pieces. Seized by panic, the people screamed and ran, but there was nowhere to go. The dock fell into dust beneath their feet.

More shocks hit, making the land around the bay roll in waves over 2 m (7 ft) high, as if it were the ocean.

> **The 23,000-ton liner was tossed from side to side like a toy boat in a bath.**

The sky was lit a sickly orange from the fires now raging across the city, and a low, near-continuous rumbling sound filled the air as hundreds of buildings collapsed into rubble.

The *Empress* had been hit by the Great Kantō earthquake. This measured 8.3 on the Richter scale and had its epicentre beneath Ō-shima Island in Sagami Bay, just 80 km (50 miles) from where the ship was moored.

The earthquake devastated Tōkyō, the port city of Yokohama and the surrounding prefectures of Chiba, Kanagawa, and Shizuoka. Between 100,000 – 142,000 people perished, either from the initial tremors, subsequent building collapses or the vicious firestorms whipped up by 110 km/h (70 mph) winds from a nearby typhoon, which struck the area soon after the earthquake. Many people died when their feet got stuck in melting tarmac. In one single incident, 38,000 people who had taken refuge in a yard at a clothing depot were incinerated by a fire whirl.

Peril in port

Individuals were facing disaster at every turn. Captain Robinson of the *Empress of Australia* had the lives of more than a thousand people on his shoulders.

Although the shocks lessened and eventually ceased, Robinson knew his vessel was in a very dangerous position.

> **What remained of the docks was engulfed in flame and the *Empress* was still tied to the wharf.**

If she stayed tied to the dock, she would burn. And if that happened, there would be nowhere for the people on board to go.

Taking action

Normally, the *Empress* would have been able to simply move astern, but a freighter, the *Steel Navigator*, was moored close behind her. Now she would need tugs to pull her out sideways, but these had been destroyed or crippled in the initial tremors. Furthermore, a ship moored to the east had lost her cable and drifted across the harbour, smashing into the *Empress* amidships.

First Captain Robinson ordered all available crew – and passengers – to turn the ship's hoses on the decks and extinguish the embers that were drifting from the burning docks.

He then had ropes and ladders cast over the side to let the survivors trapped on the crumbling dock climb aboard. Next he tried a risky manoeuvre, engaging the *Empress*'s engines to shove the *Steel Navigator* enough to allow them to manoeuvre away from the flaming docks.

With metal grinding on metal the *Empress* managed to shift the freighter, inch by agonizing inch. But just as she was slowly pulling away her port propeller fouled in the *Steel Navigator's* anchor cable.

She had edged about 18 m (60 ft) away from the flames; it probably wasn't going to be enough. Sparks and embers continued to rain down on the deck. Then, fortunately, the wind turned and eased. The ship was safe – for the moment.

Now the captain turned to helping other people. He had the ship's lifeboats lowered and formed rescue teams of crew and volunteer passengers. They then set out to shore, working through the night to ferry survivors to the ship.

The burning waters

By Sunday morning the *Empress* was a haven for 2,000 people, but now they faced another danger. A huge slick of burning oil was moving across the harbour towards the ship. The fouled propeller meant the *Empress* was still unable to steer. Captain Robinson asked the captain of a tanker, the *Iris*, to help. This vessel managed to tow the bow of the *Empress* round, allowing her to move slightly out of port to a safer anchorage.

The rescue teams kept working despite the blazing sea.

Staying behind

On 4 September, three days after the earthquake, the *Empress*'s fouled propeller was freed by a diver from the Japanese battleship *Yamashiro*, which had arrived at the harbour. The propeller was undamaged and the *Empress* was now free to leave.

Damage caused by the Great Kantō earthquake in Tōkyō.

But Captain Robinson decided that she should stay to help with the relief work.

> **For the next week the *Empress* of Australia re-entered the devastated harbour every morning and sent her boats ashore.**

The lifeboats continued the trips, returning full of refugees, who were then either transferred from the ship to other vessels or taken to Kōbe. The ship's crew and most of the passengers donated their personal belongings to help the survivors.

Sailing into history

Finally, on 12 September 1923, the *Empress of Australia* departed Yokohama. The heroism of her captain, crew and passengers was not forgotten. Captain Robinson received many awards, including the CBE and the Lloyds Silver Medal.

A group of passengers and refugees commissioned a bronze memorial tablet, which they presented to the ship in recognition of the relief efforts. When the *Empress* was scrapped in 1952, this tablet was handed on to Captain Robinson, then aged 82, in a special ceremony in Vancouver.

The Long Walk Home

In 1931, three young girls were among thousands of children forcibly taken from their families by the Australian government and sent to a harsh native settlement. Molly, Daisy and Gracie immediately escaped and followed a rabbit-proof fence for 1,600 km (1,000 miles) through the burning western deserts to get home.

DATE:
1931

SITUATION:
Three children run from a state home

CONDITION OF CONFINEMENT:
Fleeing the authorities through the Australian bush

DURATION OF CONFINEMENT:
2 months

MEANS OF ESCAPE:
Hiding in the bush, begging for help

NO. OF ESCAPEES:
3

DANGERS:
Exhaustion, starvation, heat stroke

EQUIPMENT:
None

ABOVE RIGHT
Old rabbit-proof fence remains along Hamersley Drive, Fitzgerald River National Park, Western Australia.

The rabbit-proof fence

Rabbits are not indigenous to Australia. In 1859 an English settler in Victoria, southeast Australia released two dozen into the wild. 'The introduction of a few rabbits could do little harm and might provide a touch of home, in addition to a spot of hunting.' But Austin seemed to have forgotten what rabbits are good at and they were soon spreading across the continent like a plague.

Between 1901 and 1907, the government constructed one of the most ambitious wildlife containment schemes the world has ever seen. The plan was simple: cordon off the entire western side of Australia so that the rabbits couldn't get into it. Three rabbit-proof fences crossed the country. They were one metre (3 ft) high and supported by wooden poles. No.1 Rabbit-Proof Fence ran for 1,833 km (1,139 miles) clear across the continent from Wallal Downs to Jerdacuttup. The total length of all three fences was 3,256 km (2,023 miles).

Bold though this act of segregation was, it was doomed to failure. Rabbits had already crossed west of the barrier and it was near-impossible to maintain such a structure in the harsh conditions of the Western Australian deserts, despite regular patrols by inspectors with bicycles, cars and even camels.

The stolen generation

The fence also acts as a metaphor for another act of segregation imposed on the country by the government of the time.

The white settlers of Australia had many different attitudes to the Aboriginal population. To some they were simply an inferior race. Others believed they could be assimilated into white society and have their heritage 'bred out' of them. Some were tolerant and understanding and of course there were many mixed-race children. It was the most divisive issue in that period of Australian history.

> From 1920 to 1930 more than 100,000 mixed-race Aboriginal children were taken from their families.

Children were relocated to be educated for a useful life as a farmhand or domestic servant. The government built harsh remand homes where Dickensian conditions were the norm. The children, many as young as three, shared prison-like dormitories with barred windows. Thin blankets gave little protection against the chill nights and the food was basic. These grim educational centres, or 'native settlements', were often many hundreds of miles from the place the children called home. Any children caught escaping would have their heads shaved, be beaten with a strap and sent for a spell in solitary confinement.

The food in the workhouse-like 'native settlements' was no better than gruel. The children had few clothes and no shoes.

Molly Craig, 14, her half-sister Daisy Kadibil, 11 and their cousin Gracie Fields, 8, arrived at the Moore River Settlement north of Perth in August 1931. They had been taken from their family in Jiggalong nearly 1,600 km (1,000 miles) away and they immediately decided to return home no matter what the consequences. Their plan was simple: they would follow the rabbit-proof fence.

Walking home

The girls only had two simple dresses and two pairs of calico bloomers each. Their feet were shoeless. The only food they had was a little bread. Nevertheless, on only their second day in the settlement they hid in the dormitory and then, when no one was looking, they simply walked out into the bush. It held far fewer terrors for them than the settlement.

❶ The girls were raised in Jiggalong.

WESTERN AUSTRALIA

Jiggalong

❸ The girls trekked north, following the rabbit-proof fence.

Wiluna

No.3

Kalbarri

Mount Magnet

Leonora

Geraldton

INDIAN OCEAN

Kalgoorlie

Fremantle

Perth

❷ In August 1931, they were sent to the 'native settlement' at Moore River.

Jerdacuttup

0   200 KM

0   100 MILES

The girls route following the rabbit-proof fence.

The fence itself was several days' walk away. Once they reached it they would then have several more weeks of trekking through dusty scrubland before they reached Jiggalong.

But the girls were confident that they could live off the land. Their biggest fear was getting caught by the inevitable search parties; all previous escapees had been found by Aboriginal trackers. To outfox them they would have to hide well and move fast: Molly set them a goal of covering 32 km (20 miles) a day.

> ❛ We followed that fence, that rabbit-proof fence, all the way home from the settlement to Jiggalong. Long way, alright. We stayed in the bush hiding there for a long time. ❜

They made good progress at first. They hid in a rabbit warren and managed to catch, cook and eat a couple of the creatures. The weather was wet, giving them water and removing their footprints. They met two Aboriginals who gave them food and matches.

Often, when they came upon a farmhouse they simply walked up to the door and asked for help. Despite the news of their escape being widely publicised, none of the white farmers turned them in. Some gave them food and warmer clothes.

The police were on their trail, now genuinely concerned for the girls' welfare as well as eager to return them to Moore River.

But by the third week in September the strain of life in the bush was beginning to show. Gracie, the youngest, was exhausted and the other two often had to carry her. Her legs had been slashed by thorny underbrush and become infected. After hearing from an Aboriginal woman they met that her mother had moved to nearby Wiluna, she crept aboard a train to travel there.

Molly and Daisy kept walking towards Jiggalong. They could now

move faster without their younger cousin to support, but it was still brutally hard going. The rains had gone, as summer crept up on them. Every day it got hotter yet every day they were determined to cover more ground to get home quicker.

At last, in early October, the two dusty, bedraggled girls walked into Jiggalong. They had trekked for more than 1,600 km (1,000 miles) through some of the most unforgiving terrain on Earth. They were still wanted by the authorities.

But now they were home.

The story wasn't over

The families of both girls swiftly moved house to stop the authorities taking their girls again. But, perhaps aware of what a powerful tale the girls had to tell, the government called off the chase a few weeks later.

However, although the girls' escape is a triumphant display of endurance and indomitable human spirit, their journey didn't bring total happiness. They were still in a land where the law discriminated against them.

Gracie's mother wasn't in Wiluna and she was sent back to Moore River. She became a domestic servant and died in 1983.

Molly also became a domestic servant, marrying and having two daughters. But in 1940, after she was taken to Perth with appendicitis, she was sent back to Moore River by a direct government order. Amazingly, she once again walked out of the settlement and trekked back to Jiggalong. Unfortunately, she could only take one of her daughters with her; her 3-year-old girl, Doris remained in the settlement where she was brought up. Doris later wrote the book *Rabbit-Proof Fence* about her mother's first journey, which was made into a film in 2002.

Daisy's story had the happiest outcome. She stayed in the Jiggalong area for the rest of her life, where she became a housekeeper, married and had four daughters.

Survival by Sacrifice

FOUR YOUNG MOUNTAINEERS WERE TRYING TO CONQUER THE UNCLIMBED
PEAK OF HARAMOSH WHEN AN AVALANCHE SWEPT TWO OF THEM OVER A
SHEER ICE CLIFF. THE OTHER TWO CLIMBERS WOULD DRIVE THEMSELVES
BEYOND THE POINT OF EXHAUSTION AND RISK THEIR LIVES IN A DARING
RESCUE ATTEMPT THAT WOULD HAVE TRAGIC AND HEROIC RESULTS.

DATE:
1957

SITUATION:
CLIMBING ACCIDENT

**CONDITION OF
CONFINEMENT:**
STRANDED BY AN AVALANCHE
AT 6,400 M (21,000 FT)

**DURATION OF
CONFINEMENT:**
2 DAYS

MEANS OF ESCAPE:
CLIMBING TO SAFETY,
RESCUE AND SACRIFICE
BY COLLEAGUES

NO. OF ESCAPEES:
2

DANGERS:
DEHYDRATION, EXHAUSTION,
FALLING TO DEATH,
HYPOTHERMIA

EQUIPMENT:
CLIMBING EQUIPMENT

ABOVE RIGHT
**The snow-covered peaks of the
Karakoram Range, Pakistan.**

The height of ambition

It was no wonder that the
young students were bursting
with enthusiasm for the climb.
Several extraordinary recent
mountaineering achievements
had fired the imaginations of all
men who loved the mountains:
Tensing and Hillary had climbed
Everest just four years previously
and the savage K2 had succumbed
the year after. It seemed that no
peak was beyond the reach of
determined and able men.

But the three lads from Oxford
University Mountaineering Club
took their enthusiasm one step
further. They wanted to be the
first men to conquer the virgin
spire of Haramosh, a towering
7,400 m (24,270 ft) mountain in
the Karakoram range of northern
Pakistan.

They would pay dearly for their
high ambition. They would also
display depths of bravery and self-
sacrifice that belied their years.

The team finds a leader

The project was the brainchild of
23-year-old Bernard Jillott, a grammar
school boy from Huddersfield. With
him were John Emery, a medic who
delayed his finals to join the expedition,
and Rae Culbert, a 25-year-old forestry
graduate from New Zealand.

The students were young, but also
wise enough to know that to get a
climbing permit they would need an
older, more experienced leader. They
asked Tony Streather, an army officer
who had been on the 1950 Norwegian
expedition that made the first ascent
of Tirich Mir, the highest peak in
the Hindu Kush at 7,690 m (25,223 ft).
Initially the expedition's transport
officer, he ended up being part of
the four-man team that reached
the summit. He had also climbed
Kangchenjunga (the world's third
highest mountain) in 1955 and two
years later he was in Oxford lecturing
on his experiences when the lads
from the university mountaineering
club collared him.

Streather was recently married and had a very small child, but it wasn't long since he had left Pakistan and he yearned to return and see his old friends.

> ❛ They got me into a bar, plied me with several whiskies, then asked if I would lead their expedition to Haramosh.... I suppose they caught me at a vulnerable moment and I said, "Yes, fine". ❜

The team starts planning

The four didn't always see eye-to-eye but good climbers are, by necessity, highly driven individuals who dislike compromise. Groups of them are rarely harmonious.

They decamped to the Streathers' army bungalow in Camberley and set up their expedition headquarters. Preparations went well and by July 1957 the team was in Pakistan.

On 3 August the climbers established their base camp below the towering northern face of the mountain. They then began working their way up a long flanking route to the east.

Although it was still late summer, the weather was turning against them. Heavy snowfall often kept them in their tents for days on end. For several frustrating weeks they made little progress and by early September it was obvious (to Streather at least) that they were not going to conquer Haramosh.

But then the weather broke. The sun shone and the team decided that they could at least climb to a new high point on the mountain. It would make all their efforts worthwhile.

A step too far

On the afternoon of 15 September 1957, the four men crested a ridge at about 6,400 m (21,000 ft) and what they saw nearly tore their hearts out. The view was beautiful: a dazzling bird's eye vista of the high Karakoram, something that only a tiny percentage of men have ever seen. No one had ever climbed higher on Haramosh. But they could also see that there was a huge, yawning gulf between them and the ultimate summit. Streather knew instantly it was time to turn back.

But Jillott insisted on continuing a little bit further, just to see over the next crest. He was roped to Emery.

Streather waited with Culbert, watching the other pair plough ahead through the crisp snow of the ridge. The north face dropped sheer away for 2,400 m (7,875 ft) on one side of the ridge but the gentle convex slope they were on seemed harmless enough. Then, suddenly, the climbers crumpled and twisted, their arms and legs flailing like marionettes.

For a split second Streather thought that Jillott and Emery were larking about. Then horror seized his heart: the whole side of the mountain was moving, dragging the two men with it. There was an eerie silence as they slid out of sight and then reality came thundering back with a roar as the avalanche cascaded over an ice cliff taking their friends into the abyss.

A spectacular view across the hundreds of mountain peaks in the Karakoram Range, Pakistan.

An avalanche in the Karakoram Range.

The rescue attempt

Streather and Culbert moved quickly. If their friends were still alive they would need supplies. They threw down a rucksack containing warm jackets and food. Agonizingly, it overshot the pair below and tumbled into a crevasse. There were more supplies cached at Camp 4, so Streather and Culbert tramped back to the tents.

Already shattered from their efforts, they had no time to rest; at that height every second counted in the race for survival. They collected vacuum flasks, food, warm clothing and rope and started to reclimb the four hour route to the accident site.

Night fell and still they kept climbing. Luckily the moon was up and the sky was cloudless so when they reached the ridge they were able to continue down into the basin.

By the time they got close to their friends the sun was rising. To their joy they heard Emery and Jillott shouting at them. Then they realized the shouts were a warning: they were about to step over the vast ice cliff

that Emery and Jillott had been swept over. The fallen men told them to traverse several hundred feet right, to a point where the cliff's steep gradient eased.

Streather had to cut steps with his ice axe all the way across the giddy traverse. They were nearly across when one of Culbert's crampons fell from his boot and disappeared into the void.

By the time they reached Emery and Jillott it was late afternoon. Both men were weakened after a night in the open and Emery had suffered the agony of a dislocated hip when he fell although mercifully this had clicked back into its socket. Streather knew they had to start climbing back out of the basin immediately, even though he and Culbert had now been continuously on the move for thirty hours.

They had climbed 60 m (200 ft) when Culbert's cramponless foot slipped. He fell from the ice wall and pulled everyone back down into the basin. The men tried again. This time the exhausted Jillott fell

asleep in his ropes and again they tumbled back to the bottom.

They tried for a third time but Culbert's exposed leather sole gave him no grip. Despite valiant efforts he slipped from the sheer ice and swung in space like a pendulum. He was roped to Streather who tried but could not hold his weight. Ripping his partner from his holds, Culbert hurtled back down the same cliff over which Emery and Jillott had tumbled two days earlier.

With savage irony the rescuers had become the victims.

Another night in the arms of death

The sun had set and now it was Emery and Jillott's turn to climb through the night, returning to the ridge to collect supplies. Meanwhile Streather and Culbert shivered in the darkness of the basin below.

At dawn on 17 August, Emery and Jillot had not returned. Culbert was very weak and frostbite had numbed all feeling in his feet. Streather knew that they had to try for a fourth time to get out of the basin; their colleagues might not have made it.

They would normally have been roped together, but Streather had lost his ice axe and couldn't have held the younger man if he had fallen. There was no point in both men perishing when one slipped, so they climbed by themselves. Now the full consequences of Culbert's lost crampon became apparent. He was unable to get the purchase he needed to haul himself up the ice wall. As he tried to follow Streather to the ridge he kept sliding back down. Streather could barely put one foot in front of the other himself; he had no choice but to keep climbing on his own. That climb was the most savage test of endurance he would ever face.

> ❛ I thought I was dead and I didn't know why I was climbing, but I just knew I had to keep moving. ❜

Streather eventually reached the ridge and found the rucksack they had left. He was frantic with thirst, but the water bottles were frozen solid. Now all he could do was crawl back to camp.

On the way he was surprised to see a set of tracks diverge from the correct route. Back at the camp he found Emery lying, utterly exhausted, with his cramponned feet sticking out of the tent.

> ❛ Streather asked where Jillott was. Emery said: "He's gone." "What do you mean – gone?" "He's dead. Over the edge." ❜

The divergent footprints had been Jillott's. He had strayed over a precipice and fallen several thousand feet down the south side.

Emery had nearly died himself: he had tumbled into a crevasse and only managed to crawl out that morning, reaching camp a few hours before Streather.

The two who were left

Streather and Emery then talked about going back up for Culbert. But in the cold light of day they knew that was out of the question.

Streather could only get to his feet by levering himself up with ski sticks. Emery was even weaker. Physically they wouldn't be able to accomplish it and the sad truth was that Culbert was almost certainly already dead after another night in the open.

It was time to face facts: Jillott and Culbert were dead. And unless they got a grip, they would soon be too. Streather got the stove going. Emery, the medic, gave them both penicillin jabs to protect their frostbitten hands and feet from infection.

It took them four more days to get down to base camp. Then they had the heartbreaking job of sending telegrams home to the families of Jillott and Culbert.

Home

The two survivors returned to England where Emery had emergency surgery. All his fingers and toes were amputated. The surgeons managed to leave enough of a stump of his thumb and first finger for him to hold a pen. He got a first in his medical finals. Incredibly he returned to climbing, but died in a fall in the Alps in 1963.

Streather escaped without any amputations. But he still had to face the families of the young men who had died. Doubts, regret and sadness would haunt him ever after.

But beside the tragedy there is another truth. Tony Streather pushed himself to the edge for his friends and Rae Culbert, tragically, gave even more. It was only thanks to their bravery that any men came off that mountain alive. Haramosh was finally climbed on 4 August 1958.

Climbers roped together in search of a way out between the crevasses.

The Inconvenient Survivor

WHEN US PILOT GARY POWERS' U-2 SPY PLANE WAS SHOT DOWN OVER THE SOVIET UNION, POWERS DID THE WORST POSSIBLE THING – SURVIVE. HIS MISSION WAS PART OF A PROGRAMME THAT PRESIDENT EISENHOWER DENIED EVEN EXISTED. IF POWERS WAS TO RETURN HOME, THE US GOVERNMENT WOULD HAVE TO ADMIT TO FOUR YEARS OF ILLEGAL ESPIONAGE.

DATE:
1960–2

SITUATION:
SPY MISSION

CONDITION OF CONFINEMENT:
US PILOT SHOT DOWN OVER THE USSR

DURATION OF CONFINEMENT:
1 YEAR, 9 MONTHS

MEANS OF ESCAPE:
BAILING FROM PLANE, PRISONER EXCHANGE

NO. OF ESCAPEES:
1

DANGERS:
EXPLOSION, FALLING TO DEATH, IMPRISONMENT

EQUIPMENT:
PARACHUTE, SUICIDE PILL

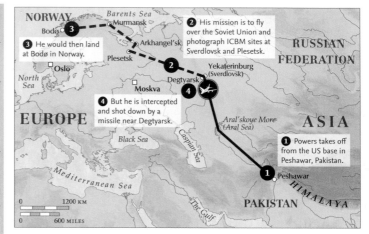

2 His mission is to fly over the Soviet Union and photograph ICBM sites at Sverdlovsk and Plesetsk.

3 He would then land at Bodø in Norway.

4 But he is intercepted and shot down by a missile near Degtyarsk.

1 Powers takes off from the US base in Peshawar, Pakistan.

Above retribution

Captain Gary Powers ought to have been very worried. He was piloting a US spy plane over the Soviet Union and taking photographs of missile silos and nuclear plants. If they spotted him, the Russians would stop at nothing to blow him out of the skies.

Worse, there was an East-West summit due to start in two weeks. If he were to be intercepted, his superiors would deny all knowledge of his existence. Powers would be expected to self-destruct his plane and take his suicide pill.

But the aircraft he was in was a U-2 spy plane. Launched in 1956, it was far ahead of any plane the Russians had.

> **The U-2 spy plane could cruise at altitudes above 21,000 m (70,000 ft), making it invulnerable to Soviet anti-aircraft weapons of the time.**

Its state-of-the-art camera could take high-resolution photos from the edge of the stratosphere. For four years the U-2 pilots had been able to fly their espionage missions above enemy countries, including the Soviet Union, unmolested. They systematically photographed military installations, nuclear plants and other strategically vital sites. So perhaps Gary Powers didn't have to worry after all.

Until the Russians did see him. And a missile did fly that high.

Operation GRAND SLAM

It was 1 May 1960 and Captain Powers had his mission: take off from the US base in Peshawar, Pakistan, overfly the Soviet Union and photograph ICBM (intercontinental ballistic missile) sites at Sverdlovsk and Plesetsk, then land at Bodø in Norway. The mission was code-named GRAND SLAM.

By now the Soviets knew that the overflights were happening, but the Americans believed they still couldn't do anything about it. They didn't know that the Soviets had been playing catch up. Although their aircraft could not yet catch the U-2, the new S-75 Dvina missile might be able to.

When Powers crossed into Soviet airspace local air force commanders were ordered 'to attack the violator by all alert flights located in the area of foreign plane's course, and to ram if necessary'.

Planes were scrambled to intercept and surface-to-air missiles were readied for launch. MIG-19s tried to climb to the U-2's altitude but failed. A newer Su-9 aircraft made it that high but was unarmed. The pilot tried to ram the US plane, but shot right by.

Powers might have fancied his chances, until three S-75 Dvina missiles were launched as he passed Degtyarsk, in the Ural Mountains. The first missile exploded in the air close behind the plane, rocking it with turbulence and causing its wings to shear off. The spinning fuselage began to fall from the sky.

Bailing out over enemy territory

His aircraft crippled, Powers started bailing out. He ejected the canopy, quickly reached back to pat his parachute and reached for the plane's self-destruct switch. His flight suited jerked him backwards.

Gary Powers, the US fighter pilot who was caught spying over the USSR in 1960.

His oxygen hose was still connected. Powers reached round and frantically tried to free it, the wind whipping him at several hundred miles an hour, thousands of feet above the Soviet Union.

One of our aircraft is missing

The US government knew that Powers was dead. There had been no contact at all since he left on his mission. Even if his aircraft had only been damaged, Powers had been trained to activate the plane's self-destruct mechanism and had been issued with the means of his own self destruction.

Powers carried a modified silver dollar that contained a poison-tipped needle. If he were captured, he could plunge this into his flesh and kill himself.

Four days after Powers disappeared, Soviet Premier Nikita Khrushchev announced to the world that they had shot down a 'spyplane'. He didn't mention the pilot.

It was bad news for Powers, but terrible news for President Eisenhower. He would be forced to admit to four years of illegal and invasive military espionage.

The US government weighed these facts and decided to launch a brazen cover up. Eisenhower made NASA issue a statement claiming a 'weather plane' had gone missing north of Turkey. The press release made so bold as to surmise that the pilot had fallen unconscious while the autopilot was still engaged and even claimed that 'the pilot reported over the emergency frequency that he was experiencing oxygen difficulties'. To back this up another U-2 plane was quickly painted in NASA colours and paraded before the media.

A bluff called

It was a bold ploy and it might have worked but for the ace up

Krushchev's sleeve: Captain Gary Powers had survived. Somehow he had freed his oxygen hose, bailed from his plane and successfully deployed his parachute. The delay in escaping had made him unable to destroy the plane. The Soviets had recovered it almost intact, even managing to develop its photographs. Powers had not killed himself.

Two days later, on 7 May, Khrushchev played his trump card. He announced:

> ❛ I must tell you a secret. When I made my first report I deliberately did not say that the pilot was alive and well... and now just look how many silly things [the Americans] have said. ❜

International embarrassment

The incident directly led to the collapse of the Four Power Paris Summit due to start on 16 May. Eisenhower, Khrushchev, Harold Macmillan and Charles de Gaulle were supposed to be round a table talking peace. But Eisenhower refused to apologize for the Powers incident and Khrushchev left the talks.

The incident was also a drastic setback for relations between the Soviet Union and Pakistan.

Powers pleaded guilty to espionage on 19 August 1960 and was sentenced to three years' imprisonment and seven years of hard labour. After serving just one year and nine months of his sentence he was exchanged for KGB Colonel Rudolf Abel on 10 February 1962. He received a hostile reception on his return to the US, where many people considered him a Russian spy. He was later cleared of any wrongdoing or cowardice in not killing himself. He became a test pilot for Lockheed.

Gary Powers died in a helicopter crash in 1977, aged 47.

Disaster on the Dark Side of the Moon

THE ASTRONAUTS OF APOLLO 13 WERE 320,000 KM (200,000 MILES) FROM EARTH WHEN AN EXPLOSION CRIPPLED THEIR SPACECRAFT. FORCED INTO THE LUNAR MODULE TO CONSERVE POWER AND OXYGEN, THEY BATTLED PROBLEM AFTER PROBLEM FOR NEARLY FOUR DAYS AS THEY SWUNG ROUND THE MOON AND RETURNED HOME.

DATE:
1970

SITUATION:
SPACE DISASTER

CONDITION OF CONFINEMENT:
LOSING OXYGEN IN LUNAR MODULE

DURATION OF CONFINEMENT:
3 ½ DAYS

MEANS OF ESCAPE:
IMPROVISED REPAIRS, METICULOUS PLANNING

NO. OF ESCAPEES:
3

DANGERS:
OXYGEN STARVATION, EXPLOSION, FREEZING TO DEATH

EQUIPMENT:
A DAMAGED SPACECRAFT

ABOVE RIGHT
The Apollo 13 prime crew onboard USS *Iwo Jima* following splashdown.
From left to right: Lunar Module pilot, Fred W. Haise, Command Module pilot, John L. 'Jack' Swigert Jr and Commander, James A. Lovell.

The mission

Apollo 13 was launched on 11 April 1970. It was to become the third manned spacecraft to land on the Moon, with a mission to explore formations near the 80 km (50 mile) wide Fra Mauro crater. The flight was commanded by James A. Lovell with John L. 'Jack' Swigert as Command Module pilot and Fred W. Haise as Lunar Module pilot.

There was a small problem on takeoff when an engine shut down two minutes early during the second stage boost. But four other engines burned longer to compensate, and the craft reached orbit successfully.

Then, on 14 April 1970, nearly sixty hours into the mission, the astronauts were 321,860 km (199,995 miles) from Earth when they heard a loud bang.

The explosion

At first the crew thought a meteoroid had hit them. As well as the noise of an explosion, the electrics were going haywire and the attitude control thrusters had fired.

In fact, a short circuit had ignited some insulation in the Number 2 oxygen tank of the Service Module. The Service Module provided life support, power and other systems to the Command Module, which held the astronauts as they travelled to and from lunar orbit. The Lunar Module was a separate, though connected, craft that would be used to ferry the men to the lunar surface and back.

The fire caused a surge in pressure that ruptured the tank, flooding the fuel cell bay with gaseous oxygen. This surge blew the bolts holding on the outer panel, which tore off free and spun into space, damaging a communications antenna. Contact with Earth was lost for 1.8 seconds, until the system automatically switched to another antenna.

The shock also ruptured a line from the Number 1 oxygen tank. Two hours later all of the Service Module's oxygen supply had leaked into the void.

As the Command Module's fuel cells used oxygen with hydrogen to generate electricity, it could now only run on battery power. The crew had no option but to shut down the Command Module completely and move into the Lunar Module. They would then use this as a 'lifeboat' for the journey back to Earth before rejoining the Command Module for re-entry.

As for the mission, the Service Module was so badly damaged that a safe return from a lunar landing was impossible. These men would not be landing on the Moon.

320,000 km from home

The Flight Director immediately aborted the mission. Now he just had to get the men home. The quickest way would be a Direct Abort trajectory, using the Service Module engine to essentially reverse the craft. But it was too late: the craft was already within the Moon's gravitational sphere of influence making it harder to 'reverse'. The engine could also have been damaged in the explosion and restarting might cause an even worse disaster.

So Mission Control opted for a 'free return', essentially using the Moon's gravity to hitch a ride and slingshot the craft back towards Earth.

First, Apollo 13 needed to be realigned; it had left its initial free return trajectory earlier in the mission as it lined up for its planned lunar landing. Using a small burn of the Lunar Module's descent propulsion system, the crew got the spacecraft back on track for its return journey.

Now they started their nerve-shredding journey round the dark side of the Moon. It was a trip that would demand incredible ingenuity under extreme pressure from the crew, flight controllers, and ground crew if the men were to make it back alive.

More problems

The Lunar Module 'lifeboat' only had enough battery power to sustain two people for two days, not three people for the four days it would take the men to return to Earth.

The life support and communication systems had to be powered down to the lowest levels possible. Everything that wasn't essential was turned off. The drama was being shown on TV but no more live broadcasts were made. Power levels were dropped so low that even voice communications were difficult.

Removing carbon dioxide from the air was another serious problem. Lithium hydroxide normally did the job but there wasn't enough of it. The only additional supply they had was in the Command Module, and its canisters were cube-shaped whereas the Lunar Module's sockets were cylindrical. It looked like the men would suffocate before they made it back.

In one of the most inspired brainstorming sessions of all time, engineers on the ground got out all the kit that the crew would have available. They then improvised a 'mailbox' that would join the two incompatible connections and draw the air through.

The air was becoming more poisonous with every breath as the astronauts followed the meticulous radio instructions to build the Heath Robinson repair. Amazingly, it worked. They would have enough clean air.

But they weren't out of the woods yet.

They needed to re-enter the atmosphere in the Command Module, but it had been totally shut down to preserve its power. Would it start up again? Its systems hadn't been designed to do this.

Again, engineers and crew on the ground had to think on their feet if their friends were to live. They invented an entirely new protocol that would power the ship back up with the limited power supply and time available without blowing the system. They also feared that condensation in the unpowered and freezing cold Command Module might damage electrical systems when it was reactivated.

It booted up first time.

Back to Earth with a splash

With Apollo 13 nearing Earth, the crew jettisoned the Service Module and photographed the damage for later analysis. Then they jettisoned the redundant Lunar Module, leaving them sitting tight in the Command Module *Odyssey* as they plunged into the atmosphere.

The enormous heat of re-entry ionized the air around the capsule causing a total communications blackout. For four and a half minutes the world held its breath. Were the men all right? Had the heat shield been damaged in the explosion? Was the craft now disintegrating in the upper atmosphere?

There must have been a few whoops of joy in Mission Control when the radio finally sparked back into life. *Odyssey* splashed down in the Pacific Ocean southeast of American Samoa and just 6.5 km (4 miles) from the recovery ship, USS *Iwo Jima*. The crew were generally in good shape. And they were home.

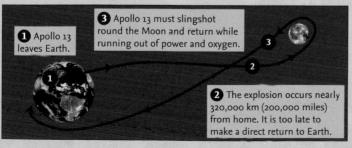

1 Apollo 13 leaves Earth.

3 Apollo 13 must slingshot round the Moon and return while running out of power and oxygen.

2 The explosion occurs nearly 320,000 km (200,000 miles) from home. It is too late to make a direct return to Earth.

Two Miles Up without a Parachute

A 17-YEAR-OLD GIRL WAS IN A PLANE OVER THE AMAZON RAINFOREST
WHEN IT WAS HIT BY LIGHTNING AND DESTROYED. SHE FELL
3 KM (2 MILES) STILL STRAPPED TO A ROW OF SEATS AND AWOKE IN
THE JUNGLE WITH MINOR INJURIES. THE ONLY SURVIVOR, SHE THEN
TREKKED THROUGH THE JUNGLE FOR TEN DAYS TO REACH CIVILIZATION.

DATE:
1971

SITUATION:
PLANE CRASH

**CONDITION OF
CONFINEMENT:**
SOLE SURVIVOR IN THE
AMAZON JUNGLE

**DURATION OF
CONFINEMENT:**
10 DAYS

MEANS OF ESCAPE:
TREKKING THROUGH
THE JUNGLE

NO. OF ESCAPEES:
1

DANGERS:
FALLING TO DEATH, DISEASE,
STARVATION, DEHYDRATION

EQUIPMENT:
NONE

ABOVE RIGHT
Amazonian rainforest, Peru.

Home for Christmas

It was Christmas Eve in 1971 and more than anything in the world, 17-year-old Juliane Köpcke was looking forward to seeing her father.

She was travelling with her mother Maria, an ornithologist. The flight in the Lockheed Electra turboprop would take less than an hour. It would leave Lima and cross the huge wilderness of the Reserva Comunal El Sira before touching down in Pucallpa in the Amazonian rainforest where her parents ran a research station in the jungle studying wildlife.

The airline, LANSA, didn't have the best safety reputation: it had recently lost two aircraft in crashes. The weather forecast was not good. But the family desperately wanted to be together for Christmas, so they stepped on board.

For the first twenty-five minutes everything was fine. Then the plane flew into heavy clouds and started shaking. Juliane's mother was very nervous.

Falling to Earth

Suddenly there was a blinding flash on the starboard wing and a fraction of a second later, a sickening explosion. The plane instantly started plummeting straight down. Christmas presents were flying around the cabin and people were screaming: it was every air traveller's worst nightmare.

> ❛ To the right we saw a bright flash and the plane went into a nose dive. My mother said, "This is it!" ❜

Lightning had hit one of the fuel tanks. The explosion tore the right wing off.

Then, suddenly, there was silence. Juliane realized there was no plane around her any more. She was in the open air, flying, and far below her she could see the jungle. It was spinning. The plane had disintegrated, throwing passengers out into the storm, 3,000 m (10,000 ft) above the Amazon.

Then Juliane blacked out. She fell more than 3 km (2 miles) into the jungle canopy but miraculously survived with only minor injuries.

For the rest of that day and the night, she remained unconscious. She woke the next morning at nine o'clock (she remembers the exact time because she noticed that her watch was still working). As she sat up she realized she was still strapped into her row of seats. And she was completely alone in the jungle.

Her ordeal was just beginning.

Water of life

Rescue planes and search crews scanned the area soon after the plane lost contact with air traffic control. But the region was so vast and remote that they couldn't find the crash site.

All ninety-one of the other passengers and crew on Flight 508 died. Remarkably, Juliane was relatively unhurt. The row of seats that she was strapped into spun as it fell, much like a helicopter, slowing her rate of descent. She also landed at a place where the jungle canopy had particularly thick foliage. This cushioned her impact with the ground. The only injuries she had were a broken collarbone, a swollen right eye, concussion and some gashes on her arms and legs.

Juliane was an intelligent, resourceful girl. She had also spent years on the research station with her parents. Her father was a practical man who had taught his daughter how to survive in the rainforest. With remarkable foresight he had prepared her for just such an emergency. He had told her that the first thing to do was find a creek and follow it downstream, because that would lead to a stream and the stream would flow into a bigger river where, eventually, there would be a human settlement.

She found a creek and started to wade downstream, but it was tough going.

Searching for her mother

As she travelled downstream, Juliane came across more wreckage – and more bodies. Her discoveries were gruesome. She came upon three women still strapped into their row of seats. They had landed headfirst and the impact had driven them nearly 0.5 m (2 ft) into the ground.

Juliane thought that one of the women might be her mother. Choking back her horror, she had to find out for certain. She couldn't bring herself to try to pull the body from the ground, so she used a stick to prise one of its shoes off. The dead woman's toes were painted with nail polish; as her mother never used nail polish, she knew it couldn't be her.

She kept walking.

At the mercy of the jungle

Juliane continued through the rainforest, wading through the jungle streams. The water was home to piranhas and poisonous fish, but none attacked her. Crocodiles lined the banks of the streams, but again Juliane's knowledge of the environment helped her: she just walked calmly by the creatures, confident that they generally do not attack humans.

The stream supplied her with ample clean water and a natural path through the dense rainforest. But it gave her no real food. The only sustenance she had was some candy she had found scattered by the wreckage. She also had several open lacerations which were vulnerable to parasites.

The plane crashed en route to Pucallpa in the Amazonian rainforest.

After a few days, Juliane became aware of an unusual sensation in one of the cuts on her arm. It felt a bit like an infection, but it became increasingly irritating, as if there was something in the wound. When she looked she discovered that a fly had laid its eggs in the hole in her arm. They had hatched and now maggots were writhing within her flesh. Terrified that she would lose her arm, there was little she could do without proper medical attention.

As each day passed she became weaker and more vulnerable. Was she right to have followed her father's advice? What if there were no human settlements for hundreds of miles? Maybe she should have waited to be rescued.

But then, on the tenth day, she stumbled out of the jungle and almost tripped over a canoe. There was a shelter beside it, and there she waited.

A few hours later, the lumberjacks who lived in the shelter finished their day's work and returned to eat and rest. They must have been astonished to see a bedraggled and exhausted young girl in a torn mini-skirt and one sandal sitting in their hut.

Although the cut in her arm was only a centimetre across, medics later removed more than fifty maggots from the hole.

They dressed her injuries and insect bites as best they could and the next morning they took her downstream in their canoe. It took seven hours to reach a lumber station in Tournavista, and from there Juliane was airlifted to a hospital in Pucallpa.

Her father was waiting for her.

And after...

Juliane returned to Germany to recuperate and continue her studies. In 1987, she earned a PhD degree in zoology, like her parents. She went on to specialize in mammalogy, studying bats in Munich, Germany.

The Cruel Cost of Survival

When their plane crashed high in the Andes, the passengers spent over two months battling brutal cold, altitude sickness and avalanches. Severe hunger forced them to eat the bodies of their dead friends. Eventually two men completed a marathon trek out of the snowy wilderness to get help.

DATE:
1972

SITUATION:
Plane crash

CONDITION OF CONFINEMENT:
In a crashed plane high in the Andes

DURATION OF CONFINEMENT:
72 days

MEANS OF ESCAPE:
Trekking to get help; rescue

NO. OF ESCAPEES:
16

DANGERS:
Avalanche, hypothermia, starvation, dehydration, altitude sickness, frostbite

EQUIPMENT:
Parts of the crashed plane; luggage

LEFT
An aerial view of the Andes, South America.

ABOVE RIGHT
On 13 October 1972, Uruguayan Air Force Flight 571 crashed in the mountains close to the Chile / Argentina border.

Impact

The first mountain tore the right wing off. The second sliced the left. Then the belly of the aircraft clipped another ridge and the tail sheared off. Now the fuselage was like a bullet flying through the rarefied air. The slim metal tube with forty-five people in it then dropped to earth and skidded to a halt in a flurry of snow and screaming metal.

Unfortunately for the passengers, the plane crash was just the start of their ordeal.

The touring team

Uruguayan Air Force Flight 571 was a chartered plane carrying five crew and forty passengers, including a rugby team and their friends and family.

The flight took off on 12 October 1972 and should have been a fairly standard hop over the Andes from Montevideo, Uruguay, to Santiago, Chile, where the rugby team was due to play a match. But a storm in the mountains forced the plane to stop overnight at Mendoza. When they took off again the next afternoon, the bad weather still hadn't cleared, but the experienced military crew were confident they could navigate through the serrated Andean peaks.

As they climbed through the pass, the mountains on either side were lost in the clouds, so the pilots had to estimate their position based on their speed and route. But they made a crucial error, failing to fully allow for the very strong headwinds. These retarded the plane's progress severely, so that when they radioed air controllers in Santiago that they were over Curicó, Chile, and asked for permission to descend, they were in fact still deep in the jagged jaws of the mountains.

The plane hit an unnamed peak between Cerro Sosneado and Volcán Tinguiririca in the remote mountains that form the border between Chile and Argentina. With both wings torn off and the fuselage ripped open, the plane came to rest in the snow at around 3,600 m (11,800 ft) up the mountain.

Death all around

Of the forty-five people on board, twelve died in the crash or shortly thereafter, including all five crew. A further five people had perished by the next morning, and one more succumbed to injuries on the eighth day.

The remaining twenty seven now found themselves in a living nightmare. Many of them were severely injured, with broken limbs and internal damage. Although there were two medical students among the survivors, they had very little equipment. They had to salvage bits of the aircraft to create makeshift splints and braces.

They had expected to be in the relatively warm climes of Santiago; now they were 3,600 m (11,800 ft) up an Andean mountain in winter. Temperatures during the day were unpleasantly sub-zero, but the nights were brutally cold. No one had cold-weather clothing or any suitable footwear. The altitude made breathing, even when stationary, very difficult. Labouring in those conditions would be a serious endeavour.

They didn't know it at the time, but they would be stranded in this barren landscape for more than two months.

Lost in a sea of white

The plane was white. The area it had crashed in was a vast, remote, snow covered mountain wasteland. Its last position wasn't known to any accuracy. Despite search parties from three countries flying over the region, the odds of them finding the survivors were very slim.

The authorities had to assume the worst. Even if anyone had survived, the simple fact was that after so long in such an environment, they would have perished soon afterwards. The main search was called off after eight days.

Survivors waiting to be rescued.

The cruellest twist was that the survivors heard this news on a small transistor radio, which they had salvaged from the plane.

Remarkably, though, one of the men managed to turn this disappointment into a source of hope:

'Nicolich came out of the plane and, seeing their faces, knew what they had heard... [Nicolich] climbed through the hole in the wall of suitcases and rugby shirts, crouched at the mouth of the dim tunnel, and looked at the mournful faces which were turned towards him. 'Hey boys,' he shouted, 'there's some good news! We just heard on the radio. They've called off the search.' Inside the crowded plane there was silence. As the hopelessness of their predicament enveloped them, they wept. 'Why the hell is that good news?' Paez shouted angrily at Nicolich. 'Because it means,' [Nicolich] said, 'that we're going to get out of here on our own.' The courage of this one boy prevented a flood of total despair.'

From *Alive: The Story of the Andes Survivors* by Piers Paul Read.

The horrors of hunger

The survivors salvaged some food from the plane. But the few handfuls of chocolate bars, snacks, and bottles of wine did not provide sustenance for long, even with strict rationing.

A raging hunger soon seized everyone left alive on the mountain. They scoured the snowy slopes for plants but found none. There were no animal tracks or burrows. Their pangs grew so voracious that they scoured the fuselage again and again in search of even the tiniest edible morsels.

In their hunger the passengers tried to consume strips of leather torn from luggage, padding from the seats and pieces of clothing.

But eventually they had to accept the truth that there was only metal, plastic, ice, and rock.

Then they made the hardest choice imaginable. They decided to eat the flesh of those who had died. Most of these were classmates or friends, and the horror of what they were being forced to do only compounded the tragedy of their situation.

Avalanche

As if they weren't suffering enough, on the morning of 29 October an avalanche suddenly cascaded down the steep rocky slopes above them and engulfed the fuselage as the survivors slept.

They remained entombed in the tiny space for three days until they managed to poke a hole in the roof of the fuselage with a metal pole. By the time they got out, eight more people had died under the snow. Three more were to die in the following weeks.

Hiking out

After they had heard the radio news about the search being called off, many passengers knew that they would have to get themselves out of the mountains if they were to survive. The avalanche expressed that fact even more plainly.

During the flight they had heard the co-pilot announce that they had passed Curicó. That meant that the Chilean countryside ought to be just a few kilometres away to the west. Probably just over the high peak they were on.

Several survivors made brief scouting missions, but their weakened state and the altitude combined to make it gruelling work. There was no way that all of them would be able to walk over and out of the mountains.

The group then decided on a new plan: a few of the fittest men would set out on an expedition to get help. They would be allocated a large ration of food and the warmest clothes, and would be excused other group duties in order to build up their strength for the trek.

> ❛ ... they would have to get themselves out of the mountains if they were to survive. ❜

The group chose Nando Parrado, a business student, Roberto Canessa, one of the two medical students and Antonio Vizintín to make the journey.

Canessa had the clearest idea of the trials they would face and he insisted that they wait as long as possible to let the warmer weather of spring get at least a foothold in the mountains. In the end they waited almost seven weeks before setting off.

The reality of their situation

Although their ultimate goal was Chile in the west, the mountain that lay in that direction towered hundreds of metres above them. Climbing it would sap their energy and expose them to great risks. The trekking team therefore decided to start out east in the hope that the valley that they were in would eventually veer round.

Shortly after starting out, the trio found the tail section of the plane, which was still largely intact. It contained luggage with extra clothing, cigarettes and even some snacks. They spent their first night in the tail in relative comfort.

But the following night they had to sleep out in the open, fully exposed to the harsh cold. They very nearly froze to death.

The valley showed no sign of turning in a convenient direction

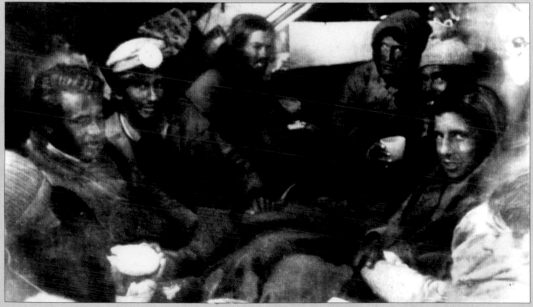

Survivors in the wrecked fuselage after rescuers reached them.

1 **FLIGHT 571**
The plane's route was over the Andes from Montevideo, Uruguay, to Santiago, Chile. Bad weather forced it to stop for a night at Mendoza.

2 **DIVERTED ROUTE**
The plane's maximum altitude was 9,000 m (29,500 ft) which, combined with the bad weather in the mountains, meant it could not take a direct route over the Andes from Mendoza to Santiago.

7 **SAN FERNANDO**
Two men continued on to the west, hiking for nine days in total to finally get help from a local huaso by the Rio Azufre. Two days later, rescue helicopters arrived to ferry the remaining survivors to hospital in Santiago.

3 **PASO DEL PLANCHÓN**
The pilots had to fly south parallel to the Andes, then turn west towards the mountains, cut through the low Planchón pass, cross the mountains and emerge on the Chilean side of the Andes south of Curicó. They would then turn north towards Santiago.

6 **HIKING WITH HOPE**
Finally a three-man expedition took the largest share of rations and set out over the mountain to the west. They realized they were deeper in the wilderness than they thought.

5 **SCOUTING MISSIONS**
The survivors initially set out east to avoid the large peak they were on, hoping to eventually loop round to Chile in the west. This proved impossible.

4 **CRASH LANDING**
In bad weather the pilots misjudged their location and the plane crashed into a mountain at 34°45'54"S 70°17'11"W.

PACIFIC OCEAN

CHILE

ARGENTINA

La Ligua

Valparaíso

SANTIAGO

Mendoza

San Fernando

Curicó

Linares

ANDES

Co de la Ramada 6410

Co Tupungato 6800

Vol. San José 5830

Co del Castillo 5485

Vol. Maipó 5290

Volcán Overo 4765

Sosneado 5160

Risco Plateado 4860

Volcán Tinguiririca 4300

Paso del Planchón 2850

Vol. Peteroa 4090

Azul 3810

Campanario 4020

KILOMETRES 0 20 40 60
MILES 0 10 20 30

and so the three men returned the next day to the tail with the plan of salvaging some large batteries they had found and using them to power the radio transmitter in the fuselage.

Out of luck

Even this bold idea failed to work. At first the batteries were too heavy for the trio to carry. Then when they brought the radio from the crash site to the tail, they found that the electrical systems were incompatible: the plane used AC, the batteries supplied DC.

Sewing for survival

It was now apparent that the only way out was to climb over the mountains to the west.

They also realized that unless they found a way to survive the freezing nights, they would die attempting the journey.

So the survivors came up with an ingenious solution. They tore out large sections of fabric from clothing, gathered padding from the plane's upholstery and got to work with a needle and thread from an emergency pack.

Eventually they created a passable sleeping bag. It would fit three men inside, but would carry the lives of all sixteen of the remaining survivors.

Hiking with hope

On 12 December 1972, Parrado, Canessa and Vizintín set out to climb the mountain to the west. It was two months since the crash. As they climbed over the first peak their bodies struggled in the thinning oxygen. It was savagely cold at night, but the homemade sleeping bag kept them alive.

After three days of trekking they met with a major disappointment. Cresting the shoulder of the mountain they expected to see the green countryside of Chile. Instead there was a sea of snow-bound peaks stretching out to the horizon. They were deeper in the mountains than they thought.

They had tens of kilometres of high altitude hiking still to go. After the initial rush of despair the men again found hope, and through that, a positive plan of action. They had further to go, so they must be stricter with their rations. That meant that one man must go back, leaving a greater share of food for the other two.

Vizintín headed back to the crash site, leaving Parrado and Canessa to hike on towards a distant shape that might, just might, be the start of a descending valley.

Vizintín improvised a sledge and descended the mountain that had taken them three agonizing days to climb in just one hour.

Five days of nothingness

Parrado and Canessa walked through the mountains for five more days. The indistinct but promising shape they had seen in the distance got closer. And, to their unspeakable relief, became a narrow valley. A river, the Rio Azufre, trickled at the base of its cradling slopes. They followed the river down, their hopes swelling with its waters. They dropped out of the snowline. They saw sparse signs of human presence: the blackened stones of an old campfire, the flattened earth of a path. Finally, nine days after setting out, they passed cows.

That evening, as Parrado gathered firewood, Canessa looked up and saw a man on a horse on the other side of the river. Parrado dropped his sticks and, although he was utterly exhausted, he galloped down to the water's edge.

The world knew first

For the fourteen people still at the crash site it was the most joyous radio broadcast they ever heard: the national news announced that Parrado and Canessa had successfully found help and rescue teams were on their way.

Parrado guided two helicopters back to the site and by the morning of 23 December 1972 the fourteen remaining passengers of Flight 571 had been plucked from the mountain.

A memorial on the crash site. Behind the memorial is the mountain that Parrado and Canessa climbed for the final push to reach rescue.

Under the Rumbling Mountain

SIX YOUNG FRIENDS WERE CAMPING BY MOUNT ST. HELENS WHEN
THE VOLCANO ERUPTED IN 1980. DESPITE BEING WELL OUTSIDE THE
DESIGNATED DANGER ZONE THEY WERE CAUGHT IN THE BURNING BLAST
WAVE AND TWO WERE KILLED. THE SURVIVORS HAD TO BRAVE SCORCHING
WINDS AND CRAWL MILES THROUGH HOT ASH TO GET HELP.

DATE:
1980

SITUATION:
VOLCANIC ERUPTION

**CONDITION OF
CONFINEMENT:**
CAUGHT IN A SCORCHING
BLAST WAVE AND TRAPPED
IN A BURNING FOREST

**DURATION OF
CONFINEMENT:**
10 HOURS

MEANS OF ESCAPE:
SHELTERING IN HOLES,
CRAWLING THROUGH
HOT ASH

NO. OF ESCAPEES:
4

DANGERS:
ASPHYXIATION, BURNT TO
DEATH, EXHAUSTION

EQUIPMENT:
NONE

ABOVE RIGHT
Mount St. Helens the day before the 1980
eruption. The view is from Johnston Ridge,
10 km (6 miles) northwest of the volcano.
The eruption removed much of the northern
face of the mountain, leaving a large crater.

At a safe distance

Everyone knew that Mount St.
Helens was a dangerous place to
be in May 1980. On 20 March, there
was a 4.1 magnitude earthquake, the
first warning sign that the volcano
had reawakened. A week later a small
explosion blew a 76 m (250 ft) hole in
the mountain and released a plume
of ash. Similar eruptions continued
for the next month and on 30 April
officials imposed a 16 km (10 mile)
'red zone' around the mountain.
No one was allowed inside without
written permission.

But the wilderness area around
the volcano is vast and the young
friends camping beside the Green
River were way beyond the danger
zone. In fact, they were 26 km
(16 miles) north of Mount St. Helens
and on the other side of two 300 m
(984 ft) high ridges. They couldn't
even see the rumbling mountain.
They could enjoy their spring
weekend in the woods no problem.
Or so they thought.

Sleeping in

There were six friends camping
in the meadow by the river in three
tents: Dan Balch and Brian Thomas;
Bruce Nelson and his girlfriend Sue
Ruff; Terry Crall and his girlfriend
Karen Varner.

Thomas had only managed to
persuade Balch to come at the last
minute; his friend had wanted to go
to the beach. But once Balch saw the
peaceful woodland meadow by the river
he loved it, and the two friends stayed
up till 3 a.m. chatting round their
campfire. At 8.32 a.m. on 18 May they
were still cosy in their sleeping bags.

Then something jolted Balch
awake. He rubbed the sleep from
his eyes to see Thomas staring out
of the tent window with his eyes
getting wider and wider.

Balch shuffled over for a look and
saw a boiling white cloud in the sky
above the ridge to the south. The
cloud quickly started turning red
and black and it was clearly heading
towards them.

Balch and Thomas sprinted from their tent and were heading for the nearest trees when the sun went out.

A furnace-like blast of heat flung Dan Balch and Brian Thomas off their feet and sucked the breath from their lungs.

A shower of ash and mud caked Balch in burning grit. He went from frozen to roasting in a heartbeat.

Balch managed to get to his feet and yelled Thomas's name. There was no answer. Then another savage burst of pain hit him: he looked down to see his hands and left leg were badly burned. He crawled over to the river to ease the pain. The water was muddy and getting warmer by the second.

He got back up onto the bank and resumed his search for his friend. As he scrambled over fallen trees he looked down and saw Thomas pinned beneath a web of torn and splintered branches.

Thomas was in agony, his hip clearly broken by the falling tree. By now the charred skin was coming off Balch's hands in chunks. The pain from his hands made him scream, but he kept working to free his friend. Somehow he was able to pull his friend up to the top of the tangle just as ash started to fall. Within seconds it was coming down so thickly that they couldn't see each other's faces though they were just inches apart.

Marshmallows toasted

Nelson and Ruff were toasting marshmallows for breakfast when the mountain exploded. For a few seconds they felt a brisk wind; the flames of their fire were blown horizontally, but they could move freely. Then daylight turned to darkness and the forest seemed to topple over.

They fled for shelter, and in the darkness and confusion they accidentally fell into a hole left by the root ball of a blown-over tree. This stroke of fortune protected them from other falling trees and undoubtedly saved their lives. After a few seconds cowering in the blackness they felt the air turn frighteningly hot. They could hear their own hair sizzling. Hair singes at 120°C and Nelson, who was a baker and worked regularly with open ovens, estimated the temperature to be about 150°C. The heatwave boiled pitch from the trees and the air was still hot enough to inflict minor burns several minutes later.

After a few minutes of darkness, the sky suddenly cleared for a few minutes and then a dense fall of ash began. Nelson and Ruff dug themselves out of the debris and called for Crall and Varner. There was no answer. Their friends were later found dead in their tent, killed by a falling tree.

Walking out of hell

Two hours after the blast, Balch and Thomas were still gathering their wits amid the debris. They had their shirt collars pulled over their noses and mouths to filter out ash, but were still nearly choking with all the caustic dust in their lungs. Then Balch saw Nelson and Ruff picking their way through the fallen trees towards them.

The eruption of Mount St. Helens on 18 May 1980, seen from West Point Peak in Gifford-Pinchot National Forest, Washington.

A panoramic image of Mount St. Helens showing miles of barren lands and destroyed landscape caused by the eruption on 18 May 1980.

Thomas was too injured to walk or be carried, so they built a makeshift lean-to in an old cabin and sheltered him there while they tried to find help.

Unfortunately for Balch, he hadn't had time to put his shoes on when they fled the tent. He now found himself scrambling from fallen tree to fallen tree trying to avoid the carpet of hot ash half a metre deep. His feet began to get severely burnt and his progress was slow. It made sense for Nelson and Ruff to hike out as fast as possible to raise the alarm.

Balch continued west, wading in the river as much as possible. After 3 km (2 miles), he ran into a local man, Buzz Smith, and his two sons. Smith lent Balch a pair of canvas tennis shoes and they trekked on. A logger joined their party and finally, after a full day's trekking, they were spotted at 6 p.m. by two rescue helicopters.

**Dan Balch walked
18 km (11 miles) barefoot
through the burning forest.**

Plucked to safety

Balch urged the rescuers to go back for his friends, but he had a tough time convincing them that Nelson and Ruff really were alive in the position he was indicating. Finally a helicopter flew off to pick them up.

> **❝ I showed them on their map where Brian was. They looked at me like I was crazy. ❞**

Nelson and Ruff had been trekking all day through the carnage and were utterly exhausted. Their relief at seeing the rescue helicopter was overwhelming, but it almost

turned to despair when the pilot didn't spot them. They had to use their clothes to stir up dust to get noticed.

Although Nelson and Ruff could now be whisked to safety, they refused to get into the helicopter unless somebody went back to pick up the injured Thomas.

Balch was airlifted to St. John Medical Center in Longview and treated for extensive burns. Thomas also was taken there for surgery on his hip. With Balch heavily sedated for his pain, it was left to hospital staff to tell his parents that their 20-year-old son wasn't at the beach after all.

Lucky to be alive

Although the world knew it was coming, the eruption of Mount St Helens surprised everyone with its violence. At 8.32 a.m. on 18 May 1980, a 5.1 magnitude earthquake rocked the volcano and the entire northern face of the mountain fell away in a gigantic rock avalanche. The avalanche created a gap in the mountain, and the pent-up pressure exploded laterally in a huge blast of pumice and ash.

The avalanche quickly grew in size as it crashed down the mountain, reaching up to 240 km/h (150 mph) and destroying everything in its path. But this was soon overtaken by the blast of pumice and ash which scorched northward at 480 km/h (300 mph) and was a raging hot 350°C. Everything within a 516 km² (200 mile²) area was devastated. The plume of ash towered 16 km (10 miles) into the atmosphere. The eruption lasted nine hours.

Fifty-seven people, mostly scientists or local residents who refused to move, were killed.

The Kindest Cut

Joe Simpson's leg was already hideously broken when he fell down a mountain crevasse and his climbing partner left him for dead. But somehow he climbed out of his icy tomb and crawled for three days and nights without food or water to reach camp only a few hours before his friends were due to leave.

DATE:
1985

SITUATION:
Climbing accident

CONDITION OF CONFINEMENT:
Stranded on an Andean peak in a storm, one climber with a broken leg

DURATION OF CONFINEMENT:
3 days

MEANS OF ESCAPE:
Crawling/climbing to safety

NO. OF ESCAPEES:
2

DANGERS:
Dehydration, falling to death, hypothermia, starvation

EQUIPMENT:
Climbing equipment

LEFT
Siula Grande seen from Cerro Yaucha, Cordillera Huayhuash, Peru.

ABOVE RIGHT
The Cordillera Huayhuash is still a popular destination for expeditions.

The dilemma

If Simon Yates cut the rope that held his friend Joe Simpson, he knew Joe would die. Simon also knew that if he didn't cut it, Joe would eventually pull him from the mountain and they would both die.

He cut the rope.

But Joe did not die.

A new route to the top

Born in 1960, Joe Simpson discovered his natural climbing ability in the hills outside his boyhood home of Sheffield. At 14 he read *The White Spider* by Heinrich Harrer, a classic mountaineering text about the first climb of the North Face of the Eiger. It fanned the flames of a passion that would push him on to ever harder ascents in the mountains of Scotland, the Alps, the Himalaya and the Andes.

In 1985, Joe Simpson was in Peru with his climbing partner Simon Yates to make a first ascent of the West Face of Siula Grande (6,344 m;

20,813 ft). With them was Richard, a traveller they had met in Lima. They trekked for two days to set up their base camp by a glacial lake. From there they would walk in and climb the peak while Richard took photos of the mountains and looked after their camp.

Descent to disaster

Several teams had previously tried and failed to climb this face. Simon and Joe were successful, but bad weather had slowed their ascent, forcing them to use all their stove's fuel. They would not be able to melt snow for drinking water on the way down. With the euphoria of their achievement fading they set out to descend via the difficult North Ridge.

Joe was leading with Simon roped 45 m (150 ft) behind him when he reached a tricky ice cliff. Joe decided to climb down the cliff using his crampons, ice axe and ice hammer. He got a good hold with the points of his crampons and dug his axe in to the ice wall. But as he was trying to get a perfect hold for his hammer, there was a crack and Joe's world turned upside down.

He fell facing the slope and both knees locked as he hit the base of the cliff. There was a crunching split in his right knee and he screamed at a surge of unimaginable pain. Thrown backwards by the impact he slid down the East Face of Siula Grande head first on his back.

> **❛ You're dead… no two ways about it! I think he knew it too. I could see it in his face. ❜**

Somehow he stopped and looked back. His left leg was tangled in the rope. His right was twisted into a sickening zigzag. The tibia had smashed up into his knee joint and shattered it. There was no way he could walk, let along climb. The pair were 5,800 m (19,000 ft) up on the ridge and alone. The mountaineer inside him knew that he had just been given a death sentence. The man who was looking at his own grotesquely swollen knee did not want to believe that.

As soon as Simon saw the damage, he knew Joe was going to die too. On his own, Simon could probably get down, but if he tried to help Joe then he might also die. Their eyes confirmed all that with each other in an instant.

But they acted differently. Joe wasn't going to lie back and die. Simon wasn't going to abandon his friend.

Joe began half dragging himself, half hopping on his ice axes across the slope towards the end of the ridge. Simon moved ahead and kicked out a trench to make Joe's job easier.

They inched themselves along for 180 m (600 ft) to the col. From here the West Face dropped away steeply in a giddy 900 m (3,000 ft) plunge of ice and rock. At the bottom, the fractured glacier led back to the base camp they had left five days before. It was four in the afternoon, it would be dark soon. It was getting colder; the men were losing feeling in their fingers. A storm was coming. They had no fuel or food. They had to keep descending.

Simon knotted their two ropes together. This gave them a length of 90 m (300 ft). By digging a seat in the snow, Simon could lower Joe straight down, slowing his descent with a belay plate. When the knot came to the belay plate, Simon would have to untie the rope to feed it through. Joe would be holding his own weight at that point.

Joe slid down the first 45 m (150 ft) quickly. Occasionally his crampon tips dug into the snow causing him to yell out in pain, but he felt amazingly positive – this was going to work!

Simon changed the rope over. If Joe fell now, he would tear Simon off the mountain too. Intense, nauseating bursts of pain wracked Joe as he was lowered. Night came and the snow howled around them, but they stuck to their routine. It was working.

With eight belays and two abseils under their belts, they had covered 825 m (2,700 ft) of the 900 m (3,000 ft) down to the glacier. They might only have two more lowers to go.

The slope had been easing, but now, as Simon paid out the rope he felt his friend rushing faster away from him. His harness bit on his flesh. What was happening?

> **❛ Then, what I had waited for pounced on me. The stars went out and I fell. ❜**

Joe knew: he was being lowered over a cliff. He tried to yell but his voice was swallowed by the thick snow clouds. Then in an avalanche of spindrift powder, he stopped, spinning on the end of the rope.

Joe looked up. The rope disappeared over the lip of an edge 4.5 m (15 ft) above. An ice wall was 2 m (6 ft) from his nose. He was dangling over the edge of an overhanging cliff that swept away from him all the way down to the glacier 30 m (100 ft) below.

Mountaineer climbing a glacier in Cordillera Huayhuash, Peru.

Directly beneath his feet was the yawning darkness of a crevasse.

There was no way Simon could pull him up. Even with a solid footing it would have required an incredible physical effort. With an unstable snow base it would be suicide. A couple of minutes of frantic yelling established that the men couldn't hear each other.

Simon wouldn't know what he had gone over. The other cliffs had been shorter. He might try to lower him further, but he would only jam when the knot reached the belay plate. Joe had to climb up – and fast.

He fished out a couple of loops of rope to tie onto the main rope with Prussik knots. These would grip the rope and enable him to climb up it. He got the first one on. But he needed two, and his fingers were now so cold they were immobile; the second loop fell tumbling into the darkness below. There was no way he could climb up now. He had been hanging for half an hour. In two more hours he would be dead; he could feel the cold was creeping over him.

> **Cold had long since won its battle. I accepted that I was to die. Sleep beckoned insistently; a black hole calling me, pain-free, lost in time, like death...**

Joe was jerked out of his contemplation of death. Up above, Simon was being dragged down the mountain. He had tried lowering Joe, hoping he might make it to the bottom, but there was no more rope to lower. The snow seat he was in was disintegrating. He couldn't hold Joe's weight indefinitely and he couldn't release the rope or he would be ripped from the slope too. His fingertips were black with frostbite. If he didn't fall he would freeze to death. He had to cut the rope.

It exploded at the first touch of the knife blade.

Glacier icefall in the high Andes, Cordillera Huayhuash, Peru.

Alive in the crevasse

In a heartbeat Joe was falling. In another he had the breath knocked from his lungs and his bones battered. There was the scuffle of falling snow then silence.

Joe looked round. He had fallen into the crevasse and landed on a ledge 15 m (50 ft) down. Blackness of hideous depth fell away from him. He hammered in an ice screw and hung on to the life that was still improbably his. He tried to climb the rough ice wall out but fell back agonizingly onto his broken leg.

Dizzy with pain he fell into a shattered sleep.

A new day

When the cold woke Joe, the sun was up and he could now see that he was on a kind of ice bridge across the top of the crevasse.

Meanwhile Simon had spent the night in a snow hole then descended to look for Joe. When he saw the ice cliff that Joe had gone over and the crevasse below, Simon knew his friend had gone. He headed numbly back to camp.

Joe had a big decision to make. He could either wait on the ice bridge for death to come or abseil down into the unknown. He hammered in

his last ice screw. But the blackness below terrified him, and it was an age before he could bear to look down. When he did, he was amazed to see not a black void, but a snow floor.

Some ragged holes made him realize this wasn't a true floor, but a ceiling above a greater abyss. At the end of his precarious cavern a slanting cone of snow rose up to the sunlight above. He would reach that sunbeam, Joe suddenly knew.

Terrified the fragile floor would give way, Joe inched his way to the ramp. It was 40 m (130 ft) high and angled at forty-five degrees rising to sixty-five degrees. Ten minutes' climbing normally. Today it was five hours before his head popped out of the ice tomb like a gopher and he took in a stunning view of sun-kissed mountains. There wasn't a cloud in the sky.

But Joe was still 60 m (200 ft) above the glacier and 10 km (6 miles) from camp. He saw Simon's rope and knew he had been left for dead. The crevasse had just been the start.

Waiting to leave

Back at the camp, Simon had dully told Richard the news. Simon then dosed himself with antibiotics and antiseptics and rested. He burnt

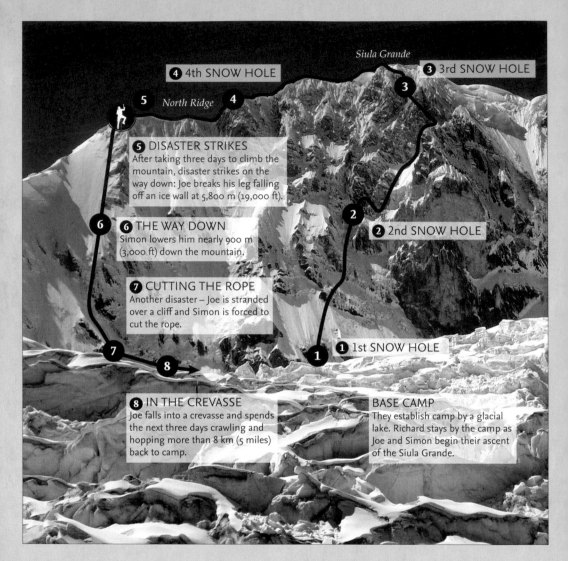

Siula Grande

4 4th SNOW HOLE

3 3rd SNOW HOLE

North Ridge

5 DISASTER STRIKES
After taking three days to climb the mountain, disaster strikes on the way down: Joe breaks his leg falling off an ice wall at 5,800 m (19,000 ft).

6 THE WAY DOWN
Simon lowers him nearly 900 m (3,000 ft) down the mountain.

7 CUTTING THE ROPE
Another disaster – Joe is stranded over a cliff and Simon is forced to cut the rope.

2 2nd SNOW HOLE

1 1st SNOW HOLE

8 IN THE CREVASSE
Joe falls into a crevasse and spends the next three days crawling and hopping more than 8 km (5 miles) back to camp.

BASE CAMP
They establish camp by a glacial lake. Richard stays by the camp as Joe and Simon begin their ascent of the Siula Grande.

Joe's clothes and gathered together the possessions that he would pass on to his parents. Guilt drooped on him like a cape.

The long crawl

Joe was lying on his side and pulling himself along with his ice axes and a push of his good leg. Occasionally he stopped to eat snow. He found Simon's footprints and for the rest of the day he hauled himself after his friend, tortured by dreams

of water, of his favourite thatched pub in Sheffield, of his mother getting ready for his return.

❛ The snow formed in patches between the rocks. It was dirty and full of grit but I ate it continually. ❜

And suddenly it was night and an avalanche was falling on him. Somehow spared again, he almost lay down and slept where he was,

but kept going until he could dig a snow hole. Outside a storm raged as Joe blacked out to spend a second night alone in the snow.

Joe awoke in the light, painfully thirsty. Frostbite had seized more of his fingers. He knew the nearest water was in the area they had called Bomb Alley, still miles away. He would be lucky to reach that today.

But at least the storm was over. And, strangely, it seemed that his leg was hurting less. Maybe it was just a muscle tear. Perhaps he could walk on it now. He stood up and passed out with the agony. He was getting delirious.

Joe reached the moraines at the end of the crevasses and made a splint from his sleeping mat and crampon straps. But he couldn't crawl on the rock, nor walk, so had to hop, a few inches at a time.

He entered a delirium of thirst, pain and hopping. Then he somehow realized he had to discipline himself. He would pick a landmark and give himself half an hour to reach it. This galvanized him into action. When he missed his target he sobbed with frustration.

He found himself scrabbling down a muddy ice cliff that he remembered from the way in. By now he was falling with every hop. But he had stopped screaming at the frequent stabs of pain. There was no one to hear him, so what was the point?

He became obsessed with getting to Bomb Alley that night and its stream of life-giving water. In his near-madness he stopped timing his landmarks and lost track of his route. Eventually he dropped to the rock and slept.

Camp

Another day had brought Simon's strength back. He didn't want to leave, but knew that they had to. Richard went down the valley to find the donkey driver and instruct him to come for them in the morning.

Another night

Joe had a bad night. He had deteriorated to the point where he could only pull himself along with his arms. The pain was at a new level of intensity. Three days and nights without water had maddened him. But somehow he made it to Bomb Alley where he drank until his stomach ached with the cold of the water, then he drank some more.

Gradually he felt his strength returning. He restarted his time

Joe Simpson, writer and climber.

targets. A strange, disembodied voice kept urging him onwards. He found Simon and Richard's bootprints in the mud and felt the buzz of being nearer to them.

Suddenly he was at the first lake, a beautifully clear pool with green shadows. Beyond was a second smaller lake and behind that were the tents. But now he was reduced to just shuffling along backwards on his bottom. He still had to climb up the moraine wall that dammed the water. What if the tents weren't there when he got to the top? Could the world be that cruel?

Another night fell and he crawled on through it. The voice told him he had to. But he lost track of where he was. Surely he should be at the camp by now? Or was he back on the glacier? Were these cactus spines digging into him? Grass? Should he sleep here?

His nostrils flared at the sharp smell of what could only be shit. He must be close to camp! He only had to stand up and shout – if they were still there…

'Simon!!'

He couldn't lift his head to see if his cries had been heard. But now

there were scuffling noises, a light, voices – not his – and then a light dazzled him.

'Joe?! Is that you?!'

Mule journey

Joe had reached camp just a few hours before Simon and Richard were due to leave with the donkey. If they had, he would have had no chance.

After an agonizing two-day mule ride they made it to Cajatambo where they hired a truck to take them to Lima.

Joe's leg was yellow and brown and swollen as thick as his thigh all the way to the ankle. Purple streaks showed haemorrhaging around the knee and ankle where it was broken. He had lost 19 kg (3 stone).

After two days waiting without painkillers in hospital while his insurance company sent clearance, he was finally operated on. Joe needed six operations on his knee. The doctors said he would never climb again and that he would have a permanent limp. After two years of rehabilitation, he was back on the mountains. All subsequent climbers have avoided the North Ridge and rappelled back down the face.

The Day the Mountain Caught Fire

THE FOREST FIRE ON STORM KING MOUNTAIN WAS SMALL AT FIRST, THEN IN SECONDS IT BLEW UP INTO A HELLISH INFERNO WITH 100-FT FLAMES THAT TRAPPED FORTY-NINE FIREFIGHTERS. STARING INTO THE HEART OF THE GALLOPING FLAMES, SOMEHOW MOST OF THEM MANAGED TO WALK AWAY FROM ONE OF THE DEADLIEST WILDFIRES IN US HISTORY.

DATE:
1994

SITUATION:
FOREST FIRE

CONDITION OF CONFINEMENT:
TRAPPED ON A MOUNTAIN ABOVE THE FIRE

DURATION OF CONFINEMENT:
A FEW SECONDS TO SEVERAL HOURS

MEANS OF ESCAPE:
RUNNING, CLIMBING, DEPLOYING FIRE SHELTER

NO. OF ESCAPEES:
35

DANGERS:
BURNING TO DEATH, ASPHYXIATION, SMOKE INHALATION

EQUIPMENT:
FIRE FIGHTING EQUIPMENT

ABOVE RIGHT
The mountains to the west of Glenwood Springs, Colorado.

A necessary danger

Fires consume 16,000–20,000 km² (1.6 million to 2 million hectares) of forest in the US every year. More often than not they are a natural phenomenon; trees are frequently ignited by lighting strikes. Regular small fires are a normal part of the forest ecosystem: they clear out dense brush, letting more sunlight through to new growth and preventing a build up of fuel that could lead to larger devastation.

Not every fire is tackled. If it starts naturally, often the policy is to let it burn itself out. But if it is ignited by human accident or arson, or if it threatens life or property, it is fought. Even in these situations, each reported fire is analysed and assigned a priority. This logical system can work well – until Nature decides to do something unpredictable.

Hot, dry and windy

Colorado enjoyed a fine spring in 1994. Sunshine and little rainfall provided balmy days for picnickers and hikers. Unfortunately the conditions were also nearly perfect for creating wildfires. The state's 98,743 km² (9.9 million hectares) of woodland were virtually bone dry, humidity was low and a warm June gave way to an equally warm July.

There was fuel and heat – two sides of the lethal 'wildfire triangle'. Now if a strong wind arose it would provide a flow of oxygen and create a potentially lethal triumvirate.

Then, on 2 July 1994, lightning struck a lone pine on a ridge near the base of Storm King Mountain, 11 km (7 miles) west of Glenwood Springs, Colorado. The tree caught fire and the flames began to spread.

The inferno smoulders

The fire was small. There were no people or property nearby. Its pinyon and juniper fuel was limited and relatively slow burning. Lightning had sparked forty fires in the district in the last two days alone. Officials gave the South Canyon fire a low priority and allowed it to smoulder.

At first, this seemed to have been the correct course of action. On 4 July, after two days of burning, the fire had consumed only 12,000 m² (3 acres) – not much by wildfire standards. But the blaze was creeping closer to the houses on the Canyon Creek Estates, and locals pressed the authorities to take action. The next day they sent in the fire crews.

Hotshots and smokejumpers

The fire crews sent by the Forest Service and Bureau of Land Management went into action on 5 July. A seven-person team hiked for two and a half hours through steep, densely vegetated terrain to the fire, cleared a helicopter landing area (Helispot 1), and started digging the firelines that would contain the burn. Meanwhile an air tanker dropped retardant on the fire.

When this crew left in the evening to rest and repair their chainsaws, eight 'smokejumpers' took over the groundwork. Smokejumpers are specialists who parachute in to fight fires in remote areas and they noticed that the fire had jumped the original fireline, so they started on a second one running from Helispot 1 downhill on the ridge's east side.

By the morning of the 6 July it was clear that the fire was growing. The fire crews and smokejumpers cleared a second landing area (Helispot 2) and were joined by eight more smokejumpers. Later on twenty 'hotshots' were called in from Oregon to help. Hotshots are an elite group of wildland firefighters known for their ability to tackle the worst fires in the toughest locations.

Now there were over forty young men and women battling the fire on Storm King Mountain. They were all experts in their profession and the crews were optimistic that they could control the fire. Then, just after 3 p.m., the weather changed.

The wall of flame

It was clear to 23-year-old firefighter Brian Lee that this fire was something different when a helicopter dropped a 180-gallon container of water on to a spot that was starting to burn and the flames roared up like it had been a squirt from a water pistol.

It was 3.20 p.m. and a dry cold front had moved into the area, bringing high winds sweeping over the mountain's contours. The resulting gusts were like high-speed injections of oxygen into the fire. Flames as high as 30 m (100 ft) were soon racing through the burn area.

Within a few minutes the fire had skipped over the bottom of the west 'drainage', or gully, and was spreading up the face of the ravine. The rapid winds also led to 'spotting' – the jumping of the fire caused when hot embers are raised by convection and carried through the air. New pockets of fire soon appeared on the east side beneath the firefighters and rapidly moved up the steep slopes into dense, highly flammable Gambel oak.

There were two groups working on that flank of the mountain: nine

The burning forest on Storm King Mountain, Colorado.

Fourteen crosses were erected on Storm King Mountain to commemorate where the firefighters lost their lives on 6 July 1994.

firefighters working on the lower slopes and eleven on the ridge line. Bryan was one of the eleven. Just before 4 p.m., Jon Kelso from the lower team radioed Bryan's team up on the ridge to say there was a spot fire below them. Nothing more was ever heard from Jon and his eight colleagues.

By now the winds on the ridge were at least 80 kph (50 mph) and were blowing the heavily laden men from their feet. Bryan and his crew were immediately ordered to get out.

Running the ridge

Wildfires can move at 22 kph (14 mph) on level grasslands; on steep slopes with high gusting

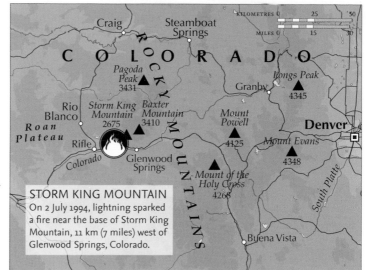

STORM KING MOUNTAIN
On 2 July 1994, lightning sparked a fire near the base of Storm King Mountain, 11 km (7 miles) west of Glenwood Springs, Colorado.

winds, the pace can be phenomenal. One firefighter estimated that the fire moved 600 m (1,970 ft) in about twenty-five seconds. Another saw flames that were 46 m (150 ft) high. No person caught in the face of such an advancing fire can realistically hope to outrun it, particularly not up a slope and wearing heavy protective clothing. Incredibly, that is just what several firefighters managed to do.

> **❛ I remember looking out from the ridge and just seeing clear. Then... as I looked back five seconds later, the whole skyline was completely black. ❜**

One of the fundamental rules of firefighting is to leave a way out. Bryan's team headed for one of the cleared helispots, which no longer had any fuel to burn. But before they could make it the blue sky turned into a boiling black wall of smoke and the apparently safe helispot was leaping with flames.

He and his colleagues had no option but to turn and run down the hill towards a saddle in the ridge. The 12-m (40-ft) high flames were only 15 m (50 ft) away and leaping closer every second. Bryan's mouth and lungs were choking with ash.

They reached the saddle but the fire was still right behind them. That is when they saw the gully dropping down off the ridge.

Going down into the gully had its own dangers. If the fire had spotted into the gully's base and the wind came, the ravine would act like a funnel, drawing the flame right up toward the men. But the smokejumpers insisted that this was the quickest route to the highway so they dropped down.

For a full mile they plunged through the ravine. The fire was roaring and crashing at their heels, as loud as a freight train. A smokejumper tumbled down from nowhere, the back of his head black and burned.

> **❛ We couldn't get the rest of our crew on the radio. We thought it was just because they were running. We didn't know they were already dead. ❜**

Half falling, half running down bare rock faces and under fallen trees they kept going and somehow managed to tumble clear of the fire onto a highway. One firefighter reported he saw two of his colleagues

actually running out of the flames. Many of the reflectors on the rear of the men's helmets had melted into black and bubbling splodges.

A hot and deadly summer

There were fourteen fatalities on the mountain that day and that year's fire season would become the deadliest in US history. Ultimately it came down to luck – where the firefighters were when the inferno turned and swept up the mountain. All of the nine in the lower team perished; some so quickly that by the time they stopped running and fell to their knees, they were dead. Bryan's team of eleven all survived.

A further twenty-four firefighters also survived. As well as those who fled in the face of the fire, many managed to cling to life inside their fire shelters. These are portable, packable cocoons made of layers of aluminium foil, woven silica, and fibreglass, which reflect radiant heat, protect against convective heat and trap breathable air. Knowing that they were going to be caught by the flames, the firefighters wrapped the shelter round themselves and sat tight until the fire raged over, around and past them.

The Miracle of Stairway B

When the 110-floor North Tower of the World Trade Center collapsed on 11 September 2001 it brought half a million tons of steel and concrete avalanching to earth. Somehow, a few floors of a stairway in that tower avoided total destruction. And within that tiny pocket, sixteen people survived the cataclysm.

DATE:
2001

SITUATION:
Terrorist attack

CONDITION OF CONFINEMENT:
Trapped in the North Tower of the World Trade Center on 9/11

DURATION OF CONFINEMENT:
102 minutes

MEANS OF ESCAPE:
Good fortune

NO. OF ESCAPEES:
16

DANGERS:
Fire, crushing, asphyxiation

EQUIPMENT:
The firemen had tools and equipment; the office workers had nothing

LEFT
Smoke billows from the Twin Towers due to impact damage from the airliners on 11 September 2001.

ABOVE RIGHT
At approximately 9.59 a.m. the South Tower of the World Trade Center collapsed after being hit by a plane.

Caught in a catastrophe

It was 10 a.m. on 11 September 2001, and Pasquale Buzzelli, a 34-year-old structural engineer, was still in his office on the 64th floor of the North Tower of the World Trade Center. The South Tower had collapsed just moments earlier after burning for fifty-six minutes. He was on the phone to his wife who was seven months pregnant and watching the horror of 9/11 unfold on TV at home in New Jersey. Pasquale told her not to worry. He was about to head down Stairwell B with a dozen colleagues. There was no smoke. He'd be fine. He put the phone down, slung his briefcase over his shoulder and led his team to the stairs.

The narrow stairs were crowded, so they could only move slowly. It took them twenty-eight minutes to walk down forty-two floors.

Then, as Pasquale reached the 22nd floor, he felt the building shake. The concrete stairs beneath his feet lurched like a ship's deck in a storm.

He heard thuds, as if heavy objects were being dropped somewhere high above. The thuds got louder, really quickly. Instinctively he dived into a corner as the walls buckled and folded on top of him. Oddly, he felt himself in free fall, and then the blackness swallowed everything.

A good turn

Captain Jay Jonas and five of his fire crew were on the 27th floor of the North Tower when they heard a sickening rumble. The staircase swayed and the lights flickered off and on. Jonas's radio crackled and a captain from another company told him that South Tower had just collapsed.

Jonas immediately decided to evacuate his men. The North Tower had been the first building to be hit by a plane. If the South Tower had just fallen, they couldn't have long to live. He didn't tell his men why they were going, he just got them moving. Despite each man

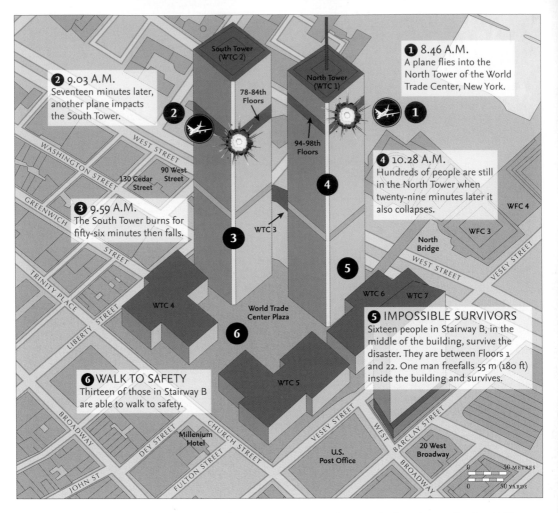

1 8.46 A.M.
A plane flies into the North Tower of the World Trade Center, New York.

2 9.03 A.M.
Seventeen minutes later, another plane impacts the South Tower.

3 9.59 A.M.
The South Tower burns for fifty-six minutes then falls.

4 10.28 A.M.
Hundreds of people are still in the North Tower when twenty-nine minutes later it also collapses.

5 IMPOSSIBLE SURVIVORS
Sixteen people in Stairway B, in the middle of the building, survive the disaster. They are between Floors 1 and 22. One man freefalls 55 m (180 ft) inside the building and survives.

6 WALK TO SAFETY
Thirteen of those in Stairway B are able to walk to safety.

South Tower (WTC 2)

North Tower (WTC 1)

78-84th Floors

94-98th Floors

WEST STREET

WASHINGTON STREET

130 Cedar Street

90 West Street

GREENWICH STREET

TRINITY PLACE

LIBERTY STREET

WTC 3

WTC 4

World Trade Center Plaza

WTC 5

WTC 6

WTC 7

North Bridge

WEST STREET

VESEY STREET

WFC 4

WFC 3

BROADWAY

DEY STREET

CHURCH STREET

FULTON STREET

Millenium Hotel

U.S. Post Office

VESEY STREET

WEST

BARCLAY STREET

BROADWAY

20 West Broadway

JOHN ST

0   50 METRES

0   50 YARDS

---

carrying close to 45 kilos (100 lbs) of equipment, they set a fast pace down the stairs.

They ticked off seven floors in a few minutes and were at the twentieth when they ran into Josephine Harris. A car had hit the 59-year-old book-keeper just a few months earlier, injuring her leg. Harris had already hobbled down fifty floors and was now moving pretty slowly.

One of Jonas's men asked what they should do. He knew that if they continued down she would be left to struggle on alone. If they

helped her, they would be risking all their lives.

'We got to bring her with us,' said Jonas.

It was a decision that would save all of their lives.

Fifteen floors further down, just five from the ground, Harris could take no more. She stopped, utterly exhausted. Jonas knew they'd have to carry her the rest of the way. As he ran into the nearest office space to look for a chair another man, David Lim, stepped up and put an arm around Harris. They helped her down one more floor.

And then the wind started.

A skyscraper in freefall

At first there was no noise, just the eerie whoosh of fast-moving air inside the building. The people in Stairway B didn't know it, but the 101-storey tower was collapsing on top of them, 'pancaking' down from the top.

The building was buckling where the planes had hit, throwing its weight onto the central columns. When these finally melted, the crown of the building dropped freely for a full floor. Had it even fallen for just 0.5 m (2 ft) it would have had sufficient force to flatten the next storey. Now it was unstoppable.

The air inside the building had to go somewhere, and much of it went blasting down the stairwells.

Fireman Matty Komorowski remembers being lifted clean off his feet: 'I was taking a staircase at a time. It was a combination of me running and getting blown down.' In the eight seconds it took the building to come down, Komorowski cleared three floors.

The people in Stairwell B couldn't see it, but the entire North Tower, half a million tons of concrete and steel, was avalanching to the ground.

Walking out of the apocalypse

For those who were conscious, the noise was a physical presence.

> 𝟞 The screaming roar of a thousand feet of building falling on top of them penetrated every atom of their bodies... 𝟫

It was like being at the bottom of Niagara Falls, except it was steel and concrete pouring over the edge.

Then, finally the roar faded. And one by one, the remaining people in Stairwell B realized that, incredibly, they were still alive. Komorowski had landed on his feet, buried to his knees in pulverized cement, but otherwise fine.

Captain Jonas coughed the dust from his lungs and radioed for help.

> 𝟞 "We're in the North Tower," he broadcast. Another firefighter answered: "Where's the North Tower?" 𝟫

From the outside, the building seemed to have been completely flattened. All that remained was an apocalyptic landscape of twisted metal, broken rubble and choking dust.

But as the thick cloud of ash began to clear, five flights of Stairwell B could be seen poking up through 100 floors' worth of rubble like a chimney. Somehow that one section had avoided destruction.

Inside, the survivors noticed a tiny shaft of sun through an opening at the top of the stairwell. They scrambled towards it.

Josephine Harris had to be hoisted out, but thirteen people in Stairway B simply climbed out of their tomb and walked across the debris to safety. Two others, including Buzzelli, were rescued from the rubble.

People walk away from the World Trade Center tower after it was hit by a plane.

The impossible survivors

Sixteen people survived inside the collapse of the World Trade Center, and they were all in Stairwell B of the North Tower between Floors 22 and 1 when the tower came down. Everyone above Floor 22 died; most who were at Floor 1 or lower also perished. Four more survivors were rescued from the underground mall.

Had the people in that stairway walked a step or two slower they would have died; so, too, if they had moved a step or two faster. Was that fate? God's will? Sheer chance?

> 𝟞 What is certainly true is that if the firemen hadn't stopped to help Josephine Harris, they would have been dead. 𝟫

One lucky guy

The light returned to Pasquale Buzzelli and he found himself sitting on top of a pile of rubble, his feet dangling over the edge, as if he were sat in his armchair at home. Astonished firemen plucked him from his perch and carried him away. He had fallen for 55 metres (180 ft) within the disintegrating building. His only injury was a broken heel.

A total of 2,752 people lost their lives on 9/11.

The rubble of the World Trade Center smoulders following the terrorist attack.

A Rock and a Hard Place

A LONE CLIMBER IS TRAPPED BY A FALLING ROCK IN THE DESOLATE CANYONS OF UTAH. AFTER FIVE DAYS OF DEHYDRATION, STARVATION AND HALLUCINATIONS, HE MAKES THE DECISION TO CUT OFF HIS OWN RIGHT ARM WITH A PENKNIFE TO FREE HIMSELF FROM THE BOULDER. ONCE FREE HE STILL HAS TO ABSEIL AND WALK HIS WAY BACK TO SAFETY.

DATE:
2003

SITUATION:
CLIMBING ACCIDENT

CONDITION OF CONFINEMENT:
TRAPPED BY A FALLEN ROCK

DURATION OF CONFINEMENT:
5 DAYS

MEANS OF ESCAPE:
CUTTING OFF HIS OWN RIGHT ARM WITH A PENKNIFE

NO. OF ESCAPEES:
1

DANGERS:
STARVATION, DEHYDRATION, BLEEDING TO DEATH

EQUIPMENT:
PENKNIFE

ABOVE RIGHT
Canyonlands National Park, Utah.

Loner's day out

He wanted to be alone for this adventure, that much was certain.

When Aron Ralston set out from home in Aspen, Colorado, he told no one where he was going. It's common climbing practice to leave a route either with friends or on a piece of paper in your car. Ralston did neither. As an experienced climber he should have known better.

Nature is king in Canyonlands. Rain, river and wind have spent millennia gouging out deep, twisting canyons from the flat desert plateau. Like veins, they offer a route through the wilderness. Like veins they are also hidden from view, lying below the surface of the plateau. It's a weirdly beautiful but also dangerous place: get stuck in a lost corner of a canyon and there is no reason why another human being would find you for days, months or years. If at all.

It was Saturday 26 April 2003 and Ralston had selected a particularly isolated part of what is already a remote area. His plan was to park at Horseshoe Canyon and mountain bike 24 km (15 miles) to Bluejohn Canyon. Bluejohn was the favoured hideout spot of Butch Cassidy and the Sundance Kid; its remoteness is one of its defining characteristics.

> **❛ It was amazing that he was walking on his own, losing as much blood as fast as he was. ❜**

He would then scramble and climb through the narrow ravine and hike back round to his pickup. By his standards, it wasn't a particularly big day. Ralston, 27, was a keen outdoorsman and climber. He had already climbed forty-nine of Colorado's fifty-five peaks over 4,300 m (14,000 ft), forty-five of them solo in winter. This outing was just a warm-up for a greater challenge: an ascent of North America's highest mountain, 6,195 m (20,320 ft) tall Mount McKinley.

Ralston had packed accordingly. All he had in his rucksack were two burritos, a litre (½ pint) of water, a cheap Leatherman-like multi-tool, a small first aid kit, a video camera, a digital camera and some climbing equipment. He was wearing just a T-shirt, shorts and baseball cap and had no spare clothing.

The accident

Ralston pedalled across the desert to the canyon trailhead and secured his bike to a juniper tree. He began 'canyoneering' down the sinuous ravine. This technique uses elements of climbing, scrambling, jumping and skidding as well as technical ropework – anything that will get you through the canyon.

It was just before lunchtime and Ralston had traversed most of the canyon. When he was just 150 m (492 ft) from the final abseil out of the canyon, he came into a 0.9 m (3 ft) wide crack. Like many of the smaller ravines it had boulders wedged in it. Most of these are stuck fast, jammed there for centuries. But the elements are constantly rearranging the desert, and many stones will rock or slide when moved.

Ralston climbed up the boulder face and stood on top. It seemed perfectly stable. Then, as he clambered down the opposite side, the 364 kg (800 lb) rock moved. It clattered and slid for several feet, throwing up dust and taking Ralston tumbling with it. Then, as suddenly as it had moved, it stopped. Dust billowed and the noise of the rockfall echoed through the wind-carved canyon. Ralston was upright and generally okay. There was just one problem – his right hand was crushed between the boulder and the rock wall.

The cruellest cut

Anger flooded through him as he pulled his hand and beat at the rock. But dwelling on the absurdity and foolishness of his situation would not help him get out. And Ralston was an extremely practical thinker. He calmed down and weighed up his options.

Another climber could find him. But the chance of that happening was very, very slim.

He had to try to free himself. Ralston began chipping away at the boulder and the wall with his cheap knife. But after ten hours of chipping, he had only a small handful of rock dust to show for his efforts. If anything, because of the way the rock was resting on his hand, his chipping was only helping the boulder settle itself more securely.

> ❛ I had the knife out and applied a tourniquet to my upper arm, using my biking shorts as the padding, and then I went to task. ❜

Next he tried using his climbing ropes to rig a hoist that would lift the boulder. But climbing ropes are designed to stretch and Ralston could generate little leverage. The rock resolutely refused to budge.

Night came, and the temperature dropped to just above freezing. Ralston wrapped himself in his ropes for added warmth and kept working to free himself.

On Sunday morning a shaft of warming sunlight found its way down to the narrow canyon floor. But it only lingered for a quarter of an hour. Ralston began forcing himself to stay optimistic. He also started rationing the precious little food and water he had.

Sunday passed, and Monday too, but he was still trapped. Now he had run out of food and water, and was starting to hallucinate. 'I believed I could see my family and friends around me, which was comforting,' he later said.

On the third day he decided to cut off his trapped hand, but his knife was so blunted from chipping at the rock that he could barely break the skin. He waited a little longer.

Ralston knew the mountain rescue protocol better than anyone; he worked in a mountaineering shop and was a volunteer rescuer. Even if his work colleagues reported him missing, the police would automatically wait twenty-four hours before declaring him lost. That would mean a rescue on Wednesday at the earliest. He started saving his urine.

Blood stains on a sandstone canyon wall show the spot where Aron Ralston's hand was trapped by the chockstone.

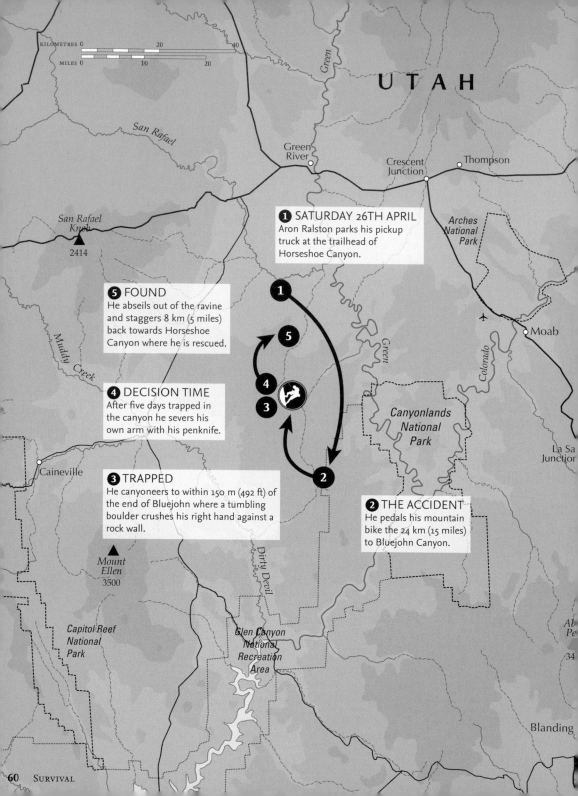

UTAH

Green River

Crescent Junction

Thompson

Arches National Park

1 SATURDAY 26TH APRIL
Aron Ralston parks his pickup truck at the trailhead of Horseshoe Canyon.

5 FOUND
He abseils out of the ravine and staggers 8 km (5 miles) back towards Horseshoe Canyon where he is rescued.

4 DECISION TIME
After five days trapped in the canyon he severs his own arm with his penknife.

3 TRAPPED
He canyoneers to within 150 m (492 ft) of the end of Bluejohn where a tumbling boulder crushes his right hand against a rock wall.

2 THE ACCIDENT
He pedals his mountain bike the 24 km (15 miles) to Bluejohn Canyon.

San Rafael

San Rafael Knob
2414

Muddy Creek

Caineville

Mount Ellen
3500

Capitol Reef National Park

Canyonlands National Park

Moab

La Sal Junction

Dirty Devil

Glen Canyon National Recreation Area

Blanding

On Wednesday, Ralston pulled out his video camera and recorded a farewell message to his parents. He also etched his name, birth date and 'RIP' into the canyon wall. By now he was sipping the urine he had previously saved.

Hallucinations haunted him. He dreamt of water, his family, friends, and finally on Thursday morning he had a vision of a 3-year-old boy running across a sunlit floor and being picked up by a one-armed man. To Ralston, the meaning of this was clear: it was a premonition of his future son. He had to get out. Now.

> **❛ I've never seen anybody who has the will to live and is as much of a warrior as Aron is and I've been doing this for 25 years. ❜**

Since his blade was too blunt to cut the bones in his forearm, Ralston knew he had to break them. Using the edge of the boulder as a fulcrum he threw his whole weight away from his hand and pushed with his legs. After a few agonizing minutes, a snap, as loud as a gunshot, echoed up and down his snaking prison. He had broken his radius. With a few more minutes of excruciating pulling, he cracked the ulna, the bone on the outside of the forearm.

Now he bound a tourniquet round his arm, twisting the strap with a karabiner to increase its bite. Then, with the dull knife blade, he began digging away at the muscles, nerves and sinews of his forearm.

It took him an hour to cut right through.

The final challenge

Ralston staggered back from the rock. There was his hand, jammed under a rock, 3 m (10 ft) in front of him. Here he was, able to move freely for the first time in five days. He had done it. But he wasn't safe yet.

He took out his first aid kit, applied antiseptic cream and

Aron Ralston pauses while answering a reporter's question as his mother Donna comforts him at St. Mary's Hospital, 9 May 2003 in Grand Junction, Colorado.

bandaged the stump as best he could. Then he rigged up a sling from his water bottle bag and gathered his climbing kit.

Bleeding heavily, Ralston got to where his side route met the main canyon. This was 25 m (75 ft) above the canyon floor. Despite only having one arm, and being on the edge of unconsciousness, Aron managed to rig his anchors and abseil safely to the dusty rock below. Leaving his rope hanging, he staggered out to rejoin the world.

Found

Dutch couple Eric and Monique Meijer and their son, Andy, had been taking photographs of the scenic Grand Gallery. They had just packed their gear and turned to leave the canyon when they heard a voice: 'Help. I need help.'

They turned to see Ralston walking towards them. Splattered with dried and fresh blood, emaciated and dehydrated he must have looked close to death. But when he spoke it was lucidly: 'Hello, my name is Aron, I fell off a cliff on Saturday and I was stuck under a boulder. I just cut off my hand

four hours ago and I need medical attention. I need a helicopter.'

The Meijers fed him biscuits and gave him water until the helicopter arrived. Ralston was able to walk unaided from the helipad to the emergency room.

> **❛ I felt very frustrated with myself for not leaving a note about my destination in my car parked at the foot of the canyon, so no one knew where I was. ❜**

When rescuers went back for his squashed hand, it took three strong men with lifting equipment more than an hour to hoist the 364 kg (800 lb) rock. There was no way that Ralston's splintered, severed hand could be stitched back on. This single fact has convinced Ralston that he made the right choice. 'That rock was going nowhere, and nor was my hand,' he said.

The premonition that Ralston had at the height of his ordeal became reality. Three years after the accident he met his future wife, Jessica. In January 2010 they had a son, Leo.

Aron Ralston continues to climb.

Bad Luck for the Good Samaritan

Ricky Megee was driving 4,800 km (3,000 miles) across Australia's northern desert when he was abducted and left for dead. With no shoes or shelter he clung to life by a remote water hole, surviving on a diet of lizards, leeches and frogs as he lost half his bodyweight.

DATE:	
2006	

SITUATION:
Abduction

CONDITION OF CONFINEMENT:
Lost in Australian Outback

DURATION OF CONFINEMENT:
71 days

MEANS OF ESCAPE:
Living on bush food, swimming a flooded river

NO. OF ESCAPEES:
1

DANGERS:
Murder, dehydration, starvation, sunstroke

EQUIPMENT:
None at first; some farm equipment later

LEFT
The Australian Outback, Northern Territory, Australia.

ABOVE RIGHT
The desolate landscape of the Australian Outback.

Bad luck for the Good Samaritan

It was a rough part of the desert, and Ricky Megee was a good man, so when he saw the three men waving down his car, he immediately pulled over. Sure, they looked a bit dishevelled, but who would not out here?

Ricky agreed to give one of them a lift, and the two men shared a drink. But he had not been driving long when the world began to fade and tilt, his senses swam and then all was blackness.

When he returned to consciousness, he was in a shallow grave under a tarpaulin and with bricks on his back. And so began seventy-one days of parched horror in the pitiless heart of the Australian Outback.

The job interview

It was January 2006 and 35-year-old Ricky Megee was making a fresh start. He had just secured a new job in a branch of the Australian Government's employment service, Centre Link, in the town of Port Hedland on the northwest coast. This would be a major life change: at the time Ricky lived 4,800 km (3,000 miles) away in Brisbane. But as he clambered into his battered Mitsubishi 4x4 on a blistering summer's day, Ricky was optimistic. A new road lay before him.

Several days and a few thousand dusty kilometres later and he was driving west on the Buntine Highway just before it crosses from the Northern Territory into Western Australia. This is a hopelessly remote part of a huge and desolate landscape. It was the end of the rainy season, which meant many roads were impassable with mud. Even the ranchers had left the huge cattle stations, waiting for the weather to become slightly more tolerable before returning to their farms. It had been a long time since Ricky had seen another soul.

It was no wonder then that as he motored along, his mind freewheeling on his future, Ricky was extremely surprised to see three men standing beside the road up ahead.

Left for dead

Exactly how events unfolded in the next few hours will probably never be known; Ricky can't remember. What is certain is that after agreeing to give one of the men a lift, he was drugged, mugged, and left for dead.

The first sensation that came to him as he regained consciousness was the smell of earth; his face was close to the dirt. As he tried to move to suck in more air, he felt something heavy on his back, pinning him down. Kicking and scrabbling his way free with increasing vigour, Ricky realised that he was lying in a shallow hole under a sheet of plastic weighted down with rocks.

He staggered to his feet and was so dazed and woozy that it took him half an hour to even pin down the basic facts of his situation. They were not good. His car was nowhere to be seen. He was dressed in only a T-shirt and shorts; his assailant having stolen his shoes and socks. The cracked and scrubby desert stretched out infinitely in every direction, with only a few twisted trees offering any sort of shade. Ricky had no idea of his location – beyond the obvious fact that he was in the middle of a desert where the daytime temperature would be around 42°C.

Ricky forced himself to concentrate and set out towards the nearest hill to get a better view of his situation.

Barefoot on the burning rocks

The panorama from the rise in the desert gave him little new information: there was no road, house or person to be seen.

Ricky knew it would take a week to walk across this desert – with full supplies and ample chance to rest in the shade – so was under no illusions about the danger he was in. But still he was hopeful; if he started walking, surely by simply covering more ground he would increase his chances of being found?

Despite still feeling ill from the after effects of whatever drug had knocked him out, he started pacing his way east – back in the rough direction he had come.

The thirst begins

With no water, no shade and no shoes, the ferocious desert sun was taking a heavy toll on Ricky's body within hours. His feet blistered, bruised and tore on the hot sand and rock. His sweat surrendered vital moisture to the whipping winds. His already confused mind received no nutrients to help repair and sustain his senses.

Ricky had no fluids at all for the first thirty-six hours of his ordeal, until he became so thirsty that he drank his own urine. Later on that second day he saw some rain clouds stacking high above the horizon and staggered towards them. He missed the downpour, but managed to suck some muddy water from puddles on rocks. Then he kept walking.

The next day he stumbled upon a river; for most of the year this would have been bone dry, but the seasonal downpours had filled the watercourse. Ricky was able to slake his burning thirst and even drift for a few kilometres with the current in the hope of finding some sign of human life.

For the next few days, Ricky used the river as his waymarker. Finally,

A highway through the barren landscape near Port Hedland, Western Australia.

when he became too exhausted to go any further, he scrabbled together a shelter near a water hole and hauled himself into its shade to rest.

Bush tucker

It was six days since Ricky had woken up under the sheet of plastic, and he still hadn't eaten. He was lying under a scrubby tree, flattened by the heat of the sun, when he saw a lizard inching its way along the branch above him. Without a conscious thought, he seized the creature and killed it. Then he impaled it on a stick and laid it out in direct sunlight to slowly cook a little. When the animal was dry enough, Ricky peeled off most of its skin and ate the rest.

This was the start of a two-month diet of bush food that was desperately unpalatable but which kept him alive.

Ricky consumed grasshoppers, caterpillars, frogs, stick insects, cockroaches and even leeches, which he pulled from water holes. He found that he had to chew these up as quickly as possible to prevent them from taking a bite out of the inside of his mouth.

Lizards became part of Ricky's diet whilst he endured weeks surviving in the Australian Outback.

> ❝ I ate the leeches raw, straight out of the dam, grasshoppers, I just ate them. ❞

He also started eating the tough, fibrous vegetation. If a plant tasted bad, he spat it out. After much experimentation he found two types that stayed down and seemed to provide some sort of nutrition.

His meagre diet was enough to keep his organs working, although it could not stop extreme weight loss. Day by day, Ricky began to fade.

A home in the wilderness

Eventually, hunger forced him to keep walking from his first camp. He passed cattle stations but no people. Ultimately he walked around 90 km (56 miles) before he found another water hole. He passed out three times en-route and could only crawl the last 500 m (1,640 ft) to his new sanctuary.

Here he found enough scattered farm equipment to build himself a tube-like shelter or 'humpy' which would keep the worst of the sun off during the day. Ricky didn't know it, but this would be his home for the next seven weeks.

Unwelcome guests

As the days rolled into weeks, Ricky established a routine that kept him sane and barely nourished. Every day he collected water and in the early evening did a 'food run', catching as many frogs and lizards as he could – six to eight on a good day. He would then peg these out to dry before he consumed them.

> ❝ I would go out just before dark and gather what I could to eat. I ate one meal a day – that is enough to survive. I just hoped and prayed that someone would find me. ❞

After a few weeks of this precarious existence he spotted a dingo. Soon he saw another, and it wasn't long before he realised that a pack was watching him. They rested at the edge of his vision during the day and circled his camp at night, snuffling and growling in their impatience for a meal. Every evening Ricky blocked up the entrance to his humpy with stones to prevent the dogs from taking him as he slept.

As he lay there in the darkness the wind would play a cruel trick of its own: whistling through the gaps in his abode, it sounded just like an approaching car.

DIY dentistry

Sixty days into his ordeal, Ricky awoke to a new type of pain. The side of his face was aching and swollen. In his dazed state he assumed that he had been bitten by one of the many poisonous spiders that live in this dangerous corner of the world. Knowing that he had no hope of counteracting the poison, he simply waited for death to take him.

When he was still alive 24 hours later and the pain was markedly worse, he investigated the problem further, feeling carefully around inside his mouth. His gums were hot with blisters and a fierce pain under one tooth told him that he had an abscess.

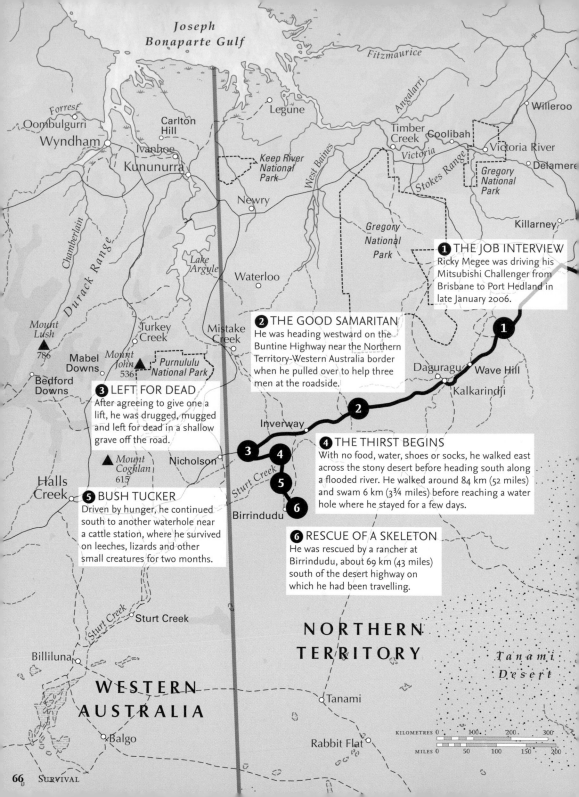

Joseph
Bonaparte Gulf

Fitzmaurice

Forrest
Oombulgurri
Wyndham
Carlton Hill
Ivanhoe
Kununurra

Legune

West Baines

Angalarri

Timber Creek
Coolibah
Victoria River
Willeroo
Delamere

Victoria

Stokes Range

Gregory National Park

Killarney

Keep River National Park

Newry

Waterloo

Lake Argyle

Mount Lush
▲
786

Mabel Downs
Bedford Downs

Turkey Creek

Mount John
▲ 536
Purnululu National Park

Mistake Creek

Gregory National Park

1 THE JOB INTERVIEW
Ricky Megee was driving his Mitsubishi Challenger from Brisbane to Port Hedland in late January 2006.

●1

Daguragu
Wave Hill
Kalkarindji

2 THE GOOD SAMARITAN
He was heading westward on the Buntine Highway near the Northern Territory-Western Australia border when he pulled over to help three men at the roadside.

●2

3 LEFT FOR DEAD
After agreeing to give one a lift, he was drugged, mugged and left for dead in a shallow grave off the road.

Inverway

▲ Mount Coghlan 615

Nicholson

●3

●4

4 THE THIRST BEGINS
With no food, water, shoes or socks, he walked east across the stony desert before heading south along a flooded river. He walked around 84 km (52 miles) and swam 6 km (3¾ miles) before reaching a water hole where he stayed for a few days.

Halls Creek

5 BUSH TUCKER
Driven by hunger, he continued south to another waterhole near a cattle station, where he survived on leeches, lizards and other small creatures for two months.

Sturt Creek

●5

●6

Birrindudu

6 RESCUE OF A SKELETON
He was rescued by a rancher at Birrindudu, about 69 km (43 miles) south of the desert highway on which he had been travelling.

Bililuna

Sturt Creek

Sturt Creek

WESTERN AUSTRALIA

NORTHERN TERRITORY

Tanami Desert

Balgo

Tanami

Rabbit Flat

KILOMETRES 0   100   200   300
MILES 0   50   100   150   200

A pack of dingos became unwelcome guests for Ricky. They circled his camp at night, snuffling and growling in their in their impatience for a meal.

just getting out of their vehicle. They stopped 100 m (328 ft) away, physically recoiling from the bearded living skeleton that was shambling towards them. The creature's skin was blistered, cracked and blackened by the sun. It was trying to articulate a plea for help, but its parched vocal cords could only produce the feeblest of whispers. The skin was drawn so tight almost every bone in the body could be counted. Only the man's eyes shone with any sort of human vitality.

> 6 "You can't imagine how remote it is out here. To be driving in the late afternoon and have a man come out of the bush is very scary." 9
> Ricky's rescuer Mark Clifford

Half the man he was

When Ricky Megee went into the wilderness he weighed 105 kg (230 lb). He was 1.91 m (6 ft 3 in.) tall. When he was flown to the hospital in Darwin he tipped the scales at only 48 kg (105 lb). Initially doctors and the police were sceptical of his story: no man could lose so much weight in such a time and survive. Moreover, no white man had ever lived for such a time that place.

But as Ricky gradually returned to normal health and lucidity, he was able to show the officials exactly how and where he had survived. Megee's crucial piece of luck was that his ordeal took place during the wet season. At any other time of year he would have been dead within days, as happens to the hundreds of people who go missing in Australia's Outback every year.

Another chance at a new life

As he slowly edged his way back to health, Ricky Megee assumed that the job he had been travelling to take up would have been long filled by someone else. But another member of staff had resigned at Centre Link and Ricky's position remained open.

Ricky knew that untreated the poison in the abscess could kill him, particularly in his severely weakened state. He started looking around for tools.

Bizarrely, despite drugging him and removing his shoes, Ricky's abductor had failed to find his car key. He also found a sharp piece of 12-gauge fencing wire. Fashioning this into a hook and using the car key as a lever, he started the operation to remove his own rotting tooth.

First he popped the blisters on his gums, then used the wire hook to dig under the tooth and the car key to jimmy it out. Twice he blacked out from the pain before he removed the offending molar.

It was around now that Ricky started to lose hope. His faith in being found, unshakeable for so long, had been worn and carved by the harsh desert conditions into a bare, sparse acceptance of his fate. He had tried so hard to survive, but now he knew he was going to die. Ricky made a cross from two sticks and placed it on top of his humpy. So his shelter would also be his grave; at least when someone did return to the farm they would find his bones and his family would have something to bury.

Rescue of a skeleton

The weeks stretched into months, and although he had said goodbye to his family, Ricky still did not lay down and die. As long as he had some energy in his body he would continue with the ordinary business of living.

One day in early April Ricky had just returned from one of his daily foraging missions and was surveying his unappetising catch in his humpy. The wind was whistling through the holes as usual, doing its best car impression. And, as usual, Ricky ignored its torturing simulacrum. Until the wind changed gear.

The sound was unmistakeable: the sudden pitch-shift that could only come from a car. Scarcely daring to believe what might be happening, Ricky tore his way out of his shelter and started to run towards the noise. His legs instantly gave way and he fell face first down the steep embankment of the water hole.

He got to his knees and staggered, crawled, hauled his way towards the two astonished ranchers who were

Alone in the Death Zone

WILCO VAN ROOIJEN WAS COMING DOWN FROM THE TOP OF THE WORLD WHEN AN ICE FALL KILLED ONE OF HIS COLLEAGUES AND SWEPT AWAY THE ROPES THAT WOULD GUIDE HIM TO SAFETY. STRANDED IN THE 'DEATH ZONE' AT 8,000 M (26,000 FT) HE HAD TO BRAVE TWO NIGHTS IN -40°C CONDITIONS TO MAKE IT BACK ALIVE.

DATE:
2008

SITUATION:
CLIMBING ACCIDENT

CONDITION OF CONFINEMENT:
STRANDED ON K2 AT 8,000 M (26,000 FT)

DURATION OF CONFINEMENT:
2 DAYS

MEANS OF ESCAPE:
BIVOUACKING OVERNIGHT, FREE CLIMBING, RESCUE

NO. OF ESCAPEES:
8

DANGERS:
DEHYDRATION, FALLING TO DEATH, HYPOTHERMIA, STARVATION

EQUIPMENT:
CLIMBING EQUIPMENT

LEFT
The snow capped peaks of the Karakoram mountains in Pakistan.

ABOVE RIGHT
Two mountaineers on the slopes of the K2 mountain in the Karakoram Himalaya, Pakistan.

The briefest taste of glory

It was 5 p.m. and -40°C when Wilco van Rooijen and Gerard McDonnell stood at the top of K2, the world's most dangerous high mountain. They hugged each other with exhilaration. Gerard gabbled with joy to his girlfriend via satellite phone. This was their moment of triumph: two years before, their summit attempt had ended in failure and a fractured skull for McDonnell. Now, here they were, on top of the 8,611 m (28,251 ft) peak with the world at their feet.

But their glory would be short-lived. Within hours an avalanche would sweep Gerard to his death and leave van Rooijen stranded at 8,000 m (26,000 ft). Ten more people would die on the mountain that day in one of the most deadly climbing accidents of modern times. Against incredible odds, Van Rooijen, 40, would survive two nights alone at the top of K2.

The backlog

No one has ever climbed K2 in winter. Its brutal weather only allows a short climbing season, from June to August; some years, no one makes it up then either. In 2008, that had been shortened further by a run of nasty weather that stopped anyone summitting during June and July.

> **For a professional, seasoned mountaineer it's more of the holy grail than Everest. There is no easy way to climb K2.**

By the end of July, there were ten expeditions camped on the mountain, all waiting eagerly for the weather to clear and give them their shot at the summit. Some had waited for almost two months and were getting edgy. The brutal peak called to them. The longer they waited in its shadow, the longer their anticipation could build into fear.

Van Rooijen, a Dutchman, and McDonnell, an Irish climber based in Alaska, were part of an international team. There was also an American-

French team, a Serbian-led expedition, a large contingent of Koreans, and smaller Italian and Norwegian groups.

But finally the weather cleared, and several groups arrived at Camp IV on 31 July, ready for the summit attempt. That night the expedition leaders sent porters ahead to fix ropes at a crucial part of the climb. Then, and at 3 a.m. on Friday, 1 August the climbers left Camp IV, 8,000 m (26,000 ft) up the mountain, and stepped towards tragedy.

The Bottleneck

At 8,611 m (28,251 ft), K2 is the second highest mountain in the world, but it is considered by climbers to be far more dangerous than Mount Everest. Only 302 people (as of July 2010) have climbed K2. More than 2,700 individuals have summitted Everest. For every four people who have reached K2's summit, one has died trying. It is known as the Savage Mountain for good reason.

There is no easy way up K2. Every route is steep, exposed and committed, making retreat very difficult. This is especially true during storms, which tend to be severe and can last for many days. Because the mountain is so high, your lungs only get a third of the oxygen they do with each breath at sea level. If you run out of your bottled supply, your body has to work at least three times as hard.

The Bottleneck is one of the most dangerous sections on this most dangerous mountain. A couloir, or narrow gully, it lies a tantalizing 400 m (1,300 ft) below the summit and its trickiest section is only 100 m (328 ft) long. But overhanging this is a terrifying wall of unstable ice towers known as seracs. These seracs frequently fall and sweep anything in their path down the steep (fifty to sixty degrees) slope of the couloir. It tightens the guts of even the most hardened mountaineers.

When Van Rooijen and his team reached the Bottleneck, they were dismayed to find that the Sherpas had prepared lines in the wrong place. The most dangerous section was still completely exposed. They had to waste several hours taking rope from the lower portion of the route and using it to prepare the lines above the Bottleneck. At this point the American group decided to abort the attempt and return to the lower camp.

The first tragedy

At 8 a.m. climbers were advancing through the Bottleneck. One of the Serbians, Dren Mandić, suddenly stopped to adjust his oxygen. He unclipped himself from the fixed rope so other climbers could pass. He slipped. He screamed. He was gone. That's how quickly it happened.

A porter who set out to retrieve the body also fell to his death.

The other climbers froze as still as the ice-cliff they were climbing. In a couple of heartbeats, two of their friends had died. Should they go on? The mountain had demonstrated its brutal power. It was also getting late. Several more climbers decided to turn back.

> ❝ My fingers were really cold and I thought, "I've already lost time and I'm not going to lose my fingers for K2, so I turned back". ❞

But many wanted to continue. There was no way they could help the dead men now. They might as well climb the mountain they had come so far to conquer. As for the time – well, the Italian party that first conquered K2 in 1954 had reached the summit at 6 p.m. If they could do it then, it was possible today.

Over the afternoon and early evening, eighteen people made it to the summit. But some did so as late as 8 p.m. (the typical time for summitting is between 3 p.m. and 5 p.m.). The Bottleneck was living up to its name.

As Van Rooijen's group took their last photos and tucked away their

The seracs above the Bottleneck on K2.

flags, McDonnell was joined by Marco Confortola, an Italian Alpine guide with whom he had struck up a friendship. Together they started down.

But K2 had more deadly games to play. By now the sun had been beating down on the ice cliffs that hung above the return route for a whole day. The seracs were at their most unstable, just as the climbers began their descent.

The Spanish climber who had been first on the summit passed back through the Bottleneck without trouble. Two hours behind him but ahead of Van Rooijen's team was the Norwegian group. Among them were Cecilie Skog and her husband Rolf Bae. When they reached the couloir at 8.30 p.m., a serac broke off from the ice field above and all hell broke loose.

The ice avalanche

Tons of ice plummetted down and smashed Bae from the ice face. He was killed instantly. The ice blocks tore the carefully laid ropes like string. Eight climbers were now trapped above the Bottleneck, including Van Rooijen, McDonnell and Confortola. Night was falling and the temperature plunging. They were caught in the 'death zone' – the brutal world above 8,000 m (26,000 ft) where there isn't enough oxygen in the air for humans to live. Acclimatization is impossible: the human body can't digest food this high. Dilly dally up here without oxygen and your body functions will shut down one by one before you slip into unconsciousness, never to wake.

The ice fall had made the climb in the Bottleneck steeper and more technical. Huge chunks of ice lay scattered along the route. Worse, since the climbers were counting on the fixed lines, they had no extra ropes; they would have to 'free climb' down.

Panic gripped some of the climbers. Several started to descend in the darkness and a few managed to navigate the Bottleneck in the dark,

An avalanche crashes through the Savoia Pass on the northwest side of K2 in the Karakoram Range, Pakistan.

including Sherpa Pemba and Cas van de Gevel, a Dutch climber. Cecilie continued descending with another climber, leaving her husband's body on the mountain. She managed to reach Camp IV during the night. A French climber and another porter were not so lucky: they fell into oblivion.

> **If you have one climber who is not so capable, you have to adapt to his speed. There were too many who weren't capable in the summit party.**

Others decided to bivouac and wait until morning before descending. Confortola and McDonnell were forced to take this tactic by brutal winds. McDonnell was weak and dangerously cold, and Confortola scraped two pitifully shallow holes for shelter – barely 40 cm (16 inches) deep – in the almost vertical slope. Despite their exhaustion they forced themselves to stay awake; they knew that if they slept they would probably tumble to their deaths. During the night, Confortola heard a roaring sound followed by screams and he

saw the lights from head torches disappear into the darkness below him.

Van Rooijen was alone as he dug himself into the mountain as best he could to sit out the bitterly cold night on the Savage Mountain.

The tangled men

Van Rooijen knew he was in trouble as soon as he woke. The fixed ropes were no more visible in the dawn light than they had been the night before. He was bone-numbingly cold and was going increasingly snow blind. If he didn't get off the mountain fast he would die up here. He started climbing down the ice field.

He had his satellite phone, but couldn't read the numbers. He started hallucinating – hearing the voices and seeing the faces of imaginary rescuers. Then he came across three real people and wished it was another hallucination – two Korean climbers and Sherpa Jumik Bhote. The three men were tangled in several ropes and had clearly been hanging there, some upside down and bloodied, for quite a while.

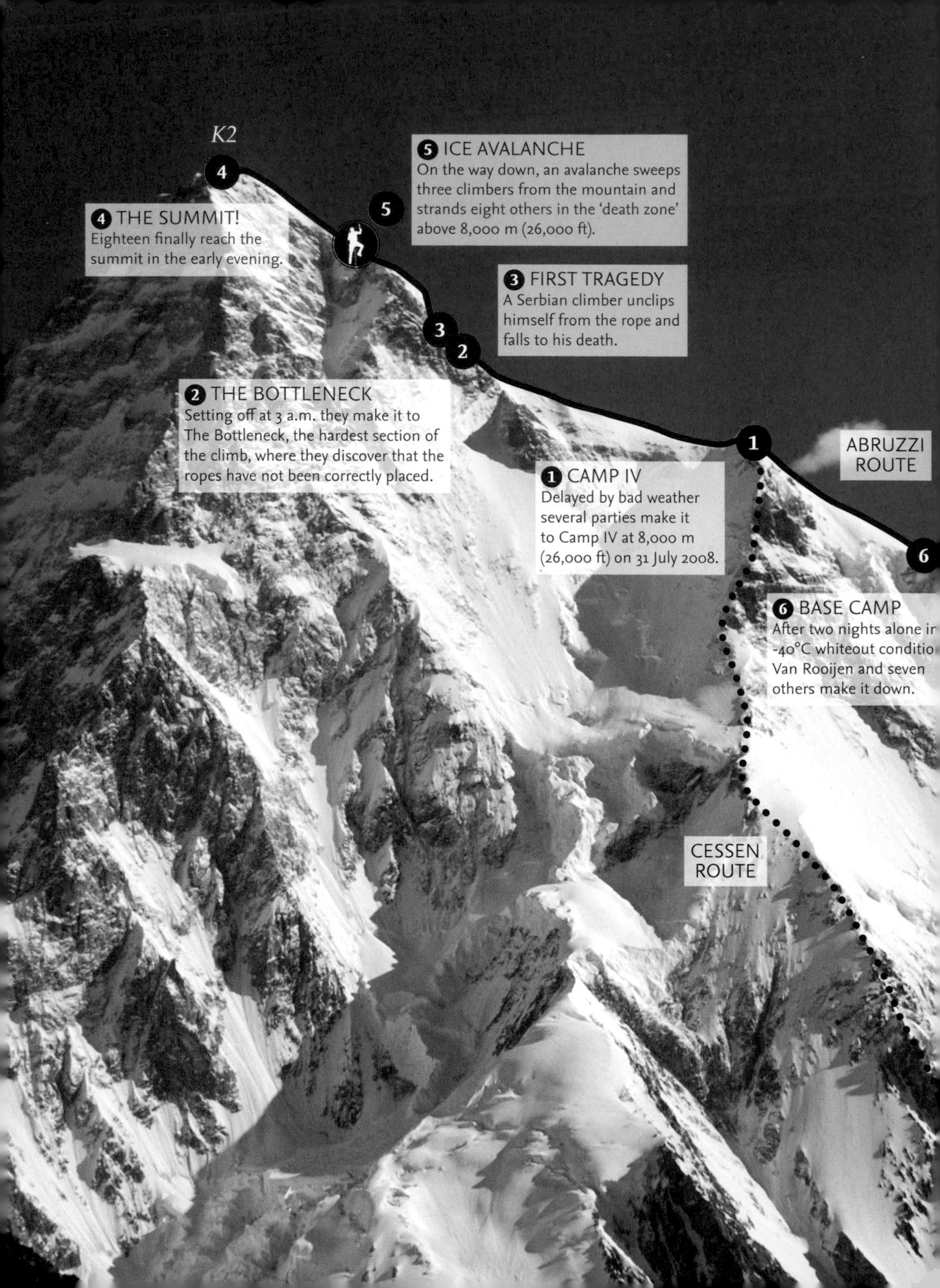

K2

4 **THE SUMMIT!**
Eighteen finally reach the summit in the early evening.

5 **ICE AVALANCHE**
On the way down, an avalanche sweeps three climbers from the mountain and strands eight others in the 'death zone' above 8,000 m (26,000 ft).

3 **FIRST TRAGEDY**
A Serbian climber unclips himself from the rope and falls to his death.

2 **THE BOTTLENECK**
Setting off at 3 a.m. they make it to The Bottleneck, the hardest section of the climb, where they discover that the ropes have not been correctly placed.

1 **CAMP IV**
Delayed by bad weather several parties make it to Camp IV at 8,000 m (26,000 ft) on 31 July 2008.

ABRUZZI ROUTE

6 **BASE CAMP**
After two nights alone in -40°C whiteout conditio Van Rooijen and seven others make it down.

CESSEN ROUTE

They had probably been the men who Confortola had seen falling. They were all alive but only Jumik could talk. Jumik Bhote informed him a rescue mission was under way from Camp IV. Van Rooijen gave him his gloves but was unable to help them any more and kept descending.

> ❛ Up there, there's no safety in numbers. ❜

Confortola and McDonnell set off slightly after Van Rooijen and also reached the three dangling climbers. They spent three hours trying to get the men the right way up, but they kept falling over. Then, bizarrely, McDonnell started climbing back up the slope on his own. Confortola assumed McDonnell had succumbed to high altitude sickness and was growing delusional.

But according to Van Rooijen, who had seen Confortola and McDonnell helping the stranded Koreans and their guide from below, McDonnell actually climbed up to the highest anchor supporting the three stranded men to try and transfer the load. This was a heroic rescue to attempt at 8,000 m (26,000 ft). The Irishman

could have gone down and saved himself, but he sacrificed his life trying to save others.

Confortola had managed to get the Koreans back into a comfortable position and was able to radio Sherpas Tsering Bhote and Pasang Bhote who were on their way up to rescue the men. But there was little else he could do. He had to get down himself or he too would die. The mountain forced him into a savage decision. He left the Koreans to their fate and continued down. After making some progress he became delirious with exhaustion and stopped, dropping into a heavy sleep.

He was woken by a huge noise – another avalanche of ice blocks. It swept past just 18 m (60 ft) from where he stood. Tumbling in the maelstrom was the body of McDonnell. Confortola saw his friend reaching out from the snow as he was swept down the mountain in a flurry of hands, boots and torn limbs.

Saturday, August 2

Just after noon, Sherpas Tsering Bhote and Pasang Bhote found Marco Confortola at the bottom of the Bottleneck, crawling on his hands and feet. They radioed Sherpa Pemba and Cas van de Gevel, asking them to come up for Confortola so that they could continue the search for Sherpa Jumik Bhote and the Koreans.

Sherpa Pasang later found Jumik Bhote and the two Koreans just above the Bottleneck – the heroic McDonnell had managed to free them after all. But, tragically, he had been killed as he followed them down.

Further tragedy struck almost immediately. Minutes after Pasang had radioed in the good news that he had found Jumik and two Koreans, another avalanche swept away the four men. Sherpa Tsering miraculously survived the avalanche, as did Pemba Gyalje and Marco Confortola at the bottom of the Bottleneck.

Eleven of the climbers who had set out that morning were now dead.

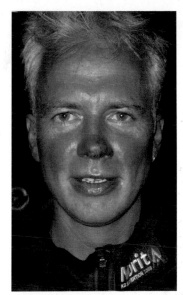

Wilco van Rooijen, the rescued leader of the Dutch climbers team.

Another night alone

Meanwhile van Rooijen was making his way down the mountain alone, but he was so confused that he went over the wrong side of the ridge. He found a route down but it took him past Camp IV. He would have to spend a second bivouac out on the mountain.

He had gone days without eating or drinking. Eating snow didn't help. Blisters covered his tongue and lips.

Finally, on Sunday 3 August, Van Rooijen crawled into camp III. He was so delirious he didn't recognize Van de Gevel and Sherpa Pemba. Third degree frostbite had crippled many fingers, all his toes and both feet. They began melting snow and gave him oxygen.

By 10 p.m. all three were back at base camp. The next day Van de Gevel and van Rooijen were evacuated from base camp by helicopter. Confortola also reached safety at Camp II, the advanced base camp.

They were lucky enough to have survived the worst single accident on one of the world's most deadly high mountains.

Italian climber, Marco Confortola, speaking to reporters at the Italian embassy in Islamabad.

The Sole Survivor of Flight 626

WHEN HER PLANE CRASHED INTO THE INDIAN OCEAN IN THE MIDDLE OF THE NIGHT, 13-YEAR-OLD BAHIA BAKARI CLUNG TO A PIECE OF WRECKAGE AND FLOATED AMID DEBRIS, DEAD BODIES AND SPILLED FUEL UNTIL SHE WAS RESCUED. SHE BEAT ASTONISHING ODDS TO BECOME THE ONLY SURVIVOR OF THE CRASH.

DATE:
2009

SITUATION:
PLANE CRASH

CONDITION OF CONFINEMENT:
CLINGING TO WRECKAGE IN THE INDIAN OCEAN

DURATION OF CONFINEMENT:
9 HOURS

MEANS OF ESCAPE:
RESCUE

NO. OF ESCAPEES:
1

DANGERS:
EXPLOSION, DROWNING, EXHAUSTION

EQUIPMENT:
NONE

ABOVE RIGHT
Chimoni Beach, Grand Comore, Comoros Islands.

The start of a holiday

Bahia Bakari was tired. It was ten to two in the morning on 30 June 2009. She was only 13 years old and not used to flying.

Her journey had been a long one: starting in Paris, she and her mother had flown to Marseille then on to Sana'a' in Yemen where they changed planes, boarding Yemenia Flight 626 with 140 other passengers and eleven crew. The flight had made a stop in Djibouti and was now on its way to its ultimate destination of Prince Said Ibrahim International Airport in Comoros.

Bahia looked over at her mother who sat beside her. Just a few more minutes and the two of them would be walking out to the welcoming arms of their relatives. They would be spending the summer together. Just think – the whole summer on an island in the Indian Ocean! Bahia wondered how warm it would be tomorrow as she pressed her forehead against the window and looked out at the velvet ocean night.

Then the Airbus 310 started its final descent and something went very wrong.

> ❛ I don't know what happened, but the plane fell into the water and I found myself in the water ... surrounded by darkness. ❜

As it made its approach, the pilot lost control. The jet made a sudden U-turn and then plunged into the ocean 14 km (9 miles) north of Grande Comore. It smashed apart on contact with the heavy swell.

Floating alone

In her initial confusion after the impact, Bahia thought she had fallen out of the plane by pressing her forehead too hard against the window. With tragic naïvety she worried that her mother – who she thought had landed safely without her – would tell her off for not wearing her seat belt.

The taste of jet fuel brought her back to reality. She was floating amid wreckage and a slick released from the aircraft's burst fuel tanks. The caustic fluid mixed with seawater burned her throat, lungs and stomach.

Yemenia Flight 626 was the deadliest sole-survivor airliner ocean crash.

There was no moon: she was in total darkness. She had no life jacket and could barely swim. There was nothing to do but clamber on top of a piece of broken fuselage and drift with the debris.

At first she could hear voices of other passengers, but one by one those voices ceased.

Bahia half slept, half passed out on her makeshift raft. Somehow she clung on despite the darkness and the heavy seas. When the sun came up, she realized she was alone in the middle of a large fuel slick. She was excruciatingly thirsty and exhausted. At one point she looked up to see a ship on the horizon, but strong winds were whipping up a rough sea. The ship didn't spot her above the waves.

Still she clung on.

Rescued by a ferry

Comoros is such a tiny country that it had no rescue ships or planes to dispatch to the crash site. In the short term all it could do was ask commercial and private vessels to help with the rescue effort. It also appealed for international help and two French military aircraft and a ship responded and set out from the islands of Réunion and Mayotte. But these were hundreds of miles away. The odds of finding any survivors did not look good.

At eleven o'clock the next morning, nine hours after the accident, the ferry *Sima Com 2* arrived at the crash site. Normally this craft carried passengers between Comoros and Madagascar, but today it was a rescue boat.

> ❛ It is truly, truly, miraculous. The young girl can barely swim. ❜

The sailors drifted disconsolately amid pieces of torn fuselage, floating luggage and the rainbow sheen of kerosene. There were many dead bodies. Then, to their astonishment, they saw a young girl clinging to a piece of wreckage. One man threw her a life ring, but as she reached out a weary arm to grab it, a large wave flipped her over and she disappeared from view.

Another sailor dived into the water to grab the girl. He plucked her from the depths and his colleagues pulled them both safely aboard the

Bahia Bakari, the sole survivor of Yemenia Flight 626.

Sima Com 2. The sailors swaddled Bahia in blankets and gave her a hot drink.

Eight hours later the *Sima Com 2* arrived in Port Moroni and Bahia rejoined the world as '*la miraculée*' – the miracle girl.

Going home

Bahia Bakari had cuts to her face, a swollen left eye, burns to her knees and a fractured pelvis and collarbone. She was the only survivor from the crash.

Bahia turned down an offer from Steven Spielberg to make a film based on her experience. She was worried that 'it would be too terrifying.'

She was flown back to France the day after the crash on a French government Falcon-900 jet. Reunited with her father and other family members, she was then taken to the Armand-Trousseau Children's Hospital in eastern Paris. She made a full recovery.

Cause of the crash

France had banned the aircraft from its airspace two years earlier after it failed an aviation inspection.

The crash has been blamed on pilot error.

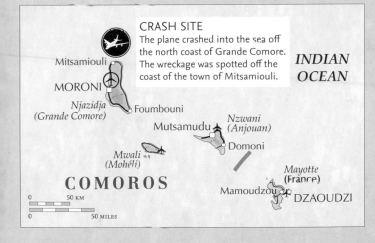

CRASH SITE
The plane crashed into the sea off the north coast of Grande Comore. The wreckage was spotted off the coast of the town of Mitsamiouli.

INDIAN OCEAN

Mitsamiouli
MORONI
Njazidja (Grande Comore)
Foumbouni
Mutsamudu
Nzwani (Anjouan)
Domoni
Mwali (Mohéli)
COMOROS
Mayotte (France)
Mamoudzou DZAOUDZI

0   50 KM
0   50 MILES

The Miracle on the Hudson

It was a freezing January day in New York and Flight 1549 was still climbing out of LaGuardia when it smashed into a large flock of geese. Birds were sucked into both engines, instantly disabling them. Captain Chesley Sullenberger safely ditched the plane into the Hudson River between Manhattan and New Jersey, saving all 155 passengers and crew.

DATE:
2009

SITUATION:
Bird strike on take-off disabled both engines

CONDITION OF CONFINEMENT:
On board a passenger jet with zero thrust

DURATION OF CONFINEMENT:
6 minutes

MEANS OF ESCAPE:
Life rafts, boats

NO. OF ESCAPEES:
155

DANGERS:
Plane crash, drowning, hypothermia

EQUIPMENT:
Pilot's skill, crew training

ABOVE RIGHT
New York City skyline over Hudson River.

A perfect day for flying

The 15th of January 2009 was cold and clear in New York City. The sheer glass and steel towers of Manhattan shone in the pale winter sunshine. The mercury showed a sharp air temperature of –7°C but the calm conditions made it a perfect day for a flight. Unfortunately for Flight 1549, it was also a perfect day for flying if you were a goose.

US Airways Flight 1549 was a domestic route from New York City's LaGuardia Airport to Charlotte/Douglas, North Carolina. In the cockpit were Captain Chesley 'Sully' Sullenberger, 57, a pilot with almost forty years' experience, and First Officer Jeffrey Skiles, 49, who was just completing his first assignment in the Airbus A320. In the cabin were three flight attendants: Donna Dent, Doreen Walsh and Sheila Dail. There were 150 passengers on board.

A few seconds before 3.25 p.m., the tower at LaGuardia cleared Flight 1549 for takeoff from Runway 4, heading northeast. First Officer Skiles took the controls for takeoff, and guided the twin-engined jet into the air.

With the undercarriage stowed and the passengers starting to think of lunch, the crew made their first report to air traffic control as they passed 200 m (700 ft). All okay.

Just a minute later, Skiles spotted a flock of geese. They were on a direct collision course with the plane. The aircraft was still climbing fast. There was no time to avoid the birds.

The plane punched right through the formation. There were several loud bangs and a flash of blood obscured the cockpit windscreen. In the cabin, passengers saw smoke and flames streaming from the engines.

Both engines had sucked in birds, tearing them apart from within. Modern turbine engines can survive the ingestion of 'swallow-sized birds', and the A320 was powered by two CFM56 engines which have additional anti-birdstrike design features. But the Canada Geese sucked into Flight

1549's engines weighed 4.5 kg (10 lb) each, and there were several of them. They damaged a spinner and inlet lip, fractured the booster inlet guide vanes and blew away the outlet guide vanes, crippling the engines.

The plane lost power in seconds. It had only just attained about 1,000 m (3,200 ft) of its initial climb to 4,500 m (15,000 ft). Captain Sullenberger took the controls as First Officer Skiles quickly ran through the emergency checklist for restarting the engines – a three-page document. Within thirty seconds, both men knew the engines weren't going to start again.

At 3:27:36, just 2½ minutes into the flight, the crew radioed air traffic control. 'Hit birds. We've lost thrust on both engines. We're turning back towards LaGuardia.'

In the cabin, passengers knew something was very wrong. The loud thuds that had rocked the engines had been replaced by a terrifying silence, with the normal engine drone completely absent. One flight attendant said it was eerily like 'being in a library'. The odour of unburnt jet fuel hung heavy in the cabin. One terrified passenger texted her husband, 'my plane is crashing'.

With zero thrust and very little altitude, every second was going to count for Flight 1549. An Airbus 320 has a maximum takeoff weight of 78,000 kg (170,000 lb), making it not the most efficient of gliders. The aircraft was close to one of the densest metropolitan areas in the world. Sullenberger had to come up with a plan, and fast. But he had very few options.

President-elect Barack Obama praised Sullenberger's 'heroic and graceful job in landing the damaged aircraft'. He also thanked the crew, and invited them all to his Presidential inauguration in Washington D.C., which took place five days later.

Air traffic control gave him a heading back to LaGuardia, with a landing to the southeast on Runway 13. Sullenberger's experience instantly told him they wouldn't make it that far.

He called the tower. Could they make an emergency landing in New Jersey? He knew that Teterboro Airport in Bergen County was quite close. Air traffic control instantly called Teterboro and cleared a landing. But by the time controllers radioed back, Sullenberger knew they wouldn't make it: a powerless glide in risked a catastrophic urban collision. 'We can't do that,' he replied. The Captain now knew exactly how serious their situation was. 'We're gonna be in the Hudson,' he said and wheeled the plane anti-clockwise to follow the river south.

The aircraft skimmed just 275 m (900 ft) above traffic on the George Washington Bridge. With the choppy grey Hudson River getting bigger by the second, Sullenberger told everyone to 'Brace for impact'. The flight attendants hurried the passengers into crash position.

Ninety seconds later, the A320 thumped into the frigid water, belly first. It was travelling at about 130 knots (240 km/h, 150 mph) and landed in the middle of the North River section of the Hudson River. Carving a deep wake, it slowed, skewed and finally stopped adjacent to 50th Street in midtown Manhattan and very near the USS Intrepid Sea-Air-Space museum.

Flight 1549 from New York to Charlotte/Douglas had lasted just six minutes.

Onlookers line the hillside as rescue workers surround the US Airways Airbus A320, Flight number 1549, which crashed into the Hudson River.

4 3.28 P.M.
The Captain radios to the tower telling them they've been hit and requesting a return to LaGuardia.

5 3.28 P.M.
Sullenberger realises they aren't going to make it to the airport. 'We're gonna be in the Hudson,' he tells control.

6 3.29 P.M.
The plane passes just 275 m (900 ft) above the George Washington Bridge.

3 3.27 P.M.
The plane loses thrust. Captain Chesley Sullenberger takes control as the First Officer quickly tries to restart the engines.

2 3.26 P.M.
Three minutes into the flight, while at 1,000 m (3,200 ft), the plane strikes a flock of Canada Geese. Several birds are ingested in both engines.

7 3.30 P.M.
Travelling at 240 km/h (150 mph), the flight ditches in the icy river.

1 3.25 P.M.
Flight 1549 takes off from LaGuardia's East runway at 3.25 p.m.

8 3.31 P.M.
Sullenberger has aimed the plane towards several boats. It comes to rest opposite the 50th Street ferry.

9 3.35 P.M.
Within four minutes, rescuers arrive to help the passengers.

NEW JERSEY

MANHATTAN

NEW YORK

QUEENS

BRON

Teterboro Airport

Hudson River

East River

Rikers Island

Wards Island

Hell Gate

Roosevelt Island

LaGuardia Airport

Flushing Bay

Ellis Island (N.Y.)

Liberty Island (N.Y.)

Governor's Island

George Washington Bridge

Lincoln Tunnel

Holland Tunnel

Brooklyn Bridge

Manhattan Bridge

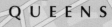

METRES 0   1000   2000
YARDS 0   1000   2000

As the wash of the impact subsided, the current caught the plane and began pulling it southwards. The impact had ripped holes in the fuselage and forced the cargo doors open. Water immediately started flooding into the cabin from the rear. The plane began to slowly sink as it floated downriver.

Now the flight attendants sprang into action. They opened the two front doors and also directed passengers to spring the four mid-cabin emergency exits. The front left slide did not immediately deploy, so the passengers, one of whom was in a wheelchair, started exiting left via the right front door and the over wing exits.

Captain Sullenberger (*left*), the pilot of the US Airways Flight 1549 that crashed into the Hudson River, accepts the Key to New York City from New York Mayor Bloomberg at City Hall, New York.

❛ These people knew what they were supposed to do and they did it and as a result, nobody lost their life. ❜

The slow going and the incoming water made a passenger panic and open one of the rear doors, causing the icy river to flood the cabin faster. The flight attendant in the rear tried unsuccessfully to reseal the door then began urging passengers forward faster, clambering over the seats to avoid the rising water.

With the cabin finally clear, Captain Sullenberger walked the entire length of the cabin to make sure that all the passengers were out. He then walked it a second time, to be absolutely certain, before stepping out onto the wing, the last man to leave the stricken aircraft.

Somehow, despite all the stresses involved in ditching an aircraft on a choppy river in winter, Sullenberger had had the presence of mind to aim the plummeting jet towards active jetties, so maximising the chance of rescue. He managed to get the plane close to three boat terminals: two ferries and a tour operator.

The first ferry reached the plane within four minutes of the ditching. Vessels from the New York City Fire and Police Departments were also on the scene shortly after.

Passengers were standing on the wings or on the inflatable slides, knee-deep in icy water as the first rescuers arrived. A few had started to swim away from the plane in case it exploded.

Captain Sullenberger advised the ferry crew to take passengers from the wing before those in the inflatable slides, as their situation was more precarious.

All the 155 passengers and flight crew were safely rescued. Five people sustained serious injuries, including flight attendant Doreen Walsh who suffered a deep laceration in her leg. A further seventy-three people were treated for minor injuries and hypothermia.

The ditching has to go down in history as a triumphant example of bad luck being overcome by skill, training and years of experience.

Sully saves the day

Of all people you'd want at the controls of your plane if it lost power from a birdstrike, Captain Chesley 'Sully' Sullenberger would have to be near the top of your list.

At the time of the incident he had been flying for US Airways for twenty-nine years, before which he had piloted fighter jets for eleven years. He had also found the time to start his own safety consultancy, Safety Reliability Methods, which applied the super-safe techniques of the airline industry to other sectors. He had recently been at the University of California studying the psychological aspect of how to keep crewmembers focused during a catastrophe. He was also an experienced glider pilot.

Jet engine vs goose

The Airbus A320 was powered by two CFM International CFM56 series turbofan engines. The CFM56 series is one of the best-selling turbofan aircraft engines in the world, with more than 20,000 of its four variants built. Each engine provides between 80 to 150 kilonewtons (18,000 and 34,000 pounds-force) of thrust. It has twenty-two fan blades which rotate at speeds of up to 25,000 revolutions per minute.

The Canada Goose (*Branta canadensis*) is a wild goose native to arctic and temperate regions of North America. It has a black head and neck with distinctive white chinstrap, and a brownish-grey body. The largest wild goose ever recorded of any species was a Canada Goose. The male usually weighs 3.2–6.5 kg (7–14 lb), but has weighed as much as 10.9 kg (24 lb) with a wingspan of 2.24 m (7½ ft).

Journey from the Centre of the Earth

Thirty-three men endure a stifling two months trapped 700 m (2,300 ft) below the surface of the earth in a collapsed mine in Chile. It is the longest ever survival in such conditions. Every man came out alive in a dramatic rescue that was seen the world over.

DATE:

2010

SITUATION:

Mine collapse

CONDITION OF CONFINEMENT:

Trapped in a tunnel 700 m (2,300 ft) below ground

DURATION OF CONFINEMENT:

69 days

MEANS OF ESCAPE:

Winched to the surface individually

NO. OF ESCAPEES:

33

DANGERS:

Crushed to death, dehydration, hunger, suffocation

EQUIPMENT:

Food and water, blankets, camaraderie

LEFT
Plan C Drilling Rig and 'Flags of Hope' in the rescue attempt for the trapped miners.

ABOVE RIGHT
The fifth rescuer, Patricio Sepúlveda, is in the rescue capsule and is being lowered into the mine, during 'Operación San Lorenzo'.

Entombed

When Luis Urzúa led his shift of thirty-two men into the mouth of the San José mine on the morning of the 5th of August 2010, he little suspected that they would next see daylight two months and eight days later.

At two o'clock that afternoon there was a catastrophic collapse in one of the galleries above where they were working. Urzúa was an experienced miner and he knew they were in serious trouble almost instantly. It wasn't just the immense noise of the rockfall pounding his eardrums. The dust cloud that blinded him was so dense and toxic that the cave-in had to be severe.

Amazingly, everyone working in the mine that day survived the rockfall. Another shift was working near the surface and they were able to evacuate the mine immediately. Unfortunately for Urzúa and his colleagues, they had been working much deeper – at 700 m (2,300 ft)

below the surface – and the falling debris had completely blocked their return route.

> There had been many previous rockfalls in the mine's 100-year history, causing several accidents and one fatality. The operators had only been allowed to re-open the mine after a previous accident on the condition that they improve safety. This they failed to do.

As shift supervisor, the responsibility for their survival now fell to Urzúa. He first tried to lead the men through the ventilation shaft that provides additional air to the main tunnel and takes a separate route to the surface. But the ladders that should have allowed them to climb this shaft had not been installed by the mining company. The miners had to return to the small and scantily equipped refuge that was their only sanctuary so far underground and set about rationing their supplies and steeling their spirits for the long black wait that lay ahead of them.

It was the 5th of August. They wouldn't even know that rescuers were looking for them for another seventeen days.

First rescue attempts

The Atacama Desert in Chile is one of the least hospitable places on Earth: in many areas no rain has fallen in the entirety of recorded history. Half a mile under its bleached and blasted sands, conditions in the San José copper and gold mine are even less welcoming. A spiral road loops and twists its way inexorably down from the surface into the darkness of the mineral-rich rocks. Although the men were trapped 700 m (2,300 ft) below surface level, because the mine is accessed by this long, winding road rather than a vertical shaft, they were actually 5 km (3 miles) from the entrance.

Rescue teams tried to bypass the rockfall through the same ventilation shafts that the men had tried to enter. But these were either blocked by fallen rock or were so unstable that entering them would seriously endanger the rescuers. When engineers brought in heavy machinery to shift the rubble, the mine collapsed again. Another way down would have to be found.

The percussion-technology drills used to make the boreholes used four hammers instead of one and moved at more than 40 metres (130 ft) a day.

No one knew if the men were still alive or exactly where they were. This meant that there was no point in starting to drill a hole wide enough to winch up a man straight away; the effort would most likely be wasted. A better plan would be to drill several smaller holes to maximize the chance of making contact. These holes would still be large enough to transport food, water, medical supplies and other necessities down to the men. The larger scale retrieval operation could then begin.

Rescue teams used hammer drills to sink eight exploratory boreholes 15 cm (6 inches) in diameter. In theory these would punch through the tunnel wall into an area where the miners might be sheltering. But the task facing the drilling teams was immense: they were aiming for targets just a few metres wide that were more than 600 m (1,970 ft) underground. Not only would it take a long time simply to penetrate to that depth, the rock in the mine is extremely hard, amplifying any drift of the drill. Furthermore, the existing maps of the mine shafts were out of date, adding further uncertainty to calculations. It would take engineering skill and a lot of luck to reach the miners.

Daily life in a half-mile deep hole

The emergency shelter was little more than a 50 m² (540 ft²) space lined with two long benches and this soon became too oppressive for the men to stay in. Fortunately the rockfall had happened far enough away from them to leave 2 km (1¼ miles) of galleries in which they could move around.

Chile's Health Minister Jaime Mañalich said: 'The situation is very similar to the one experienced by astronauts who spend months on end in the space station.' And on 31 August, a team of NASA specialists including two physicians, one psychologist and an engineer arrived to provide their expertise.

Finding water and food was the first big problem. The miners used their tools to dig for naturally occurring water in the walls and floor of the mine. There were a few vehicles in the tunnel with them, and they drained their radiators for water. The men also used the trucks' batteries to power their helmet lamps. The emergency food supplies they had were only enough for two to three days, but the miners were able to eke them out to last for a full

President Piñera holds the message sent by the miners 'Estamos bien en el refugio los 33'. (We are all right in the shelter, the 33 [of us].)

two weeks. Each miner was given two small spoonfuls of tuna, a sip of milk, a biscuit and a scrap of peach to last him forty-eight hours. By the time they were rescued, each man had lost an average of 8 kg (18 lb) in weight.

Facing such hardship above ground would have been exhausting; enduring it in the hot and humid darkness half a mile underground put near-unbearable physical and mental strain on the men. Somehow they had the foresight and fortitude to support each other no matter how hard things got. One of the miners, Mario Sepúlveda, later said:

'All 33 trapped miners, practicing a one-man, one-vote democracy, worked together to maintain the mine, look for escape routes and keep up morale… We knew that if society broke down we would all be doomed. Each day a different person took a bad turn. Every time that happened, we worked as a team to try to keep the morale up.'

Breakthrough

On the 19th August, fourteen days after the men were sealed into the earth, one of the probes stopped grinding rock and started spinning free. Engineers on the surface waited for a tapped signal or other response but heard no signs of life. Rescuers began to fear what had so long been expected: after all, who could survive so long in such a place?

But they kept drilling and three days later the eighth probe broke into a tunnel at 688 m (2,257 ft) below the surface of the earth. Pulling out the drill bit, engineers were amazed to see a handwritten note fastened to it with insulating tape. It read:

'Estamos bien en el refugio los 33.'

(We are all right in the shelter, the 33 [of us].)

Agonized with hope, the men had been able to hear the drills inching closer and had started preparing their messages should one manage to reach them. The drill that finally did break through appeared just 20 m (66 ft) from their refuge.

SAN JOSÉ MINE

The San José Mine is about 45 km (28 miles) north of Copiapó, in northern Chile.

The breakthrough meant that rescuers could send the men aid almost immediately. Rescuers used 1.5 metre long (5 ft) blue plastic capsules – nicknamed *palomas* ('doves') after carrier pigeons – to ferry supplies to the miners. Each shipment took an hour to descend the hole, and engineers had to grease the borehole to ease the passage of the capsules. A video camera was also sent down and soon the first grainy, silent images of the exhausted, dirty and unshaven men were filling TV screens all over the world.

The miners needed help to organize the uplift so several rescuers had to descend into the mine hole before anyone could come up. Manuel González, the first rescuer down, ended up spending twenty-five hours in the mine.

Doctors reported that although the miners were tired and malnourished, there were few major medical problems and they were in better health than could be expected after spending so long in such high temperatures and humidity.

Rescuers sent down high-energy glucose gels, rehydration tablets, medicines and oxygen. It would be another two days before solid food was lowered. Two other boreholes were completed to pipe down oxygen-enriched air and a permanent communications link so that miners could enjoy morale boosting daily video chats with their family.

But there was still a long way to go before the men could actually be rescued.

Getting ready for the rescue

To get the men out the hole needed to be enlarged in two stages, first to 30 cm (12 inches) in diameter and then again to 71 cm (28 inches). Going straight from a 14 cm (5¾ inches) hole to a 71 cm (28 inches) hole would create too much torque and put potentially dangerous pressure on the drill bits.

Furthermore, the instability of the ground above the cave-in meant that engineers had been forced to site their drilling rig slightly to the side. The shaft they drilled was therefore at a slight angle, which caused extra wear on the neck of the drills and that added time to the operation.

Cross section of the San José mine

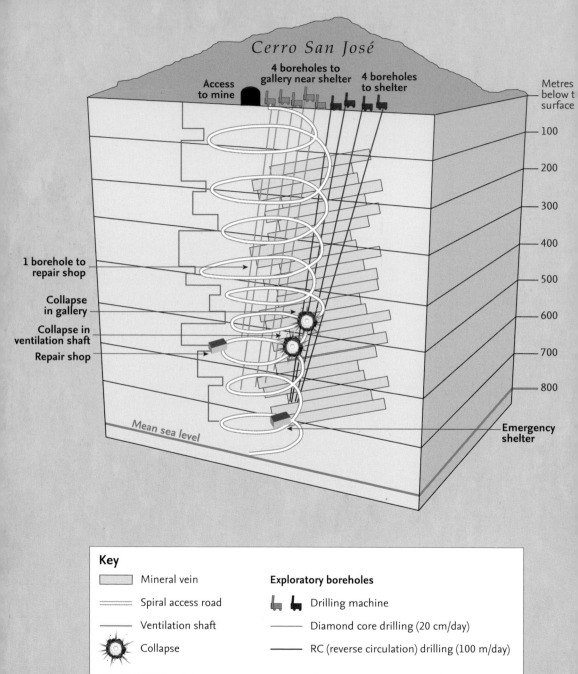

Cerro San José

Access to mine

4 boreholes to gallery near shelter

4 boreholes to shelter

Metres below the surface

— 100
— 200
— 300
— 400
— 500
— 600
— 700
— 800

1 borehole to repair shop

Collapse in gallery

Collapse in ventilation shaft

Repair shop

Mean sea level

Emergency shelter

Key

Mineral vein

Spiral access road

Ventilation shaft

Collapse

Exploratory boreholes

Drilling machine

Diamond core drilling (20 cm/day)

RC (reverse circulation) drilling (100 m/day)

The rescuers also had to proceed carefully to avoid drilling into the production tunnels that wind above the shelter.

Conservative estimates said the rescue might take until Christmas – five long months away. Such a lengthy incarceration would be a huge challenge for the men both physically and mentally.

Discipline, routine, work and mutual support became the cornerstones of their daily lives. Fluorescent lights with timers helped keep the men on a day and night schedule. Doctors sent down vaccines for tetanus, diphtheria, flu and pneumonia, which the men administered themselves. Psychologists encouraged them to play as active a role as possible: the miners split themselves into three eight-hour shifts to look after the *palomas*, maintain communications, check mine safety and organize the sanitation.

Hour by hour, day by day, they kept themselves busy staying alive, as hundreds of feet above them, the giant drill crunched ever closer.

Extraction

The drilling went much faster than had been expected, and in early October the giant tube in the planet's crust was complete. After a lengthy series of safety checks, the rescue effort – dubbed 'Operación San Lorenzo' (Operation St. Lawrence) after the patron saint of miners – began on Tuesday, 12 October 2010.

The ascent would not be without its risks and the four healthiest miners were to go first; they could best tell the rescue team about the conditions of the journey and of the remaining miners. After they were up, the least healthy men would then be rescued.

Six hours before his rescue, each miner started on a NASA-recommended liquid diet rich in sugars, minerals and potassium. He had a girdle strapped round his waist

Luis Urzúa, the leader of the trapped miners and the last of the thirty-three to be lifted to freedom, celebrates with President Piñera.

to maintain stable blood pressure, and took an aspirin to help prevent blood clots.

Each miner wore a green moisture-resistant tracksuit with sunglasses to avoid retinal damage from sudden exposure to sunlight. He was then strapped into a harness inside the 53 cm (21 inches) wide bullet-shaped capsule that was lined with masks, heart monitors and video cameras.

The miners survived underground for a record sixty-nine days, from 5 August to 13 October 2010 when the 33rd miner reached the surface. An estimated one billion people around the world watched the live rescue on television.

At 11.16 p.m., the final checks had been completed and Florencio Ávalos was strapped into his harness. The capsule door was closed, Ávalos gave the thumbs up and somewhere an engineer pressed the button that started his climb through 700 m (2,300 ft) of solid rock. The thirty-two remaining miners watched Ávalos

disappear into the hole and the world held its breath.

The capsule rose steadily at 1 metre per second (2.2 mph) and fourteen minutes later it popped out of the ground. The door was opened and Ávalos stepped out to hug his family in front of a blaze of camera lights and a wall of cheers.

Less than twenty-four hours later, all thirty-three miners had been rescued. Two were suffering from silicosis, one had pneumonia, and a few others had dental infections and corneal problems. The rest were in good medical condition and all were expected to recover fully.

The last man out of the blocked mine was Luis Urzúa, the shift supervisor. He stepped away from rescuers, greeted his son and then threw his arms around Chile's President, Sebastián Piñera, saying, 'I've delivered to you this shift of workers, as we agreed I would'. The president replied, 'I gladly receive your shift, because you completed your duty, leaving last like a good captain.'

The Survivor of Circumstance

RUBEN VAN ASSOUW WAS FLYING BACK FROM A HOLIDAY IN SOUTH AFRICA WITH HIS PARENTS, BROTHER AND 100 OTHER PEOPLE WHEN THEIR PLANE SMASHED INTO THE GROUND ON LANDING. THE CRASH WAS SO VIOLENT THAT THE AIRCRAFT DISINTEGRATED COMPLETELY, FLINGING WRECKAGE OVER A WIDE AREA. SOMEHOW RUBEN SURVIVED THE CATASTROPHIC IMPACT.

DATE:
2010

SITUATION:
AIR DISASTER

CONDITION OF CONFINEMENT:
STRAPPED TO SEAT IN A CRASHING PLANE

DURATION OF CONFINEMENT:
IMPACT AND WAIT FOR RESCUE SERVICES

MEANS OF ESCAPE:
SEAT POSITION, BODY MASS, LUCK

NO. OF ESCAPEES:
1

DANGERS:
PLANE IMPACT, POTENTIAL FIREBALL, FLYING DEBRIS

EQUIPMENT:
NONE

ABOVE RIGHT
The tail section of the Afriqiyah Airways Airbus A330 passenger plane which crashed on landing at Tripoli airport.

Why did one boy survive?

All extreme survivals have some element of mystery to them. Indeed, it is the fact that they cannot be explained rationally, that they are outside our everyday comprehension that makes them so fascinating. How could a person live in those conditions? What made them hang on? How did they know where to walk to? Why him or her?

There is no one clear reason why 9-year-old Ruben van Assouw survived and all the 103 other people on board Flight 771 died when it smashed into the ground 900 m (980 yd) short of the runway at Tripoli International Airport, in Libya on 12 May 2010. He was not alone in a particular section of the plane; his family were beside him. He did nothing unique at impact. There were other children of his size on the flight. The answer can only be that even though an extreme event created an extreme set of dangers, every element of Ruben's situation somehow combined to help him avoid them all. Exactly *how* they combined will never be known.

Countdown to a dream

It was to be a dream safari. Patrick and Trudy van Assouw of Tilburg, Holland, had been married for 12½ years, and since that was halfway to their 25th anniversary they decided to mark the occasion with an unforgettable family adventure. They would take their sons Enzo, 11, and Ruben, 9, through South Africa's Kruger Park to Swaziland and the wetlands of the Indian Ocean coast. The trip would last a fortnight and the wildlife-mad boys would see nature's most spectacular animals.

> **‘ The boys are counting the days and minutes and can hardly wait. ’**
> **Patrick van Assouw, Ruben's father, in his blog just before the holiday.**

The holiday was nearly cancelled

because of the eruption of the Icelandic volcano Eyjafjallajökull. The uncertainty only added to the boys' fevered anticipation.

But the skies cleared and the adventure went ahead. The boys saw buffalo, ostrich and gnus, and enjoyed close encounters with monkeys and elephants. Ruben hugged his brother Enzo by South Africa's beautiful Mac Mac falls and the family watched the setting sun set the waters of an African river on fire.

The van Assouws uploaded stunning snaps of all these sights to their blog, so their friends and family could share their adventure even before it was over. Cruelly, their cheerful picture diary would become a memorial to a family tragedy.

No reason to crash

Late in the evening of 11 May 2010, the van Assouw family boarded Afriqiyah Airways Flight 771 in Johannesburg for the first stage of their journey home. It was a new aircraft and only around half full, there were ninety-three passengers and eleven crew on board. There was plenty of room to stretch out and catch some much-needed sleep or enjoy a midnight movie.

Everything on the flight went normally and the plane was smoothly making its final approach to the airport when, for some reason, it smashed into the ground 900 m (980 yd) short of the runway.

6 **Until the very last moment things were normal between the pilot and the control tower.** 9

There was no unusual weather in Tripoli that day. The pilot reported no technical problems before the jet struck the ground nor was there any fuel shortage. The Airbus A330-200 had only been delivered to the airline eight months previously and had flown just 1,600 hours. Authorities recovered the cockpit voice recorder

and flight data recorder and ruled out terrorism as a cause of the disaster.

Sand and mist may have hampered visibility and caused the pilot to misjudge his manual landing, but the definitive cause of the crash remains a mystery.

Catastrophic damage

The impact was so sudden and violent that the captain didn't have time to communicate a single syllable of their danger. The plane disintegrated so quickly that there wasn't even a fireball from igniting fuel. The destruction was utterly catastrophic: much of the plane was reduced to football-sized chunks of debris.

Rescuers found seats, luggage and souvenirs scattered over a wide area of dusty scrubland. It was clear that the passengers stood no chance. So they were astonished to find a young boy, still strapped into his seat 0.8 km (½ mile) from the aircraft's tail section. His legs were clearly broken but he was breathing.

6 **The child has several breaks in both legs and is under intensive care but is stable.** 9

The saddest day

For the Netherlands, this was the country's worst disaster since the floods of 1953. In total seventy Dutch holidaymakers were among the victims and the government declared a day of mourning.

Friends and strangers laid flowers on the van Assouws' doorstep in Batavia Street, Tilburg.

6 **Words can't express how sorry I am for your loss. So many people around the world are grateful for the miracle of your survival.** 9

A few days after the crash, Ruben's aunt and uncle flew to Tripoli to be with their nephew and to break the news of the remarkable and terrible event that had befallen him.

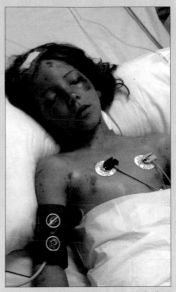

Nine-year old Ruben van Assouw at El Khadra Hospital in Tripoli, Libya on 20 May 2010, before his transfer to The Netherlands.

Many little strokes of luck

Some areas of aircraft fare better that others in crashes. But even this fact depends on circumstances. The seats above the wings may be safer if the plane strikes the ground nose first, but if the fuel tanks explode there may be a higher number of fatalities there.

Ruben's size could have helped him: children's lower mass can lessen the damage to their bodies caused by a severe impact.

No two crashes are alike; each plane will break up in a different way. The way the plane fractured may have caused Ruben's seat to separate from its row and catapult him through the disintegrating fuselage.

There was no warning of the crash so no one had time to adopt the brace position. Ruben might have been accidentally sitting in a way that maximized his chances of avoiding serious injury.

Together, these little factors added up to make him the only survivor of a crash that was so utterly tragic for so many other people.

The Wife in the Wilderness

When Rita and Albert Chretien's van became stuck in the snow in a remote Nevada forest they knew they were in trouble. After Albert disappeared in a savage storm trying to get help, Rita was left to face the cruel wilderness alone for seven long weeks.

DATE:
2011

SITUATION:
LOST IN THE WILDERNESS

CONDITION OF CONFINEMENT:
STRANDED ALONE IN A VAN IN A SNOWBOUND FOREST

DURATION OF CONFINEMENT:
49 DAYS

MEANS OF ESCAPE:
RESCUE

NO. OF ESCAPEES:
1

DANGERS:
HYPOTHERMIA, STARVATION, EXHAUSTION

EQUIPMENT:
A MINI-VAN, SPARE CLOTHES, SOME FOOD, WATER BOTTLES

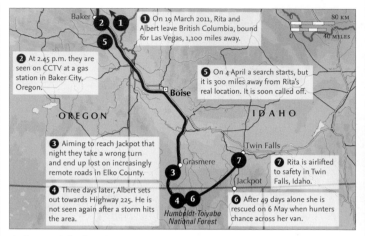

❶ On 19 March 2011, Rita and Albert leave British Columbia, bound for Las Vegas, 1,100 miles away.

❷ At 2.45 p.m. they are seen on CCTV at a gas station in Baker City, Oregon.

❸ Aiming to reach Jackpot that night they take a wrong turn and end up lost on increasingly remote roads in Elko County.

❹ Three days later, Albert sets out towards Highway 225. He is not seen again after a storm hits the area.

❺ On 4 April a search starts, but it is 300 miles away from Rita's real location. It is soon called off.

❻ After 49 days alone she is rescued on 6 May when hunters chance across her van.

❼ Rita is airlifted to safety in Twin Falls, Idaho.

A date with destiny

It was 6 May 2011 and Rita Chretien decided that today she would die. She had been stranded in a snowbound forest for the previous 49 days without seeing a single soul. She circled the date in her mud-stained diary and said her prayers.

The road trip

Rita, 56, and her husband Albert, 59, ran an excavating business in Penticton, British Columbia. In mid-March they decided to travel to Las Vegas for a trade convention. This was a journey of 1,100 miles, but the couple were used to travelling long distances together. Besides, spring was just around the corner. With a few provisions and an easy schedule, they'd be just fine in their sturdy Chevrolet Astro van.

Stranded

The couple set off from home on 19 March, stopping to fill up at a gas station in Baker City, Oregon, where they were seen on CCTV around 2.45 p.m. Although they didn't know it, this would be their last contact with civilisation.

As the miles rolled by, it began to get late. They decided to drive to Jackpot, Nevada, that night and find a rest-stop. Albert programmed this instruction into their new GPS and they turned south off Interstate 84.

Albert soon realised he'd turned too early. They weren't on US 93 but Idaho 51: they needed to be further east to make Jackpot. That's when Albert decided to take a short cut through the remote Humboldt-Toiyabe National Forest, and again he trusted his GPS. Unfortunately for the Chretiens, this time the most direct route to Jackpot was along a series of increasingly remote forestry roads. The Astro's rear-wheel drive didn't help matters, and as the snow and mud got deeper, they soon heard the unsettling whizz and splatter of tyre treads spinning free. They were stuck.

The quiet forest

For hours Albert tried to free the van from its forest prison. It became obvious that they were going nowhere.

By the time night fell, Albert was anxious, almost frantic. Rita tried to calm him, suggesting they get some rest and work out what to do in the morning. The couple curled up on the floor of their van, throwing their spare clothing over themselves to retain body heat. It was a cold, uncomfortable night.

The next morning they tried in vain to dig themselves out and every hour that passed made them more aware of the extreme remoteness of their location.

Another night and day came and went. Then another. After three days they had still seen no-one. They would have to do something.

Walking into the wilds

Albert believed they were about 10 miles from State Highway 225. Even in the heavy snow, that should be trekkable in a day or two. He would get there quicker on his own, and once he had reached civilisation he could easily direct rescuers to Rita. So he took the GPS, kissed his wife goodbye and set off alone in search of help. He had only been gone a couple of hours when the storm blew in.

The hard business of survival

Luckily Rita had a suitcase of clothes packed for their trip, and an emergency blanket. She also had some books and her journal. But she had precious little to eat.

> ❦ I figured I'd be out of there at least in a week, and I had some candies so I'd eat a candy a day and that was it. But I ran out... ❧

She had some scraps of beef jerky and trail mix; she rationed herself to a tablespoon a day. When the trail mix ran out after a week, she found

The Chevrolet Astro van, in which Rita Chretien spent 49 days before being rescued.

some candies so ate one of those a day. When the candies ran out, she ate her fish oil tablets. Again, one a day. Every other day she walked to collect water in plastic containers.

A rescue is launched... and called off

The Chretiens' relatives back in Canada knew something was amiss when the couple hadn't called after two weeks. They raised the alarm on 4 April.

The police found no trace of the couple in Nevada so began to check CCTV footage from stops on their route. This led them to the gas station near Baker City.

Although this was the last place the couple had been seen it was fully 300 miles from where Rita was shivering in her van in northern Nevada. After searching for a few weeks, police abandoned the search in mid-April.

Death by degrees

For Rita the long days and nights settled into a cold, lonely routine. By forcing herself to gather water, write in her journal and pray daily she at first kept her spirits aloft. But as March became April and then turned into May, her pitiful rations ran out completely.

Rita had felt physically quite strong considering her desperate situation. What she didn't realise was that although her deterioration had been gradual, it was severe.

The final day

When Rita went to get water on 6 May, she found it nearly impossible to get back to the van. She was almost crawling and was struggling to breathe. She thought she was going to have a heart attack. When she finally managed to haul herself back into her cold metal sanctuary she decided that maybe that was that.

Rita cleaned herself up as best she could, gathered her blanket around her and prayed the prayer she had learned as a child: 'Now I lay me down to sleep, I pray the Lord my soul to keep, if I should die before I wake, I pray the Lord my soul to take.' She then lay down in the back of the van and let sleep take her.

Around two hours later, she woke up to a loud roaring noise... Hunters. On quad bikes.

Sole survivor

Rita was airlifted to hospital in Twin Falls, Idaho, where it was discovered she had lost nearly 30lb (14kg) during her ordeal.

A huge team of searchers, including Canadian Mounties, spent months combing the Nevada wilderness for Albert Chretien. Sadly no sign of him was ever found.

Rita made a full recovery. She was reunited with her children in hospital and later returned to the family business. She still drives the same Chevrolet Astro van she lived in for 49 days.

PRISON

Charmed by a Renegade Queen

A BEAUTIFUL QUEEN, LIVING IN TURBULENT TIMES, IS ALREADY TWICE
WIDOWED AND IS NOW FORCIBLY SEPARATED FROM HER NEW HUSBAND
AND IMPRISONED AGAINST HER WILL IN THE TOWER HOUSE OF AN ISLAND
CASTLE. SURROUNDED BY ENEMIES AND COURT POLITICS, HER GALLANT
RESCUE DEPENDS UPON THE HELP OF HER JAILER'S LOVESTRUCK BROTHER
AND ANOTHER YOUNG ADMIRER.

DATE:
1567–8

SITUATION:
IMPRISONMENT

**CONDITION OF
CONFINEMENT:**
IN A CASTLE ON A REMOTE
SCOTTISH ISLAND

**DURATION OF
CONFINEMENT:**
10 MONTHS

MEANS OF ESCAPE:
DISGUISE, HELP FROM
JAILER'S FAMILY

NO. OF ESCAPEES:
1

DANGERS:
RECAPTURE, BETRAYAL

EQUIPMENT:
CHARM, GUILE, AN EARRING

The queen in the high castle

An escape from Lochleven Castle would have been a serious undertaking for a man in 1568. The heavy stone building had a five-storey keep with just a few tiny windows. Surrounding this was an outer curtain wall with a lookout tower and only one gate. A few hundred feet beyond this lay the waters of Loch Leven, a broad, deep and cold lake that completely surrounded the island on which the castle was built.

The task would have been harder still for a woman, encumbered with her more voluminous clothing. As for a woman who was also a queen and probably the most recognizable face in the country, such an escape would require an extraordinary effort.

Luckily for Mary Stewart, Queen of Scots, she was no ordinary woman.

Background to Mary's imprisonment

Mary's life was characterized by intrigue, captivity, plots and revenge. Born on 8 December 1542, her father, King James V of Scotland died just six days later. Mary was his sole legitimate child and she was crowned Queen of Scotland at the age of nine months.

Her first marriage, aged 15, was to Francis, the Dauphin of France. She ascended to the French throne with him in 1558. But he died the following year and Mary was forced out of her royal life in France and had to return to Scotland.

For the next four years she travelled extensively round Scotland, both building the support and arousing the suspicions of varying factions of the country's most powerful lords. She married again in 1565, but this union with her first cousin, Lord Darnley, was both unhappy for Mary and unpopular at court. In 1567 Darnley was found strangled following an explosion at their house.

When Mary then married the Earl of Bothwell, the man widely believed to be Darnley's assassin, it was a step too far for many Scottish nobles. They raised an army, confronted Mary and Bothwell and subsequently imprisoned her in Lochleven Castle on 15 June 1567. Although she was also forced to abdicate the Scottish throne in favour of her one-year-old son James, her presence in the world at large would be a thorn in the side of the faction opposing her. It was highly unlikely that her enemies would release her in the near future.

The inside men

The castle belonged to Sir William Douglas, one of the nobles who opposed Mary. He lived there with his family, but it was as much a fortress as a residence, with a high tower, thick walls and the extra security of being built on an island in the middle of a broad Scottish loch.

Moreover, Mary was a deposed queen, instantly recognizable and ill-suited for feats of physical adventure. If she were to escape it must be through acts of guile and contrivance.

But while she still had a few loyal servants and some political friends in the outside world, Douglas and her most powerful adversary, the Earl of Moray, forbade her any contact with potential supporters.

So it fell to Mary herself to find the help she needed. Her first accomplice was a surprising but convenient choice: George Douglas, brother of her jailer Sir William. A dashing, spirited young man, George was apparently charmed by the imprisoned queen and actually fell in love with her. Her second ally was another young Douglas lad called Willie, who also decided to risk his neck for her.

George and Willie agreed to smuggle letters from Mary to her supporters. George also began enthusiastically planning a daring escape. But the Earl of Moray got wind of George's plotting and banished him from the island. Keen to cling to any leverage she had, Mary

gave him a farewell gift of one of her pearl earrings, asking him to return it to her as a sign that he had her escape worked out.

By March George had come up with an idea. Mary borrowed clothes from a laundress and took her place on the boat that ferried these servants back to the mainland. The escape would have succeeded but for an eagle-eyed boatman who spotted Mary's fingers on her muffler: they were too long and white to be those of a hard-working servant girl. He removed the muffler, discovered the truth and returned the queen to her prison.

The diversion

Sir William Douglas was aghast at how close he had come to losing Mary and to enraging the fearsome Earl of Moray. He increased security on the island and dispatched young Willie ashore with George.

But George was in too deep to give up that easily. He started a ruse, telling his mother that he was off to France to make a fresh start and somebody else would need to look after young Willie.

Out of affection for Willie, Sir William decided to allow him to return to the island. George then had an inside connection to Mary and he began to plan a second breakout in earnest.

In May, a boatman arrived at the castle bearing Mary's pearl earring. He told a rambling story about how another boatman had found the earring and tried to sell it on, and this allayed suspicion Sir William might have had. Only Mary knew that this was the pre-agreed signal.

Meanwhile Willie had asked Sir William for permission to organize the traditional May celebrations. One element of these festivities was the appointment of the Abbot of Unreason, the overseer of the revelries with the right to give orders to whomever he chose.

Willie ensured that everyone, particularly Sir William, made the most of the alcohol laid on for the

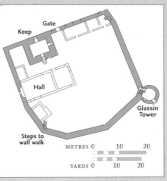

Ground floor plan of Lochleven Castle

occasion. He also securely staked down all the castle's boats except one. Willie still had to get hold of the keys to the main gate, which never left Sir William's sight.

Fortunately, drink had played its part and Willie was able to drop a napkin over the keys as they lay on the dining table and whip them away before the inebriated Sir William could notice.

He dashed into the courtyard and signaled to Mary. Dressed as a servant girl she scurried across the courtyard and through the now-open gates. Willie locked the gate behind him and threw the keys in the mouth of a cannon. They jumped into the only unsecured boat and rowed ashore.

George Douglas was waiting for them with open arms.

After the escape

Unfortunately for Mary, this tale does not have a happy ending. She never saw Bothwell again. After her escape, she managed to raise a small army but this was defeated at the Battle of Langside on 13 May. She then fled south into England, seeking the protection of her cousin, Queen Elizabeth I. Mary had previously taken Elizabeth's throne and the worried English queen had her arrested. For the next nineteen years, Mary was detained in several castles and manor houses throughout England before being tried and executed for treason on 8 February 1587.

Flight of the Philosopher

In 1619 the philosopher Hugo Grotius found himself embroiled in a ruthless struggle for political power in the Netherlands. Convicted of treason, he was sentenced to life imprisonment and locked up to rot in the dank castle at Loevestein. With his wife's help he made an ingenious escape hidden in a wooden chest.

DATE:
1619–21

SITUATION:
Falsely imprisoned

CONDITION OF CONFINEMENT:
Locked in a medieval fortress

DURATION OF CONFINEMENT:
20 months

MEANS OF ESCAPE:
Hiding in a chest of books

NO. OF ESCAPEES:
1

DANGERS:
Capture, betrayal, suffocation

EQUIPMENT:
A wooden chest

ABOVE RIGHT
The Nieuwe Kerk (New Church) in Delft, final resting place of Hugo Grotius.

The academic action hero

Hugo Grotius was a hugely influential sixteenth century thinker and academic. Born in Delft in 1583, he was a child prodigy who went to the University of Leyden aged 11 and earned his doctorate by 15.

A true polymath, he wrote seminal texts on legal matters, politics, the arts and philosophy. His volume *The Law of War and Peace* is a pioneering work that earned him the title 'the father of international law'.

His academic accomplishments are rightfully respected, but to many people his most remarkable achievement was a daring escape from a harsh prison sentence.

A dangerous philosophy

In the early seventeenth century the Netherlands was going through a period of political and religious instability. There were two religious factions vying for power. Maurice of Nassau, Prince of Orange, led a strict Calvinist group of nobles. Grotius' former tutor and mentor Johan van Oldenbarnevelt was a major figure in the other faction. Both sides saw the potential for great wealth and influence and the struggle for ultimate power would be a bloody one.

When Oldenbarnevelt advocated an official policy of religious tolerance in 1613, he asked Grotius to draft an edict expressing this position. Hostilities flared on its publication and when Oldenbarnevelt later proposed that local authorities be given the power to raise troops, Prince Maurice had had enough.

On 29 August 1618, Grotius and van Oldenbarnevelt were seized and tried on trumped up charges in a court organized by Prince Maurice himself. Unsurprisingly, both men were convicted of treason. Van Oldenbarnevelt paid for his opinions with his head. Grotius, 36, was sentenced to life imprisonment in the dank surroundings of Loevestein Castle. His home and property were also confiscated.

Imprisoned

Loevestein is an imposing mediaeval fortress 8 km (5 miles) from Gorinchem in South Holland, built on an island formed by the Waal and the Maas rivers. The castle has high-walled towers with a few tiny windows and is surrounded by a moat. Grotius would have suffered in dark, damp conditions and the round-the-clock guards and position of the fortress made escape unlikely.

Many of his political friends petitioned to have Grotius' sentence appealed. They were all unsuccessful. Maurice had prepared his move thoroughly. But Grotius did have an ally of unexpected power – his wife Maria. As soon as he was arrested, she petitioned the court to share her husband's confinement. This request was flatly denied. But Maria seems to have made something of a pest of herself, and the authorities finally agreed to admit her into prison with Grotius, on condition that she should remain there for the duration of his imprisonment.

Maurice and his circle probably thought they were ridding themselves of an irritation, but it was a concession that they would later come to regret.

The forgotten philosopher

Grotius' life became one of hidden exile. His cell was spartan and although he was allowed to write letters, he was forbidden to correspond with his friends on the topics that most interested him. All his communications were thoroughly censored.

Gradually his jailers allowed small numbers of books to be brought to their prisoner. These were conveyed to his cell in a wooden chest, along with his clean linen. The chest was brought by boat from Gorinchem.

For twenty months Grotius remained in this state of forgotten confinement. He refused to allow his imprisonment to break his mind. He wrote a summary of Dutch law, *Introduction to the Jurisprudence of Holland*, entirely from memory. This text later became a legal standard.

However, although his study brought him some solace, Grotius knew that at any time the political forces that had detained him could probably find it within their power to execute him. And with the religious unrest continuing, this was becoming more and more likely.

Maria knew this too, and she began to plan a daring escape.

Sowing the seeds

There were several guards in the prison and they checked everything that went in and out of Grotius' cell, including the wooden box that was used to transport his linen and his precious books.

But, over time, the guards became more lax in their inspection of this container. As they never saw anything in it but books and linen, after many months they waved it through unchecked more often than they examined its contents. Maria decided this was the key to her husband's freedom.

She began a campaign of misinformation, cultivating a friendship with the prison governor's wife and complaining vociferously to this woman that Grotius' imprisonment had made him seriously ill. The confinement had

2 THE ESCAPE
After twenty months he climbs into a wooden chest and is carried away on a boat bound for Gorinchem. Here he meets up with a friend who smuggles him away via another boat.

1 IMPRISONED
Hugo Grotius is sentenced to life imprisonment in Loevestein Castle, 8 km (5 miles) from Gorinchem in South Holland.

3 FREE AT LAST
Grotius travels on to Antwerp, then into France where he is reunited with his wife.

NORTH SEA

NETHERLANDS

Gorinchem

Breda

Tilburg

Roosendaal

Antwerpen (Antwerp)

BELGIUM

KILOMETRES 0 5 10 15

MILES 0 5 10

The medieval castle of Loevestein (Slot Loevestein) in the Netherlands.

affected his brain, she said, causing him to work almost manically. She thought it best if she took his books from him and returned them to their owners.

She went on to spread this story around more widely. Soon everyone in the vicinity of the castle was aware that Grotius was suffering greatly and had been confined to his bed. Maria was making physical preparations too. She cleared the chest out and bored several small holes in it to provide ventilation.

Maria then brought her maid into the plan and made her final preparations.

The escape

On 22 March 1621 the chest arrived in Grotius's cell as normal. When he began to pack it with the books that he no longer required, his wife stopped him. She explained that it was he who should be getting into the wooden container.

At first Grotius refused, considering the plan to be foolhardy in the extreme. Maria persisted, and her powers of wifely persuasion eventually won through: Grotius agreed to climb into the box.

This was easier said than done. The chest was little more than 0.9 m (3 ft) long and by doubling himself up, Grotius put heavy pressure on his lungs. He was barely able to draw enough breath to keep himself conscious. As Maria secured the locks, she must have known it was likely she would not see her husband alive again.

Maria remained in the cell, watching as guards took the chest with her husband in it to the boat. It was much heavier than usual and the plan nearly failed at the first hurdle: one of the soldiers on the boat noticed the apparent increase in weight and demanded that it be opened. Only a piece of quick thinking from the maid saved the enterprise. She distracted the man and the box was loaded aboard the boat unchecked.

As the boat journeyed from Loevestein to Gorinchem, Grotius was in a state of barely controlled panic within the chest. Desperately short of air, he wanted to take deep breaths but could not afford to make any noise. If he were detected he would certainly end up at the bottom of the river Waal.

Grotius was in a state of barely controlled panic within the chest... For hours he lay cramped and gasping for life.

Finally, the boat reached Gorinchem. The chest was now supposed to be taken to the home of David Bazelaer, one of Grotius' most trusted friends. But when the boat reached the shore, there was no way of getting the heavy chest to Bazelaer's house without arousing suspicion. Again the maid came to the rescue, improvising a tale that the chest contained glass, and it must be moved with particular care. Helpful bystanders quickly located two porters and they carefully moved it on a horse cart.

With the box safely in his study, Bazelaer dispatched his servants from the house to ensure total security, and opened the locks. He threw open the lid and was delighted to see his old friend crammed within, wheezing and disorientated, but otherwise all right.

The men knew they weren't out of the woods yet: Grotius would soon be missed and a search launched. They had to move fast if he was to find sanctuary. Bazelaer had prepared a disguise, and he dressed Grotius as a mason before hustling him out the back door.

Along with the maid he hurried through the bustling marketplace to where a boat was waiting to take them to Brabant. The intrepid serving girl meanwhile travelled all the way back to Loevestein and passed on the good news to Maria.

Incredibly, no one in the castle had yet noticed that the philosopher

Statue of Hugo Grotius, made by Franciscus Leonardus Stracké in 1886 and placed at Grote Markt in Delft.

was missing. It was Maria who informed the guards of his escape. The furious governor promptly put her in solitary confinement.

Grotius had now made it to Antwerp and soon after his arrival in that city, he sent a letter to the States General which assured them that he had used neither violence nor corruption during his escape. He solemnly protested his innocence and that the persecution he had suffered would never lessen his patriotism.

Perhaps there had been a change of policy towards Grotius during his escape, or maybe the authorities were simply impressed with his ingenuity; what is certain is that a few days later Maria was set free and the joyous couple were reunited in France.

Together in exile

Grotius and his wife spent ten years in exile in France. During this time he enjoyed the patronage of King Louis XIII who called him 'the miracle of Holland'. He also wrote his most important work, *The Law of War and Peace*.

Escape from Devil's Island

HENRI 'PAPILLON' CHARRIÈRE WAS SENTENCED TO LIFE IMPRISONMENT
AND HARD LABOUR IN THE NOTORIOUS PENAL COLONY OF FRENCH GUIANA.
AFTER A SERIES OF INGENIOUS BREAKOUT ATTEMPTS HE FINALLY ESCAPED
FROM THE BRUTAL DEVIL'S ISLAND BY FLOATING TO VENEZUELA ON A RAFT
OF COCONUTS AND TREKKING THROUGH THE JUNGLE.

DATE:
1932–45

SITUATION:
IMPRISONMENT (CLAIMED
TO BE FALSELY)

**CONDITION OF
CONFINEMENT:**
HARD LABOUR AND
SOLITARY CONFINEMENT

**DURATION OF
CONFINEMENT:**
14 YEARS

MEANS OF ESCAPE:
RAFT OF COCONUTS,
TREKKING THROUGH
THE JUNGLE

NO. OF ESCAPEES:
1

DANGERS:
RECAPTURE, DROWNING,
DISEASE

EQUIPMENT:
COCONUTS, STOLEN BOATS

ABOVE RIGHT
Devil's Island, French Guiana.

Escape from Devil's Island

Henri Charrière was born on
16 November 1906 in Saint-
Étienne-de-Lugdarès in France's
Ardèche region. His mother died when
he was 10 years old. In 1923, at the age
of 17, he enlisted in the French Navy.
After serving for two years he began
a colourful life as a member of the
Paris underworld. Charrière became
known as Papillon, from the butterfly
tattoo he had on his chest (*papillon* is
French for butterfly).

On 26 October 1931, Papillon was
convicted of the murder of a pimp
named Roland Le Petit. Papillon
claimed he had been framed, but he
was sentenced to life in prison and
ten years of hard labour, to be served
in the penal colony of St-Laurent-du-
Maroni in French Guiana.

The prison colony was established
by Napoleon III in 1852 as a kind of
cellar of the French Empire; a place
where the irredeemable criminals
could be put and forgotten about.
The colony's principal camp was
on the mainland, surrounded by
mosquito-infested swamps and semi-
jungle. There were also three offshore
jails on the islands of Royale, St Joseph
and, notoriously, Devil's Island.
Although these were several miles
out into the Atlantic and so harder to
escape from, these island prisons had
a healthier environment, being aired
by the trade winds. St-Laurent-du-
Maroni remained in use until 1952.

> **I was innocent of the killing
> for which a public prosecutor,
> some cops and the twelve
> bastards of the jury had
> sent me to penal.**

This would be Papillon's home for
the next fourteen years, during which
his life would be defined by extreme
conditions of imprisonment and
resourceful escape attempts.

First escape

On board the ship for South
America, Papillon learned of the brutal

life that awaited him in St-Laurent-du-Maroni. Conditions were bestial and prisoners routinely murdered each other for petty grudges and meager sums of money. Papillon resolved to escape as soon as possible.

As soon as he arrived at the colony, Papillon claimed to be ill. He was sent to the infirmary where he met two fellow escape enthusiasts Joanes Clousiot and André Maturette. Together they hatched a plan to club their Arab wardens and scale the wall. They would then hide in the jungle with a convict whom they had bribed and then sail to safety in a dugout canoe.

They dealt with the wardens as planned, but Clousiot broke his leg jumping from the wall and the canoe was too rotten to carry them far.

Papillon acquired a boat from the leper colony on nearby Pigeon Island. The three men sailed into the current of the Maroni River and drifted out into the Atlantic Ocean. Clear of the penal colony, they then turned north-west and journeyed more than 1,600 km (1,000 miles) to Trinidad.

There they were helped on their journey by a British family, the Dutch Bishop of Curaçao and some other French fugitives. They planned to go to Curaçao and then on to British Honduras, but as they approached the Colombian coastline, they were spotted. The wind had died in their sails and they were soon behind bars in Colombia.

Breakout from a Colombian prison

Falling in with a local smuggler, Papillon managed to escape from the prison at Ríohacha, making to the Native American settlements on the Guajira peninsula. There he went to ground in a pearl diving village, where he earned the trust of the locals. He lived with two teenage sisters and acquired a stash of 572 pearls. But after only months in this relative paradise, Papillon decided to leave on a quest for vengeance.

> ❛ The coming in of the water, the rats, the centipedes and the tiny waterborne crabs, was the most revolting, the most depressing thing a human being could possibly have to bear. ❜

Soon after leaving the village he was betrayed by a nun who recognized him and thrown into jail at Santa Marta. For twenty-eight days he was

Solitary confinement cells once used to hold some of France's worst criminals, stand overgrown with jungle vegetation on the island of St Joseph off the French Guiana coast.

locked in the hideous Black Hole, an underground block of slimy, filth-covered cells that flooded twice a day with the tide.

Now reunited with Clousiot and Maturette he was transferred to a prison at Barranquilla. The men tried four times to escape, organizing a riot in the chapel, drugging a sentry, causing a blackout and even managing to procure some dynamite, but all the attempts failed. In November 1936, Papillon was returned to French Guiana.

His escape earned him two years in solitary confinement on the island of St Joseph. His only companions were the 23 cm (9 inch) long centipedes. Clousiot and Maturette were similarly incarcerated. A rule of strict silence was brutally enforced in the rows of tiny cells. Men routinely went mad or hung themselves with their trousers. Caught receiving cigarettes and tiny morsels of coconut from a friendly fellow prisoner, Papillon feigned amnesia to avoid punishment. He survived his term. Clousiot did not.

On his release, Papillon was transferred to Royale. He promptly

Cells of the penal colony in St-Laurent-du-Maroni, French Guiana.

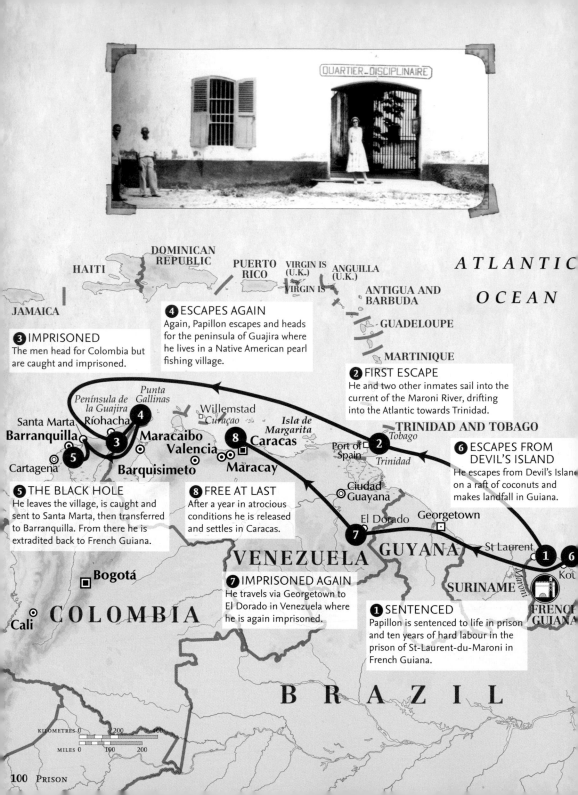

QUARTIER-DISCIPLINAIRE

4 ESCAPES AGAIN
Again, Papillon escapes and heads for the peninsula of Guajira where he lives in a Native American pearl fishing village.

3 IMPRISONED
The men head for Colombia but are caught and imprisoned.

2 FIRST ESCAPE
He and two other inmates sail into the current of the Maroni River, drifting into the Atlantic towards Trinidad.

6 ESCAPES FROM DEVIL'S ISLAND
He escapes from Devil's Island on a raft of coconuts and makes landfall in Guiana.

5 THE BLACK HOLE
He leaves the village, is caught and sent to Santa Marta, then transferred to Barranquilla. From there he is extradited back to French Guiana.

8 FREE AT LAST
After a year in atrocious conditions he is released and settles in Caracas.

7 IMPRISONED AGAIN
He travels via Georgetown to El Dorado in Venezuela where he is again imprisoned.

1 SENTENCED
Papillon is sentenced to life in prison and ten years of hard labour in the prison of St-Laurent-du-Maroni in French Guiana.

ATLANTIC OCEAN

DOMINICAN REPUBLIC
HAITI
PUERTO RICO
VIRGIN IS (U.K.)
VIRGIN IS
ANGUILLA (U.K.)
ANTIGUA AND BARBUDA
JAMAICA
GUADELOUPE
MARTINIQUE

TRINIDAD AND TOBAGO
Tobago
Port of Spain
Trinidad

Punta Gallinas
Península de la Guajira
Willemstad
Curaçao
Isla de Margarita
Santa Marta
Ríohacha
Barranquilla
Maracaibo
Caracas
Cartagena
Valencia
Barquisimeto
Maracay
Ciudad Guayana
El Dorado
Georgetown
St Laurent
Kou
SURINAME
FRENCH GUIANA
Maroni

VENEZUELA
GUYANA
Bogotá
COLOMBIA
Cali

B R A Z I L

KILOMETRES 0   200   400
MILES 0   100   200

tried to escape again, but was betrayed by an informant (who Papillon later stabbed to death). His reward was eight years in solitary, although this was reduced to nineteen months when a doctor intervened on his behalf.

> ❛ I should never have believed or imagined that a country like… France, the mother of freedom throughout the world, …could possibly possess an establishment of such barbarous repression as the St Joseph solitary confinement prison. ❜

The 'insane' escape

It was 1940 and officials in French Guiana decided to support the pro-Nazi Vichy Regime. This meant that anyone caught trying to escape would be executed.

To avoid such a fate, Papillon feigned insanity and was sent to the asylum on Royale. He tried escaping from the asylum with another prisoner, but their boat was smashed against rocks. The other prisoner drowned and Papillon nearly suffered the same fate.

Henri Charrière, 'Papillon' (1906–73).

Papillon ended up on Devil's Island, the smallest and reputedly most escape-proof jail in the penal colony. But by studying the waters around the island, Papillon found a rocky inlet surrounded by high cliffs that had escape potential. He discovered that every seventh wave was large enough to carry something on the water far enough out into the sea to drift towards the mainland. He proved his theory by throwing sacks of coconuts into the ocean.

Papillon roped a pirate named Sylvain into his plan and they threw themselves into the crashing waves with sacks of coconuts to float on. As predicted, a larger wave carried them out into the Atlantic. They drifted for days under the burning sun with only coconut pulp to eat. Eventually they washed up on the mainland. But Sylvain left his coconut sack too early and was swallowed by quicksand.

Papillon made his way to Georgetown in Guyana by boat. He could have lived there as a free man,

but he continued northwesterly towards Venezuela. Here he was caught and imprisoned in El Dorado, a small mining town in the Gran Sabana region. He suffered for a year in appalling conditions, facing regular beatings and enduring forced labour.

Finally, on 18 October 1945, after fourteen years of incarceration, he was then released. Papillon became a Venezuelan citizen, married a local woman and opened restaurants in Caracas and Maracaibo. He was treated as a minor celebrity, regularly appearing on television.

He returned to France in 1969 when he published his memoir, *Papillon*. The book sold over 1.5 million copies in France and was made into a Hollywood movie starring Steve McQueen, much to the chagrin of a French minister who attributed 'the moral decline of France' to mini-skirts and Papillon.

Henri Charrière died of throat cancer in Madrid, Spain, on 29 July 1973.

ABOVE
Papillon's prison cells, Devil's Island, French Guiana.

ABOVE LEFT
The prison of St-Laurent-du-Maroni in 1954.

The Escape from Alcatraz

Alcatraz's reputation as a formidable island fortress had been fairly earned. Its sheer walls held over 300 of America's most dangerous criminals securely in the middle of San Francisco Bay. Then, in June 1962, three men put a daring and ingenious plan into action and pulled off what is possibly the only successful escape from the prison they called 'The Rock'.

DATE:
1962

SITUATION:
Incarceration in Alcatraz

CONDITION OF CONFINEMENT:
Locked in an 'escape-proof' island penitentiary

DURATION OF CONFINEMENT:
Several years

MEANS OF ESCAPE:
Tunnelling, climbing, paddling rafts

NO. OF ESCAPEES:
3

DANGERS:
Drowning, guard detection, police capture

EQUIPMENT:
Cutlery, common implements, homemade rafts

ABOVE RIGHT
The Rock is a small island located in the middle of San Francisco Bay in California, United States. It served as a lighthouse, then a military fortification, then a prison.

A route off the rock

Alcatraz was the ultimate in escape-proof prisons. It was built on a scrubby rock island 2.4 km (1½ miles) from the city of San Francisco. The curved bay around the island has a fierce tide, the water is cold even in the height of summer and the depths are home to eleven species of shark including the Great White.

In all its years as a prison its security had never been breached. Then, in June 1962, four men thought they had a plan that would succeed where so many others had failed. Three of them may well have pulled it off.

The escapees

Four men planned the Alcatraz escape: Frank Morris, Allen West and the Anglin brothers, Clarence and John. They were not the most heroic of characters, but the careful planning, ingenuity and sheer audacity of their Alcatraz escape attempt has captured the world's imagination.

John Anglin was born on 2 May 1930 in Donalsonville, Georgia. His brother Clarence came into the world the following year on 11 May. As young men they worked together on Georgia farms before turning to the more lucrative career of robbing banks. Police caught up with them in 1956 and they were both sentenced to 15–20 years. They tried to escape several times from their first prison, the Atlanta Penitentiary, and after spells in Florida State Prison and Leavenworth Federal Penitentiary they were sent to Alcatraz in the winter of 1960–1.

Frank Lee Morris (born in Washington, D.C. on 1 September 1926) was a troubled boy, who spent most of his young life moving in and out of foster homes. He was only 13 when convicted of his first crime and by his late teens his rap sheet listed a variety of offences from possession of narcotics to armed robbery.

Allen Clayton West (born c. 1929) was a specialist hijacker and car thief. He was sent to the Atlanta Penitentiary from where he tried unsuccessfully to escape, earning himself a one-way ticket to Alcatraz in 1957.

Planning the escape

Frank Morris, Allen West and Clarence and John Anglin had originally met in the late 1950s in the Atlanta Penitentiary. West was the first to be transferred to Alcatraz following an attempted breakout. Over the next few years the other three joined him in the maximum security jail. Between them the men had many escape attempts under their belts and it was no surprise that the reunited foursome soon started plotting a route off the Rock.

Of course, what they were attempting to do was widely regarded as impossible. By 1962, thirty-six Alcatraz inmates had tried to escape the island. None had been remotely successful. Nor was there anything to suggest that Morris, West and the Anglins would be the ones to buck this trend. They had failed on all of their previous breakouts at lower security prisons.

If they become the first men to defeat the Rock, the quartet knew they had to pull off something truly special. They needed a plan that was creative, audacious and utterly methodical in its execution.

Alcatraz put several formidable barriers between an escaping prisoner and his freedom. First, there was the problem of how to exit his cell. These windowless boxes were just 1.5 x 2.7 m (5 x 9 ft) in size and had thick concrete walls. And a front 'wall' of hardened steel bars. In 1934 the prison had been remodelled and all the old iron bars replaced with 'tool-resistant' steel that could withstand the teeth of a hacksaw. Guards made frequent checks, even at night. The prison itself was built on solid rock. Only one prisoner lived in each cell.

Alcatraz became a maximum security federal prison in 1933 and for the next twenty-nine years held some of America's most notorious criminals including Al Capone, George 'Machine Gun' Kelly, Mickey Cohen and Bumpy Johnson.

Even if a man did get out of his cell, next there was the question of how to get out of the cell block. Cells had no contact with the outside walls: each cell block was like a prison inside a prison. After that there was the small matter of the outer perimeter wall: 3 m (10 ft) of concrete topped by a fence and barbed wire, and watched by armed guards. Finally, the greatest barrier of all came courtesy of Mother Nature: the swirling depths of San Francisco Bay. The waters here are particularly treacherous. The water is usually below 16°C and with the ebbing tide, the current pulls out towards the Pacific.

The four men knew they had a near impossible challenge on their hands and they dedicated themselves whole-heartedly to their endeavour, spending nine long months nurturing their plans before the escape came to fruition.

The preparations began around September 1961. The prisoners were housed in Cell Block B. Behind their cells was an unguarded 0.9 m (3 ft) wide utility corridor. Accessing this would normally have been impossible, but the prisoners noticed that the concrete around the air vents in their cells had been damaged by moisture.

Night after night they chiseled this away using homemade tools – a metal spoon soldered with silver from a dime and an electric drill improvised from a stolen vacuum cleaner motor. They did much of their digging during music hour, when accordions drowned out their scraping. They used false cardboard walls painted to look like the original grate to cover up their handiwork. They also stole soap, toilet paper, prison issue raincoats, a carborundum rod from the prison workshop and hair clippings from the prison barber.

By late May 1962, Morris, West, and the Anglins had finished cutting through the walls of their cells. They made their final preparations, gathered their equipment and set their sights on a date. The night of the 11th of June would see them try to outfox Alcatraz.

The plan in action

The cells had long been locked down and the lights were low when Frank Morris rolled softly out of his bed for what would be the last time. He reached under his bunk and removed the papier-mâché model of his own head that he had spent the last few weeks constructing. Made of soap and toilet paper that had been mashed together and reformed,

Mug shots of the three prisoners that made a rare escape from Alcatraz Island.
From left to right: Clarence Anglin, John William Anglin and Frank Lee Morris.

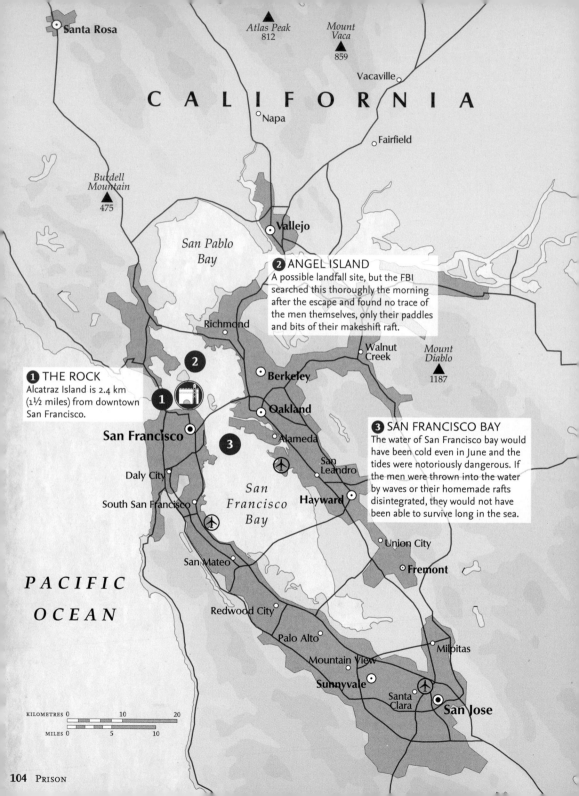

CALIFORNIA

Santa Rosa

Atlas Peak 812

Mount Vaca 859

Vacaville

Napa

Fairfield

Burdell Mountain 475

San Pablo Bay

Vallejo

2 ANGEL ISLAND
A possible landfall site, but the FBI searched this thoroughly the morning after the escape and found no trace of the men themselves, only their paddles and bits of their makeshift raft.

Richmond

Walnut Creek

Mount Diablo 1187

1 THE ROCK
Alcatraz Island is 2.4 km (1½ miles) from downtown San Francisco.

Berkeley

Oakland

San Francisco

Alameda

3 SAN FRANCISCO BAY
The water of San Francisco bay would have been cold even in June and the tides were notoriously dangerous. If the men were thrown into the water by waves or their homemade rafts disintegrated, they would not have been able to survive long in the sea.

Daly City

San Leandro

Hayward

South San Francisco

San Francisco Bay

PACIFIC OCEAN

Union City

San Mateo

Fremont

Redwood City

Palo Alto

Milpitas

Mountain View

Sunnyvale

Santa Clara

San Jose

KILOMETRES 0   10   20

MILES 0   5   10

it was trimmed with real hair and was authentic enough to fool a guard's glance in the midnight gloom. He tucked it between the edges of his still-warm blankets.

He then knelt down to the ventilation grille and removed it. For the last eight months he had been scrabbling at this opening with a spoon and it was now big enough to allow his body to pass through. He squeezed himself through the enlarged opening and into the maintenance shaft.

Squeezing past pipes and conduits, Morris's escape route then headed up through a fan vent. In the last few days, once they had gained access to the shaft, the men had removed the fan's blade and motor. Only a steel grille blocked the passage now. And the prisoners had earlier removed this grille's metal rivets with the carborundum rod and substituted dummy rivets made of soap. They had also used the space to construct life vests and an inflatable raft from the several stolen raincoats. Morris collected this kit and climbed further up the shaft.

After what must have been a back-breaking, skin-tearing struggle in the most cramped of conditions, Morris reached the point where the shaft met the top of the roof. The lights of San Francisco must have twinkled particularly beautifully across the water as he hauled himself out onto the rooftop. The summer night air must have smelled particularly sweet as he stood looking down on the walls that had held him prisoner for so long. And as he saw his old pals the Anglins come up to join him he must have felt a surge of elation.

But there was still a very long way to go and where was West? The fourth member of their team was not on the roof. Had he been caught leaving his cell? Were the guards onto their plan already?

Morris and the Anglin brothers must have paused here, waiting for their colleague. But, friend though he

One of the escape holes created behind a ventillation grille in the cells.

was, they knew they must press on if they were to stand any chance.

What the three didn't know was that down in his cell, West was scratching furiously at his ventilator grille. His false wall had started slipping some days before, so he had used cement to hold it in place. Unfortunately this set and although West desperately chipped away at the wall, by the time he did his companions were gone.

> The day after the escape a man claiming to be John Anglin called a lawyer in San Francisco. He wanted to arrange a meeting with US Marshals. The lawyer refused to help the man who then hung up. Whether this was the real Anglin or a hoax caller has never been established.

Meanwhile the trio used the height of the roof to help them clear Alcatraz's formidable fence. Not a single guard saw them go. They then scrabbled over the rocky ground to the northeast coast of the island where they took out their escape rafts. In theory the rafts would be strong enough to carry them the couple of miles to the nature reserve of Angel

Island. But since there had been no way of testing the craft, as the men climbed aboard for the first and only time, they were truly launching themselves into the unknown.

Did they make it?

Exactly what happened after the men paddled away from Alcatraz will probably never be known. Their plan was to steal clothes and a car on the mainland, but no such thefts were reported in the area after the escape. The FBI found some plywood paddles and parts of the raincoat raft on Angel Island, but did the men leave them there or the tide? If the sea took the men, it took them completely; no bodies were ever found. If they escaped, they covered their tracks extremely well.

The men were on the FBI's Most Wanted list for seventeen years until the case was finally closed in 1979. The FBI believes the men drowned in San Francisco Bay.

West, the unescaped prisoner, helped the FBI and prison authorities, giving them full details of the escape plan. He was never charged for trying to escape from Alcatraz and was transferred the next year.

The Dan Cooper Hijack

 On a stormy November night in 1971 a man known as Dan Cooper hijacked a Boeing 727 bound for Seattle using a bomb in his briefcase. The FBI met his demand for a $200,000 ransom and parachutes. Cooper then evaded agents by leaping from the jet at 3,000 m (10,000 ft) and more than 320 km/h (200 mph). It remains the only unsolved hijack in US history.

DATE:

1971

SITUATION:

Plane hijack

CONDITION OF CONFINEMENT:

Wanted by police and federal agents

DURATION OF CONFINEMENT:

18 hours

MEANS OF ESCAPE:

Parachuting from a Boeing 727

NO. OF ESCAPEES:

1

DANGERS:

Falling to death, police intervention

EQUIPMENT:

Parachute, explosives, coolness

LEFT
Boeing landing at Portland, Oregon.

ABOVE RIGHT
Crew members of the hijacked Northwest Airlines 727 jet. Stewardess Tina Mucklow (*right*), 22, described the hijacker as 'not nervous.' 'He seemed rather nice, and he was never cruel or nasty,' she said. Captain Bill Scott (*centre*) said, 'We first knew he was not aboard when we arrived in Reno.' Also in the picture is First Officer Bill Rataczak (*left*).

The hijack

Flight 305 was going to be just like any one of the hundreds of other flights – thousands maybe – that Florence Schaffner had made as an attendant for Northwest Orient. A short 280 km (175 mile) hop from Portland, Oregon to Seattle, Washington on a dull day in late November. Tomorrow was Thanksgiving and the passengers were in good spirits. In a few hours they'd be uncorking a bottle of wine with their loved ones and savouring the holiday spirit. As the jet climbed into the clouds, Florence unbuckled her lap belt and rose from her jump seat by the aft stair door. Just a few more smiles, a few more meals and she too could look forward to the holiday.

So when the smartly dressed man in Seat 18C slipped her a piece of paper, she popped it unopened into her pocket. They would only be in the air for less than an hour and she had a lot of passengers to serve. Besides, it wasn't the first time a

lonely businessman had passed her his phone number. But then the man leaned closer and whispered in her ear, 'Miss, you'd better look at that note. I have a bomb.' And Florence knew this flight was going to be anything but routine.

She looked again at the man. He was about 45 years old, maybe 2 m (6 ft) tall and his skin seemed unusually well tanned for this time of year. He was dressed in a dark suit and raincoat, a neatly pressed white shirt and black tie with a mother of pearl tiepin. He was wearing black sunglasses. The passenger manifest would say that his name was Dan Cooper.

Florence scrabbled in her pocket for his note. It read, 'I have a bomb in my briefcase, I will use it if necessary. I want you to sit next to me. You are being hijacked.' The note also demanded $200,000 in unmarked bills, a refuelling truck and four parachutes to be ready on the tarmac when the plane touched down (at Seattle-Tacoma International Airport) or Dan Cooper would blow the plane sky high.

Not wanting to alarm the passengers, Florence moved as calmly as she could to the cockpit and told the pilot, William Scott, about the note. He radioed air traffic control who in turn alerted the Seattle police and the FBI.

The next step was to find out if Cooper was bluffing. Captain Scott asked Florence to return to Row 18 to see if the bomb was real. She slid into a seat next to the skyjacker, who had moved over to a window seat, and quietly asked: 'What's this about a bomb?'

The man opened the case and closed it again quickly. In that brief glimpse, Florence saw red cylinders, wires and a large battery. It looked real enough. Cooper now demanded that the plane must not land until his money and parachutes were ready at Seattle. Florence reported back to the flight deck and the captain radioed SEA-TAC Airport.

Cooper had played his hand and it was a good one. How could the authorities respond? The FBI called Northwest's president at home in Minneapolis and he made a quick decision: 'Do whatever the man demands'.

❛ He seemed rather nice ❜

They did, and used unmarked bills as per Cooper's instructions, but they also played a few trump cards of their own. They packed bills from 1969, most of which had serial numbers starting with L, making them easier to identify. Agents also used a Recordak microfilm device to quickly photograph all 10,000 $20 bills.

With the FBI busy and the plane circling Seattle, Cooper sat coolly in his seat, enjoying a cigarette. He also ordered a bourbon and soda from the flight attendants, which he offered to pay for.

It was 5.24 p.m. when the message came from airport traffic control that the money and parachutes were on their way. Fifteen minutes later the plane was on the ground in Seattle.

The passengers didn't know what was going on. For them the flight was ordinary, if a little longer than expected. Cooper seemed happy not to alarm them and he let them disembark. Florence Schaffner also got off at Seattle, ending the most memorable flight of her life.

Cooper insisted that Captain Scott, First Officer William Rataczak, flight attendant Tina Mucklow and flight engineer H.E. Andreson remain on board. He asked the tower to send some fresh food out for the crew. Then he ordered Scott to taxi the plane to a far corner of the airfield and dim the cabin lights. There, out of sight of the police and out of range of any marksmen, the passenger from Seat 18C waited for his money.

The escape

The lights of the airport control tower shone wetly against the blue-black November sky. The wind was picking up. It was going to be a stormy night.

In the 727, Cooper was getting a little jumpy. The refuelling was going too slowly; he threatened to detonate his device then and there unless the fuel crew picked up their pace.

At last the headlight beams of a Northwest Orient vehicle swung out over the tarmac. A shaking airline employee pulled up at the aft stairs and handed the cash and parachutes to flight attendant Mucklow.

With refuelling completed, Cooper checked the ransom and

The FBI released this artist's drawing of 'Dan Cooper,' the suspected skyjacker, who parachuted from a Northwest Airlines 727 jet after collecting $200,000 ransom in Seattle.

parachutes, established a flight plan and set the aft stairs. He then ordered the crew to taxi the plane back to the runway and prepare for take off. Destination: Mexico City.

Despite the smooth progress of his plan so far, the odds were stacked heavily against Cooper. The FBI might have delivered the ransom, but they weren't going to just let him fly off into the sunset with the money. Seattle-Tacoma airport was crawling with agents. United States Air Force F-106 fighters had been scrambled to shadow the 727 when it took off. No one had yet been crazy enough to even attempt parachuting from a speeding jetliner, but if Cooper did jump, the fighter pilots would see him go and could pinpoint his landing zone.

Cooper ordered Captain Scott to fly at just 170 knots (200 mph) and 3,000 m (10,000 ft) - normal cruising altitude is between 7,500 m and 9,000 m (25,000 and 37,000 ft) - to minimise the dangers of jumping. But flying so low and so slow would limit the plane's range to just 1,600 km (1,000 miles). If he didn't jump, they would have to refuel at Reno where the authorities would no doubt be ready to pounce.

The weather was also turning against him, with a heavy rainstorm lashing the state of Washington. It was nearly December and the skies above the Pacific North West coast were far from hospitable.

Cooper told Captain Scott to leave the cabin unpressurized. This would lessen the rush of air if he did open the rear door to attempt a parachute escape.

The plane was still rising through the rainclouds when Cooper turned to Tina Mucklow who was sitting beside him and told her to walk up to the cockpit and stay there.

Tina obeyed, but just as she stepped behind the curtain into the first-class seats, she looked back. Cooper seemed to be tying something to his waist with rope. A few moments later in the cockpit, a red 'door open' warning light flashed on. It didn't

FBI agent Ralph Himmelsbach (*2nd right*) asks questions of Mr. and Mrs. Harold Dwayne Ingram (*left*) at FBI offices where it was announced that the Ingram's son Brian, 8, had found the Dan Cooper hijacking money while on a family outing on the north shore of the Columbia River.

indicate a specific door, but the crew suspected it was for the stairs in the aft section, beneath the tailplane and the rear-mounted engine. The 727 was the only plane in which a passenger could access this stair.

> The Boeing 727's airstair was not designed to be deployed in flight. It was gravity-operated and when Cooper opened it, the stair remained down until the aircraft landed.

At 8.10 p.m., 24 minutes into the flight south, the 727 crossed the Lewis River in southeast Washington, about 40 km (25 miles) north of Portland. As it passed over the river, the crew noted that the plane performed an 'odd little curtsy'. The pilot had to trim it back to level flight.

The Boeing 727's airstair was not designed to be deployed in flight. It was gravity-operated and when Cooper opened it, the stair remained down until the aircraft landed.

Perhaps Dan Cooper jumped as soon as the door was down. Or maybe he stood on the threshold for a few moments, staring out at the black eye of the storm and

wondering at the dangers of the step he was about to take. Nobody knows. But what is certain is that he strapped on a parachute, took his money and leapt into the teeth of the gale at 320 km/h (200 mph). Sometimes fortune does indeed favour the brave: the rain was so heavy that the F-106 fighter pilots tracking the plane didn't notice him going.

He was never seen again.

The manhunt

Just after ten o'clock that evening, the Boeing 727 landed in Reno, with its lowered aft stairs dragging on the runway. FBI agents stormed the plane and found only two of the four parachutes, Cooper's tie with its mother-of-pearl pin and some fingerprints by his seat. He had taken the two military parachutes and left behind the two more maneuverable sport parachutes.

Investigators knew the plane's flightpath and speed and had a rough idea of the time that Cooper jumped – the time of the 'curtsy'. But with the plane moving at 90 m (300 ft) per second and the turbulent weather of the 24th of November, even a few

CANADA

USA

③ RANSOM MONEY
The aircraft circles Seattle in a holding pattern while the FBI gathers the ransom.

④ HOLD-UP
The plane lands at Seattle-Tacoma International Airport. The passengers are allowed to disembark. Cooper holds the four crew members. An airline employee delivers his ransom and the parachutes.

Seattle

③

④

Tacoma

W A S H I N G T O N

⑥ SEARCH
The search for Cooper initially focuses on countryside south eas of Ariel, near Lake Merwin, 48 km (30 miles) north of Portland.

⑦ THEORIES
Later theories built on weather reports from another pilot flying just 1,200 m (4,000 ft) above and four minutes behind Flight 305 suggested that the landing zone wa up to 32 km (20 miles) further east

Mount St Helens

⑧

2550

Cougar

⑤ COOPER JUMPS
The plane is passing low over the Lewis River when Cooper lowers the aft stairs and jumps.

⑤

Lake Merwin

Lewis

⑥ **⑦**

Lookout Mountain

1735

Columbia

⑧ FOUND
In 1978, a hunter finds the instruction placard from the plane's aft stairs a few minut flying time to the north of th initially proposed landing sit

⑨

② Washougal

Portland

①

② HIJACK
Shortly after takeoff, Cooper starts the hijack.

⑨ MONEY FOUND
Eight-year-old Brian Ingram finds $5,880 in decaying $20 bills from the ransom in the waters of the Columbia River

① START
Portland, Oregon where Flight 305 originated.

P A C I F I C   O C E A N

O R E G O N

KILOMETRES 0   25   50   75

MILES 0   25   50

seconds of doubt over the exact time of his leap made it impossible to predict his landing zone with 100 per cent accuracy. Police had to spread the net wide, exhaustively searching 73 km² (28 miles²) of remote country. From late 1971 into spring 1972, the FBI co-ordinated one of the most intense manhunts in the history of the northwestern US. Their agents worked in teams with local police and more than 200 US Army troops, scouring the countryside on foot, in boats and by helicopter.

They didn't find a single trace of Cooper, his parachutes, his money or the briefcase with the bomb.

Investigators also contacted banks, savings companies, businesses and newspapers with the serial numbers of the 10,000 $20 bills. Scotland Yard and other international law enforcement agencies were on high alert. Northwest Airlines offered a reward of $25,000 for information leading to recovery of the money. The Oregon Journal offered $1,000 to the first person who identified a single note from the haul.

No one ever claimed any of the rewards.

If Cooper had survived, why did none of the money ever turn up? The FBI were becoming increasingly adept at solving major financial crimes by

The badly decomposed $20 dollar bills were shown to newsmen after a check of their serial numbers showed that they were identical to the bills given to hijacker Dan Cooper. The money was found by Brian Ingram, 8, on the north shore of the Columbia River, partially buried in the sand.

tracking stolen bills. And they certainly had the publicity to help them spot notes if they were spent. But if the fall had killed him, where was the body? Even if it had plummeted into a ravine or a lake, surely a piece of the parachutes or some of the money would have been discovered?

With every lead turning into a dead end and no further evidence coming to light, the trail began to cool.

It wasn't until late 1978 that a significant clue turned up. A hunter

found an instruction card from the aft stairway of the hijacked plane just a few minutes' flying time from Cooper's predicted landing area. It refocused a new set of searches, but nothing further was discovered.

Then in February 1980, eight-year-old Brian Ingram was enjoying a family picnic by the banks of the Columbia River when he found $5,880 in rotting $20 bills. They were bound with rubber bands and turned out to be part of the ransom paid nine years previously.

The FBI believed the money could have washed into the river from one of its tributaries, many of which run through the drop zone. It reinforced their belief that Cooper had not survived the jump. But if that was the case, why had it taken so long for the money to appear? The discovery only seemed to add to the mystery.

When the FBI announced in October 2007 that it had gathered a partial DNA profile of Cooper from his tie it seemed they might be close to solving the case. But so far the profile has only served to rule out a few of the more likely suspects.

Dead or alive, Dan Cooper escaped.

FBI agents dig in sand on the north shore of the Columbia River, where a portion of the Dan Cooper hijack money was found by the Harold Dwayne Ingram family.

The Storming of Fresnes

In one of the most brazen assaults on a prison in history, a commando-like team blitzed the doors and watchtowers of a prison in Paris to free their leader, Antonio Ferrara. Then the search began for one of the most wanted men in Europe.

DATE:
2003

SITUATION:
Prison breakout

CONDITION OF CONFINEMENT:
Incarceration in solitary confinement

DURATION OF CONFINEMENT:
8 months

MEANS OF ESCAPE:
Commando-style assault

NO. OF ESCAPEES:
1

DANGERS:
Shooting, explosion, other police intervention

EQUIPMENT:
AK-47s, grenade launchers, dynamite

Six cars burst into roaring flames, lighting up the night on the suburban Paris street. A few sleepy local residents, woken by the noise, watched in frightened awe as the fire took hold. Somewhere a radio crackled with barked orders. Far-off police sirens wailed closer. Fire appliances rattled through the narrow thoroughfares. It was four o'clock in the morning. Was this the start of a riot? A chemical accident? A terrorist assault?

No one could have guessed it was just a sideshow.

Little big man

Antonio Ferrara was born into a poor family on 12 October 1973, near Naples in Italy. His parents emigrated to France with his six brothers and sisters in 1983 and he grew up in the Parisian suburb of Choisy-le-Roi. He left school at 16 and after a few months working in menial jobs he embarked on his life of crime.

By the mid Nineties, Ferrara had specialized in robbing security vehicles. He became famous throughout the French underworld for his knack of rigging just the right amount of dynamite needed to blast open an armoured car without damaging the bank notes inside.

In a robbery typical of his style, a Valiance security van was attacked in Toulouse by a gang of eight to ten men equipped with Kalashnikovs and FAMAS (French assault rifles). The van's staff were threatened, its doors quickly blown and the masked perpetrators would vanish into the back streets in fast cars. It is thought Ferrara pulled off around fifteen such heists successfully.

He began to mix in the most influential of criminal circles and cultivated a reputation for violence. Rising swiftly through the underworld ranks, he was a member of a group of expert bank robbers, nicknamed 'The Dream Team' by the French press and referred to as the 'most dangerous gang in Europe' by Interpol.

Police came to recognize his trademark heist techniques and he became one of the most wanted robbers in Europe. He was also wanted for an attempted murder committed in 1996.

Ferrara was called 'El Niño' ('little boy' in Spanish) because he stood just 1.65 m (5 ft 5 inches) tall, although presumably only by people who knew him very well.

Playing cops and robbers

Ferrara seemed to have an aptitude for prison breaks. He was arrested in 1997 but escaped the following year when accomplices freed him during a hospital visit. After four further years on the run he was recaptured and sentenced in January 2003 to eight years imprisonment for two bank hold ups. He was sent to La Santé, the high-security prison in central Paris.

One thing that made Ferrara particularly dangerous was his ability to find a guard or cop on the inside who was open to persuasion. Lucien Aimé, a former head of France's Central Office for the Repression of Banditry, said gangsters like Ferrara would willingly pay £1.5 million or more for help in escaping.

Ferrara had only been in La Santé for a month when prison officials found more than 0.5 kg (1 lb) of plastic explosives and five detonators that had been smuggled into his cell. This little cache got him transferred to Fresnes, supposedly one of the most secure prisons in Europe.

The assault on Fresnes Prison

At 4.30 a.m. on 12 March 2003, six men, masked and very heavily armed, drove up to the huge gates of Fresnes Prison.

The men got out of the car, and the guards in the prison watchtowers would have noticed that they were

La Santé Prison (centre), Paris.

wearing gloves and police armbands. But this cursory nod at a subtle disguise was immediately rendered immaterial by the bazookas and AK-47s, which the men produced and pointed at the jail.

Without a moment's hesitation, two of the men raked the surveillance towers with automatic gunfire, sending the guards diving for cover and causing extensive damage. Another team member launched bazookas and AK-47 gunfire while the rest used rocket-propelled grenades to punch a massive hole in the heavy prison gate. Dynamite and another grenade took care of a second inner armoured door.

Meanwhile Ferrara was blowing the bars of his cell. He used explosives provided by his lawyer Karim Achoui and passed to him by a corrupt prison guard in a tennis ball. Had Ferrara been in his usual cell he would have been too far from the prison gates to escape. But the previous evening he had refused to let his cell be searched during the normal rounds.

To the guards it had seemed like a show of insolence typical of the proud outlaw. They duly sent

him for a cool down in the solitary confinement wing. This building was situated near the rear door of the jail. So when the dynamite blew out his cell wall, Ferrara was easily able to hook up with his accomplices. All the men sped away from the jail in their three 'police' cars with sirens wailing and lights flashing. The operation had taken less than ten minutes.

The nearest police and fire crews were still dealing with the diversion of the six burning cars, giving the gang a few crucial extra minutes to get clean away.

One attacker was believed to have been wounded in the eye, but no guards were hurt in the breakout. Officials described the escape as a 'military-style operation using weapons of war' and a 'millimetre-precision attack'.

But the clinical operation wasn't perfect. A handgun, an assault rifle, a stick of explosives, detonators and blood traces from the eye injury were all left behind. Ferrara himself made a mistake: he left his mobile phone in his cell. Police would ultimately use this to trace him and his accomplices.

2 PARIS
Ferrara's trademark armoured car assaults take place all over France, including Paris, Toulouse and Marseille.

7 ARRESTED
He is finally arrested in a bar in Paris's 12th arrondissement in an undercover sting.

4 RECAPTURED
Four years later he is recaptured and sent to La Santé, a high-security prison in central Paris.

5 TRANSFERRED
One month later, prison guards find dynamite in his cell and he is transferred to Fresnes.

1 CHOISY-LE-ROI
The Parisian suburb of Choisy-le-Roi where Antonio Ferrara and his family settled after their move from Italy.

6 ON THE RUN
Following his dramatic escape from Fresnes he flees south, presumably to the criminal underworld of Marseille.

8 BACK BEHIND BARS
Ferrara is finally sentenced to seventeen years, much of which he spends in total isolation back in Fleury-Mérogis.

3 BREAKOUT
After his first arrest he is sent to Fleury-Mérogis prison. He escapes during a medical examination.

KILOMETRES 0   1   2   3
MILES 0   1   2

Flight and recapture

Ferrara fled to the south of France and threw himself under the plastic surgeon's knife, dramatically altering his features in an attempt to stay permanently disguised. Despite also dying his hair and changing locations every night, his new-found freedom only lasted four months.

Nicolas Sarkozy, the tough-talking interior minister, declared Ferrara to be the most wanted man in France. The man who would go on to be French president mounted one of the biggest manhunts in French history, making Ferrara's recapture his top personal priority.

As the months ticked by, one by one Ferrara's accomplices were captured. Fourteen would eventually be brought to justice.

Finally, in the early evening of 10 July 2003, Ferrara entered a packed bar in Paris' 12th arrondissement to meet a friend. Tourists and regulars jostled for space in the lively atmosphere as the master criminal sat down with a drink to discuss business.

Suddenly he was surrounded by police. Almost every drinker in the

French lawyer Karim Achoui *(centre)* arrives at the Paris courthouse on 2 October 2008 before the beginning of the trial of his former client, Antonio Ferrara.

bar was an undercover officer – forty agents in total swooped on him. It was the culmination of a massive undercover operation and Ferrara was caught. 'You again?' is all he said.

Paying the price

On 14 December 2008, Antonio Ferrara, 35, was sentenced to seventeen years in prison for his spectacular

escape from prison in Fresnes. Several accomplices were also sentenced including Karim Achoui, the dynamite-handling lawyer, who got seven years.

The French police may have been two steps behind Antonio Ferrara for several years, but they finally got the measure of their man. Ferrara was incarcerated in the prison at Fleury-Mérogis in the southern suburbs of Paris. Although this is the largest prison in Europe, with 3,800 prisoners, Ferrara was held alone in a section of the prison built specially for him. He has been in solitary confinement since 2003. Twenty-three armed guards keep him under constant surveillance. The neighbouring cells are kept empty, to prevent any contact with other inmates. He is not allowed to talk to anyone, nor to study or do any work. He never sees the light of day; even the 12 m (40 ft) lane he exercises in is covered with a metal vault. When he showers it is in front of guards dressed in flak jackets and equipped with tear gas and Tasers. Every day he is moved into a different cell and his old cell is searched. He also undergoes a full, daily body search. He will not be eligible for parole until 2033.

The Paris courthouse on 31 August 2010 before the beginning of the appeal trial of Antonio Ferrara and seven other people.

WAR

The Man who Might be King

'BONNIE PRINCE CHARLIE' MAY HAVE BEEN VAIN AND FOOLISH, BUT AFTER
DEFEAT AT CULLODEN HE PROVED HIMSELF A MAN OF GREAT ENDURANCE
AND RESOURCEFULNESS. FOR FIVE MONTHS HE LIVED IN THE WILDS OF THE
SCOTTISH HIGHLANDS AND BRAVED THE SAVAGE SEAS OF THE HEBRIDES,
SUCCESSFULLY EVADING THE MASSED FORCES OF ONE OF THE MOST
POWERFUL NATIONS ON EARTH.

DATE:
1746

SITUATION:
LEADER OF A FAILED
REBELLION

**CONDITION OF
CONFINEMENT:**
PURSUED BY GOVERNMENT
FORCES

**DURATION OF
CONFINEMENT:**
5 MONTHS

MEANS OF ESCAPE:
HIDING IN THE WILDS OF
SCOTLAND, FLEEING BY BOAT

NO. OF ESCAPEES:
1

DANGERS:
CAPTURE, BETRAYAL,
EXHAUSTION

EQUIPMENT:
GUILE, LOYALTY

ABOVE RIGHT
Memorial cairn commemorating the Battle of
Culloden in 1746 at which the Jacobite forces
were routed by Government troops ending the
Stuart dynasty's campaign for power.

Downfall of a dream

Culloden was a bloodbath. The last pitched battle fought in Britain, it was also one of the most one-sided. The violence began at 1 p.m. on 16 April 1746 and within forty minutes the disciplined rows of Redcoats had braved the wild charge of the Highlanders and rebuffed it. Muskets and grapeshot tore the rebels limb from limb and the Government soldiers then set about slaughtering the wounded and the vanquished on the bleak, rain-sodden moor.

> **the soldiers' bayonets were stain'd and clotted with the blood of the rebels up to the muzzles of their muskets**

And so began the desperate escape of the man they called Bonnie Prince Charlie. Over the next five months this 25-year-old dandy would display nerve, tenacity and guile and would earn the fierce loyalty of many supporters, despite a huge price on his head.

The Young Pretender

Charles Edward Stuart was the grandson of James II and VII, the exiled king of England, Scotland and Ireland. With French backing, the Catholic 'Young Pretender' launched a Jacobite rebellion against the Protestant rule of King George II in 1745.

Landing in the west of Scotland he gathered the support of leading clans and marched south, taking Edinburgh and routing the Government's only army in Scotland at the Battle of Prestonpans. His army grew in size and confidence, marching as far south as Derby in December 1745.

Following false reports of a Government army amassing to the south the prince retreated northwards, giving the English time to muster a real army. Commanded by the Duke of Cumberland, son of George II, this force caught up with the Young Pretender at Culloden. Charles Stuart had little in the way of a back-up plan. With his army dying in the mud before his eyes, he took to his heels with a few loyal supporters.

The Government, however, most certainly did have a plan: catch the Prince and obliterate all traces of the rebellion. They posted a reward of £30,000 (approximately £44 million today). A Prince could not travel undetected by other persons, even in a wild land like the Scottish Highlands. People would know him. People would hide him. And surely one of them would be tempted to make themselves rich with a single word.

The prince made for Fort Augustus, at the southwest end of Loch Ness, where he expected to find a rally of the clans. On the way he visited Lord Lovat, head of Clan Fraser and a wily man known as Simon the Fox. Once loyal to the Jacobite cause, Lovat could sense the tide had turned. He apparently welcomed the prince with a glass of wine and sent him onwards after two more.

There was no gathering at Fort Augustus. Disappointed, the prince and his small party headed further down the Great Glen then headed into the wilderness west of Loch Lochy.

This is a desolate place even now; then it was a near-trackless wilderness. The fugitives had to abandon their horses and move on foot. Sleeping in remote shepherds' cottages by day and moving at night, they made it through the mountains of Glenfinnan to Arisaig and the shores of Loch nan Uamh on the west coast. It was here, just nine months earlier that the prince had arrived aboard the French brig *Du Teillay*, ready to stake his claim to the throne.

By now the only path open to him was a return to France where he might be able to persuade the French to mount a large-scale invasion. His Highland allies would have to fare as best they could.

But he had no ship. The great chiefs of Skye, the MacLeods and

MacDonalds had also seen which way the wind was blowing and turned their backs on the Pretender. With all the available vessels of the Royal Navy dispatched to intercept him, it looked bleak.

However, a vital piece of misinformation had found its way to the Government forces: the prince had reportedly fled to the remote islands of St Kilda, 80 km (50 miles) beyond the Western Isles in the Atlantic. The Royal ships set their course there, allowing Charlie to slip away from the mainland to the Outer Hebrides.

Rowing into the storm

In a tiny open boat with a storm rising, the journey from Arisaig to the Western Isles made for a terrifying ordeal. The skipper of the boat was 68-year-old Donald MacLeod of Gualtergill, who knew the waters as well as anyone.

The old man later said he had never sailed in a storm as bad and that the passengers expected every wave they met to be the one that would smash them against rocks or overwhelm the boat and send them straight to the bottom.

❛ I had rather face cannons and muskets than be drowned in such a storm as this. ❜

But they made it through the Cuillin Sound between Skye and Rum and out into the Minch, one of the fiercest stretches of water around the British Isles. Running their sail before the southeasterly gale they sped through the storm in almost pitch-blackness for eight hours. At dawn they saw they were by the coast of Benbecula, having put 100 km (60 miles) between them and their pursuers.

The net closes

The next two months were a game of cat-and-mouse. The navy by now knew the Prince wasn't on St Kilda, so the Royal ships returned to patrol the

The Anthony Stones sculpture of Bonnie Prince Charlie in Derby, England.

waters around the Outer Hebrides, ready to pounce on any French vessel that might try to whisk the Prince to safety. A force of Redcoat soldiers had also landed at Barra in the south and was sweeping north.

Meanwhile Donald MacLeod piloted Charlie north to Lewis and Harris, then south again to the Uists and Benbecula, always just one step ahead of their hunters.

❛ [the Prince was] now encompassed by no less than three or four thousand bloody hounds, by sea and land, thirsting for the captivity and noble blood of their Prince. ❜

This deadly game continued for two months until the Prince and his advisers hit upon a new and daring strategy.

The prince in petticoats

Flora MacDonald was a young lady from South Uist with an Irish maidservant, Betty Burke. The Prince swapped his royal fineries for Betty's gown, stockings, shoes and quilted petticoats and stepped aboard a tiny rowing boat with Flora and four oarsmen.

Their destination was Skye, and they believed that their plan's boldness

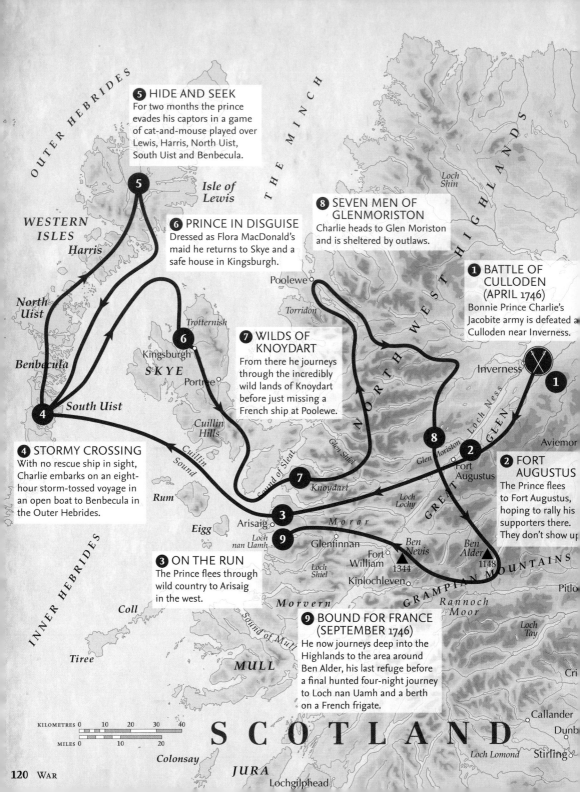

5 HIDE AND SEEK
For two months the prince evades his captors in a game of cat-and-mouse played over Lewis, Harris, North Uist, South Uist and Benbecula.

6 PRINCE IN DISGUISE
Dressed as Flora MacDonald's maid he returns to Skye and a safe house in Kingsburgh.

8 SEVEN MEN OF GLENMORISTON
Charlie heads to Glen Moriston and is sheltered by outlaws.

1 BATTLE OF CULLODEN (APRIL 1746)
Bonnie Prince Charlie's Jacobite army is defeated a Culloden near Inverness.

7 WILDS OF KNOYDART
From there he journeys through the incredibly wild lands of Knoydart before just missing a French ship at Poolewe.

4 STORMY CROSSING
With no rescue ship in sight, Charlie embarks on an eight-hour storm-tossed voyage in an open boat to Benbecula in the Outer Hebrides.

2 FORT AUGUSTUS
The Prince flees to Fort Augustus, hoping to rally his supporters there. They don't show up

3 ON THE RUN
The Prince flees through wild country to Arisaig in the west.

9 BOUND FOR FRANCE (SEPTEMBER 1746)
He now journeys deep into the Highlands to the area around Ben Alder, his last refuge before a final hunted four-night journey to Loch nan Uamh and a berth on a French frigate.

OUTER HEBRIDES

THE MINCH

Loch Shin

Isle of Lewis

WESTERN ISLES

Harris

North Uist

Poolewe

Torridon

NORTH WEST HIGHLANDS

Inverness

Benbecula

Trotternish

Kingsburgh

SKYE

Portree

South Uist

Cuillin Hills

Cuillin Sound

Sound of Sleat

Glen Shiel

Knoydart

Glen Moriston

Fort Augustus

GREAT GLEN

Loch Ness

Aviemor

Rum

Eigg

Arisaig

Loch nan Uamh

Morar

Glenfinnan

Fort William

Loch Shiel

Kinlochleven

Ben Nevis 1344

Ben Alder 1148

Loch Lochy

GRAMPIAN MOUNTAINS

Pitlo

Rannoch Moor

Loch Tay

Cri

INNER HEBRIDES

Coll

Tiree

MULL

Sound of Mull

Morvern

Loch Lomona

Callander

Dunb

Stirling

Colonsay

JURA

Lochgilphead

S C O T L A N D

KILOMETRES 0 10 20 30 40

MILES 0 10 20

was its strength: the Government forces would hardly suspect that such a tiny and ill-guarded vessel was the Prince's. It worked. Once they were spotted by a group of soldiers, but since they didn't act like runaways, the soldiers' suspicions dissipated. Their major battle was with more atrocious sailing conditions. For three days they rowed through fog, gales and wild seas.

Skye was no safe haven: Redcoats swarmed over the island. Flora and the Prince were forced into the wildest, boggiest quarters of the Trotternish Peninsula in order to reach the home of MacDonald of Kingsburgh where they found shelter.

MacDonald's wife was quite astonished when the visibly unshaven Miss Betty Burke appeared in her hallway and gave her a grateful kiss.

Hounds at his heels

The respite on Skye was brief. In early July the Prince was forced to cross the dangerous Sound of Sleat to the mainland. There was nothing regal about his bearing now. He fled into the Rough Bounds of Knoydart, which even to this day is an untamed land. Sleeping wild in the heather, protected from the elements and insects by nothing by a length of plaid, he tracked north over the high ridges of Glen Shiel and up through the steep Torridon peaks to Poolewe where a French ship had slipped through the navy cordon to collect him. He missed the vessel by hours.

Here his fortunes turned a little. He was given shelter by some men who had served in his army and been outlaws ever since. These Seven Men of Glenmoriston hid the prince in a cave high up in the hills. The £30,000 bounty could have solved all their problems, but they never once considered collecting it.

A heroic deception

It was around this time that a loyal Jacobite called Roderick Mackenzie was travelling through Glen Moriston. Redcoats mistook him for the prince and shot him. Fatally wounded, the wily and brave Mackenzie compounded their error, exclaiming, 'Alas, you have killed your Prince!' with his last breath. Mackenzie's severed head was sent to the Duke of Cumberland at Fort Augustus who believed he had his man. The deception gave the real Prince some vital room to manoeuvre.

Charlie slipped south again to allies near Ben Alder. They hid him in a tree house, high on the slopes of the mountain beneath a steep cliff.

Finally the Prince got word that a French frigate had been seen off Arisaig. With some loyal guards he made a four-night forced march past the treacherous bogs and braes of Rannoch Moor, skirting the foothills of mighty Ben Nevis.

On 19 September they reached Loch nan Uamh, the same spot where he had landed fourteen months previously, so full of hope and endeavour. The royal fugitive, exhausted and defeated, climbed aboard the ironically named *L'Heureux* ('Happy' in English) and by midnight they were at sea, bound for France.

A rebellious spirit crushed

Lord Lovat's caution in welcoming the prince had been wise but did not stretch far enough: he was executed for treason on Tower Hill in London the next year, the last man in Britain to be beheaded.

Other sympathisers, noble and common, were hanged or imprisoned in filthy, rotting hulks on the Thames. Many died in the appalling conditions.

The boatmen who helped him escape were tortured into confessing.

> **6 Thirty thousand pounds!... I could not have enjoyed it eight and forty hours. Conscience would have gotten up upon me... And tho' I could have gotten all England and Scotland for my pains I would not allow a hair of his body to be touch'd if I could help it. 9**
> Donald MacLeod, the boatman, on why he was not tempted by the enormous reward.

Flora MacDonald was arrested but later released. She married and lived on Skye, apart from five years spent in the United States, until 1790.

The prince tried to persuade the French government to mount a second, better prepared invasion, but these plans came to nothing. Bonnie Prince Charlie had had his moment of glory. For the next forty years he lived a life of slightly sad and drunken disappointment.

The Glenfinnan Monument, on the shore of Loch Shiel, was erected in 1815 as a memorial to the soldiers who died for the Jacobite cause.

The Last of the Sixteen Thousand

The 16,500 men, women and children who set out from Kabul knew their journey would be dangerous. But they had little idea of the scale of the tragedy that would befall them. Frozen in the ice-bound passes and cut down by hostile Afghan tribesmen, only one soldier, William Brydon, would reach safety in Jalalabad.

DATE:
1842

SITUATION:
War

CONDITION OF CONFINEMENT:
Surrounded by the enemy in Afghanistan

DURATION OF CONFINEMENT:
7 days

MEANS OF ESCAPE:
Fighting, fleeing on horseback

NO. OF ESCAPEES:
1

DANGERS:
Being killed in battle, capture, exhaustion, freezing to death

EQUIPMENT:
Rifle, sword, horse

ABOVE RIGHT
Modern Kabul, situated 1,800 m (5,900 ft) above sea level in a narrow valley, wedged between the Hindu Kush mountains along the Kabul River.

The man on the dying horse

The British soldiers behind the dusty walls of Jalalabad watched in astonishment as the dying horse inched its way towards them. Its rider was slumped almost double in his saddle. Blood had seeped from beneath his hat and was covering his face. As he got closer they could see his uniform: he was British too. But was he dead?

Then the rider dismounted. His horse collapsed and breathed no more. The man moved his swollen, bloody lips for several seconds before any sound came out. Finally a rasping voice announced that he was Assistant Surgeon Brydon, 5th Native Infantry, Bengal Army.

Now the soldiers were dumbfounded. It was not Brydon himself who caused their amazement, but the fact that he was not accompanied by a single one of the 4,500 native and British soldiers and 12,000 civilians who ought to have been with him.

Auckland's folly

Since defeating Napoleon in 1812, Britain had regarded Russia as its greatest foe. India, the jewel in the imperial crown, seemed particularly vulnerable to the Russian bear. Lord Auckland, the governor general of India, proposed a bold military scheme: occupy Afghanistan and hold it as a buffer state between India and Russia.

In 1839, an army duly went over the Khyber Pass, reached Kabul and ousted the prickly Amir Dost Mohammed Khan, replacing him with a ruler more sympathetic to British goals.

The occupiers began to settle in, establishing a garrison of 4,500 native Indian soldiers led by British officers. It seemed that all was well. The soldiers brought their wives and families to Kabul.

When Major General William Elphinstone took control of the garrison in 1841, his predecessor gave him easy assurances: 'You will have nothing to do here.'

But the Afghans viewed this as an invasion. They would soon fight back in earnest.

Massacre

The British were complacent considering their situation. They had built their main stronghold on marshy ground surrounded by Afghan-occupied hill forts. Their main food depot was outside the base. Elphinstone was a bad commander: riddled with gout and rheumatism, he was also teetering on the brink of dementia.

The Afghan people hated the puppet government and turned their anger on the British. Soldiers on patrol were attacked with increasing frequency. Snipers began shooting into the base itself.

Then on 2 November 1841, a mob stormed the British residency and murdered the deputy envoy, Sir Alexander Burnes.

Elphinstone did nothing. It was left to the envoy, Sir William Macnaghten to attempt negotiations with Akbar Khan, son of the ousted leader. Macnaghten must have suspected the mood would be frosty when he and three officers met Akbar on 23 December. But he couldn't have suspected what was about to happen. No sooner had the men greeted each other than Akbar pulled out a pistol and shot the envoy. The officers were also killed.

The four bodies of the envoy and officers were sliced up and their heads and limbs paraded through the streets of Kabul.

Even Elphinstone now knew that they had to get out.

The long road ahead

The road from Kabul to Jalalabad was a hard journey at the best of times. It was high with many passes, and in midwinter with hostile Afghan tribesmen swarming the heights it was like walking into a lions' den.

Worse, it wasn't just professional soldiers who had to make the 140 km (90 mile) journey, there were 12,000 civilians including thousands of women and children.

The British thought they had managed to broker an agreement with the Afghans: they would leave behind their artillery if their people could be guaranteed a safe passage. But the Afghans had no intention of keeping this promise; they wanted to send a message that the great powers would be sure to understand.

Death in the icy passes

Snow had been falling for three weeks as the 16,500 men, women and children of the Kabul garrison set out on 6 January 1842.

They were barely out of the gates when the attacks started. Snipers in the Kabul ramparts fired on the backmarkers as they left the city.

The column only managed 8 km (5 miles) that day and was forced to spend the night in the snow. Hundreds died of cold.

Akbar Khan stepped up his assault at the Khoord Kabul Pass. This 8 km (5 mile) gorge made the travellers sitting ducks for the tribesmen in the heights on either side. The soldiers fought back bravely, but could do little to stop the deaths of 3,000 of their fellows. More died of exposure that night.

After five days of carnage, Elphinstone agreed to hand himself over as a hostage. He might have thought this would guarantee safe passage for the rest of the column, but the very next day the Jagdalak pass was blocked allowing thousands of tribesmen to cut the rearguard to pieces.

The modern Jalalabad Road from Kabul to Jalalabad, Afghanistan.

HINDU KUSH

Tūnel-e Sālang

Bāzārak

AFGHANISTAN

Jabal as Sirāj

Chārīkār

Maḥmūd-e Rāqī

Kashmund

① THE LONG ROAD AHEAD
On 6 January 1842 the 16,500 men, women and children of the Kabul garrison set out to travel the 140 km (90 miles) to Jalalabad.

② TRAPPED
The travellers become sitting ducks at the Khoord Kabul Pass, a narrow 8 km (5 mile) gorge.

⑥ SOLE SURVIVOR
Brydon continued on to Jalalabad alone.

Mehtar Lām

Kābul

Sarowbī

① KĀBUL (Kabul)

②

Jagdalak

⑥ Jalālābād (Jalalabad)

⑤

Meydān Shahr

Kowt-e Ashrow

③

③ MASSACRE
The Jagdalak pass was blocked allowing thousands of tribesmen to cut the rearguard to pieces.

Gandamak

Sikaram
▲
4761

④

⑤ FATEHABAD
They reached Fatehabad, just 6 km (4 miles) from their destination, but five of the men were killed.

④ THE LAST STAND
Twenty officers and forty-five British soldiers make a final stand at Gandamak. Six officers escaped heading for Jalalabad.

Pol-e 'Alam

Barakī Barak

Gardēz

PAKISTAN

Khowst

Thal

KILOMETRES 0   20   40

MILES 0   10   20

William Brydon, the sole survivor of the massacre of Kabul, finally reaches Jalalabad.

And then there was one

Twenty officers and forty-five British soldiers stood on a scrubby, snow-covered mound near Gandamak. They shivered as they loaded their rifles and fixed bayonets. Death was coming, of that they were sure, but they would not sell their lives cheaply. It was on the morning of 13 January 1842 and they were all that remained of the 16,500 people who had set out from Kabul. William Brydon was among them.

The Afghans circled them and at first seemed to suggest a peaceful outcome could be achieved, assuring the besieged men that no harm would come to them. But then the snipers opened fire. As the foreigners dropped the Afghans closed in for the kill, surging at the soldiers in waves.

The men were quickly cut down and soon there were only six mounted officers left. With a glance and a shout they gathered together and dug their spurs into their blood-splattered mounts. Somehow they broke through the enemy cordon and rode like the wind for Jalalabad.

By the time they reached Fatehabad, just 6 km (4 miles) from their destination, the Afghans fell on them again. Five of the officers were cut down; only Brydon galloped on.

Sole survivor

By the afternoon of 13 January the British troops in Jalalabad were eagerly watching for their comrades of the Kabul garrison. They probably guessed that something had gone very wrong, but nothing could have prepared them for the scale of the massacre.

By the time Brydon arrived at the dusty walls of Jalalabad that afternoon he was nearly dead himself. He had bad injuries to his knee and left hand and part of his skull had been sheared off by an Afghan sword. The magazine padding in his hat had deflected most of the blow, saving Brydon's life.

> **The only reason his brains were still in his head was because he had earlier stuffed a copy of Blackwood's Magazine into his hat to keep out the intense cold.**

Although Brydon was the only Briton to complete the trek from Kabul to Jalalabad he was not the only ultimate survivor. A Greek merchant called Baness made it to Jalalabad two days after Brydon but he died a day later. Fifty people held as hostages by the Afghans were later released.

Not safe yet

The Khyber Pass was still in Afghan hands, isolating Jalalabad from the rest of British India. The next month an earthquake devastated the city's fortifications and Akbar Khan tried to finish off the garrison.

But the defenders put up a remarkable fight and even managed to counter-attack, forcing Khan back to Kabul. Finally a relief force arrived from India on 16 April.

The British regained some of their pride by sending a large force back to Kabul in the autumn. They rescued some prisoners and burnt down the citadel and the Great Bazaar.

But the world's greatest power had learned a hard lesson in Afghanistan.

A peaceful life

After another narrow escape in the Indian Mutiny of 1857 when a bullet grazed his spine, Brydon decided enough was enough. He left the army and retired to the quiet of northern Scotland. He had eight children and died peacefully in 1873.

Back to the Fatherland

GUNTHER PLÜSCHOW WAS A CELEBRATED FIRST WORLD WAR GERMAN AVIATOR. HE FIRST ESCAPED FROM THE BRITISH IN CHINA, AND FLED ACROSS THE UNITED STATES ONLY TO BE CAUGHT AT GIBRALTAR. INTERRED IN A PRISONER OF WAR CAMP IN ENGLAND, HE BECAME THE ONLY GERMAN POW EVER TO SUCCESSFULLY ESCAPE FROM THE UK DURING EITHER WORLD WAR.

DATE:
1915

SITUATION:
CAPTURED DURING THE FIRST WORLD WAR BY THE BRITISH

CONDITION OF CONFINEMENT:
IN A PRISONER OF WAR CAMP NEAR DERBY

DURATION OF CONFINEMENT:
4 WEEKS

MEANS OF ESCAPE:
SCALING A FENCE, WALKING THROUGH OPEN COUNTRY, DECEPTION

NO. OF ESCAPEES:
1

DANGERS:
BEING SHOT, RECAPTURE, DROWNING

EQUIPMENT:
CIVILIAN CLOTHES, TOILETRIES, MONEY

ABOVE RIGHT
Donington Hall, Leicestershire.

Hero on the run

Gunther Plüschow was every inch the dashing German hero. Tall, blonde and muscular, he made his name as an aviator during the early days of the First World War, operating from the East Asian Naval Station at Tsingtau (Qingdao), a German colony in China.

Tsingtau was besieged by the Japanese and British and on 6 November 1914, Plüschow tried to escape to China by plane. He crashed into a rice paddy but managed to make his way to Shanghai. A diplomat friend helped him secure false papers and a ticket on a ship leaving for San Francisco. In January 1915 he made his way across America to New York where he managed to get travel documents for a ship that left for Italy.

However, a storm forced the vessel to dock at Gibraltar where he was arrested by British soldiers.

Stately imprisonment

On 1 July 1915 Plüschow arrived at the camp for officer prisoners of war at Donington Hall in Leicestershire.

Although the men here lived in fairly civilized conditions, the camp's security was tight. There were two 2.7 m (9 ft) high barbed wire fences with entanglements in between them, and an electrified inner perimeter wire. There was also a watchtower, searchlights and an outer guardhouse that protected the main road. Beyond that lay mostly open country. The nearest town and railway station were several miles away.

> ❛ He thought, "Where that got in here then I can get out." ❜

The accidental escaper

Plüschow didn't actively plan his escape: he was lying on his back in the summer sun when he watched a young deer scramble through the wire fence and the notion of a breakout dropped into his head.

On 4 July he and Oskar Trefftz, a fellow officer who spoke English, made a break for it. It was a stormy night and the men deliberately selected a part of the fence where the sheltering guards were unlikely to spot them.

At 11.00 p.m. they heard a loud cheer from the main hall: this coded call told them that their colleagues had successfully duped the night-time roll call. They would not be missed until morning. After the next guard change Plüschow and Trefftz crept out of cover and approached the electrified fence.

Using a homemade ladder and some spare planks, they managed to scramble over all the fences at the expense of a few cuts and scratches.

The athletic men scampered past the gatehouse, leapt over streams, and jumped stone walls before bolting into the woods.

They made it to an open road and, after Trefftz determined the correct direction by feeling a signpost with his hands, set off to walk the 24 km (15 miles) to Derby.

Down and out in London

The men had no false papers or ration books, just civilian clothing, some toiletries and a little money. They separated and caught different trains to London.

Plüschow made it to St. Paul's Cathedral where the men were to rendezvous, but Trefftz didn't show up. The next day's papers confirmed that his friend had been arrested at Millwall docks; they also gave a detailed description of Plüschow.

He quickly had to alter his appearance. Plüschow removed his tie and handed his coat in at the cloakroom at Blackfriars station. The attendant asked: 'What name is it?' Plüschow automatically replied in German 'meinen' (mine). The half-asleep attendant merely wrote Mr Mine on the receipt.

Plüschow then daubed his face and hair with a mix of Vaseline, soot and coal dust to transform his high-bred blonde Germanic looks into those of a dark haired ordinary working man.

For the next three weeks he lived like a vagrant in the capital, trying to find an opportunity to stow away on a ship. In his spare moments he kept his mind busy by reading books about Patagonia. He also spent several nights hiding inside the British Museum.

> **Plüschow was so emboldened by his success, he even had souvenir photographs taken of himself at London docks.**

But he was running out of time and money. He needed a quick way out of Britain. For security reasons, there were no published notices announcing the departure of ships, but Plüschow overheard two men talking about a Dutch ship, the SS *Princess Juliana* due in at Tilbury.

The stowaway

He caught a train to the Essex port. The SS *Princess Juliana* was in the harbour but all the wharves were guarded.

Plüschow waited until darkness then swam into the fierce currents of the Thames. His plan was to reach a boat and then row out to the moored ship but the riptide was too strong and he was washed ashore exhausted. Plüschow spent four more days and nights making several attempts to reach the vessel before he was able to steal a boat, drift past the guards, shin up a thick mooring rope and crawl exhausted into a lifeboat.

The next morning he awoke to find the ship docking at Flushing in Holland. The former naval officer slid from his hiding place, melted into the crowd of passengers and disappeared.

Within hours he was back in Germany where, ironically, he was initially arrested as a spy. This mix-up was soon redressed and within a few weeks Plüschow was receiving an Iron Cross from Kaiser Wilhelm II.

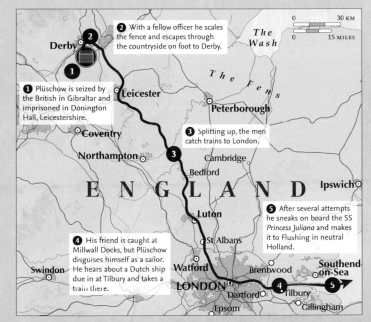

1 Plüschow is seized by the British in Gibraltar and imprisoned in Donington Hall, Leicestershire.

2 With a fellow officer he scales the fence and escapes through the countryside on foot to Derby.

3 Splitting up, the men catch trains to London.

4 His friend is caught at Millwall Docks, but Plüschow disguises himself as a sailor. He hears about a Dutch ship due in at Tilbury and takes a train there.

5 After several attempts he sneaks on board the SS *Princess Juliana* and makes it to Flushing in neutral Holland.

The War on the Run

WHEN LEO BRETHOLTZ FLED FROM THE ANTI-JEWISH VIOLENCE IN PRE-WAR VIENNA, HE LITTLE REALISED HE WOULD BE SPENDING THE NEXT SEVEN YEARS EVADING THE CLUTCHES OF THE NAZIS. HE MADE SEVERAL DARING ESCAPES, AND BECAME ONE OF THE FEW PEOPLE TO SUCCESSFULLY BREAKOUT OF A TRAIN BOUND FOR AUSCHWITZ.

DATE:
1938–44

SITUATION:
WARTIME PERSECUTION

CONDITION OF CONFINEMENT:
ON THE RUN AS A JEW IN NAZI EUROPE

DURATION OF CONFINEMENT:
7 YEARS

MEANS OF ESCAPE:
SWIMMING AN ICY RIVER, TUNNELLING, CROSSING THE ALPS, JUMPING FROM A MOVING TRAIN

NO. OF ESCAPEES:
1

DANGERS:
CAPTURE, EXECUTION, BETRAYAL

EQUIPMENT:
FALSE PAPERS, DISGUISES, UNDERGROUND CONTACTS

LEFT
The entrance to Auschwitz II-Birkenau extermination camp.

ABOVE RIGHT
Hitler in Vienna, March 1938.

Violence in Vienna

Leo Bretholtz had told his mother the river would be shallow – 'not like the Danube'. He had half believed his comforting words himself. But as he stood on the bank of the Sauer, looking over towards Luxembourg and freedom, the true danger of his planned escape was now terrifyingly clear. A week's lashing rain had swollen the watercourse into a seething torrent. It was nearly winter and the water was sharply cold. But there was no going back now.

Clutching the battered case that held all his belongings, Leo waded into the river and swam out into the current.

The surge of hate

Although the Second World War was still a year away, Vienna in 1938 was a hard place to be Jewish. Leo Bretholtz was 17 and had seen even his closest friends turn into Jew-haters who screamed insults

in his face. Brownshirts raided Jewish shops, the Hilter Youth sniggered as they watched Jewish men and women scrub pavements and rabbis had their beards set on fire.

Leo's mother knew it was time to act. She encouraged him to contact the Ezra Committee, a group that helped Austrian and German Jews find refuge in Luxembourg. Leo's aunt and uncle lived there, so it seemed like viable plan. The major downside was that Leo would have to go alone: his father had died in 1930 and his mother had to stay to look after his two sisters, one of whom was in hospital.

> **A week's lashing rain had swollen the watercourse into a seething torrent.**

The Ezra Committee helped Leo safely negotiate the 20-hour train journey from Vienna to Trier in Western Germany, close to the border with Luxembourg. Here he managed to swim the Sauer river, dragging himself to safety on the opposite bank before meeting up with his relatives.

This would just be the first of many daring escapes that Leo would make.

The joy of meeting his uncle and aunt was short-lived. Gendarmes challenged him in a café a few days later and when he could not produce the correct papers, they had him declared an illegal alien. He was not arrested, but he was persona non grata as far as the Luxembourg authorities were concerned, and he would have to move on.

Calm before the storm

The Ezra Committee helped him to get to Antwerp and, although the war began on 1 September 1939, Belgium initially remained neutral. Leo enjoyed a period of relative calm working as an electrician. Then on 10 May 1940, as he was lying in hospital awaiting a hernia operation, the Germans launched their *blitzkrieg* against the Low Countries.

Leo was among the hundreds of 'illegal aliens' rounded up and sent to an internment camp at St Cyprien in France near the Spanish border. But France soon fell to the Nazis and the French collaborationist government began to make life harder for Jews.

Leo's second escape

Leo and his colleagues began to worry that the Vichy government would soon follow the Nazi's lead in its persecution of Jews. He decided to try his luck on the run. Leo escaped from the camp at St Cyprien by digging his way out under the barbed wire fence.

He met up with an old friend who advised him to travel to Luchon in the Pyrenees. There he registered as a refugee and met up with many other familiar faces from Antwerp.

But the Jews' worst fears about the

Trier, where Leo arrived after fleeing Vienna, and from where he crossed the Sauer to Luxembourg.

French government began to come true. The authorities moved Leo and all other Jews in Luchon to Bagnères-de-Bigorre in the foothills of the Pyrenees. Food was restricted here, and they heard dire stories about mass deportations to the east. Leo managed to contact some relatives in America, begging them to help in any way possible.

Thwarted by a new war

In November 1941, his relatives managed to procure him a truly golden ticket: a visa to America. Full of hope, Leo went to collect it from the US consulate in Marseille on 8 December 1941, only to be told that all visa processing had been suspended – the attack on Pearl Harbor had happened just the day before.

More bad news

Returning to Bagnères, Leo was devastated by news from Vienna: his mother, sisters, grandmother and two aunts had all been deported

to Auschwitz. He would never see any of them again.

The Vichy government was now restricting Jews to certain locations. Leo was among many ordered to live in Cauterets, a town in the mountains to the southwest of Bagnères.

The food was nothing more than rancid cabbage water which gave everyone diarrhoea.

The persecution increased. Jews were soon being rounded up and sent to Drancy, a suburb of Paris, and from there, although no one was sure exactly what was happening, it was clear that anyone who went east was never heard from again. With the help of his friends, Leo managed to acquire some false papers establishing his credentials as a Frenchman. He joined up with a man called Albert Hershkowitz and the two of them set off on another daring escape plan, this time aiming to flee to neutral Switzerland.

Into Switzerland

Leo and Albert made it to Evian-les-Bains on Lake Geneva where they paid nearly all their money to a guide who promised to help them flee across the mountains. After an exhausting 24-hour march, and with their feet torn to bloody shreds, they made it to the border only to be turned back by frontier police.

They were handed back over to the Vichy police and taken to an internment camp at Drancy. Leo didn't know it, but this was to be his last stop before Auschwitz.

The hell-hole at Drancy

Conditions at Drancy were abysmal. Around 7,000 Jews, homosexuals and Gypsies lived here at any one time before being sent to Auschwitz. The food was nothing more than rancid cabbage water which gave everyone diarrhoea. There was little water for washing and bedding extended to straw scattered on concrete. Filth was everywhere. Children wailed through the night for their mothers.

The camp authorities knew the reason for this, even if the inmates did not: every soul in the compound was just one train ride away from certain death.

All Leo knew was that he had to escape.

Jumping from the Auschwitz Express

On 5 November 1942, Leo was told to gather his belongings. With hundreds of other internees he had his head shaved and was herded onto a truck. At the railway station, they were packed into cattle wagons, fifty people in each, twenty wagons in all. There was little food and no water. A single bucket served as a latrine. Within a short time the floor was awash with filth and vomit.

Leo and a friend, Manfred Silberwasser, set to work on the bars of one of the windows. Some people begged them to stop – they would be shot, or would get everyone else shot in their place. Others insisted that they were right to try. After hours spent scrabbling, their fingers bloody, they finally managed to shift the bars. Leo and Manfred said farewell to their Drancy friends and clambered out into the night, clinging to the top of the train in the buffeting darkness. As the train slowed for a curve they jumped.

After hours spent scrabbling, their fingers bloody, they finally managed to shift the bars.

Bullets whistled over their heads – some guards must have seen them leap. The train began to slow and shouts echoed into the night. Leo and Manfred ran for it. Perhaps the fact that the train had a schedule to keep meant that the guards could not look for long. Maybe they simply ducked and dived the right way. However they did it, Leo and Manfred eventually heard the noises of their pursuers getting fainter. Then train started back on its journey. They had escaped their trip to the gas chambers.

Eventually they found sanctuary in a village, where the priest took them in for the night. This man passed them on to a colleague of the cloth who also shielded them and displayed immense kindness and courage in giving them two train tickets to Paris. They made it there and stayed with Leo's Aunt Erna for two weeks, managing to get hold of some new forged papers. Leo took the name of Marcel Dumont. Two weeks with Aunt Erna was a blessed relief after the hardship of Drancy, but it was too risky for them to remain in Paris.

Leo – or rather, 'Marcel' – and Manfred took a train south. After they crossed the Loire, Manfred went to meet his brother in the Dordogne, while Leo aimed to return to Bagnères. Unfortunately, he pushed his luck a little too far and was picked up by the police.

As the officers escorted him to prison, they stopped at a café. Leo asked to use the lavatory and

Leo found refuge in Antwerp until May 1940.

7 Leo is imprisoned in the hellish camp at Drancy, the last stop before Auschwtiz. He is packed on a train to this final destination but manages to dismantle the bars on a window and climb out.

2 Authorities force him to move on, and he eventually finds safety and work in Antwerp.

9 Again he escapes from a train before heading to Paris. This time he keeps a low profile and spends the rest of the war in Limoges working for a Jewish resistance group. After the war he emigrates to America.

1 Leo flees anti-Semitic violence in Vienna, taking a train to Trier in Western Germany then swimming over the River Sauer to refuge in Luxembourg.

6 Leo gets some false papers and escapes to Evian-les-Bains on Lake Geneva from where he crosses the mountains, only to be turned back at the Swiss border.

8 He flees to Paris, then heads south, but is recaptured and sent to a labour camp at Septfonds.

3 The Nazis sweep into Belgium in 1940 and Leo is sent to an in internment camp at St Cyprien in France.

4 He tunnels out and travels to Luchon in the Pyrenees.

5 The anti-Jewish crackdown intensifies and the authorities move Leo and all other Jews in Luchon to Bagnères-de-Bigorre.

promptly escaped through its window. But his freedom was short-lived; he was recaptured and suffered a savage beating which damaged his still-untreated hernia. Leo was sentenced to a month in solitary confinement, which he spent largely in agony.

Another escape

He was eventually transferred from prison to a labour camp at Septfonds, where he spent his days in the pointless, humiliating and wearying work of breaking rocks. His escape partner Manfred had avoided prison and he managed to make contact with Leo, promising him a new set of papers if he could manage to escape.

Within a month, Leo had his opportunity. Along with several other inmates he was to be transferred to a camp on the Atlantic coast to help build fortifications. As soon as he was put on the train, Leo noticed that the guards stayed on the platform, so he popped a window on the opposite side of the carriage and fled along the tracks.

Manfred proved as good as his word, supplying a new birth certificate and by Christmas, Leo was back with his aunt in Paris.

From there he journeyed to Limoges, where he joined an underground group of Jewish resistance fighters called La Sixième (the 'Sixth'), so-titled in reference to the Nazi collaborator Fifth Columnists. Within this operation Leo helped forge papers, aid escapers and reunite scattered families. With typical bravado, he did much of his work wearing a uniform of a Vichy paramilitary youth organisation, the Compagnons de France.

One last close call

Leo continued his dangerous double life until May 1944 when he came perilously close to disastrous discovery. His hernia, which had

A railway wagon used to transport prisoners to Auschwitz II-Birkenau extermination camp.

required an operation before the war even began, now became strangulated. One minute Leo was walking through a park, the next he was prostrate on a park bench in agony. He passed out with the pain and remembered nothing more until he came round in hospital the next morning.

A stern-faced nun appeared and stared down at him. Leo knew his worst fears had been realised.

A passer-by had called an ambulance, and Leo had been operated on, which had saved his life. For that, Leo was grateful. But he also knew he had almost certainly been discovered as a Jew – the operating surgeon would have seen that he had been circumcised.

As he flushed with pain and panic, a stern-faced nun appeared and stared down at him. Leo knew his worst fears had been realised. Then the nun smiled gently, and introduced herself as Sister Jeanne d'Arc, assuring Leo that as long as he remained on her ward, his secret would be safe.

The sister's kindly silence undoubtedly saved his life, and by the end of May, Leo was fit enough to be discharged. A week later, the D-Day invasion signalled a turning point in the fortunes of Nazi Germany.

In August, the Resistance in Limoges mounted a massed assault on the occupying German forces, capturing the entire garrison. Leo continued his work with La Sixième, and when the end of the war came, he enjoyed the reward he had sought for so long – freedom. Leo was once again granted his visa for America, and he sailed for New York in January 1947.

A Midget Submarine and Malaria

FREDDY SPENCER CHAPMAN PERSONIFIED A VERY BRITISH BLEND OF RAW
COURAGE, DETERMINATION AND ECCENTRICITY. FOR NEARLY THREE AND
A HALF YEARS OF THE SECOND WORLD WAR HE SURVIVED ASTONISHING
HARDSHIPS, DEEP IN THE HARSH JUNGLES OF MALAYA BEHIND ENEMY
LINES. THERE HE DIVIDED HIS TIME BETWEEN BLOWING UP JAPANESE
TRANSPORTS AND OBSERVING RARE WILDLIFE.

DATE:
1941–5

SITUATION:
WARTIME SURVIVAL AND
ESCAPE

**CONDITION OF
CONFINEMENT:**
IN OCCUPIED ENEMY
TERRITORY IN THE
MALAYAN JUNGLE

**DURATION OF
CONFINEMENT:**
3 YEARS, 5 MONTHS

MEANS OF ESCAPE:
TACTICS, TRICKERY,
A MIDGET SUBMARINE

NO. OF ESCAPEES:
1

DANGERS:
DISEASE, STARVATION,
ENEMY ACTION

EQUIPMENT:
WEAPONS, EXPLOSIVES,
SURVIVAL SKILLS

ABOVE RIGHT
Naturalist, adventurer and unsung hero of the
Second World War, Freddy Spencer Chapman
(far left).

The born survivalist…

Many people are born survivors.
In a few rare instances these
extraordinary individuals actually
thrive under extreme conditions
and perform acts that are almost too
remarkable to be believed. Without
doubt, Lieutenant Colonel Frederick
'Freddy' Spencer Chapman was one
of the greatest of these exceptional
fighters.

He spent the last three and a
half years of the Second World War
behind enemy lines in the jungles
of Malaya. In some of the densest
and most disease-ridden terrain
on the planet, where a man could
march for an entire day and cover
less than a mile, Chapman took on

the Japanese occupying forces with
an almost supernatural display of
determination and creative military
endeavour.

In one two-week period he and
two colleagues blew up fifteen railway
bridges, derailed seven trains and
destroyed at least forty military
vehicles. Chapman designed his
own bombs, his favourite being a
gelignite-packed bamboo stick,
which he would leave on the open
road like debris from the jungle.
In this ferocious fortnight he got
through 455 kg (1,000 lb) of explosives,
100 grenades and caused between
500 and 1,500 enemy casualties.
Chapman later found out that the
Japanese command had dispatched

2,000 troops to confront his three-man band, believing the jungle to be packed with 200 highly trained Australian commandos.

His evasions and escapes are remarkable because they lasted for years. Virtually every day he was either suffering from a horrendous jungle fever, being shot at, hiding with Chinese guerillas or hunting Japanese patrols. Very often he was doing all of these things at once.

Chapman was also the very definition of the British eccentric. Because despite all the sabotage he performed, the perils he escaped and the diseases he suffered, he still made sure he devoted plenty of time to his hobby – birdwatching.

...and naturalist

Imagine James Bond but, rather than having the alter ego of a playboy to accompany his secret agent personality, instead having that of a naturalist. The man you have in mind is Freddy Chapman.

While Freddy was busy battling malaria, blowing up bridges, derailing trains, killing enemy soldiers by the squad load and training local insurgents he was also taking detailed notes on the local birdlife and collecting seeds to send back to Kew Gardens.

> **6 Colonel Chapman has never received the publicity and fame that were his predecessor's lot 9**

He had a profound love of nature and wildlife, gained from his boyhood spent in the Lake District. And he wasn't about to let a war get in the way of his passion. As he so beautifully put it, 'I don't see why the Japanese should be allowed to inconvenience me.'

Born tough

Freddy Chapman's mother died shortly after he was born and his father was killed in the First World War. He was brought up by an elderly clergyman and his wife on the edge of the Lake District in Cumbria.

Chapman was tough to the point of foolhardiness from an early age. In his spare time he picked up a few extra shillings poaching wildlife from under the noses of local gamekeepers. He encouraged his school friends to wallop him on the head with a cricket bat 'to see how hard he could take it'.

At Cambridge University, Chapman put more effort into climbing spires at night than he did into his studies. After graduating with a geography degree, he joined the 1930–1 British Arctic Air-Route Expedition and Greenland Expedition in 1932–3 as a ski expert and naturalist. This was where he perfected his survival skills. He led a three-man team across the bleak Greenland icecap, the first European to do this since Nansen. He lost several finger- and toenails, and survived more than twenty hours in a sealskin kayak during a ferocious storm at sea. He also managed to find time to learn Inuit and to father an illegitimate son with a local woman.

Before heading north to Scotland for a short time of quietness as a teacher of geography and outdoor activities at Gordonstoun school in 1938 (where Prince Philip was one of his pupils), Chapman even managed to make the first ascent of Mount Chomo Lhari in the Himalayas. This 7,134 m (23,400 ft) peak is so dangerous it would not be climbed again until 1970.

He also made detailed notes on unusual birds, collected dried seeds and pressed more than 600 interesting plants.

Life in a wartime jungle

By 1939, Chapman was almost eager for war. As he wrote at the start of his autobiography, *The Jungle Is Neutral*:

'In the early summer of 1939... when I was a housemaster at Gordonstoun School, Morayshire, it became obvious even to me – who rarely seemed to find time to read a newspaper – that war was coming...'

Chapman's fieldcraft was superb and he spent the early months of the war in Scotland passing on his expertise to specialist soldiers. One of his colleagues at this time was David Stirling who would go on to found the SAS.

In 1941, Chapman was deployed to Singapore. He proposed the organization of 'stay-behind' parties of soldiers to act as guerillas should the Malay peninsula and Singapore fall to the Japanese. His superior officers practically scoffed in his face at the very notion that such an event could happen. When it did, they quickly asked Chapman to proceed with his plan, but the short notice left him much less preparation time than he would have liked. Singapore fell in early 1942, and Chapman disappeared into the mountains virtually on his own. He was not to emerge again until May 1945.

> **6 On three of the four days since my escape I had travelled furiously, with hardly any rest, from dawn till dusk 9**

For all his sabotaging success in these years, Chapman's life was one of excruciating hardship. He was almost permanently sick with malaria, blackwater, beriberi or some other jungle fever and at one point spent 17 days in a coma. He only knew this from the absence of any notes in his diary. Festering ulcers from leech bites and injuries covered his body. At one point, his fever was so severe that he had to bound his mouth shut to stop his chattering teeth giving away his position to a Japanese patrol.

His understanding of nature was key to his strength as a survivalist. He believed that 'the jungle is neutral'. It was not out to get him personally,

THAILAND

PERLIS

Alor Setar

KEDAH

Malay Peninsula

Pinang

PINANG

George Town

Kota Bharu

SOUTH CHINA SEA

Kuala Terengganu

3 THE CHEMOR RIVER
This is where he was captured by the Japanese.

KELANTAN

TERENGGANU

2 TANJUNG MALIM
The area where Chapman had his furious fortnight of sabotage.

3

2

MALAYSIA

5

5 PANGKOR LAUT
The small island off Pangkor where Chapman escaped on the mini-sub.

PERAK

Teluk Intan

1

PAHANG

Kuantan

1 SUNGEI SEMPAN
The first campsite behind Japanese lines.

SELANGOR

KUALA LUMPUR

Klang

PUTRAJAYA

NEGERI SEMBILAN

Seremban

4 BATU PUTEH
This is where Freddy spent a year living with Chinese guerillas.

STRAIT OF MALACCA

MELAKA

Melaka

4

INDONESIA

JOHOR

Johor Bahru

SINGAPORE

SINGAPORE

Tanjungpinar

KILOMETRES 0   50   100   150

MILES 0   50   100

so there was no need to get worked up; much better to maintain a steady, resolute state of mind no matter what trials he faced. Likewise, there were bounties to be had courtesy of the wilds, but they were not put there by a benign providence especially to reward him. Chapman felt that this calm, accepting outlook was of the utmost importance in ensuring that his physical health and will to live were reinforced on a daily basis. He expressed this more philosophically: 'There is neither good nor bad, but thinking makes it so.'

A most gentlemanly escape

In 1944, fatigued by malaria, Chapman mistakenly walked into a Japanese camp. He was instantly arrested. Many men would have given up at this point, but not Chapman.

To make conversation (and perhaps an impression), Freddy asked the Japanese officer if he knew the whereabouts of two Japanese he had known at Cambridge: Prince Hashisuka the ornithologist and Kagami the skier. Whether Chapman was being deliberately charming or not, the officer was sincerely flattered by Chapman's kind words about his countrymen and gave the Englishman as much rice and salt fish as he could eat, apologized for not having any whisky and, as Chapman himself put it, 'showed no inclination to do anything so unmannerly as to tie my hands'.

Chapman settled down amid his captors in a large, securely pegged-down tent with a large fire burning by the tent opening. First he thought about simply dashing into the jungle while relieving himself outside. But the Japanese sentries stood so closely to him that he was unable to either run or indeed let nature take its course, and the guards became too suspicious for him to try that idea again. Next he tried to set the officer's clothing alight with his pipe (which he had been allowed to keep) and escape in the ensuing chaos, but

The submarine HMS *Statesman* on which Freddy made his final escape.

there wasn't enough of a draught to make his spilt tobacco embers flare up.

Finally he made a convincing show of vomiting, and asked to move a little further from the heat of the fire. In the half-darkness at the back of the angled tent wall he was able to work the bottom of the canvas loose by pretending to stretch and turn over in his sleep.

> **We had a bath, shaved off our beards and moustaches, sent our Chinese clothes to the incinerator, and drank large quantities of pink gin.**

He yanked the canvas wide, pinging the pegs free and creating enough of a gap for him to bolt into the jungle.

Although never in any doubt that he would escape, Chapman felt a pang of regret about having to do so: he thought it would appear very rude of him.

He then spent more than a month living wild in the jungle and avoiding the numerous Japanese search parties before joining the camp of a party of Chinese guerillas.

Rescued by a mini-sub

Chapman met up with two members of Force 136, John Davis and Richard Broome, but due to continued Japanese attacks they remained isolated among the Communist Guerillas until early 1945. Finally, with the help of the Malayan Chinese Communists they repaired their radio and made contact with their headquarters in Colombo.

Disguising themselves as Chinese labourers they made a remarkable 60-mile trek through the mainland jungle to the island of Pangkor off the Malay west coast. There they made contact with the navy and managed to escape from occupied Malaya in the mini-submarine HMS *Statesman*.

Canoeing into History

In one of the most daring raids of the Second World War, twelve Commandos set off to canoe 97 km (60 miles) upriver to bomb ships deep in German occupied France. Although successful, they faced fierce seas, enemy sentries, betrayal and a terrifying flight on foot. Only two men made it home.

DATE:
1942–3

SITUATION:
WARTIME MISSION

**CONDITION OF
CONFINEMENT:**
CARRYING OUT A COMMANDO
RAID IN ENEMY TERRITORY

**DURATION OF
CONFINEMENT:**
2½ MONTHS

MEANS OF ESCAPE:
CANOEING DOWNRIVER;
FLEEING ON FOOT

NO. OF ESCAPEES:
2

DANGERS:
CAPTURE, EXECUTION,
DROWNING, HYPOTHERMIA,
BETRAYAL

EQUIPMENT:
CANOES, LIMPET MINES,
RATIONS, OTHER COMMANDO
EQUIPMENT

Big problems in wine country

In 1942 the picturesque harbour of Bordeaux was a thorn in the Allies' side. The port was a major supply base for the German military with merchant ships bringing in thousands of tons of valuable raw materials including oils, crude rubber and food. U-boats also used the area as a base. It meant that German vessels didn't have to run the gauntlet of the English Channel, keeping them out of reach of the Royal Navy.

Something would have to be done about Bordeaux.

An audacious plan

A bombing raid would have likely been successful, but it would have led to high numbers of civilian casualties in what was an Allied country under occupation. This plan was ruled out.

Bordeaux is not on the open ocean, which also ruled out an open assault from warships. But its unusual geography did offer another gap in

its defences. Perhaps a small team of commandos could approach the port up the snaking Gironde estuary.

They could plant mines on as many vessels as possible, sinking or damaging enough ships to block the harbour with wreckage. By keeping the assault force small and maintaining the element of surprise there was a chance they could pull it off and make good their escape overland.

And so Major Herbert 'Blondie' Hasler came up with the idea for Operation Frankton.

The Cockleshell Heroes

The first problem was how to get the men up the Gironde to Bordeaux. The river would be heavily guarded. A motorboat would instantly draw attention. But perhaps human-powered vessels, moving under cover of darkness, could sneak past the sentries. The problem with that was that the journey was 97 km (60 miles) – a huge distance to paddle, especially against the flow of a river.

ABOVE RIGHT
Canoeing in open waters.

The men chosen would need to be the toughest of the tough. Even then they would have to undergo intense specialist training for the mission.

> *It would take them four nights of constant paddling with days spent hiding out in enemy territory.*

Twelve Royal Marine Commandos were selected for Operation Frankton. Since the canoes that they were to use were nicknamed 'cockles', these twelve men would become known as the 'Cockleshell Heroes'.

The worst possible start

The sun had long set on 7 December 1942 when the submarine HMS *Tuna* surfaced 16 km (10 miles) from the mouth of the Gironde estuary. A few minutes later her crew popped open her hatch, stepped out into the chilly night and started lifting out six collapsible Mark II canoes.

These were 4.6 m (15 ft) long semi-rigid craft with canvas sides and a flat bottom. Each vessel had to transport two men, eight limpet mines, two hand grenades, rations and water for six days, a camouflage net, a torch and other combat equipment. The men also carried a .45 Colt pistol and a combat knife.

As one of the canoes – the *Cachalot* – was being passed through the submarine's hatch, she was accidentally holed. The two Royal Marines who were to have paddled her, Fisher and Ellery, were in tears at their disappointment. But the hole in the canoe probably saved their lives.

Into enemy waters

There were now five canoes left, code-named *Catfish*, *Conger*, *Coalfish*, *Cuttlefish* and *Crayfish*. 'Blondie' Hasler led the mission from *Catfish*, which he paddled with Marine Bill Sparks.

The angled mouth of the Gironde is notoriously dangerous, and as the men turned into the river they hit

a violent rip tide. Waves 1.5 m (5 ft) high slammed into their bows and soaked the men to the skin. The canoe *Conger* was swamped and sank in the turbulent waters.

The *Cuttlefish* also capsized. Its crew, Lieutenant John Mackinnon and Marine James Conway, grabbed onto other canoes and were towed in to shore. Now unable to take any further part in the mission, they set out for Spain on foot.

The run upriver

The raiding party now consisted of six commandos in three canoes. After slipping past three German frigates set as a checkpoint in the river, they covered 32 km (20 miles) in the remaining five hours of darkness and landed near St-Vivien-de-Médoc.

Unfortunately, the crew of *Coalfish*, Sergeant Samuel Wallace and Marine Jock Ewart, were acting as backmarkers but were discovered at daybreak near the Pointe de Grave lighthouse and arrested.

That left the raiding party with only two canoes: *Catfish* crewed by Hasler and Sparks, and *Crayfish*, which was crewed by Marine William Mills and Corporal Albert Laver. They still had many miles to travel and now the Germans might be waiting for them.

Having captured two of the commandos, the Germans now knew that some sort of mission was underway, although their captives gave up very little information under interrogation. Patrols along the river were stepped up.

But the raiders avoided detection on the night of 8–9 December and paddled a further 35 km (22 miles) in six hours. They covered 24 km (15 miles) the next night and despite encountering a strong ebb tide on 10–11 December they were now within striking distance.

With the tide so strong, Hasler decided to hide for another day and launch the final stage of the mission on the night of 11–12 December.

Major Herbert 'Blondie' Hasler *(left)* and Corporal Bill Sparks *(right)*, visit the English Church of St Nicholas in Bordeaux for a memorial service to the Cockleshell Heroes, 3 April 1966.

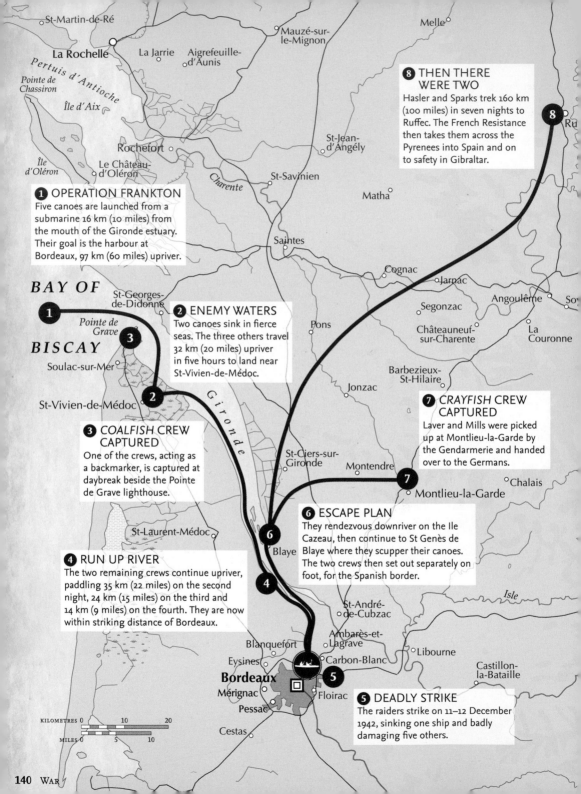

❽ THEN THERE WERE TWO
Hasler and Sparks trek 160 km (100 miles) in seven nights to Ruffec. The French Resistance then takes them across the Pyrenees into Spain and on to safety in Gibraltar.

❶ OPERATION FRANKTON
Five canoes are launched from a submarine 16 km (10 miles) from the mouth of the Gironde estuary. Their goal is the harbour at Bordeaux, 97 km (60 miles) upriver.

❷ ENEMY WATERS
Two canoes sink in fierce seas. The three others travel 32 km (20 miles) upriver in five hours to land near St-Vivien-de-Médoc.

❸ COALFISH CREW CAPTURED
One of the crews, acting as a backmarker, is captured at daybreak beside the Pointe de Grave lighthouse.

❼ CRAYFISH CREW CAPTURED
Laver and Mills were picked up at Montlieu-la-Garde by the Gendarmerie and handed over to the Germans.

❻ ESCAPE PLAN
They rendezvous downriver on the Ile Cazeau, then continue to St Genès de Blaye where they scupper their canoes. The two crews then set out separately on foot, for the Spanish border.

❹ RUN UP RIVER
The two remaining crews continue upriver, paddling 35 km (22 miles) on the second night, 24 km (15 miles) on the third and 14 km (9 miles) on the fourth. They are now within striking distance of Bordeaux.

❺ DEADLY STRIKE
The raiders strike on 11–12 December 1942, sinking one ship and badly damaging five others.

KILOMETRES 0   10   20

MILES 0   5   10

Deadly silent

At 9 p.m. the two canoes slipped into the calm river beneath a clear sky. After another hour of paddling, they were inside the walls of the harbour. The commandos got to work.

Hasler and Sparks placed eight limpet mines on four ships in the western side of the dock. A sentry on deck of one of the boats spotted movement and shone his torch down on them, but the men remained motionless and the camouflage net hid the canoe perfectly.

Laver and Mills placed another eight limpet mines with eight minute fuses on two merchant vessels in the south basin.

The commandos left the harbour at 12.45 a.m.

❦ **Eight minutes later flames licked the sky over Bordeaux and a volley of explosions rolled across the ocean as *Crayfish* and *Catfish* escaped on the tide.** ❧

A monument commemorating Operation Frankton, overlooking the Gironde estuary at Saint-Georges-de-Didonne, France.

Escape

The men wouldn't have heard or seen the limpet mines detonate, although they assumed their mission had been successful. Soon the Germans would be swarming over every inch of countryside looking for them. The most dangerous part of the raid was only beginning.

The four men met on the Ile Cazeau and then continued down river until just before dawn when they came ashore near St Genès de Blaye, just north of Blaye and sunk their canoes.

The two crews then set out separately on foot. The Germans would expect the men to travel directly south to the relative safety of Spain. Instead the plan was to head north, link up with the French Resistance, and then make their way south.

Hasler had worked out that they would be less obvious to the locals if they stopped outside the towns they passed through, and memorized the maps before entering, then they could walk through confidently as if they were meant to be there.

And then there were two

Laver and Mills only made it as far as Montlieu-la-Garde before they were picked up by the Gendarmerie and handed over to the Germans.

Hasler and Sparks covered 160 km (100 miles) in seven nights, reaching the town of Ruffec on 18 December 1942. Here they made contact with the French Resistance, who hid them at a farm for eighteen days. They were then guided across the Pyrenees into Spain.

Finally, on 23 February 1943 a message reached England that Hasler and Sparks were safe in Gibraltar. Hasler flew back home on 2 April and Sparks was sent back by sea later.

The fate of their fellows

The crew of *Conger*, Corporal George Sheard and Marine David Moffat, eventually made it to shore, but they had been too long in the brutally cold water and they perished from hypothermia.

Sergeant Samuel Wallace and Marine Jock Ewart were executed on 11 December in a sandpit in a wood north of Bordeaux.

MacKinnon and Conway evaded capture for four days, but they were betrayed and handed over to the Germans at La Réole hospital 48 km (30 miles) south east of Bordeaux. Along with Corporal Laver and Marine Mills they were shot by the Gestapo.

A worthy sacrifice

The mission succeeded in sinking one ship and crippling five others. This damage severely disrupted the use of Bordeaux harbour.

❦ **[It was] the most courageous and imaginative of all the raids ever carried out by the men of Combined Operations.** ❧

Winston Churchill said that the Cockleshell raid helped to shorten the Second World War by six months.

The Incredible Journey of Jan Baalsrud

JAN BAALSRUD WAS A SECOND WORLD WAR COMMANDO WHOSE
UNDERCOVER MISSION WAS BETRAYED. AFTER SHOOTING A GESTAPO
OFFICER AND ESCAPING INTO THE SNOWY WILDS OF NORWAY, HE SPENT
EIGHTEEN DAYS COWERING IN A SNOW HOLE. FORCED TO AMPUTATE NINE
OF HIS TOES, HE FINALLY ESCAPED ACROSS A FROZEN LAKE INTO SWEDEN.

DATE:
1943

SITUATION:
A COMMANDO MISSION
COMPROMISED BY THE
GESTAPO

**CONDITION OF
CONFINEMENT:**
HUNTED BY GERMAN
SOLDIERS IN NORTHERN
NORWAY

**DURATION OF
CONFINEMENT:**
2 MONTHS

MEANS OF ESCAPE:
HIDING IN A SNOW HOLE,
TREKKING ACROSS A
SNOWBOUND PLATEAU,
SELF-AMPUTATION

NO. OF ESCAPEES:
1

DANGERS:
CAPTURE, HYPOTHERMIA,
GANGRENE

EQUIPMENT:
SKIS, A SLEDGE, A POCKET-
KNIFE, HELP FROM THE
LOCAL RESISTANCE

ABOVE RIGHT
The snow-covered landscape in north Norway.

The wrong man

The four commandos waited until nightfall before starting the next stage of their mission. Then Sigurd Eskeland left their fishing boat and slipped ashore while the others took up watch positions and waited for his return.

Eskeland made his way to the local shop where he was to meet their contact, a local resistance sympathizer. This man had agreed to help them with their mission and galvanize local resistance efforts.

Unfortunately, the shopkeeper Eskeland introduced himself to, only shared the name of their contact, not the sympathies. They had the wrong man. Panicked, he refused to help and as Eskeland hurried back to the boat the terrified shopkeeper passed his details on to the Gestapo.

It was 28 March 1943 and the four-man team of Norwegian commandos had come from Scotland to blow up a vital air control tower in their German-occupied homeland.

They were far in the frozen north, a brutal land of rocky islands and sheer fjords, where the few tough inhabitants scraped a living from the sea and what little land that wasn't ice-bound.

Eskeland made it back to the boat, but the next day the Norwegians watched as a German gunboat motored into the bay. Their mission was over. But they could still save their skins.

On the run

They attached a time delay fuse to the 8 tons of explosives that should have destroyed the air control tower and instead used it to send *The Brattholm* to the bottom of the fjord.

The Norwegians then fled in a small boat, but the German gunners blew it out of the water. So the commandos plunged into the ice-cold arctic waters and swam for shore. They made it to land, but as they scrabbled up the snow-covered rocks on the beach, the Germans shot three of them. Only one man, Jan

Baalsrud, got away and he was still in deep trouble: freezing, soaking and without one of his sea boots he found himself at the bottom of a steep 60 m (200 ft) snow gully with four Germans shooting at him.

Baalsrud scurried behind a boulder and pulled out his pistol. He shot and killed the leading Gestapo officer and wounded a second soldier. He took his opportunity and scrambled up the slope, shots thumping into the snow around him.

He made it to the top and ducked behind another boulder. The Germans were nowhere to be seen and for a second he thought he had got clean away. Then he looked down to see that the big toe on his bootless foot had been half shot off.

Evasion

Baalsrud was on a tiny offshore island; the enemy would soon be all over it, so he had to get off. For the next few hours he hobbled over the frozen interior to its south coast. He could see another island to the east, but only one way to get to it. Baalsrud waded into the water and swam for 183 m (200 yards) through the heart-stoppingly cold Arctic Ocean.

As he hauled himself ashore, shudders wracking his body, he saw two small girls approaching. Their mother and their neighbour took him in and sheltered him for the night. At dawn they risked their necks to row him to Ringvassøya, a larger island nearby.

Sympathetic locals then smuggled him from house to house for the next six days, but Baalsrud knew that his luck would soon run out. He had to make it to the mainland and then cross the high, snow-bound plateau into neutral Sweden.

Lost in the storm

On 5 April Baalsrud made it to the mainland. The next part of his plan was to reach Lyngenfjord to the east. He was on skis, which would make his journey easier, but he still had

The Lyngen Alps, a mountain range east of Tromsø, in north Norway.

to cross the icy Lyngen Alps, 900 m (3,000 ft) high.

He was high in the hills when a storm hit and Baalsrud became utterly lost. Snow-blind, ravaged by frostbite and delusional, he shambled helplessly around the freezing heights for four days.

Eventually he staggered into a house in a tiny village of Furuflaten. He found immediate succour from a woman and her two children. He also recruited a vital ally: the woman's brother was a man named Marius Grönvold, a farmer and part-time journalist who had just the connections Baalsrud would need to continue his journey.

Grönvold spent four days helping Baalsrud recover, but the commando had suffered greatly in the mountains and could not continue alone. It was also far too dangerous to remain where he was.

Two weeks in the Hotel Savoy

On the night of 12 April Grönvold and some fellow patriots smuggled Baalsrud on a stretcher past the German garrison and across the fjord to a humble wooden hut at Revdal. Baalsrud christened his new home the Hotel Savoy.

For two days he recovered alone, then Grönvold returned with a plan.

When Baalsrud could walk they would head to the neighbouring village of Mandal where some colleagues would help him climb up onto the 900 m (3,000 ft) plateau behind Revdal. From there it was a 40 km (25 mile) trek across the exposed high ground to Sweden. Not easy, but possible.

Unfortunately, Grönvold was kept away from the hut for a week by another storm. In the meantime Baalsrud went rapidly downhill.

> ❛ After five days, he could only believe that he was condemned to lie in the desolate hut until the poisoning killed him or till he wasted away through starvation. ❜

His injured and frostbitten feet became poisoned. His toes turned black and began 'oozing a foul-smelling liquid'. Barely conscious, Baalsrud took out his pocketknife and drew out a substantial amount of blood.

This was how Grönvold found him on 21 April. It was obvious that Baalsrud needed a hospital and to get there as soon as possible. And since there was no way he could climb to the plateau himself, he would have to be taken there.

NORWEGIAN SEA

Sørøya

Lopphavet

① THE MISSION
On leaving Scotland, the four-man commando team set sail for Norway, landing at Tottefjord, high in the unpopulated north, beyond the Arctic Circle.

② ON THE RUN
Two women risk the wrath of the Gestapo to row Baalsrud to Ringvassöy.

③ LOST IN THE STORM
He spends four days lost in a storm in the Lyngen Alps before stumbling into the tiny village of Furuflaten.

④ HOTEL SAVOY
Sympathizers smuggle him across the fjord to a wooden hut at Revdal.

⑤ DIY SURGERY
He is dragged up onto the plateau where he spends eighteen days in various snow-holes and amputates nine of his toes.

⑥ BID FOR FREEDOM
From there the local Lapp people take him on a sledge across Finland and into neutral Sweden.

⑦ SAFE AT LAST
At Saarikoski he is picked up by a Red Cross seaplane and flown to Boden in Sweden.

NORWAY

SWEDEN

FINLAND

TROMS

Senja

Across the frozen plateau

Four days later, Grönvold and three other men strapped the still-delirious Baalsrud onto a sledge and hauled him 900 m (3,000 ft) up the snow-covered mountain. At the top, they expected to rendezvous with the team from Mandal. But there was no one there.

The Gestapo must have caught their colleagues; the trek was off. But they couldn't take Baalsrud back down the hill either – the Nazi patrols would soon discover him. They would have to dig him into the best shelter they could and trust him to the elements until they could reformulate a new plan.

Grönvold and his colleagues put him in the lee of a boulder and built a snow wall around him. Still on the sledge, Baalsrud was wrapped in two blankets and put in a canvas sleeping bag. Then they gave him the few rations they had and left him.

Although Baalsrud was entombed, immobile, in a chilly snow hole, this protected him from the savage extremes of the weather raging outside. He lay in this chamber of ice for four or five days, shivering and sick, but alive.

The men from Mandal had been delayed because German troops had chosen that very morning to make their first visit to their town. When they finally did manage to sneak up to the plateau, two days later, they couldn't find Baalsrud – fresh snow had completely covered him.

It would be a full week before Grönvold could return to the plateau. There was still no sign of the commando, so they had to pick the most likely part of the snow and just start digging. They found him.

He was lying pale and waxy in his icy coffin. 'He's dead,' said Grönvold. 'I'm not dead, damn you,' replied the corpse.

For the next seven days, teams from Mandal began to haul him towards the frontier. But the relentlessly bad weather again forced them to leave him alone in a snow hole on the plateau.

DIY surgery

Meanwhile, his toes had taken another turn for the worse. Gangrene had set in and if it wasn't checked, it would spread to his feet. Baalsrud decided that he would have to amputate his own toes. He got out his pocket-knife and set to work, slicing off all but one of the useless digits. Brandy was his only anaesthetic and he sealed the bloody stumps with castor oil.

> ❦ He still had his pocket-knife and he still had some brandy. With the brandy as anaesthetic and the knife as a scalpel... he began carefully to dissect them [his toes] one by one. ❦

The operation checked the gangrene, but Baalsrud's health was as fragile as an icicle. In total he had spent eighteen days on his back in a hole in the inhabitable wastes of the plateau.

Over the ice to freedom

Finally, on 31 May he woke to see a native Lapp carefully watching him. Reindeer were all around. His Mandal contacts had brokered a deal with the local Sami tribe to transport Baalsrud towards the border with Finland and from there across Finland and into neutral Sweden.

But they nearly fell at the final hurdle. When his rescuers reached Lake Kilpisjärvi, they initially refused to cross the uncertain ice. Sweden lay on the far bank, but the men would not risk it. Then a German ski patrol appeared, opened fire and Baalsrud's story had a dramatic final act: the Lapps, the reindeer and his sledge all skidded wildly over the groaning ice to the safety of Sweden.

Aftermath

Baalsrud was rushed to a Swedish hospital where doctors said that his act of self-amputation had undoubtedly saved his feet. He needed seven months of recuperation before he was flown back to Britain. He later returned to Scotland where he helped train other Norwegian commandos.

On 25 July every year, hikers gather in Tromsø to follow the route of Baalsrud's escape on a nine-day march in his honour.

Lake Kilpisjärvi, Finland.

The Great Escape

In March 1944, seventy-eight allied prisoners of war tunnel out of Stalag Luft III. The escape's incredible planning and boldness severely embarrassed Hitler. Seventy-three prisoners were recaptured of which fifty were shot. Five men made it to freedom. It is one of the most famous wartime escapes in history.

DATE:
1944

SITUATION:
Held as prisoners of war

CONDITION OF CONFINEMENT:
In Stalag Luft III

DURATION OF CONFINEMENT:
Months or years depending on the individual

MEANS OF ESCAPE:
Tunnels

NO. OF ESCAPEES:
78

DANGERS:
Discovery by guards, tunnel collapse, suffocation, being shot

EQUIPMENT:
Improvised tools, meticulous planning, forged documents

ABOVE RIGHT
Prisoner of war camp Stalag Luft III which was run by the Luftwaffe for captured airmen until its liberation on 29 April 1945.

The camp

Stalag Luft III opened on 21 March 1942 and was originally run by the Luftwaffe as a camp for captured officers of the British RAF and Fleet Air Arm. It later expanded, taking officers and non-commissioned officers from other services and nationalities.

It had an impressive range of sports and recreational facilities as well as a library. The prisoners built a theatre and put on two shows a week. They broadcast a news and music radio station and published two newspapers.

But despite the relative decency of camp life, it was the duty of all prisoners to escape.

The master plan

The idea for the escape from Stalag Luft III came from Squadron Leader Roger Bushell. In the spring of 1943, he presented a plan of unprecedented boldness to the Escape Committee. Bushell wanted to dig three tunnels simultaneously instead of one, reasoning that even if one tunnel were discovered, the Germans would be unlikely to suspect that another two were being dug.

Three tunnels would also enable more men to escape. Bushell believed he could get 200 men out, more than ten times as many as any previous attempt. The men would all be dressed in civilian clothes and have meticulously forged identification papers.

The Committee approved the daring plan and Bushell, or 'Big X' as he was code-named, began the job of organizing the Great Escape.

The problems

The prison camp had been deliberately designed to thwart tunnelling. It had been sited on land with yellow, sandy subsoil, which could easily be spotted if anyone dumped it on the much darker surface soil. This loose sand also made it much harder to build a structurally sound tunnel.

The prisoners' barracks were raised several inches off the ground, making it easier for guards to detect tunnels. The Germans also installed seismograph microphones around the perimeter, which would detect sounds of digging.

> ❛ Everyone here in this room is living on borrowed time. By rights we should all be dead! The only reason that God allowed us this extra ration of life is so we can make life hell for the Hun... ❜

Bushell had the problem of finding the equipment and organizing the manpower to actually dig the tunnels. Plus there was the constant security headache of keeping three major construction projects completely secret from the many guards who were constantly patrolling the compound.

Tunnel construction

The three tunnels were code-named 'Tom', 'Dick' and 'Harry'. Tom was sited in a gloomy corner of a hallway in one of the buildings. Dick started beneath a drain sump in a washroom while Harry's entrance was hidden under a stove.

The tunnellers dug deep – going about 9 m (30 ft) below the surface. This would stop the perimeter microphones picking up vibrations. The tunnels were as narrow as possible, only 0.6 m (2 ft) in diameter, to minimize the amount of earth that must be moved. But several larger chambers were dug underground, housing the air pump, a workshop, and staging posts for each tunnel. The prisoners bolstered the sandy tunnel walls with scavenged wood from their beds, among other sources.

Over 600 prisoners in total worked on the tunnel construction.

Many other materials were pilfered and re-tasked to aid the escape effort. The 'Klim' tin cans in which the Red Cross supplied powdered milk proved particularly versatile. These were fashioned into digging tools, earth scoops, candle holders and were used to construct a ventilation system in all three tunnels. Air pumps were built from Klim tins, hockey sticks, bed slats and knapsacks to supply the digging men with air.

There seemed to be no end to the ingenuity. Prisoners skimmed the fat from their soup to use as candle-wax and unraveled threads

from old clothing to make wicks. They fitted each tunnel with electric lighting and installed rail car systems to shift the spoil more quickly. The men also used the railway to reach the digging faces.

Meanwhile the forgers managed to persuade some friendly guards to lend them railway timetables, maps, and many official papers. Prisoners obtained civilian clothes by bribing German staff with cigarettes, coffee and chocolate.

The disposal problem

Some sand could be scattered on the surface. The prisoners carried the spoil in small pouches made from old socks, which they hung inside the bottom of their trouser legs. They would then don greatcoats to disguise the bulges and walk calmly about the compound, releasing their cargo by means of a string. Their slightly awkward gait earned them the nickname 'penguins'. More than 200 penguins made around 25,000 trips.

Prisoners also dumped sand into the small gardens they were allowed to tend. As work progressed Dick was partly filled in, sacrificed as a good place for soil dumping and a place to store maps, forged travel permits and civilian clothing.

It was inevitable that the Germans would suspect something, and in September 1943, guards hiding in the woods saw the 'penguins' taking sand from the hut where Tom was located. They discovered the tunnel. The Gestapo also visited the camp and instantly transferred nineteen of their prime escape suspects to Stalag VIIIC.

As a precaution, Bushell ordered that work on the last tunnel, Harry, should cease. It restarted in January 1944. Bushell had planned to escape in the fair weather of summer, but now he ordered the attempt be made as soon as the tunnel was ready. Harry was finally finished in March.

The end of the 'Harry' tunnel, showing how close the exit was to the camp fence.

Neubrandenburg

Neustrelitz

Prenzlau

Oranienburg

BERLIN

Potsdam

Strausberg

Fürstenwalde

Luckenwalde

Fläming

GERMANY

Eisenhüttenstadt

Finsterwalde

Spremberg

Senftenberg

Riesa

Döbeln

Meißen

Freital

Freiberg

Pirna

CHEMNITZ

Teplice

Most

Litoměřice

CZECH REPUBLIC

Ústí nad Labem

Děčín

Česká Lípa

Oderhaff

Zalew Szczeciński

Police

2 **NORWEGIAN PILOTS**
Bergsland and Müller travelled
to neutral Sweden by boat.

2 Szczecin

Stargard Szczeciński

Gryfino

Jezioro Miedwie

4 **DUTCH RESISTANCE**
The Lambrecs returned to the
Netherlands and rejoined the
Dutch Resistance.

4 *Schorfheide*

Schwedt
an der Oder

Eberswalde-
Finow

Oder

Odra

Warta

**Gorzów
Wielkopolski**

Puszcza Natecka

P O L A N D

Frankfurt
an der Oder

Międzyrzecz

Poznań

Lub

Świebodzin

Ś

Odra

Guben

Kościan

Cottbus

Forst

Zielona Góra

Gosty

Leszno

Cottbus

Żary

1 STALAG LUFT III
The camp was near the town of
Sagan in the German Province
of Lower Silesia, now Żagań in
Poland.

1 Żagań

Rawicz

Hoyerswerda

Weißwasser

Polkowice

3 DUTCH PILOT
Van der Stok headed via Dresden
through France and eventually
found safety at a British consulate
in Spain.

Lubin

Legnica

3

Dresden

Görlitz

Zgorzelec

Bolesławiec

Jawor

Wrocław

Zittau

Jelenia
Góra

Świebodzice

Świdnica

Kamienna
Góra

Jablonec
nad Nisou

Liberec

KILOMETRES 0   20   40   60

MILES 0   10   20   30

Trutnov

Szczecinek

Wałcz

Piła

Chodzież

148 WAR

Crawling to freedom

The plan was for 202 men to escape. They were split into two groups, each of 101 men. The first group was nicknamed 'serial offenders', and included men with a history of escapes, German speakers, and the seventy men who had put in the most work on the tunnels. They were guaranteed a place.

The second group of 101, known as 'hard-arsers', had to draw lots to determine inclusion. Bushell thought these men would be unlikely to succeed as their limited German meant they would have to travel by night. They only had the most basic fake papers and equipment.

> The camp Kommandant was appalled by the shooting of the fifty escapees by the Gestapo and allowed the prisoners to build a memorial. It still stands today.

A moonless night was essential if the men were to maximize their chances of escape. Clear skies kept their nerves ragged for a week until on Friday, 24 March 1944, the escape was declared 'go' and the chosen men moved into Hut 104.

Setbacks

Unfortunately, it was the coldest March for thirty years and Harry's trap door was frozen shut, which delayed the start of the escape by an hour and a half. When the first man did exit the tunnel, he found it hadn't reached the forest as planned. It came up just short of the tree line and close to a guard tower.

Rather than have a man leave every minute, this slowed the escape rate to ten per hour.

Worse luck was to follow. An Allied air raid knocked out the camp's power, shutting down the tunnel lights. Then a section of tunnel collapsed and had to be repaired.

Despite these problems, seventy-eight men managed to crawl through Harry to freedom.

Then, at 4.55 a.m. the guards spotted the seventy-ninth man as he climbed from the tunnel mouth.

Tough going

Many escapees planned to catch a night train, but in the darkness they were unable to find the station entrance and ended up stuck on the platform until daylight, when they were rounded up.

Those who went cross-country faced an even harsher obstacle. Thick snow – 1.5 m (5 ft) deep in places – forced the escapees to leave the cover of woods and fields and use roads, making it easier for the pursuing Germans to spot them.

After the escape

All but five of the seventy-eight escapees were captured. Hitler initially ordered them all to be shot, along with

Kommandant Friedrich Wilhelm von Lindeiner-Wildau, of Stalag Luft III.

the camp's Kommandant, its architect and the guards who were on duty.

> After the war, several Gestapo officers responsible for the executions of the escapees were executed or imprisoned following the Nuremberg Trials.

In the end, fifty prisoners were executed, singly or in pairs. Roger Bushell was shot by the Gestapo near Saarbrücken, Germany.

The five who made it

Per Bergsland and Jens Müller, both Norwegian pilots, caught a train to Stettin in Germany (now Szczecin, Poland). There they met two Swedish sailors who smuggled them past harbour authorities and onto a ship bound for Gothenburg, where they sought out the British consulate.

Bram van der Stok, a Dutch pilot, bluffed his way through several German checkpoints and travelled via Dresden to Belgium. He then passed through France before finding safety at a British consulate in Spain.

Ryone and Mikail Lambrec, members of the Dutch Resistance, found their way back to the Netherlands and rejoined their underground comrades.

The memorial to 'The Fifty' Allied airmen executed after the 'Great Escape'.

Across the Roof of the World

WHEN MOUNTAINEER HEINRICH HARRER ESCAPED FROM A POW CAMP IN INDIA HE HEADED FOR THE HIMALAYA, RATHER THAN THE PLAINS. HIS JOURNEY TOOK HIM OVER THE WORLD'S MOST FEARSOME MOUNTAINS AND THROUGH ITS MOST SECRETIVE COUNTRY, BEFORE HE FINALLY REACHED THE GOLDEN CITY OF HIS DREAMS, LHASA.

DATE:
1939–46

SITUATION:
CAPTURED BY BRITISH FORCES IN INDIA

CONDITION OF CONFINEMENT:
HELD IN PRISONER OF WAR CAMP; ON THE RUN IN HOSTILE TIBET

DURATION OF CONFINEMENT:
6½ YEARS

MEANS OF ESCAPE:
TREKKING THROUGH THE HIMALAYA

NO. OF ESCAPEES:
2

DANGERS:
CAPTURE, EXPULSION, STARVATION, HYPOTHERMIA, MURDER

EQUIPMENT:
ESCAPE EQUIPMENT; THE CLOTHES AND BELONGINGS OF A POOR TRAVELLER

LEFT
The holy Mount Kailas in Tibet.

ABOVE RIGHT
A river in the Spiti Valley, Himachal Pradesh.

Height of ambition

Heinrich Harrer was a German Olympic ski champion and keen mountaineer who in 1938 became one of the first men to climb the deadly north face of the Eiger.

This prodigious achievement earned him a place on the 1939 expedition led by Peter Aufschnaiter to the unclimbed Nanga Parbat in the Himalaya.

There had been four attempts to climb this 8,126 m (26,660 ft) mountain. All had failed, costing many lives. Harrer and his colleagues would find a new way up and make an attack on the peak the following year.

But trouble was brewing between the nations of Europe, and British-controlled India was no place to be if you were German. In early September 1939 war broke out. Aufschnaiter, Harrer and the other members of the team were seized by Indian forces.

Imprisoned in India

They were interned in the biggest POW camp in India at Dehra Dun in Uttarakhand. This had seven separate sections each surrounded by a double barbed-wire fence. Two more lines of wire entanglement enclosed the whole camp. Guards constantly patrolled the space between the lines.

Harrer immediately vowed to escape. The jagged wall of the Himalaya to the northeast held more promise for him than India, where he would need money and perfect English to evade capture. After several failed escape attempts, he joined a group of six other like-minded POWs and set about plotting an all-or-nothing breakout.

Escape

Harrer knew he had to keep himself fit for the attempt and he exercised relentlessly in rain and burning sun alike. He also scrabbled together all the money and provisions he could, gathering such useful items as a compass, watch, shoes and even a small mountaineer's tent.

On 29 April 1944, Harrer and four others, Aufschnaiter, Bruno Treipel, Hans Kopp and Sattler darkened their faces with make-up, shaved their heads and donned turbans. Two other men dressed as English officers and, posing as an Indian barbed-wire repair squad, the seven men walked out of the camp's main gate.

> ❛ I was covered with scratches and bruises and owing to my heavy load had walked through the soles of a pair of new tennis shoes in a single night. ❜

Heading for Tibet

The two 'officers' boarded a train for Calcutta and made their way to the Japanese army in Burma. The other five headed for the border with Tibet. This was, in theory, a neutral country and should offer them sanctuary.

Kopp, Aufschnaiter, Treipel and Sattler went by the main road, but Harrer struck out alone, travelling by night and sleeping by day.

For more than two weeks Harrer shunned all human contact. His path took him through the remote Jumna and Aglar valleys and he frequently found himself face to face with wild animals, including big cats and an aggressive bear, which he managed to scare off with a stick. On the one occasion when he ran into a local woman he escaped by scaling the 3,022 m (9,915 ft) peak, Nag Tibba.

> ❛ As I was loping along in the grey of dawn I found myself facing my first leopard. ❜

On 10 May he once again bumped into his four colleagues at Nelang. They had not been detected, but their journey had been punishing. Now Sattler came down with altitude sickness and gave up the escape attempt. He gave his colleagues a two-day start before turning himself in.

Frustratingly, the four remaining escapees soon got lost. Harrer and Aufschnaiter had to climb a 5,500 m (18,000 ft) mountain just to see where they were. Forced to go back on their tracks, their mistake cost them three days and much of their rations.

But after seven days of near-constant marching they reached the 5,896 m (19,350 ft) Tsang Chok-la Pass that formed the border between India and Tibet.

Fugitives in an unknown country

No Englishman could now arrest them, but their final objective, the Japanese lines, lay thousands of miles away in Burma. To reach it they would have to travel for many months through the high mountains and wind-whipped plains of Tibet. Few foreigners had penetrated the interior of this country and little was known about it. Would the Tibetans show them any hospitality? The Germans had no knowledge of the language and little money.

Their introduction to this strange land was not cordial. The empty mountain heights and deserted valleys forced them to endure brutally cold temperatures and the men were soon exhausted and close to starvation.

Tibet had remained isolated thanks largely to its geographic remoteness, but also due to its extremely efficient administrative network. It was impossible to survive in this harsh land without trading and receiving help from locals. Even the tiniest village had either a head monk or secular leader who would demand to see their travel permit.

The first Tibetans they met were wary of strangers and refused to trade with them. Eventually they had to resort to intimidation simply to buy meat.

The Germans made it as far as Shangtse before the head monk refused them permission to go on any further. He denied their claims of asylum. The villagers were forbidden from selling the men supplies or from offering hospitality. They had no option but to travel back to India via the Shipki Pass.

On 9 June 1944 they were, heartbreakingly, back at the Indian border – the land of the enemy. They realized that it was simply not possible for foreigners to live in Tibet without a permit. If they were to achieve their goal they would need to act more wisely.

'The Roof of the World' at Lhasa-Xining, Tibet.

Again into Tibet

The men soon vowed to try again. They believed that the officials they had encountered had not had the authority to decide their case; if they could just talk to a high enough judiciary they ought to be granted the refuge they sought.

The four men split into pairs to increase their chances. Aufschnaiter and Treipel went down the trade road that flanked the Sutlej. Harrer and Kopp headed through the Spiti valley back up towards the Himalaya, passing themselves off as pilgrims bound for the holy mountain of Kailas.

On 17 June Treipel was too exhausted to go any further and he bought himself a horse and rode back to the lowlands. Harrer and Kopp joined up again with Aufschnaiter.

The Potala Palace and Buddhist stupas in Lhasa, Tibet.

After five days' marching along the upper Indus, the trio reached Gartok. Here they met the local Viceroy and although he forbade them from journeying to the interior of Tibet, he did give them a permit to the Nepal border. With this valuable concession came an entitlement to servants and yaks.

On 13 July they set off and travelled for weeks through deserted lands. They were ill-prepared for the alternately freezing and hot weather: their tent could be covered with snow during the night only for this to melt in the morning. At last they reached Gyabnak, the limit of their permit.

Here they were summoned into the next settlement, Tradün, by two high officials. The route gave them a beautiful view of the wonders that the interior of this most mysterious land might hold: the golden towers of a monastery gleaming in the sun and beyond that the high ice walls of Dhaulagiri, Annapurna and Manaslu.

The whole population of Tradün was out in the streets to see these strange men for themselves. The officials could not believe they were German POWs, but they agreed to send their petition to remain in Tibet to higher authorities in Lhasa. The men were given generous supplies of flour, rice and *tsampa*, a powdered meal that formed the basis of the local diet.

For three long months they waited while their petition made its way across the country's vast interior, was considered and a verdict returned. In the meantime, Kopp had had enough: he left to try his luck in Nepal. Out of the seven who had broken out of the internment camp, five had made it to Tibet, and from those five now only Aufschaitner and Harrer remained.

> **We were the only mountaineers in the group and consequently physically and mentally best fitted for the lonely and strenuous life in this bleak land.**

On 17 December 1944 word came back – their petition had been denied. Harrer and Aufschaitner were forced to leave for Nepal.

But it was now winter and the weather was bitterly cold. The thermometer never once moved from its measure of -30°C; the lowest it could show. After seven savage days and nights they reached Dzongka on Christmas Day 1944. Thick snow prevented their further progress for a month.

On 19 January 1945 they started again and after another week of hard trekking they reached the beautiful village of Kyirong.

The Village of Happiness

It's likely that Aufschnaiter and Harrer were the first Europeans ever to visit Kyirong. The name means 'Village of Happiness' and Harrer fell in love with its Alpine situation and quaint wooden houses. But as beautiful as the place was, they were still stuck there. The Tibetan officials were eager to push them on to Nepal, where they would be handed over to the British – which had been Kopp's fate.

Even the fact that the war ended in the summer of 1945 did not lessen their desire to avoid Nepal: after the First World War the British had kept POW camps going for two years and they had no desire to fall into their hands even now.

Burma was no longer the longed-for physical sanctuary; Tibet had become their spiritual goal and Lhasa, the capital and inner heart

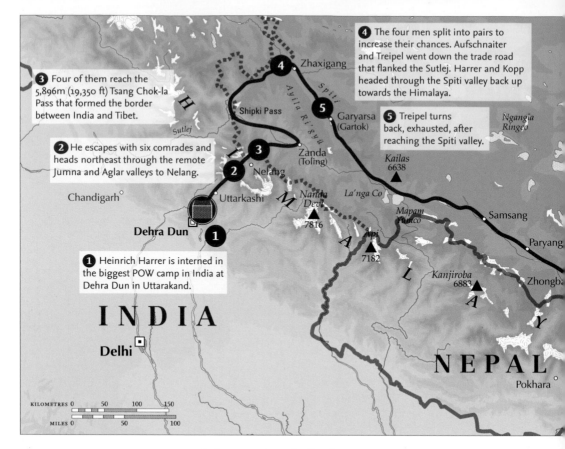

③ Four of them reach the 5,896m (19,350 ft) Tsang Chok-la Pass that formed the border between India and Tibet.

② He escapes with six comrades and heads northeast through the remote Jumna and Aglar valleys to Nelang.

① Heinrich Harrer is interned in the biggest POW camp in India at Dehra Dun in Uttarakand.

④ The four men split into pairs to increase their chances. Aufschnaiter and Treipel went down the trade road that flanked the Sutlej. Harrer and Kopp headed through the Spiti valley back up towards the Himalaya.

⑤ Treipel turns back, exhausted, after reaching the Spiti valley.

of this magical country, had seized control of their imaginations.

Harrer and Aufschnaiter determined to start out for the border as they had promised their hosts before veering round and heading northeast towards the Tibetan interior. They would approach Lhasa from the Changthang plain to its northwest. This would be harder than the usual pilgrims' road, but it would avoid administrative centres.

They laid a cache of supplies 19 km (12 miles) away on the road they would take. Winter was coming, but they could not stay any longer; they would have to risk it. Aufschnaiter went first, but villagers became suspicious and Harrer could not get away. He eventually brazened his way through the protests.

A detour towards death

They made good progress despite carrying 36 kg (80 lb) of supplies each and having to move in the dark with a feeble light. They edged across icy bridges spanning bottomless gorges. Fifteen degrees of frost chilled the air in their lungs as they became probably the first Europeans to traverse the 4,876 m (16,000 ft) Chakhyungla Pass. Now they were so far out in the wilderness that they dared to travel in daylight.

By now Harrer and Aufschnaiter looked so wild and weathered that they could pose as Indians and trade with locals for supplies. But still they had to avoid main routes as much as possible. After glimpsing the mighty bulk of Everest they decided to head into territories so harsh that the local

nomads tried to dissuade them from going. Their proposed route would take them in the territory of the Khampas, notoriously violent robbers.

They ignored these warnings and actually walked into just such a bandit camp. The Khampas tried to separate the men to pick them off more easily, but the Germans boldly faced them down and marched swiftly out of the settlement. They escaped by choosing an escape route so severe that even the hardy Khampas gave up following them.

The last stage of the flight to Lhasa was the hardest journey Harrer ever endured. The temperature was constantly around -40°C and their hands and feet were seized rigid with the cold. Harrer had been struck by an attack of sciatica from constantly

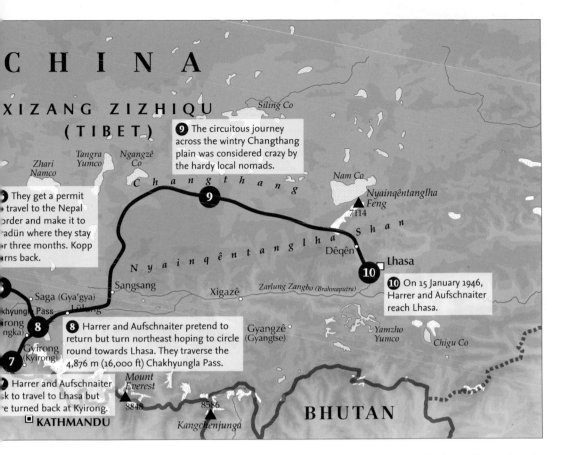

C H I N A

X I Z A N G   Z I Z H I Q U
(T I B E T)

Siling Co

9 The circuitous journey across the wintry Changthang plain was considered crazy by the hardy local nomads.

Zhari Namco

Tangra Yumco

Ngangzê Co

Nam Co

C h a n g t h a n g

Nyainqêntanglha Feng
7114

9

3 They get a permit to travel to the Nepal border and make it to adün where they stay r three months. Kopp rns back.

N y a i n q ê n t a n g l h a   S h a n

Dêqên

Lhasa

10

10 On 15 January 1946, Harrer and Aufschnaiter reach Lhasa.

Sangsang

Xigazê

Zarlung Zangbo (Brahmaputra)

Saga (Gya'gya)

khyung Pass

Lü ng

rong

ngka

8

Gyirong (Kyirong)

7

8 Harrer and Aufschnaiter pretend to return but turn northeast hoping to circle round towards Lhasa. They traverse the 4,876 m (16,000 ft) Chakhyungla Pass.

Gyangzê (Gyangtse)

Yamzho Yumco

Chigu Co

Harrer and Aufschnaiter k to travel to Lhasa but e turned back at Kyirong.

Mount Everest
8848

8586

■ KATHMANDU

Kangchenjunga

BHUTAN

---

sleeping on cold hard ground. When they ate, their spoons stuck to their lips and they had to tear their flesh away.

> **❬ an evening in a warm tent was more important than if, in the safety of our homes, we had been given a racing-car as a New Year's gift. ❭**

Eventually they reached the relatively busy Tasam Highway and with Lhasa fifteen days' march ahead of them fell in with an official caravan, again bluffing their credentials.

On 15 January 1946 they set out on their last march. Since leaving Kyirong they had marched for seventy days and rested for five. But as they paced through a broad valley they rounded a corner and saw the golden roofs of

the Potala, the Dalai Lama's winter residence and the most famous landmark of Lhasa. It was everything they had dreamed it would be and more.

Taken in by royalty

They looked more like brigands from Changthang than Europeans and they fully expected to be detained by the guards at the gate to Lhasa. But, to their astonishment, they were able to walk into the inner city without being stopped.

It was almost as if, having made it so far, they were above suspicion. Not even bearded Europeans were suspect because no one had ever made it into Lhasa without a pass before. Speechless with relief, awe and gratitude they passed into the innermost streets of the Forbidden City.

At first the alarmed locals shooed them away. When the men collapsed with utter exhaustion, the Tibetans saw their ruined feet and relented, bringing them butter-tea and other refreshments. And then Harrer and Aufschnaiter heard themselves addressed in perfect English. A senior Tibetan noble stood looking down at them. He took them into his own house and for the first time in seven years they found themselves enjoying a meal cooked on a stove.

The start of a greater adventure

Harrer went on to become a friend and tutor to the eleven-year-old 14th Dalai Lama, who spotted him in the streets below the palace through his telescope.

Escape from a Siberian Gulag

In 1945, German POW Cornelius Rost was sent to a Siberian gulag. Facing an unbearable life of beatings, starvation and hard labour in a lead mine, he escaped. For the next three years he would brave the savage Russian landscape and the constant danger of recapture on an epic 13,000 km (8,000 mile) journey home.

DATE:

1949–52

SITUATION:

A German POW sent to a Siberian gulag

CONDITION OF CONFINEMENT:

Imprisoned in a Siberian lead mine, alone on the run in Stalinist Russia

DURATION OF CONFINEMENT:

3 years

MEANS OF ESCAPE:

Trekking, skiing, living as a nomad, hitching lifts

NO. OF ESCAPEES:

1

DANGERS:

Capture, betrayal, starvation, hypothermia

EQUIPMENT:

Some supplies, skis and a gun at the start; later, none

LEFT
The snow covered coast near Cape Dezhnev on the Chukchi Peninsula, the most easterly point in mainland Asia.

ABOVE RIGHT
The mountain landscape of the Chukchi Peninsula in Siberia.

The unbelievable journey

Some escapes seem so incredible that they defy belief. For years Cornelius Rost had to contend with people who doubted his tale. Could he really have escaped from the forced labour camp of a gulag and trekked 13,000 km (8,000 miles) through Stalinist Russia? If so, why had he changed his name in the book about his exploits to Clemens Forell?

The truth seems to be that Rost did indeed make this epic journey, and his name change adds credence to his tale: he took on one of the most powerful and brutal dictatorships in history and lived to tell the tale. It was natural that he would fear reprisals.

The forgotten soldiers

At the end of the Second World War, 20,000 defeated German soldiers were trapped in the Soviet Union, a country keen to get revenge for its millions of fallen men.

Cornelius Rost was one of these unlucky soldiers. Captured by the Russians in 1944, he was held as a normal Prisoner Of War for a year. Then he was sentenced to twenty-five years' hard labour in a lead mine in a far, frozen corner of Siberia.

In October 1945, he was among 3,000 prisoners who boarded cattle wagons in Moscow station for the journey to East Cape (Cape Dezhnev), just south of the Arctic Circle by the Bering Strait.

> The journey to the gulag lasted nearly a year. More than half the men who started it died – from exhaustion, malnutrition or dysentery. Many just froze to death.

Their destination was incredibly remote – so remote in fact that the journey took nearly a year, moving by cattle train, horse-drawn sledges and finally dog sledges. Only 1,236 men made it – less than half of those who started.

The end of the Earth

The prisoners lived in the lead mine itself, in caves lit by a single lamp. Guards forced them to work brutally hard for twelve hours every day. Bread, potatoes and water barley gruel was all they had to sustain their efforts.

> **Once a week, if they were lucky, they would see the sun for an hour. If the men didn't die of exhaustion, they would certainly succumb to lead poisoning.**

Rost's sentence of twenty-five years was clearly nominal; he would be dead long before then.

It was an existence almost beyond endurance. Rost knew he would soon be emaciated and exhausted. And despite being surrounded by hundreds of miles of frozen nothingness, he thought it would be better to at least try to escape.

He fled almost immediately. But after he went missing, guards cut the rations of his fellow prisoners to almost nothing. When they recaptured Rost eleven days later, they made him run between lines of the nearly starving men. His fellows beat Rost so badly he almost died.

Three more years passed before Rost found another opportunity to break out.

The surrogate escapee

The camp doctor was a fellow German who had been using his more privileged position to put together an escape plan. He had stashed a map, food, money, clothing, a pair of skis and, remarkably, a gun.

He then made a heart-breaking self-diagnosis: he had cancer. There was no way he would make it. He asked Rost to take his place, on the condition that he contact his wife in Germany when he made it to freedom.

On 30 October 1949, the doctor distracted the guards long enough for Rost to slip out of the hospital. For the next three years he would be on the run in a savage landscape ruled by an even more brutal dictatorship.

Out of the frozen east

His plan was simple: go west as far and as fast as he could. Pursuit was a certainty, but Rost believed that if he could put 320 km (200 miles) between himself and the gulag then the guards would probably give up trying to find him. From there he could head south into Manchuria.

Rost set himself a punishing daily target of at least 32 km (20 miles), although he often topped 48 km

(30 miles) – an incredible achievement in the savage terrain of Siberia. But while the icy winds and frozen terrain stretched his endurance to the limit, the environment also protected him: there were very few people out here.

Life as a nomad

Nevertheless, he took specific care to avoid human contact. He didn't dare light a fire, so the little food he had was solid with cold. A whole month passed before he met two nomadic reindeer herders. Rost was convinced they would either kill him or turn him in, but it seems the men felt they had more in common with the fugitive than they did with Moscow. They welcomed him into their camp, looking after him for nearly three months.

That winter with the herdsmen was invaluable for learning practical skills.

> **Rost learned how to live in the Siberian wilds: how to fish and hunt; how to improvise a tent; the knack of lighting a fire from moss.**

He also learned the importance of help from others. But the very necessity of seeking such a trust would bring him danger as well as aid.

The prospectors

Rost spent two more months with another group of herdsmen. Then in June 1950 he encountered three fellow fugitives – Russians who had fled prison to eke out a living as hunters in the winter and gold prospectors in summer.

He threw in his lot with them for a year, and adopted the Russian name Pyotr Jakubovitsch. The men worked as a team, panning for gold twelve hours a day from June till October. It was punishing work but by autumn they had gathered a small pile of gold dust, which they divided into even shares.

With the days shortening, the men stole six reindeer to drag their

Ruins of the gulag on the Chukchi Peninsula in Siberia.

sledges and headed for the plains to hunt for fur. It was perhaps inevitable that greed and death would be close companions to men in such a situation, and they duly arrived to turn Rost's world upside down again.

Left for dead

One of Rost's colleagues, a man named Grigori, had a gold nugget that he had filched during his days as a prisoner working in a gold mine. His colleagues discovered the nugget and there was a deadly battle that left Rost alone with Grigori. The man had seemed mad to start with; now he was also highly paranoid.

Five days later Grigori stole Rost's gold too and shoved him off a cliff, leaving him for dead.

Rost very nearly died, but he was saved again by another group of sympathetic herdsmen. They tended to his wounds and helped him recuperate before sending him on his way with one of their huskies, which Rost named Willem.

It was summer 1951 and Rost had been out of the lead mine for twenty months. But he was still a long way from home: even the border with Manchuria lay 1,280 km (800 miles) away.

But as he began to pass more signs of civilization, he knew had to develop a cover story. He claimed to be a Latvian who had finished his eight-year sentence in a labour camp and been ordered to Chita, a city near Manchuria. This explained his limited Russian and his battered physical condition.

Riding the rails

His tale passed muster with some woodcutters who had a cargo of timber to send to Chita. They offered Rost the job of escorting the shipment and even gave him a travel permit. Rather than getting off at Chita, Rost stayed on the train until the end of the line at Ulan Ude and

his good fortune kept running: a drunk Chinese truck driver gave him a lift to the Manchurian border.

Here his lucky streak came to a sad end. The border was fortified and impassable. A suspicious guard shot Willem and Rost once again had to take to his heels.

For the next few weeks he lived a precarious existence, hiding by day and sneaking onto trains at night, stealing food when he could.

It was clear he would need a sympathetic ally if he were to make any significant progress across the vast Soviet Union. He met a forestry worker whose father was an Austrian captured by the Russians in 1914. This man instantly recognised Rost's German accent. But rather than hand him over to the authorities, he helped him plot out a route to the border with Iran, some 2,400 km (1,500 miles) away.

A false step

By early 1952, Rost had made it to Novo-Kazalinsk, east of the Aral Sea. He briefly lived with the members of a local underground movement who promised to smuggle him out of the country by heading north round the Caspian Sea and then passing into Iran through the Caucasus. But Rost scented a trap and he abandoned the group, striking out south on his own, the most direct route to Iran.

It was a bad decision. Rost spent the next five months trekking south to no avail. He lost a dangerous amount of weight, became utterly exhausted and in the end was forced to retrace his steps.

In June he made it back to Novo-Kazalinsk and decided that this time he would trust the underground. He was passed from safe house to safe house on a northwest route towards Uralsk, then southwest to Urda. By November he had reached the Caucasus.

As he closed in on his goal, so the risks increased. He was travelling through more populous regions now, making his chance of being caught

by the police much higher. Although he was thousands of miles from the gulag, this was still Stalinist Russia and if caught Rost would be arrested as a German spy and returned there.

Even when his smuggling companions told him they had crossed the icy river that marked the border with Iran, Rost felt sure he would be caught.

But the unbelievable story had come true: he had made it out of the Soviet Union.

Last throw of the die

Three days later he was in the nearest town, Tabrīz. He walked into the police station and told them his story. It was so incredible they assumed he was a Soviet spy and arrested him.

Rost was taken to Tehrān where he endured weeks of daily interrogation. He stuck to his story, but still the Iranians were convinced he was a spy.

Rost's uncle had moved to neighbouring Turkey before the war. Rost begged that his captors bring this man to Tehrān to identify him as a German. The Iranians agreed and a week later, Rost's uncle stepped into his cell.

It looked like fate had played a final cruel trick on Rost: he was so exhausted and emaciated from his years on the run that his uncle didn't recognise him.

But he had brought a photograph album that had belonged to Rost's mother. Rost told him to look at a particular picture of his mother. On the back he claimed that he, in a different lifetime, had written his mother's birthday – the day he had presented her with the photo.

The Iranian officers pulled out the photo and flipped it over. Written on the back was: '18 October 1939'.

Rost was released and flew with his uncle to Ankara. He then flew via Athens and Rome to Munich.

He walked into his home city on 22 December 1952, nearly three years and 13,000 km (8,000 miles) after his journey started.

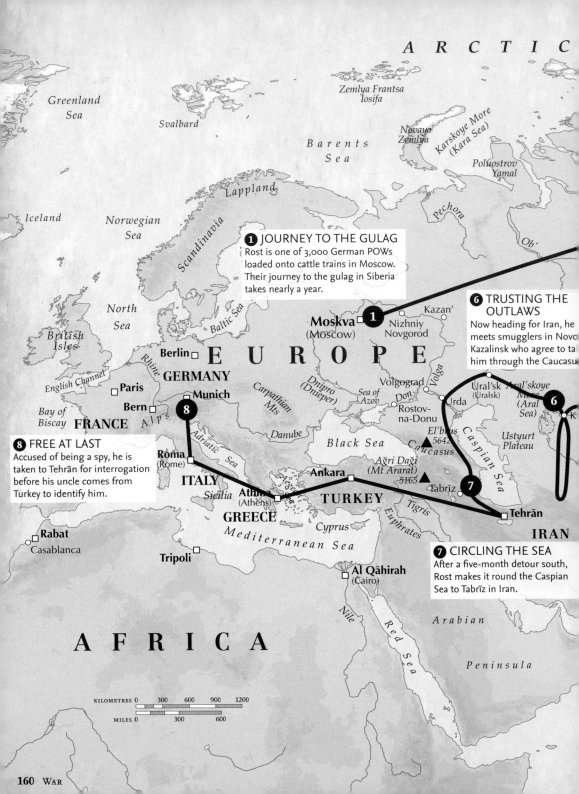

1 JOURNEY TO THE GULAG
Rost is one of 3,000 German POWs loaded onto cattle trains in Moscow. Their journey to the gulag in Siberia takes nearly a year.

6 TRUSTING THE OUTLAWS
Now heading for Iran, he meets smugglers in Novo Kazalinsk who agree to take him through the Caucasus

8 FREE AT LAST
Accused of being a spy, he is taken to Tehrān for interrogation before his uncle comes from Turkey to identify him.

7 CIRCLING THE SEA
After a five-month detour south, Rost makes it round the Caspian Sea to Tabrīz in Iran.

ARCTIC

Greenland Sea

Svalbard

Zemlya Frantsa Iosifa

Novaya Zemlya

Karskoye More (Kara Sea)

Barents Sea

Poluostrov Yamal

Lappland

Iceland

Norwegian Sea

Scandinavia

Pechora

Ob'

North Sea

British Isles

Baltic Sea

EUROPE

Berlin
GERMANY

Munich

Rhine

English Channel

Paris

Bern

Bay of Biscay
FRANCE

Alps

8

Roma
(Rome)
ITALY

Sicilia

Adriatic Sea

Carpathian Mts

Danube

Athina
(Athens)
GREECE

Ankara

TURKEY

Dnipro (Dnieper)

Sea of Azov

Don

Volgograd

Rostov-na-Donu

Black Sea

El'brus 5642 ▲
Caucasus

Ağri Daği (Mt Ararat) 5165 ▲

Tabrīz

7

Volga

Urda

Moskva
(Moscow)
1

Kazan'

Nizhniy Novgorod

Ural'sk (Uralsk)

Aral'skoye More (Aral Sea)
6

Ustyurt Plateau

Caspian Sea

K

Cyprus

Tigris

Euphrates

Mediterranean Sea

Tehrān

IRAN

Rabat
Casablanca

Tripoli

Al Qāhirah
(Cairo)

Nile

Red Sea

Arabian Peninsula

AFRICA

KILOMETRES 0 300 600 900 1200
MILES 0 300 600

O C E A N

ernaya
mlya

uostrov
aymyr

Novosibirskiye
Ostrova

Vostochno-Sibirskoye
More

More Laptevykh
(Laptev Sea)

② THE ESCAPE
After three years' forced labour
in a lead mine, Rost flees the
gulag and heads west into the
frozen Siberian wilderness.

② *Bering*
Sea

S I B I R
(SIBERIA)

Verkhoyanskiy Khrebet

Indigirka

Kolyma

Khrebet Kolymskiy

Vilyuy

Lena

Yakutsk

R U S S I A N   F E D E R A T I O N

③ **③ LIFE AS A NOMAD**
He is helped westwards by
nomadic herdsman.

Poluostrov
Kamchatka
(Kamchatka
Pen.)

Novosibirsk

Krasnoyarsk

Ozero Baykal
(Lake Baikal)

Chita

Sakhalin

Novokuznetsk

Ob'

Irkutsk

④ THE PROSPECTORS
After a spell panning for gold,
he travels by timber-train to
Ulan Ude.

Khabarovsk

Irtysh

na

④ *Ulan Ude*

Hövsgöl
Nuur

Selenga

M a n c h u r i a

Vladivostok

Hokkaidō

⑤

⑤ RIDING THE RAILS
Unable to cross the border
to Manchuria, he treks and
hitchhikes west.

G O B I

Sea of
Japan
(East Sea)

Ozero
Balkhash

A S I A

Bo
Hai

Yellow
Sea

Honshū

Korea Strait

Pamir

Hindu Kush

▲
K2
8611

Qingzang
Gaoyuan
(Plateau of Tibet)

Huang He
(Yellow River)

Chang Jiang
(Yangtze)

East
China
Sea

Kyūshū

H I M A L A Y A

Brahmaputra

▲
Gongga
Shan
7514

Indus

▲
Mt Everest
8848

Ganga
(Ganges)

Irrawaddy

Salween

Xi Jiang

Taiwan

Luzon
Strait

INDIA

Bay
of
Bengal

Mekong

G. of Tongking

Hainan

Luzon

Philippine
Sea

abian
Sea

Andaman
Sea

Gulf
of
Thailand

South
China
Sea

Philippine
Islands

The Six Escapes of 'Farra the Para'

WHEN CAPTAIN ANTHONY FARRAR-HOCKLEY WAS CAPTURED DURING THE KOREAN WAR HE DEDICATED ALL OF HIS CONSIDERABLE INTELLIGENCE, BRAVERY AND RESOURCEFULNESS TO ESCAPING. HE BROKE OUT SIX TIMES AND DESPITE THE INCREDIBLY HARSH JOURNEYS, THE FRUSTRATION OF CAPTURE AND THE SICKENING TORTURES HE SUFFERED, HE NEVER GAVE UP HIS QUEST FOR FREEDOM.

DATE:

1951–3

SITUATION:

CAPTURED BY THE CHINESE IN THE KOREAN WAR

CONDITION OF CONFINEMENT:

SEVERAL BRUTAL PRISON CAMPS

DURATION OF CONFINEMENT:

28 MONTHS

MEANS OF ESCAPE:

TUNNELLING, DIGGING THROUGH WALLS, EVASION ON FOOT, SWIMMING ICY RIVERS AND MORE

NO. OF ESCAPEES:

1

DANGERS:

ENEMY ACTION, EXECUTION, DISEASE, EXHAUSTION, TORTURE

EQUIPMENT:

ARMY UNIFORM, SOME STOLEN TOOLS AND EQUIPMENT

LEFT
Pyongyang, the capital of North Korea.

ABOVE RIGHT
Freedom Bridge over the Imjin River between North and South Korea

The battle that started it all

The Battle of the Imjin River was a key conflict in the Korean War. On 22 April 1951 forces from the People's Republic of China attacked United Nations positions on the lower Imjin River in an attempt to breakthrough and recapture the South Korean capital Seoul.

During three days of intensive fighting, the men of the Gloucestershire Regiment put up a fiercely determined resistance that severely disrupted the Chinese offensive. Among many of the heroes of the battle was Captain Anthony Farrar-Hockley. After his company had suffered devastating losses, he helped his men retrench and hold on for some time. Nevertheless they became surrounded, ran out of ammunition, and after hand-to-hand fighting with bayonets, Farrar-Hockley organized an orderly withdrawal. He was one of the last to leave the position and was captured.

Captain Anthony Farrar-Hockley started planning his escape immediately.

Escape No. 1

He took his first opportunity as they were being marched north by their captors. As they forded the Imjin River just below Choksong, he slipped away into the water.

> ❛ When I surfaced about thirty yards downstream, I half expected to hear the sound of shots and the cries of the guards coming after me. ❜
>
> From *The Edge of the Sword* by A. Farrar-Hockley.

For the next seven hours he half-swam, half-crawled along the shallow but icy cold river.

'My clothes were saturated and my boots were filled with water. I began to sink: I realized that I was drowning.'

In the morning he was spotted by two Chinese soldiers, but he lay still and rigid, with his jaw hanging low to feign *rigor mortis*. His ploy, combined with his genuinely frozen state, worked and the men moved on.

Farrrar-Hockley now had about 16 km (10 miles) to travel back to the British lines. That was too far to float down the increasingly swift river so he started across the paddy fields and scrub-covered hill. He dressed in a discarded rice sack and muddied his face to look like a peasant. When he was challenged by a Chinese sentry he bluffed his way past with the few words of Korean he knew. Agonizingly, he was just 550 m (600 yards) short of the lines when he ran into a soldier of the North Korean Army who didn't buy his trickery.

Escape No. 2

After being marched north for several days towards Pyongyang, Farrar-Hockley managed to tiptoe out of the camp at night with two fellow English prisoners.

They hid out in a monastery with a sympathetic Korean family until the Chinese found him hiding in a tool shed.

He was tied up with a noose round his neck and hands bound in the small of his back. But he was careful not to give away the two comrades who were still hiding in the monastery. He even managed to let slip a coded phrase as he was marched past their hiding place to let them know that the Chinese had not spotted them.

Unfortunately, Farrar-Hockley had left his boots behind and the long march north on stony roads that he was now forced to endure slashed his feet nearly to the bone.

Farrar-Hockley was taken to a Chinese army camp in Munha-ri, south of Sunch'ŏn. His foot became very badly swollen, and Farrar-Hockley agreed to let his comrades 'operate' on him.

> **❢ Doug got to work with a Schick razor blade; and I regret to say I swore a great deal. ❣**
>
> From *The Edge of the Sword* by A. Farrar-Hockley.

The conditions in this prison were abysmal. The men were rarely allowed to wash, getting increasingly sick with dysentery and fevers. They had little food, were often forbidden from going to the latrine and were denied medical treatment.

It was here that Farrar-Hockley received his first dose of political lecturing. The Chinese believed they could 'educate' their captives into becoming revolutionary Marxists. Farrar-Hockley disagreed.

But gradually his foot healed and escape was soon uppermost in his mind again.

Escape No. 3

After three months they were marched south for ten days, passing through the broken streets of the North Korean capital, Pyongyang.

Their new home was at an army's company headquarters and, if anything, conditions were worse.

> **❢ The only way in which four of us could lie down simultaneously... was to overlap legs and hips, taking it in turns as to whose legs should be on top... ❣**
>
> From *The Edge of the Sword* by A. Farrar-Hockley.

They were deep behind enemy lines in a military camp and the security was less strict than it might have been. Farrar-Hockley soon spotted an opportunity, and with a colleague, Duncan, he slipped away from the camp in the dead of night.

They drank from muddy streams and ate raw maize as they moved constantly for three nights. They were nearly swept away crossing a river but kept going and were shielded by a sympathetic family who gave them breakfast.

But as they were sheltering to eat their boiled corn, five soldiers passed close by. Duncan decided to run for it, but he tripped on a root and fell. Farrar-Hockley managed to get away, but he realized that Duncan had been captured without his warm clothes. Knowing he would die in the cold without them, Farrar-Hockley handed himself in at the local headquarters.

Escape No. 4

They were put in bunkers dug into the earth of a hillside, the doors of which where stopped up with oil

Lt. Col. Anthony Farrar-Hockley (*left*) with Major Anthony Ward-Booth (*right*), during military operations.

drums. Farrar-Hockley immediately started tunnelling through the earth floor of the bunker. After narrowly avoiding detection, he dug his way clean out over the course of several nights and made a run for it, heading west towards the sea.

This was a real slog: he was almost constantly swimming rivers and slogging through muddy paddy fields. His cut foot had become re-infected and he had a nasty case of tonsillitis. He was also coming down with jaundice.

He was only managing 10 km (6 miles) a day at most and the countryside was packed with troops and arms depots. Still, he managed to trek undetected for fifteen days and finally made it to within sight of the coast.

But his feet had split into a mass of raw wounds and he was so sick and exhausted that he passed out in his tracks as he crossed a field. He awoke in the mud house of a Korean family. Despite the overwhelming numbers of soldiers in the area and the potential punishment that they faced for hiding him, they nursed him back to a semblance of health.

❛ I stayed in that house for another six days, during which they fed and cared for me as if I was one of their own. ❜
From *The Edge of the Sword* by A. Farrar-Hockley.

The sea, and a possible boat, was only a kilometre or so away. But just as Farrar-Hockley decided to make his final break for it, a North Korean soldier stumbled upon him. After a hot pursuit through a cornfield he was cornered by more soldiers.

Escape No. 5

He was first taken to a brutal police jail, where prisoners lived in atrocious conditions and constant fear of random beatings.

Then he was moved to an interrogation camp, which had its own forms of unpleasantness. The daily ration was just boiled millet and thin soup with a single bean in it. This meagre allowance was diminishing and their captors often used starvation as an interrogation technique. The men were forced to do hard labour, building shelters and emptying the camp latrine by hand after which they would be refused permission to wash.

Winter was coming: it was getting bitterly cold at nights and Farrar-Hockley's clothes were reduced to little more than rags. He had planned to break out in the spring, but now decided he had to go earlier.

He broke out with two comrades, Ron and Jack, by cutting a hole in the wattle and mud wall of their cell. They managed to steal some padded clothing and then ran into the night, covering 19 km (12 miles) before dawn. Their goal was the coast north of Namp'o.

Again, though, his bravery was not rewarded with good luck. A sentry spotted him and the best Farrar-Hockley could do was walk forward and occupy the man's attention so that the other two could escape.

❛ One [Chinese soldier] … said a few words to me in what I believed to be elementary Russian, and I replied heartily in gibberish, ending as many of my words as possible with 'ski', 'sh', 'ish' and 'off'. ❜
From *The Edge of the Sword* by A. Farrar-Hockley.

Torture

He was taken to Pyongyang and interrogated, the Chinese demanding he tell them where Ron and Jack were. Farrar-Hockley refused and the Chinese finally lost patience.

They took him along a corridor and opened a door of double-plated steel with thick padding in between. Behind it was a square concrete cell. Ropes hung down from metal rings in the ceiling. There were more rings in the left-hand wall and a barrel of water in front of the right. There was a tiny chair, like a child's, in the centre of the room, with more ropes on it. The floor and walls were darkened with splashes of dried blood.

❛ As I stripped off my filthy, lousy shirt and jersey, I knew that I was in a torture chamber. ❜
From *The Edge of the Sword* by A. Farrar-Hockley.

Farrar-Hockley was made to strip to the waist and was tied to the chair. A boot on his chest knocked him flat back onto the concrete. He was doused with a few ladles of icy water and a towel was slapped over his mouth. More cold water was poured on this. As the sopping towel clung to his face and he dragged in vital breaths, water gathered in his nostrils, mouth and lungs. The more he breathed the more water came in and the less air he took in. This savage cycle of ever-shortening breaths rapidly flooded him with panic. Utterly unable to move, he had never been as scared in his life. He was drowning and he knew for certain that death would soon take him. Eventually, blessedly, the darkness took him. He had just undergone what is now known as 'waterboarding'.

He came back to the light – and raw pain. His torturers had brought him back to life by applying a lighted cigarette to his back. Water coursed from his mouth and nose.

They asked him where his colleagues were. He refused to tell them. They repeated the procedure. He experienced the same terror and expectation of death. Again, he felt the breath dying in his lungs. Again, he refused to tell them anything. Three times they repeated the torture and still Farrar-Hockley gave them no information. Exhausted and in agonies, he was thrown in a dark cell and bound hand and foot.

That was day one.

The procedure was repeated on the second, fourth and sixth days of his confinement. In this time he was given maize but no water. He was not allowed to use the latrine and as he

CHINA

Yalu

NORTH KOREA

11 ESCAPE NO. 6
During spells in camps at Changsong and Pyŏktong he attempts to escape for a sixth time, and a seventh plan is betrayed before it can be implemented.

Pyŏktong

7 RECAPTURED
He is taken to a brutal Korean jail at Sinŭiju and then to an interrogation centre near Pyongyang.

Dandong (Andong)

Sinŭiju

10 MARCHED NORTH
After a short time in a POW camp at an old coal mine at Kang Dong, he endures a near-deadly march of 322 km (200 miles) north in November.

Hamhŭ

Chŏngju

Sinanju

Sunch'ŏn

Taedong-gang

9 TORTURED
He is caught and taken to Police HQ in Pyongyang where he was tortured for seven days. He refuses to betray his comrades.

4 CAPTURED
Caught again he is taken north to a camp at Munha-ri.

Yangdok

Wŏnsan

KOREA

P'YŎNGYANG (Pyongyang)

Kangdong

Imjin-gang

8 ESCAPE NO. 5
This time he cuts a hole in the wall and escapes with two colleagues, heading for the coast north of Namp'o.

Songnim

Namp'o

1 BATTLE OF THE IMJIN RIVER
Captain Farrar-Hockley is captured at the Battle of the Imjin River in April 1951.

Sariwŏn

Cho-do

BAY

P'yŏngsan (Namch'ŏn)

6 ESCAPE NO. 4
Caught near Namch'ŏn he is thrown into a pit dug in a hillside. He tunnels his way out and heads west, nearly making it to the coast. He is rescued by a local family before being caught.

5 ESCAPE NO. 3
After three months they pass south through Pyongyang to a new camp from where Farrar-Hockley flees for a third time.

Kŭmch'ŏn

Choksong

2 ESCAPE NO. 1
He escapes from the prisoners' column south of Choksong, but is soon recaptured

Kaesŏng

Ŭijŏngbu

Kuri

12 FREEDOM!
When the war ends in the summer of 1953, Farrar-Hockley is taken south by train and repatriated near Kaesong.

Koyang

SŎUL (Seoul)

3 ESCAPE NO. 2
He escapes again near Ŭijŏngbu and hides in a monastery.

SOUTH KOREA

KILOMETRES 0   25   50
MILES 0   15   30

had contracted enteritis his clothes were soon horribly fouled. With the blackest of humour, Farrar-Hockley noted that this did not put the lice off their meal.

On the seventh day of his torture routine, just as he thought he might finally be able to take no more, one of his captors came in and spoke to him: 'You are very lucky,' the man said. 'Tomorrow you will be shot.'

Escape No. 6

As promised, Farrar-Hockley was taken out the next day to see a file of armed soldiers – this had to be it. He also saw Ron and Jack. But, amazingly, they got away with a warning: try to escape again and you *will* be shot. They were then marched through Pyongyang and beyond to an old coal mine turned POW camp.

From there they had to endure a 322 km (200 mile) march north in wintry conditions with very little clothing. Farrar-Hockley was in a terrible condition from his tortures, he had no shoes and his feet were freezing solid. Unable to walk, he at one point fell into a coma and he was only roused by his colleagues rubbing some warmth back into him. He was one of the lucky ones: other men were dropping in their tracks from dysentery, beriberi and sheer exhaustion.

Even when they made it to their new prison camp at Changsong, for many of them it was already too late.

> **Someone died almost every day; men whose skeleton bodies had been starved or maltreated beyond the point of response to their improved circumstances.**
> From *The Edge of the Sword* by A. Farrar-Hockley.

Farrar-Hockley took a long time to recover. At first he could barely stand but he forced himself to walk a few paces, which he increased by five paces each day.

Soon he was part of an eight-man escape party. They gathered together

The Demilitarized Zone between North and South Korea looking from south to north.

as much stolen and scrounged kit as they could. One of the men even managed to make a compass. They hid this gear in a maize field which they passed on their way to collect water. But they were spotted by a sentry and Farrar-Hockley was sent to solitary confinement.

Betrayal

By Christmas 1952 his sentence in solitary confinement meant he missed the 'escaping season' of summer. Mid-winter had been ruled out before: conditions were too harsh for men in their weakened condition. But they were a little stronger now. Farrar-Hockley and three other men planned to escape in February along the frozen Yalu river.

But, on the night of the attempt, as they were readying their kit, the Chinese discovered them. It was too much of a coincidence. The men were forced to countenance an unbearable thought: someone on their own side had betrayed them.

This was a very harsh reality for Farrar-Hockley to swallow as he was thrown in an outhouse in thin clothes for two snow-bound days and nights.

Final steps to freedom

After recovering from the frostbite sustained in this ordeal, Farrar-Hockley, and the other men at the camp, entered into a new stage of

their captivity. The Chinese began to seem less confident; a sense of nervousness, even fear, was evident in some of their actions. They began giving the men more rations and asking them to tell the Red Cross that they had been well treated. The reason for their unease was simple: peace was coming.

By summer 1953 the belligerents in the Korean War had agreed on a truce. Fighting stopped and the Korean Demilitarized Zone was established at the 38th parallel, the strip of land 248 x 4 km (155 x 2.5 miles) that now divides North and South Korea.

Farrar-Hockley's bravery may not have resulted in a successful escape, but it undoubtedly kept him alive long enough to see this day. On 17 August 1953 he and his fellows left their prison compound forever. They were taken to a station and soon travelled back south of the Imjin River, an area they had battled so hard to defend, in the comfort of a train.

Farrar-Hockley spent a few days in a repatriation camp catching up with familiar faces. Then, on 31 August 1953 he climbed out of the back of the truck he was in, leaving his bag of meagre belongings behind, and walked into the sunshine of a very warm day.

An American soldier slapped him on the back.

'Welcome to Freedom,' he said.

This story is a brief retelling of the events in *The Edge of the Sword* by Anthony Farrar-Hockley, published by Pen & Sword Military. Reproduced with permission.

Across the Killing Fields

DITH PRAN WAS A CAMBODIAN INTERPRETER WHO RISKED HIS LIFE TO
HELP AN AMERICAN JOURNALIST COVER THE ARRIVAL OF THE KHMER
ROUGE IN PHNOM PENH IN 1975. HE THEN ENDURED FOUR YEARS OF
TORTURE AND STARVATION AT THE HANDS OF THE MURDEROUS REGIME
BEFORE TREKKING THROUGH THE WAR-TORN JUNGLE TO FREEDOM.

DATE:
1975

SITUATION:
GENOCIDE

**CONDITION OF
CONFINEMENT:**
IN A FORCED LABOUR CAMP

**DURATION OF
CONFINEMENT:**
4½ YEARS

MEANS OF ESCAPE:
DECEPTION, WALKING
THROUGH A WAR ZONE

NO. OF ESCAPEES:
1

DANGERS:
EXECUTION, TORTURE,
STARVATION, EXHAUSTION

EQUIPMENT:
NONE

ABOVE RIGHT
Angkor Wat Temple, Siem Reap, Cambodia.

The life of an interpreter

Pran was born on 27 September 1942 in Siem Reap, Cambodia, near the temple complex of Angkor Wat, which is now a popular destination for backpackers. The area was then part of French Indochina, occupied by the Japanese.

Pran's father was a senior public works official and the boy enjoyed a comfortable upbringing. He learnt French at school and taught himself English. In 1960 Pran became an interpreter for the US military, a job he held for five years until the Americans left Cambodia. He then worked for a British film crew and in the travel industry.

Caught in the civil war crossfire

In 1970, the US was still heavily involved in the conflict in neighbouring Vietnam. With the backing of the US, the dictator Lon Nol seized power in Cambodia. Rising in opposition to Nol was the newly born Khmer Rouge, a hard line Communist group. Civil war was soon tearing Cambodia apart.

Tourism vanished almost overnight, and Pran moved with his family to the capital to look for employment. He began working with journalists and in 1972 became the personal interpreter and close friend of New York Times reporter Sydney Schanberg.

In the next few years the Khmer Rouge became ever more powerful and ruthless. By spring 1975 the US had withdrawn from Vietnam and Cambodia was becoming increasingly unstable. With Phnom Penh expected to fall any day, the US began evacuating its citizens.

On 12 April, US personnel left Phnom Penh. With the increasingly bloodthirsty Khmer Rouge on the doorstep, thousands of Cambodians were also desperate to leave. Pran managed to get his wife and their four children onto a US truck, but he decided to stay behind to help Schanberg cover the story.

Schanberg and Pran thought that when the Khmer Rouge had taken Phnom Penh there would at least be a form of peace. They could not have been more wrong. Gaining control was just the first step in the Khmer Rouge's strategy for a social revolution that would be defined by atrocities on an appalling scale.

A life-saving intervention

When the Khmer Rouge soldiers took the capital they went on a spree of looting, rape and indiscriminate killings on the streets. Schanberg and Pran were among several journalists observing the mayhem in a hospital when a squad of troops pulled up. The soldiers threatened the men, forcing them into an armoured vehicle. Schanberg and his Western colleagues complied, but Pran began arguing furiously with the troops. Schanberg initially thought that Pran was arguing because he did not want to get on the truck.

The journalists were later released and Schanberg found out how close he had come to death: the soldiers had been taking the Westerners away to shoot them. Pran had risked his neck by refusing to get on the truck – his intervention saved their lives.

Skulls from a mass grave of Khmer Rouge victims in Choeung Ek, the Killing Fields near Phnom Penh, Cambodia.

It was clear that Schanberg would have to leave. He tried to get Pran out as well by faking a German passport, but at the last minute the Khmer Rouge saw through the ploy and Pran was kept behind as his friend returned home.

Year Zero

The Khmer Rouge, under the extreme leadership of Pol Pot, began implementing a social plan of extraordinary scope and brutality. Their aim was to turn Cambodia into a classless, agrarian society by forcing the urban population into agricultural communes. The country isolated itself internationally and obliterated all signs of Western influence. People who wore glasses, perfume, makeup or even watches were executed. Teachers, merchants, doctors and other members of the educated classes were also killed. Schools, hospitals, banks and factories were all closed and the currency and financial system abolished. All religions were banned and all private property confiscated.

The new regime called itself Democratic Kampuchea. It decreed that 1975 was 'Year Zero'.

To avoid execution, Pran reinvented himself as a peasant.

He changed the way he spoke, restricting his vocabulary and adopting an uneducated accent. He hid all evidence that he had known Americans and claimed to have been a taxi driver. What little money he had he threw away and he also discarded his Western shirt and slacks, dressing instead in a peasant's simple attire. It was an act he would have to maintain every minute of every day for the next four and a half years.

Living a lie

Pran joined a forced labour farm 32 km (20 miles) from Siem Reap. He and other villagers had to perform backbreaking work in the rice paddies, often for twelve hours a day non-stop. At night they were indoctrinated in the political values of the new state. Many of his colleagues were executed, usually with a pickaxe to save bullets.

Estimates vary, but probably 1.5–2 million Cambodians were killed by the Khmer Rouge, around 30–40 per cent of the population.

Their food ration was just one tablespoon of rice per day. People were constantly dropping dead from

A mass grave of the Killing Fields victims in Choeung Ek, Cambodia.

THAILAND

LAOS

Nakhon Ratchasima (Korat)

Buriram

Ubon Ratchathani

Pakxé

④ THE KILLING FIELDS
Eventually he walks 96 km (60 miles) through the 'killing fields' and booby-trapped jungle to freedom in Thailand.

③ LABOUR FARM
He works on a forced-labour farm 32 km (20 miles) from Siem Reap.

Angkor Wat

Siemréab (Siem Reap)

Bătdâmbâng

Chanthaburi

① SIEM REAP
Dith Pran starts out as an interpreter in Siem Reap near the temples of Angkor Wat.

CAMBODIA

Tônlé Sap

Mekong

Kâmpóng Cham

PHNUM PÉNH (Phnom Penh)

Choeung Ek

② PHNUM PÉNH
He is working with journalist Sydney Schanberg when the Khmer Rouge seize power in 1970.

Tây Ninh

Thu Dâu Môt

Biên Hoa

Hô Chi Min (Saigon)

GULF OF THAILAND

Long Xuyên

Rach Gia

Cân Thơ

Vinh Long

Tân An

My Tho

Bên Tre

Vung Ta

Tra Vinh

Soc Trăng

Mouths of the Mekong

Ca Mau

Băc Liêu

VIETNAM

KILOMETRES 0   50   100   150
MILES 0   50   100

hunger. Pran and the other villagers resorted to eating bark, snakes, insects, snails and rats. Sometimes they were forced to eat the flesh of the recently deceased.

On one occasion, Pran tried to sneak out and eat some raw rice. He was caught. The guards made his fellow villagers beat him severely and leave him lying injured in a storm.

Despite the daily beatings, backbreaking labour and systematic starvation, Pran survived.

Sydney Schanberg received a Pulitzer Prize in 1976 for his Cambodia reporting, which he accepted on behalf of his friend Pran.

Meanwhile in New York, Schanberg was helping Pran's family, who had made it to the US. The reporter also contacted intermediaries at border camps in Thailand to circulate photographs of his lost friend. But for years there was no news of Pran.

There was a rumour that Pran had been fed to alligators, but this was untrue. It was his brother who had suffered that fate.

The Vietnamese restore control

By January 1979, Vietnam was a unified Communist nation and the paranoid Cambodian leadership feared its power. Pol Pot ordered pre-emptive military action; it was just the pretext the Vietnamese needed. They invaded Cambodia and removed the Khmer Rouge from power.

Pran went back to Siem Riep and found his hometown had been devastated. Wells were filled with skulls and bones; the fields around the town had become huge mass graves; fifty members of Pran's family had been killed.

The Vietnamese made him village chief, but when they learned of his US connections, Pran knew he had to try to escape.

A commemorative stupa filled with the skulls of the victims at Choeung Ek, Phnom Penh.

Walking to the west

On 29 July 1979 Pran set out to walk to Thailand across the 'killing fields' and through the jungle. His journey took him across 96 km (60 miles) of booby traps, unexploded bombs and past still-skirmishing Vietnamese and Khmer Rouge forces. His two companions were blown up by a land mine.

Exhausted and nearly starving, Pran crested a ridge on 3 October and saw a Red Cross tent at the edge of the jungle below him. Within a week he was in the arms of an overjoyed Sydney Schanberg who flew to join his friend in Thailand.

Aftermath

Pran moved to the United States and was reunited with his family. He got a job with The New York Times as a photojournalist, and became a US citizen in 1986. He died of pancreatic cancer in 2008, aged 65.

Dith Pran and Sydney Schanberg in New York, 28 November 1984.

SHIPWRECKS

The Trials of the *Wager*

In 1740 Commodore George Anson led a squadron of eight ships on a mission to seize a share of Spain's Pacific possessions. The sailors were ravaged by disease and pounded by storms and when one vessel was wrecked its crew faced a nightmare fight for survival on the savage Patagonian coast.

DATE:
1740–44

SITUATION:
Sea voyage

CONDITION OF CONFINEMENT:
On board overcrowded and disease-ridden ships; wrecked on shore

DURATION OF CONFINEMENT:
Several years, depending on the sailor

MEANS OF ESCAPE:
Sailing in lifeboats, trekking through jungle, by canoe

NO. OF ESCAPEES:
1 in 10 of the original crews

DANGERS:
Drowning, mutiny, murder, hunger, dehydration, disease

EQUIPMENT:
Some ship's stores, small boats

ABOVE RIGHT
Cape Horn, South America.

The voyage of pride and greed

It was 1739 and Great Britain was envious of the riches that Spain was milking from her New World empire: silver from Peru and Mexico, luxury goods from Manila, sugar, tobacco, dyes and spices from the Caribbean.

Britain had the sea power but not the trade agreements; action would have to be taken. Unfortunately for the 1,900 crew and troops enlisted for Commodore Anson's venture, it would be a scheme of action undone by greed and poor planning that would lead to death, misery, murder and disaster.

George Anson's mission was ambitious to say the least. He was to lead six warships through the fearsome waters of Cape Horn and up the west coast of South America where he was to capture Callao in Peru (the port that served Lima) and if possible take Lima as well. He was to then capture Panama, seizing any rich galleons that he could and lead a revolt of the Peruvians against Spanish colonial power.

He had a squadron of six warships: the *Centurion* (400 crew), *Gloucester* (300 crew), *Severn* (300 crew), *Pearl* (250 crew), *Wager* (120 crew), *Tryal* (70 crew). Two other vessels, the *Anna* and *Industry*, would carry supplies.

To achieve his goals Anson would also have the modest resource of 500 additional troops. But no regular troops were available so the 500 were to be drawn from the invalids of the Chelsea Hospital – men too sick, wounded or old for active duty. When these soldiers heard about the details of the proposed voyage, those able to run away promptly did. Only 259 came aboard, many on stretchers, and the numbers were made up with fresh recruits from the marines, most of who had yet to fire a gun.

Disease runs rampant

The squadron left England on 18 September 1740 and immediately encountered delays, finally reaching Madeira on 25 October. After taking three days at sea to transfer supplies, the *Industry* turned back on 20 November.

> **‹ By now, food had started to rot and the ships were infested with flies. ›**

The ships were overcrowded and typhus thrived in the hot, humid and unsanitary conditions. The men also came down with dysentery.

The squadron reached Isla de Santa Catarina off the coast of Brazil on 21 December and the sick were sent ashore. Anson then ordered the ships to be thoroughly cleaned. First the below-deck areas were scrubbed clean, then fires lit inside and the hatches closed so that the smoke would kill rats and other vermin. Finally, everything was washed down with vinegar.

The main mast of the *Tryal* needed repairs that took almost a month, far longer than Anson had hoped to stay. The men were stuck on shore all this time in makeshift tents and at the mercy of mosquitoes. It wasn't long before malaria joined the roll-call of diseases culling the men. The *Centurion* lost 28 men while in port and the number of sick taken back on board when they left on 18 January 1741 had risen from 80 to 96.

Soon after the ships started round Cape Horn on 7 March 1741 they were struck by another violent storm. Fighting gale force winds and huge seas while weakened by typhus and dysentery, the crew now also had to contend with the horrors of scurvy. One man who had been wounded at the Battle of the Boyne fifty years earlier but had made a complete recovery found that his wounds reopened and a broken bone fractured again. Hundreds of men died of various diseases in the weeks during and immediately after battling around the Horn.

> **‹ Life is not worth pursuing at the expense of such hardships. ›**

The wreck of the *Wager*

The squadron was scattered after it rounded Cape Horn. All the vessels would go on to face further hardship, but the men aboard the *Wager* probably faced the stiffest trials.

The captain, David Cheap, had been sick during much of the voyage and was below decks when the storm scattered the squadron near Cape Noir. He then mistakenly sailed the ship into a large bay, which blocked their passage north. Struggling to turn the boat around with just twelve men fit for duty, a large wave smashed into the ship. Cheap tumbled down a ladder and dislocated his shoulder. The surgeon gave him opium and he retired below.

Instead of taking command, his lieutenant Baynes started drinking. The ship was dashed onto the rocks and discipline completely broke down as the crew helped themselves to liquor and arms.

Of the ship's original 300 crew and troops, 140 were now alive on the beach. Cheap tried to maintain control but the men were furious, blaming him for the loss of the ship and their current awful situation. They salvaged a little food from the wreck, but it was now winter and the men had little shelter against the driving winds and rain. Cheap only made things worse by shooting a drunken sailor and refusing to allow him any treatment. His victim lingered in agony for two weeks before dying, turning many of his remaining supporters against him.

They would all die eventually if they stayed where they were; their only hope was to take to sea again in the ship's boats which had not been damaged. The ship's carpenter set about lengthening the longboat and adding a deck so that most of the men would fit on board.

But there was a disagreement about where to go next, and a mutiny was brewing. Cheap insisted on heading to the rendezvous of Socorro Island, off the coast of Mexico, to find Anson. The gunner John Bulkeley thought their only viable option was to head 640 km (400 miles) south to the treacherous Strait of Magellan and sail north to Brazil. He convinced half the men to join him.

Cheap tried to win supporters for his plan with bribes of liquor, but when the modified longboat was ready on 9 October 1741, Bulkeley had him arrested on the charge of murder.

The *Centurion* off Cape Horn, South America.

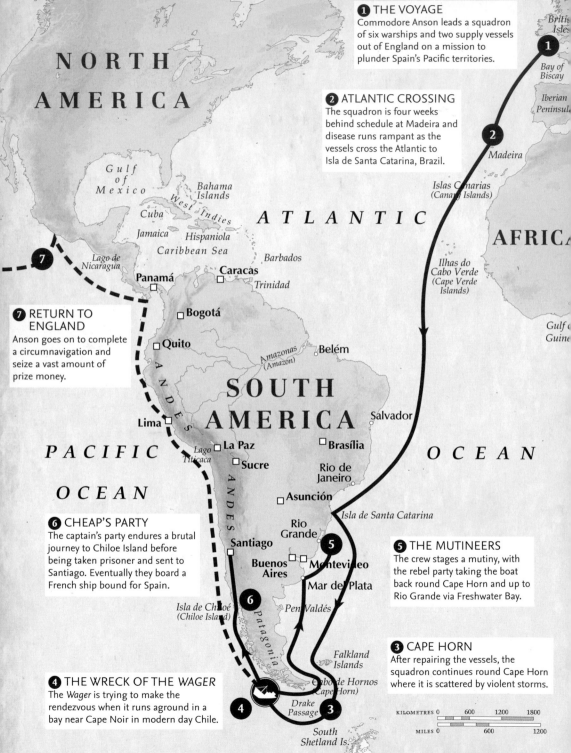

❶ THE VOYAGE
Commodore Anson leads a squadron of six warships and two supply vessels out of England on a mission to plunder Spain's Pacific territories.

❷ ATLANTIC CROSSING
The squadron is four weeks behind schedule at Madeira and disease runs rampant as the vessels cross the Atlantic to Isla de Santa Catarina, Brazil.

❼ RETURN TO ENGLAND
Anson goes on to complete a circumnavigation and seize a vast amount of prize money.

❻ CHEAP'S PARTY
The captain's party endures a brutal journey to Chiloe Island before being taken prisoner and sent to Santiago. Eventually they board a French ship bound for Spain.

❺ THE MUTINEERS
The crew stages a mutiny, with the rebel party taking the boat back round Cape Horn and up to Rio Grande via Freshwater Bay.

❸ CAPE HORN
After repairing the vessels, the squadron continues round Cape Horn where it is scattered by violent storms.

❹ THE WRECK OF THE WAGER
The *Wager* is trying to make the rendezvous when it runs aground in a bay near Cape Noir in modern day Chile.

NORTH AMERICA

SOUTH AMERICA

AFRICA

ATLANTIC OCEAN

PACIFIC OCEAN

British Isles

Bay of Biscay

Iberian Peninsula

Madeira

Islas Canarias (Canary Islands)

Ilhas do Cabo Verde (Cape Verde Islands)

Gulf of Guinea

Gulf of Mexico

Bahama Islands

West Indies

Cuba

Jamaica

Hispaniola

Caribbean Sea

Barbados

Trinidad

Lago de Nicaragua

Panamá

Caracas

Bogotá

Quito

Amazonas (Amazon)

Belém

Salvador

Brasília

Lima

Lago Titicaca

La Paz

Sucre

Rio de Janeiro

Asunción

Rio Grande

Santiago

Rio de Janeiro

Buenos Aires

Montevideo

Mar del Plata

Pen. Valdés

Isla de Chiloé (Chiloe Island)

Patagonia

Falkland Islands

Cabo de Hornos (Cape Horn)

Drake Passage

South Shetland Is.

KILOMETRES 0   600   1200   1800

MILES 0   600   1200

Four days later, the modified longboat, now-christened *Speedwell*, sailed south with fifty-nine men aboard under the command of Lieutenant Baynes. Following this was a cutter with twelve men, a barge with ten and another small boat with Cheap, a lieutenant and the surgeon.

About a dozen men had fled the camp (to avoid Cheap's frequent punishments) and were left behind on the island.

But more storms hit the boats, and the cutter was lost. The men on the barge decided to throw their lot in with Captain Cheap, so the mutineers sailed off on the *Speedwell* leaving them to their fate.

The Pacific coastline of Chiloe Island, Chile, South America.

The mutineers

The *Speedwell* was the biggest boat, but this worked against the mutineers: it was too dangerous to land the vessel to look for food. Men had to risk their necks and swim through the icy water to do this job. They bickered over navigation, currents and weather, and it took a month to reach the Atlantic and many men died.

On 14 January 1742 the *Speedwell* entered Freshwater Bay, in what is today the resort city of Mar del Plata. Eight men swam ashore and found fresh water and seals. As they looked back out to sea they saw the boat leaving without them, Bulkeley claimed it was the wind; the men knew they had been abandoned to save rations.

Eventually the *Speedwell* reached the Portuguese waters of the Rio Grande on 28 January. Only thirty men were still alive and they were little more than skeletons.

The eight men left at Freshwater Bay spent a month eating seal meat before they decided to make for Buenos Aires, 480 km (300 miles) further north. After a couple of failed attempts at this journey, two of the sailors murdered a pair of their fellows and ran off with the group's guns, flints and other supplies.

The remaining four were later enslaved by Indians.

Cheap's party

Meanwhile, Captain Cheap found that the deserters had returned to the camp, putting him in charge of a party of nineteen men. They tried rowing up the coast but lashing rain, brutal headwinds and huge waves made it very hard going. One boat was lost and a man drowned. It was impossible for everyone to fit in the remaining boat, so four marines were left ashore with muskets to fend for themselves. With one more death on the journey, there were now thirteen in the group.

A local Indian agreed to guide these men up the coast to Chiloe Island on payment of their boat on arrival. But three more men died en route and six of the seamen stole the boat never to be seen again. This left Cheap with three other officers and the Indian, who was finally persuaded to take them on by canoe in return for their only remaining possession, a musket.

They made it to Chiloe Island only to be taken prisoner by the Spanish. Eventually they were moved to the capital of Santiago where they were released on parole. They stayed there

till late 1744 when three of them joined a French ship bound for Spain.

Of the 300 men originally on the *Wager*, twenty-nine crew and seven marines made it back to England.

Return to England

Whilst the men of the *Wager* were facing their ordeal, Anson continued with his journey, crossing the Pacific and taking many ships. One galleon was carrying 1,313,843 pieces of eight and 35,682 ounces of silver.

Of the 1,900 men who set out in the original squadron, only 188 made it back to England.

Anson became famous and was invited to meet the King. Huge crowds turned out to see the treasure he took as it was paraded through the streets of London.

He personally took three-eighths of the galleon's £91,000 (about £130 million today) prize money and earned £719 (about £100,000 today) as captain during the three year, nine month voyage. A seaman would have earned around £300 in prize money (about £440,000 today), equivalent to 20 years' wages.

Anson later became an Admiral.

After the Mutiny

When Fletcher Christian cast Captain Bligh and eighteen loyal sailors adrift in the Bounty's tiny, overcrowded longboat with few provisions, he knew they were as good as dead. But, in an astonishing feat of seamanship, Bligh guided them across 3,618 nautical miles (6,700 km) of treacherous seas to reach safety forty-seven days later.

DATE:
1789

SITUATION:
Mutiny

CONDITION OF CONFINEMENT:
Cast adrift in a longboat

DURATION OF CONFINEMENT:
47 days

MEANS OF ESCAPE:
Exceptional seamanship, discipline

NO. OF ESCAPEES:
18

DANGERS:
Drowning, starvation, killed by natives

EQUIPMENT:
Some supplies, a compass, a quadrant

ABOVE RIGHT
Tropical beach on Tahiti.

An unfamiliar tale

The story of the mutiny on the *Bounty* is a familiar one: the valiant mate Fletcher Christian leads the crew in a justified mutiny against the brutal Captain Bligh. But the truth is both less simple and more interesting, and includes a fascinating chapter that is often omitted: Bligh's supreme captaincy of the cast-adrift longboat across 3,618 nautical miles (6,700 km; 4,165 miles) of open ocean to safety.

The voyage out

On 23 December 1787, *Bounty* sailed from England for Tahiti (then known as 'Otaheite') on a mission to procure breadfruit for transport to the West Indies. The crew ran into atrocious weather at Cape Horn, which blocked their progress. Bligh duly turned the ship about and went round the world the other way, heading east round the Cape of Good Hope and crossing the Indian Ocean. After ten months at sea, *Bounty* reached Tahiti on 26 October 1788.

All is ship shape

For five months all went well. Bligh and his crew collected 1,015 breadfruit plants and stored them safely on the *Bounty*.

> **I had a Ship in the most perfect order and well Stored with every necessary both for Service and Health.**

By 4 April 1789 the *Bounty* was full of cargo, supplied with provisions and in good trim. It was ready to set sail for England. But half of its crew were not.

Tempted by paradise

Bligh has long had a reputation as a harsh disciplinarian, but this may have been exaggerated over the years. He certainly had an acid tongue and did not suffer fools gladly, but he was brave under fire and an outstanding seaman. He was also quite lenient compared with other British naval officers when it came to punishing wayward men.

He had allowed the crew to live ashore with the Tahitians and the men had perhaps enjoyed a little too much tropical hospitality. The seamen sported native tattoos; many had fallen for island women.

Bligh himself wrote in his log: 'It is certainly true that no effect could take place without a cause but here it is equally certain that no cause could justify such an effect. It, however, may very naturally be asked what could be the reason for such a revolt, in answer to which I can only conjecture that they have ideally assured themselves of a more happy life among the Otaheitans than they could possibly have in England, which joined to some female connection, has most likely been the leading cause of the whole business.'

The revolt in paradise

At daybreak on 28 April 1789, Fletcher Christian (originally the master's mate but promoted to Lieutenant by Bligh on the voyage out) made his move, mustering an armed party and seizing Bligh while the captain slept. The mutiny was well planned: Christian also placed guards stationed outside the cabins of officers whom he knew would be loyal to the captain. Bligh was dragged at bayonet-point onto deck in just his nightshirt.

> ❛ Christian… with several others came into my cabin while I was asleep, and seizing me, holding naked bayonets at my breast, tied my hands behind my back, and threatened instant destruction if I uttered a word. ❜

Bligh berated Christian for his villainy and appealed to the crew to reconsider, to no avail. The mutineers soon had control of the ship's arms and Bligh was put into the launch with five loyal officers. Thirteen other men voluntarily joined their captain.

The party of nineteen were then cast adrift 30 nautical miles (56 km; 35 miles) off Tofua, a tiny island in what is now known as Tonga. With nineteen men in it the tiny boat – just 7 m (23 ft) long – sat so heavy in the water that the gunwales were just a few inches above the water. Four other sailors wanted to join Bligh but there was no room in the boat.

One of the men had managed to gather some clothes for Bligh. For provisions they had sixteen pieces of pork, three bottles of wine, five quarts of rum, 68 kg (150 lbs) of bread and 106 litres (28 gallons) of water: enough for a few days.

Christian allowed them to take four cutlasses but no firearms. He refused Bligh's request for his maps and navigational equipment.

More hostility

The captain's party immediately set out towards Tofua in search of supplies. But the natives were hostile and after a couple of days they realised that the Englishmen had no weapons and launched an all-out assault, attacking the crew with clubs and stones. They killed one sailor and injured almost all the others, forcing them to scramble back into their boat and push out to sea. The natives continued the pursuit in canoes, stoning the sailors with painful accuracy, and it was only when night fell that they were able to completely escape.

The captain to the rescue

The men begged Bligh to take them towards home and now their lives were literally in Bligh's hands: only he had the knowledge and skill to navigate them to safety. Luckily for them, Bligh was a superlative seaman. He had joined the Royal Navy at the age of 7 as a cabin boy and had sailed with Captain Cook on his third voyage to the Pacific in 1776, under whose tutelage he had perfected his navigational skills.

The captain spoke plainly about their chances: unless they could make it to the nearest European outpost, which was in Timor, 3,618 nautical miles (6,700 km; 4,165 miles) away, they would certainly die.

Only Bligh knew how hard this was going to be. The journey would be arduous and their situation was more desperate than before: they had lost a portion of their provisions in

Jagged rocks surround the rim of Bounty Bay, Pitcairn Island.

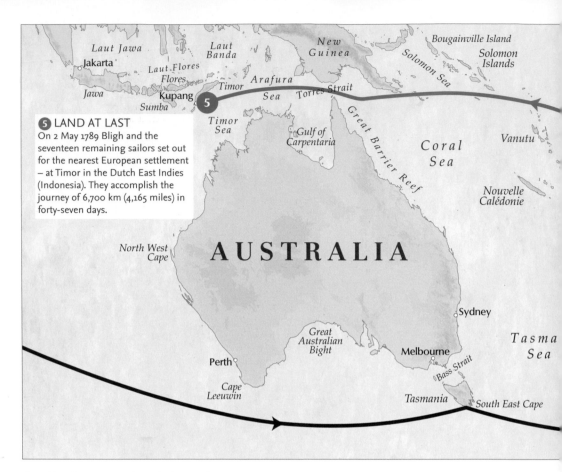

5 LAND AT LAST

On 2 May 1789 Bligh and the seventeen remaining sailors set out for the nearest European settlement – at Timor in the Dutch East Indies (Indonesia). They accomplish the journey of 6,700 km (4,165 miles) in forty-seven days.

the pell-mell escape. Bligh made the crew solemnly swear to a ration of just one ounce of bread a day and 142 ml (1/4 pint) of water.

Sailing blind

With the oath fresh in their minds he set course for Timor across a sea that was then little known. Bligh had a quadrant and compass but Christian had taken his maps, charts, instruments and watch. The only things between them and certain death were Bligh's navigational skills, knowledge of the sea and memory of the area they were in from previous study of his maps.

Bligh steered them to the west-north-west and almost immediately they ran into ferocious gales and heavy rains. Huge waves constantly

threatened to swamp the boat and the men had to bail for their lives. They passed Fiji but dared not stop: without weapons Bligh feared they would be massacred on arrival. Indeed, they were chased by natives whom they believed to be cannibals.

Land at last

But on the 28 May they sighted the then-uninhabited northern coast of Australia, passing it to the north on 4 June and steering for Timor.

Now the men were glad of Bligh's iron discipline: although they were at death's door, without his foresight and strict rationing they would have crossed that portal already. They sighted land on 12 June and two days later Bligh brought the longboat into

the port of Kupang in the Dutch East Indies (now Indonesia). Despite being severely malnourished, every man who had set out from Tofua got out of the boat alive. The journey had taken them forty-seven days and they had travelled 3,618 nautical miles (6,700 km; 4,165 miles).

> **❛ Perhaps a more miserable set of beings were never seen. ❜**

Out of the frying pan...

Meanwhile the mutineers tried to settle on the island of Tubuai, but after suffering three months of attacks by ferocious natives, they returned to Tahiti. Most of the mutineers decided to stay there.

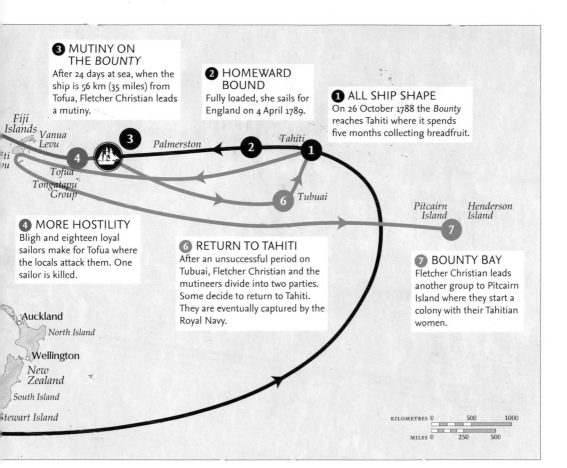

❸ MUTINY ON THE BOUNTY
After 24 days at sea, when the ship is 56 km (35 miles) from Tofua, Fletcher Christian leads a mutiny.

❷ HOMEWARD BOUND
Fully loaded, she sails for England on 4 April 1789.

❶ ALL SHIP SHAPE
On 26 October 1788 the *Bounty* reaches Tahiti where it spends five months collecting breadfruit.

Fiji Islands
Vanua Levu
Palmerston
Tahiti
Tofua
Tongatapu Group
Tubuai
Pitcairn Island
Henderson Island

❹ MORE HOSTILITY
Bligh and eighteen loyal sailors make for Tofua where the locals attack them. One sailor is killed.

❻ RETURN TO TAHITI
After an unsuccessful period on Tubuai, Fletcher Christian and the mutineers divide into two parties. Some decide to return to Tahiti. They are eventually captured by the Royal Navy.

❼ BOUNTY BAY
Fletcher Christian leads another group to Pitcairn Island where they start a colony with their Tahitian women.

Auckland
North Island
Wellington
New Zealand
South Island
Stewart Island

KILOMETRES 0   500   1000
MILES 0   250   500

Fletcher Christian took the remaining eight crewmen as well as six Tahitian men, eleven women and one baby, and sailed on in *Bounty*. They passed through the Fiji and Cook Islands, but feared that the Royal Navy would find them there. Desperate for a safe haven, on 15 January 1790 they rediscovered Pitcairn Island, which had been lost from the Royal Navy's charts, and settled there. To avoid detection and remove the temptation of escape, they burnt the ship on 23 January 1790 in what is now called Bounty Bay. The Pitcairn colony started out well, but in 1793, a conflict broke out between the mutineers and the Tahitian men who sailed with them. Fletcher Christian and four other sailors were killed by

the Tahitians, all of whom were also killed, some by the widows of the murdered mutineers. In 1808, when an American ship visited Pitcairn Island, only one sailor, nine women, and some children still lived.

Fourteen of the mutineers who remained on Tahiti were later captured by the Royal Navy. Four died in a shipwreck on the way back to England. Of the rest, four were acquitted (these were the men who had wanted to get into the overcrowded longboat with Bligh), three were convicted but later acquitted and three were hanged.

The loyal men return

Bligh and his loyal sailors were welcomed in Kupang where most of

them recovered from their ordeal, although five men died, mostly from malaria, in the next few months.

Bligh reached England on 15 March 1790, two years and eleven weeks after he left. In October 1790, Bligh was honourably acquitted at the court-martial inquiring into the loss of the *Bounty*. For him the mutiny was little more than a blip in what was an illustrious career. He would go on to command eleven other ships, become Governor of New South Wales and eventually achieve the rank of Vice Admiral.

In 1791 he went on a second voyage to transport breadfruit from Tahiti; this one was successful and breadfruit is a popular food in the West Indies to this day.

Shipwreck, Slavery and the Burning Sand

On 28 August 1815 the US brig *Commerce* was wrecked on the western coast of the Sahara. Its eleven crewmen survived but, crippled by the brutal desert conditions and enslaved by hostile tribesmen, they faced a savage battle for survival that would tear their flesh and nearly crush their spirits.

DATE:
1815

SITUATION:
Shipwrecked on the Saharan coast

CONDITION OF CONFINEMENT:
Enslaved by nomads, trapped in the desert

DURATION OF CONFINEMENT:
2½ months

MEANS OF ESCAPE:
Sailing, walking, riding camels

NO. OF ESCAPEES:
7

DANGERS:
Capture, dehydration, murder, starvation, sunburn

EQUIPMENT:
Some supplies at first; later, nothing

LEFT
Sahara Desert, Western Sahara.

ABOVE RIGHT
Essaouira (Swearah), an old Portuguese city in Morocco.

Trading places

It was early May in 1815 and Captain James Riley of the US brig *Commerce* was ready for adventure.

The War of 1812 against the British had severely disrupted his usual trans-Atlantic shipping business but it was finally over. Now it was time to get back to work and earn some money; he and his ten crewmen had families to support.

They cast off from Middletown in Connecticut and sailed to New Orleans to pick up a cargo of flour and tobacco. From there they crossed the Atlantic in six weeks, arriving at Gibraltar where they sold their goods and loaded up with brandy, wine and Spanish dollars.

Their plan now was to sail down West Africa towards the Cape Verde islands to trade for salt. With any luck and a fair wind they would be back in New England by harvest-time, their pockets bulging with their wages.

But as they passed Rabat, Morocco, thick fog cloaked the ship. Riley couldn't see land or navigate. He was forced to judge their progress by dead reckoning: taking a fix and then using the ship's speed to calculate their position, a technique rendered inaccurate by strong currents or winds.

On 28 August the clouds parted long enough for Riley to take observations. Aghast, he discovered they were 190 km (120 miles) further south than he had thought they were. Was it possible that they had accidentally threaded their way through an 80-km (50-mile) wide channel in the dark foggy night, missing Tenerife with its 3,600 m (12,000 ft) mountain range entirely?

In actual fact, they were much further east, nearer the West African coast and caught in the grip of the strong Canary Current. This was a very dangerous stretch of coast: at Cape Bojador alone there had been thirty known wrecks between 1790 and 1806.

It was a dark night with no moon. The sea was high and the wind violent. They sounded 219 m (120 fathoms) but Riley still had a nagging sense of something wrong. Then, at nine o'clock, he heard a roar that made his guts sink: breakers. A sickeningly violent jolt threw every hand to the deck. They were being swept onto rocks – every sailor's worst nightmare.

Waves crashed over the deck, flooding the ship and they struck the rocks, the vessel jamming fast. They just had time to load provisions, water, charts and Riley's navigational aids into a boat, then the crew scrabbled ashore.

With dawn came a break in the weather. Riley assessed their situation. All eleven crewmen were alive. They had food, drink, some tools and 2,000 Spanish dollars. The lifeboat had been damaged, but they could repair it, wait for calmer seas, and set out to find a friendly ship.

Just then they saw a man approaching them along the sand. His hair and beard were matted and his eyes were wild. He did not look at all friendly.

Trading people

The Arab tribes, Sahrawis, who lived a harsh life in this unforgiving land, believed that shipwrecks were rightfully theirs. Sailors told many tales of them subjugating Christian infidels who were stranded: they would burn what they didn't want from the wreck and then enslave the crew to a life in some of the most brutal living conditions imaginable. That was simply the way things were in the desert.

The wild man approached and started snatching things from the wreckage. The temptation to fight him off was strong, but he would only return with others. They let him take some goods. He left but soon came back with more wild-looking people –too many to fight.

The crew had to watch in impotent despair as the Sahrawis plundered their goods and burned their charts and instruments.

As the raiders were occupied, the crew tried to escape on the damaged lifeboat. The Sahrawis managed to take one man captive. The Captain traded himself for this prisoner then bravely made his own bolt for freedom. Somehow the eleven men made it to sea in the boat.

Life in the boat

The damage to the boat meant they had to constantly bail water. With only improvised sails they were at the mercy of the current. They would try to head out to sea where they might meet another vessel, but the ocean was vast and their chances would be slim.

The sailors had rescued a pig, the only animal to make it from the wreck alive, and after three days adrift they killed it. They drank its blood and ate its meat, skin and bones too. The relentless African sun gave them enough of a fear of thirst to make them fill their empty water and wine bottles with urine.

More stormy weather hit them with gale force winds driving high waves over the boat. Only constant bailing kept them afloat.

They mixed urine with water and sipped it. Some men had hardly any clothing and the sun burned them so badly the skin came off in sheets. They were also rubbed raw from the friction with wood and saltwater. The boat was falling apart from the pounding.

After four days they hadn't seen a single other vessel and they agreed to head back to the coast, rather than face certain drowning.

After four more days they landed on a tiny beach backed by a cliff. They

A camel train in the unforgiving Sahara Desert landscape.

had only some salt pork, a few bottles of water and urine and some silver. The urine was worth more to them than the silver.

The cliffs that formed the coast were almost impassable. In a whole day's walking and climbing they managed only 6.4 km (4 miles).

> **‘ A harder day's travel was never made by man. ’**

Eventually they hauled themselves to the top of a cliff to gaze out on a barren plain without tree or shrub as far as the eye could see. They were at the western edge of the Sahara, the world's largest desert. It rolled away from them for 4,830 km (3,000 miles) to the Red Sea and stretched 1,930 km (1,200 miles) from the Sahel savannah in the south to the Atlas Mountains in the north.

By the time Riley and his men reached the desert, the shared urine which they were drinking had passed through their bodies twelve times.

Finally they saw a campfire. After waiting till dawn so that they didn't unduly alarm anyone they crossed a massive dune and saw an Arab tribe at a well. Exhausted, they threw themselves submissively at the tribe's feet.

The Arabs tore their clothes from their bodies and fought over these new possessions ferociously, wounding each other with their scimitars. The men were now slaves of the Oulad Bou Sbaa, a notoriously warlike desert tribe.

They drank from the cattle trough, taking on about half a gallon of green water without rising. Diarrhoea and violent cramps instantly seized their bodies. For the first time in days, they began sweating.

> **‘ Our skins seemed actually to fry like meat before the fire. ’**

They were now raging with hunger, but their new masters had nothing to offer them. Nomadic Arabs rarely ate solid food. Their staple fare was *zrig*,

camel's milk mixed with water – 0.7 litres (1½ pints) of this a day was all the nourishment the slaves could expect.

A savage journey

The crew were now divided up among different masters and they began a long, brutally painful ride on camels to the next well. The men's clothing had been stripped from them and their white skins were naked in the burning Saharan sun.

> **‘ I searched for a stone intending, if I could find a loose one sufficiently large, to knock out my own brains with it. ’**

The Bou Sbaa forced them to sleep outside their tents on the open stony ground. The first mate was so badly burned that the inside of his legs 'hung in strings of torn and chafed flesh'.

They plunged on for more than a week, covering 48 km (30 miles) a day southeast into the desert, but they found no water. Even the nomads were suffering. They ate a few roots and herbs, but their water was running out and the camel's milk began to fail.

Riley had been pricking his leg with a thorn to keep track of time. On 18 September the Bou Sbaa held a *yemma* or tribal meeting. They decided to return to the well by the sea. They could find no water here. The sailors were about to do the 320 km (200 mile) journey all over again.

Now the seamen began to suffer as they had never suffered before. They tried to eat tiny desert snails but their bodies didn't have enough water to digest them. The only thing they could get to drink was camel's urine. At one point two of the men greedily devoured a cyst taken from a camel. Deranged by hunger, others were reduced to eating the peeling skin from their arms, biting off chunks of their own flesh.

The desert trader

Riley was sold to a man named Sidi Hamet for two dollars' worth of goods. By now Riley could make himself understood in Arabic and as he told Hamet about the family he had left behind, tears filled in his eyes. Desert-hardened men did not cry, but Riley saw that his words made Hamet well up too. Riley sensed a sliver of hope.

The captain told his new master a bold lie. He said he had a friend in Swearah, the largest sizeable town, who would ransom him for 100 Spanish dollars. But he actually knew no one there.

Hamet was tempted – he owed his ruthless father-in-law, Sheik Ali, a large sum of money. Hamet agreed to try to ransom Riley, but he warned that he would personally cut his throat if he found him to be lying. He would be undertaking a dangerous journey by going to Swearah with white slaves: for 1,300 km (800 miles) they would be vulnerable to bandits and warlords, and sheikhs who would insist on tribute for transporting the Christians.

Riley also persuaded Hamet to buy four of his shipmates. He promised his consul friend would redeem them too. Hamet used up all of his money doing so. His very last purchase was an old male camel, which he slaughtered to feed the sailors for the journey to Swearah.

But the sailors didn't get much meat. Desert tradition meant that anyone and everyone was allowed to share in the feast. When the rest of the tribe descended on the carcass Riley and the others had to make do with some of the blood and a drink from the camel's rumen. This is the creature's first stomach, which held the lumpy green semi-digested soup that the camel would have later regurgitated as cud.

Sidi Hamet had to share more than a meal: now all the nomads knew he had slaves and what he was intending to do with them.

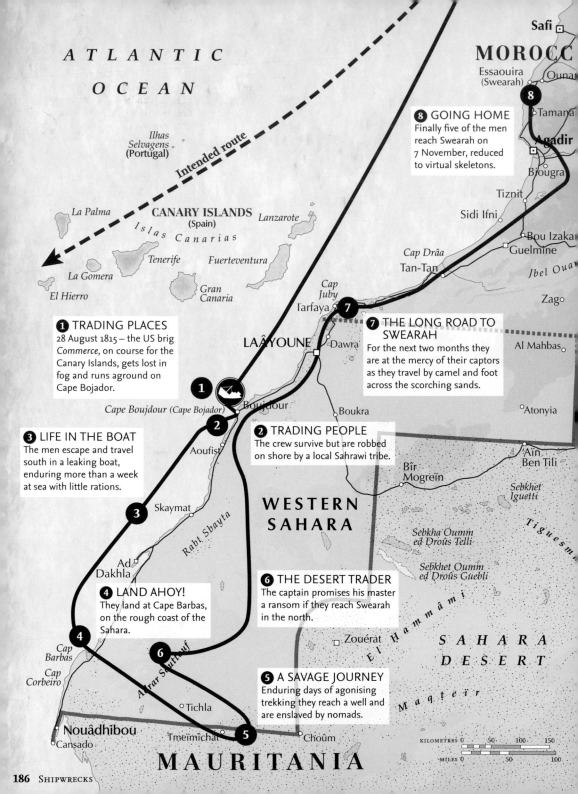

ATLANTIC
OCEAN

MOROCC

*Ilhas
Selvagens*
(Portugal)

Safi

Essaouira
(Swearah)

Ouna

8 GOING HOME
Finally five of the men
reach Swearah on
7 November, reduced
to virtual skeletons.

Tamana

Agadir

CANARY ISLANDS
(Spain)

Islas   Canarias

Lanzarote

B'ougra

La Palma

Tiznit

Tenerife

Fuerteventura

Sidi Ifni

La Gomera

Gran
Canaria

Bou Izaka

El Hierro

*Cap
Drâa*
Tan-Tan

Guelmine

Jbel Oua

Zago

*Cap
Juby*
Tarfaya

7

1 TRADING PLACES
28 August 1815 – the US brig
Commerce, on course for the
Canary Islands, gets lost in
fog and runs aground on
Cape Bojador.

LAÂYOUNE

Dawra

**7 THE LONG ROAD TO
SWEARAH**
For the next two months they
are at the mercy of their captors
as they travel by camel and foot
across the scorching sands.

Al Mahbas

1

Boujdour

Cape Boujdour (Cape Bojador)

Boukra

2

2 TRADING PEOPLE
The crew survive but are robbed
on shore by a local Sahrawi tribe.

Atonyia

3 LIFE IN THE BOAT
The men escape and travel
south in a leaking boat,
enduring more than a week
at sea with little rations.

Aoufist

Aïn
Ben Tili

Bîr
Mogreïn

*Sebkhet
Iguetti*

3

Skaymat

**WESTERN
SAHARA**

Rabt Sbayta

*Sebkha Oumm
ed Droûs Telli*

Tiguesm

Ad
Dakhla

*Sebkhet Oumm
ed Droûs Guebli*

6 THE DESERT TRADER
The captain promises his master
a ransom if they reach Swearah
in the north.

4 LAND AHOY!
They land at Cape Barbas,
on the rough coast of the
Sahara.

4

*Cap
Barbas*

*Cap
Corbeiro*

6

Zouérat

El Hammâmi

**S A H A R A
D E S E R T**

Afrar Souttouf

5 A SAVAGE JOURNEY
Enduring days of agonising
trekking they reach a well and
are enslaved by nomads.

Nouâdhibou

Cansado

Tichla

Maqteir

Tmeimichat

5

Choûm

KILOMETRES 0   50   100   150

MILES 0   50   100

MAURITANIA

The long road to Swearah

It was 27 September, nearly a month since the sailors had been shipwrecked. Hamet left the Bou Sbaa who were heading back to the coast and struck out east, deeper into the desert to avoid as many other humans as possible.

Although he had shown some feeling towards Riley, he was still a man of the desert who pushed his slaves hard. It was only after many more days of hard riding that they found more water.

> **The remaining flesh on our posteriors, and inside of our thighs and legs, was so beat, and literally pounded to pieces, that scarcely any remained.**

The camels had not drunk for twenty days and each beast took on 227 litres (60 gallons). They would need the water: as Hamet turned northwest the desert changed from rocky barrenness to dunes hundreds of feet high.

Within three days of having all the water they wanted, Riley and his four crewmen were dried to husks again. A two-day windstorm pulverized them to the point of madness, the whipping sand nearly blinding them and rubbing their sunburnt skin to a bloody mess.

It was now mid-October and they were walking through sand so hot it felt like embers. Riley collapsed one evening in a near-comatose state. He awoke near midnight to hear the noise of another hurricane wind approaching them. Eventually, to his astonishment, Riley realised it was the sea. They were back by the coast near Cape Bojador where their misfortunes had begun. Hamet pushed them on.

One of the sailors ate some weeds against Riley's advice and was poisoned. He lagged behind and the traders beat him – they had to move fast if they were to avoid the bandits

who lurked in this area. At one point Hamet's brother was going to execute the man and Riley stepped in and butted him, inflaming his anger.

Hamet stopped the killing and calmed his brother. He respected Riley's boldness and feeling for his men.

> **Some of my comrades, as if their taste had become depraved by the rage of hunger, declared that putrid meat was far preferable to fresh.**

They reached Wednoon where Hamet gave the men a share in a honeycomb he had bought. The men wolfed down the honey, the waxy comb and even the young bees that were still in the cells, tears of joy rolling down their sunken cheeks.

Now they had to pass through the territory of the notorious Sidi Hashem, a greedy overlord who demanded tribute from traders. This was a land of bandits and cutthroats.

A posse of thieves duly harassed them, but when they survived the encounter, Hamet became convinced that Allah was with Riley, and he began to look even more favourably on the captain.

The bluff is called

When they were within a few days' ride of Swearah, Hamet made Riley write a letter to his consul friend to ask for his ransom. Not only did Riley not know the man, but the consul was English and Riley was American; the two nations had only recently made peace.

The one advantage Riley had was that none of the men around him could read his words. He poured his heart and soul into the letter, begging the unknown consul for aid and leaving the issue of his nationality vague.

However, as Hamet took the note to the consul, he had to leave the sailors. Despite being so close to salvation, the scheming Sheik Ali

chose this moment to arrive and stake his own claim for the men.

It took much plotting, counter-plotting and bold effrontery from Sidi Hamet and his allies to scare off his powerful father-in-law and get the ransom that would earn the sailors their freedom.

After two months of trekking the men were so exhausted they could barely stay upright.

One day the emaciated Riley rounded a hill and looked up to see the dreamlike walls and towers of a city on a low peninsula in the distance. Anchored just off the town was a brig flying the Union Jack. Ten months' before, seeing those colours would have enraged the Americans, now it made them drop to their knees and weep with joy.

As the sailors lay numbly looking out at the picturesque scene, an English gentleman in an immaculate riding coat with tails stepped up and held out a hand. It was the consul, William Willshire. 'Come my friends, let us go to the city', he said.

Going home

Riley and his four companions reached Swearah on 7 November. They sailed to Gibraltar and then on to the United States. Riley was reunited with his family on 19 March 1816.

Two more sailors from the *Commerce* were eventually ransomed by different Arab masters and also made it home.

The other four men were never heard from again.

Riley wrote a bestselling book about their exploits and the survivors became famous. However, they were to pay a heavy price. When Riley came out of the desert his weight had dropped from 109 kg (240 lb) to just 41 kg (90 lb) and all the men suffered from health problems for the rest of their lives. Two sailors died within seven years of returning home.

The Whale and the Pacific

In 1820, the crew of the whaler *Essex* abandoned ship after being rammed by a huge whale in the South Pacific. For nearly three months they drifted in open boats with few supplies. Racked with hunger and madness they were reduced to cannibalism in an effort to survive a horrific journey before eventually reaching the Chilean coast.

DATE:
1820

SITUATION:
Ship sunk by a whale

CONDITION OF CONFINEMENT:
Marooned on an uninhabited island; adrift in open boats

DURATION OF CONFINEMENT:
90/95 days

MEANS OF ESCAPE:
Cannibalism

NO. OF ESCAPEES:
8

DANGERS:
Drowning, hunger, dehydration, being shot and eaten

EQUIPMENT:
Some ship's equipment, weapons

ABOVE RIGHT
A sperm whale blowing at sea.

Hard work on the open sea

The whaling industry was a vital part of life in the nineteenth century. Whale oil provided fuel for lamps and candle wax, and spermaceti had many pharmaceutical uses. Whaling offered a solid financial reward to men who had no cultural scruples about killing cetaceans.

But it was a brutally hard life.

The men knew they would face almost daily dangers: towering seas, savage gales and hungry icebergs.

The American whaling industry was based in Nantucket, Massachusetts, but the richest whaling grounds were in the South Pacific. This meant the men faced an arduous journey of 6,500 nautical miles (12,000 km; 7,460 miles) through the North and South Atlantic Oceans and round the notorious Cape Horn before they even started work. When the *Essex* left Nantucket,

they accepted that they would not see their families for two and a half years.

What they couldn't have guessed is the tortures and sufferings that one of the beasts that they normally killed with impunity would bring down upon them.

The whale that fought back

The *Essex* was small for whaleships of the time, although she had recently been refitted. She was 27 m (87 ft) long, measured 238 tons, and was captained by 28-year old George Pollard, Jr. She sailed out of Nantucket on 12 August 1819.

Just two days out of port, the ship was almost sunk by a violent squall, which the crew considered a bad omen. The ship reached Cape Horn on 18 January 1820, but it took five weeks for the *Essex* to navigate these dangerous waters and reach the South Pacific.

Once there, the voyage initially went well, with the ship hunting successfully until 20 November.

On that fateful day, the *Essex* had found a pod of sperm whales and was picking off individuals when the unthinkable happened. One of the whales, a huge creature much larger than average (estimated to be the same length as the *Essex*), peeled away from its fellows and turned towards the boat.

It rammed the vessel hard and there was the sickening crunch of splintering wood. The sailors fell sprawling to the deck. The captain tried to muster a response, but the ship was barely under his control. Meanwhile the whale had turned and was again swimming fast towards them. Its mighty back smashed into the hull for a second time, and the vessel gave a wild lurch. So violent was the blow that the men knew instantly that they were doomed.

The twenty sailors piled into three smaller whaleboats with such meagre supplies as they could gather in their flight. Within ten minutes the *Essex* had capsized, but the crew managed to retrieve some provisions before she finally sank.

The captain estimated them to be 2,000 nautical miles (3,700 km; 2,300 miles) west of South America. He thought they might manage the journey in fifty-six days. Rationing their provisions for that length of voyage gave them each a few ounces of bread, a little hard biscuit and half a pint of water per man per day. This is about one third of the minimum required food intake and half the minimum water intake for a healthy adult.

But by 30 November, the boats had travelled around 770 km (480 miles) and the provisions were holding out. The men were hungry and tired but in good spirits and Pollard was optimistic that they would survive the trip.

On 20 December, the men landed on uninhabited Henderson Island, now part of the British territory of the Pitcairn Islands.

A rocky hard place

At first it seemed like Henderson Island was the sanctuary that would save them. The island had birds, fish and vegetation. The men even found a small freshwater spring. At first they ate relatively well and built up their strength after the shock of the sinking.

But Henderson Island is just 10.4 km (6½ miles) long and 5.6 km (3½ miles) wide and by Christmas Day, they had exhausted its natural resources. There was no reason for other ships to visit the island; the men knew they would have to leave if they were to survive.

Seventeen of the twenty *Essex* crewmen decided to get back into their whaleboats. Three men stayed behind to take their chances on Henderson.

Drifting with death

Rations were now halved, and the men were severely starved and dehydrated. Excess sodium in their bodies was having a terrible effect. They were ravaged by diarrhoea, their skins erupted in weeping boils and oedema affected their limbs. They suffered blackouts and their behaviour became bizarre and, when they had the energy, violent. They stole food from each other.

On 10 January 1821, crewman Matthew Joy was the first man to die. Others soon followed. The first six to perish were sewn into their clothes and slipped over the side.

On the night of 28 January the three boats separated. One, with three crewmen aboard, was never seen again.

The beach at Henderson Island, Pitcairn Islands.

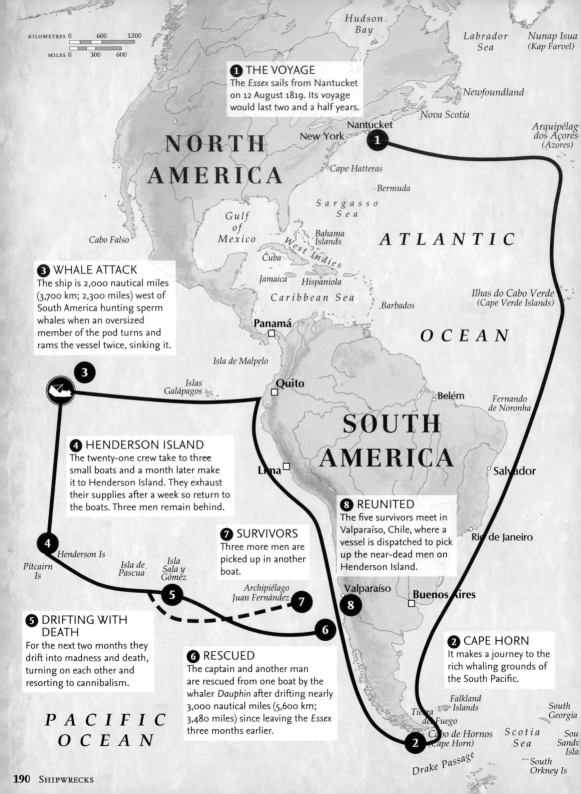

① THE VOYAGE
The *Essex* sails from Nantucket on 12 August 1819. Its voyage would last two and a half years.

③ WHALE ATTACK
The ship is 2,000 nautical miles (3,700 km; 2,300 miles) west of South America hunting sperm whales when an oversized member of the pod turns and rams the vessel twice, sinking it.

④ HENDERSON ISLAND
The twenty-one crew take to three small boats and a month later make it to Henderson Island. They exhaust their supplies after a week so return to the boats. Three men remain behind.

⑦ SURVIVORS
Three more men are picked up in another boat.

⑧ REUNITED
The five survivors meet in Valparaíso, Chile, where a vessel is dispatched to pick up the near-dead men on Henderson Island.

⑤ DRIFTING WITH DEATH
For the next two months they drift into madness and death, turning on each other and resorting to cannibalism.

⑥ RESCUED
The captain and another man are rescued from one boat by the whaler *Dauphin* after drifting nearly 3,000 nautical miles (5,600 km; 3,480 miles) since leaving the *Essex* three months earlier.

② CAPE HORN
It makes a journey to the rich whaling grounds of the South Pacific.

Those who still lived knew that they might still be many days, if not weeks from land. The little food they had would soon run out.

When the next man died, Captain Pollard ordered his body remain in the boat.

Their shipmate's corpse would be the men's next meal.

The most horrible lottery

Three more men would die and be eaten before 1 February when the survivors ran out of food again. They now faced an unthinkable crisis. In Pollard's boat four men lived: Brazillai Ray, Charles Ramsdell, the captain and Pollard's young cousin, Owen Coffin. In their depths of desperation, the men decided that unless one of them was sacrificed, they would all die long, lingering deaths. The chance to live became a lottery.

They agreed to draw lots to determine who would give his life for the survival of his fellows.

Every man had a one in four chance of drawing the black spot. The man who pulled it from the bag was the unfortunately named Owen Coffin.

Horrifically for Coffin, the three remaining men then drew lots again to see who would execute him. This hideous duty fell to Coffin's friend, Charles Ramsdell. Ramsdell shot Coffin. The boy's remains were consumed by Pollard, Ray and Ramsdell.

Shortly after, Ray also died. For the rest of their tortuous days in the boat, Pollard and Ramsdell survived by gnawing on the bones of Coffin and Ray.

Skeletons and bones

On 23 February 1821 the Nantucket whaling ship *Dauphin* was scanning the horizon for its quarry when it spotted the tiny boat. Her captain ordered her to sail alongside. The

An illustration by A. Burnham Shute, for the novel *Moby Dick* by Herman Melville.

sailors looked down to see the two survivors.

The *Dauphin* found two skeletal men crouched in their boat amid a pile of gnawed human bones.

It was 95 days since the *Essex* sank and the men were so confused that they had not even noticed the bulk of the *Dauphin* sailing beside them.

The British merchant brig *Indian* picked up the other boat. Three men still lived in it; they had also resorted to cannibalism to survive. The five men were reunited in the port of Valparaíso in Chile, where they told officials about the men they had left

on Henderson Island. These sailors were picked up on 5 April 1821, more dead than alive.

Eight men lived to tell the tale of the whaleship *Essex*. Six were lost or buried at sea. Seven were eaten.

Fact as strange as fiction

First Mate Owen Chase wrote an account of the disaster, the *Narrative of the Most Extraordinary and Distressing Shipwreck of the Whale-Ship Essex*. Chase's son also served on a whaleship and he lent his copy of his father's story to a young man he met at sea. This young sailor was Herman Melville and the true-life tale of the *Essex* inspired his novel Moby-Dick.

The Teenage Captain

In late 1893, William Shotton was the 18-year-old third mate on the *Trafalgar* when its captain and other officers died of fever on a voyage from the Dutch East Indies to Australia. The only man on board with any navigational skills, Shotton took command and steered the disease-ridden ship 5,200 km (3,220 miles) to safety.

DATE:
1893

SITUATION:
Senior officers dead of a mystery fever

CONDITION OF CONFINEMENT:
On board a diseased ship in the Indian Ocean

DURATION OF CONFINEMENT:
50 days

MEANS OF ESCAPE:
First class seamanship

NO. OF ESCAPEES:
18

DANGERS:
Disease, mutiny, foundering, storms

EQUIPMENT:
Ship's equipment, some navigational theory

ABOVE RIGHT
The *Trafalgar*.

Alone at the wheel

One by one, the terrifying sickness seized the *Trafalgar's* officers. A wild fever ravaged their bodies and they lost their senses rapidly, in some cases within hours, invariably dying soon after.

For the crew of twenty-three men, living in close quarters in the belly of a ship it must have been a dreadful ordeal to watch your fellows die and know that in all likelihood you would be next. For William Shotton it was worse: he was responsible for the vessel and he was only 18 years old.

A strong ship

The *Trafalgar* was built at Glasgow as a four-masted iron ship in 1877 and later converted into a barque of 1,768 tons. She measured 82.8 m (271½ ft) long, had a beam of 12 m (39½ ft) and needed twenty-four crew to handle her as well as a captain and three officers.

When the *Trafalgar* sailed from New York with a cargo of kerosene in the summer of 1893, it seemed like it was going to be just another voyage for its experienced crew. But nothing could have prepared them for what happened at their destination of Jakarta (then known as Batavia) in the Dutch East Indies, now part of Indonesia.

The port of death

Jakarta was then surrounded by swamps and had a reputation for being disease-ridden. As the cargo was landed, the crew were ordered not to go on shore. Despite this precaution, Captain Edgar soon fell ill with a virulent disease known as 'Java fever'. His condition deteriorated by the hour and the chief officer, Mr Richard Roberts, eventually rowed to the Dutch guard ship to ask for medical assistance. It was too late to save their captain.

When he returned three hours later the captain was dead.

Captain Edgar was buried in Jakarta Cemetery the next day, with the steward and six of the crew taking part in the hurried service. This was just a taste of the deadly horrors yet to come.

Many of the men began to complain of feeling ill, but the new captain Richard Roberts, reasoned that there was little hope of the men recovering while in such a foul place. Roberts was a young man with a lot to live for: he had only just been married before the vessel left Cardiff on the first stage of its journey. He determined that they should start for Australia as soon as possible. The ship sailed on 29 October 1893 with the twenty-three crew seized almost rigid with unease and dread.

A rough journey into manhood

They were barely clear of the island of Java when a seaman succumbed to the fever and died. Captain Roberts fell ill next. He never would see his young wife again.

Mr Norwood the first officer was also ill by now and although he seemed to improve a little at first, he weakened again, lost his reason and died on 21 November. The second mate, who had been promoted from the crew, was worse than useless.

The choice to command the ship now was young William Shotton. He had only recently completed his apprenticeship and earned a commission as third officer, mainly because of his theoretical knowledge of navigation.

The whole responsibility for the working of the ship fell to a lad of just eighteen.

The only other man on board who had the remotest knowledge and confidence to take control of the barque was a sailmaker called Hugh Kennedy. While Shotton snatched a few hours' rest from his long and arduous duties, Kennedy nervously guided the ship.

A seaman was also transferred to the poop deck to keep occasional watch, though he knew very little about navigation.

Shotton faced a formidable task. The rest of the crew were terrified into idleness and mutinous mutterings. Shotton faced up to them dauntlessly.

> **❛ ...the reality was that, young and inexperienced as he was, he alone could take them to port. ❜**

As they crossed the Indian Ocean the cook fell ill and died, the fifth victim of the passage. The crew's morale plunged even further. Melbourne was still hundreds of miles distant and the idea of reaching it seemed hopeless. But Shotton never

lost heart; he faced up to the disaffected crew and, with Kennedy as an unexpected ally, learnt how to sail a ship the practical way. At the same time, Shotton sensed some of the men's fear was based on superstition. He placed a light in the cabin the crew thought was haunted, alarming and distracting them. With growing courage he refused the demand to head for Fremantle, and made for Melbourne.

In the teeth of the tempest

In mid-December, they sighted the coast of Australia, and Shotton hoped they would pass another vessel. But they saw none, so he decided to make land to determine their position.

No sooner had he identified their position as just off Port Fairy in Victoria than a wild westerly gale blew up. There was only one way to survive the tempest's violence, Shotton decided, and that was to run before it. He ordered all hands on deck, gradually shortened the sail as the gale rose and for several heart-stopping hours the ship scudded before the storm.

The *Trafalgar* was smashed by huge waves and ripped by vicious winds: the topsail and the main lower-topsail were blown clean out of the bolt ropes.

At last the wind eased a little and the heaving sea fell; Shotton took his chance and stood the ship in towards the Victoria coast. He piloted the vessel through the entrance to the Bass Strait and brought the seamen safely into Port Phillip about a week before Christmas.

The modest hero

The story of his accomplishments made newspapers all over the world and the Victorian Government presented Shotton with a gold watch and chain in recognition of his gallantry. He also later received Lloyd's Silver Medal.

But Shotton himself seemed astonished that his exploits should have earned such high regard. He bore the attention modestly; after all, he was merely doing his duty.

❶ The *Trafalgar* arrives in Batavia (now Jakarta), but the captain succumbs to Java fever and dies while the ship is still in harbour.

❷ After three weeks sailing the first officer dies. William Shotton, the 18-year-old third officer, is now in charge of all the crew.

❸ Within sight of their goal the ship is lashed by a ferocious storm.

❹ Shotton guides the *Trafalgar* safely into Port Phillip.

0   1000 KM
0   500 MILES

INDONESIA
Sumatera
Jakarta
Surabaya   Dili
Jawa   Timor
New Guinea
Solomon Sea
Arafura Sea   Cape York
Timor Sea
Darwin
Coral Sea
North West Cape
Cairns
INDIAN OCEAN
AUSTRALIA
Perth
Brisbane
Cape Leeuwin
Great Australian Bight
Canberra
Port Fairy
Sydney
Melbourne
Bass Strait

Not a Man was Lost

WITH THEIR SHIP, *ENDURANCE*, CRUSHED BY ICE, ERNEST SHACKLETON
AND FIVE OTHER MEN SAILED 1,300 KM (800 MILES) ACROSS THE MOST
SAVAGE SEAS ON EARTH IN A TINY LIFEBOAT TO GET HELP. FACING
HURRICANE WINDS AND 18 M (60 FT) WAVES, THEIR VOYAGE IS ONE OF
THE GREATEST OPEN BOAT JOURNEYS EVER ACCOMPLISHED.

DATE:
1914–16

SITUATION:
SHIPWRECK

**CONDITION OF
CONFINEMENT:**
STRANDED IN THE
ANTARCTIC

**DURATION OF
CONFINEMENT:**
19 MONTHS

MEANS OF ESCAPE:
SEA JOURNEY AND
FORCED MARCH

NO. OF ESCAPEES:
28

DANGERS:
DROWNING, FREEZING TO
DEATH, STARVATION

EQUIPMENT:
LIFEBOATS, SOME
FOOD AND FUEL

ABOVE RIGHT
**Ernest Shackleton's ship, *Endurance*, trapped
in the ice.**

The Endurance

There has probably never been a more fittingly named vessel than Sir Ernest Shackleton's *Endurance*. When it sailed from South Georgia on 5 December 1914 on the first leg of the Imperial Trans-Antarctic Expedition, the crew were prepared for a tough adventure. They were going to cross the most extreme continent on earth. Little could they suspect just how much they would be forced to endure. Or how much heroism they would perform to return them all home safely.

Shackleton was leading the crew to Vahsel Bay, the southernmost explored point of the Weddell Sea at 77°49'S. There he would land a shore party and prepare to make the transcontinental crossing.

But disaster struck before they could reach their goal. The pack ice was thickening with every mile they sailed south and, by 14 February 1915, the *Endurance* was seized tight in a frozen vice.

There was nothing the men could do but sit and wait as, for the next eight months, the drifting ice took the ship back northwards. Then on 27 October, the ice stopped toying with the men and crushed the *Endurance*. The vessel sank from sight on 21 November, leaving the party stranded on the moving ice.

> **We knew it would be the hardest thing we had ever undertaken, for the Antarctic winter had set in, and we were about to cross one of the worst seas in the world.**

They were not going to cross Antarctica, but the adventure that the continent had thrust upon them was going to be every bit as incredible as what they had planned.

First steps to safety

Shackleton's priority now was simply how to save the lives of his twenty-seven-man crew.

In theory they could march across the pack ice to the nearest land and then trek to a harbour that ships were known to visit. But the ice was too broken up and dangerous to travel across. The party established 'Patience Camp' on a flat ice floe, and waited as the drift carried them further north, towards open water.

Another three months passed. Then, on 8 April 1916, the ice broke up enough to allow them to launch their three lifeboats. For seven perilous days they sailed and rowed through stormy seas and dangerous loose ice, reaching the temporary haven of Elephant Island on 15 April.

They were on solid ground, but their fortunes looked bleak. Elephant Island wasn't on any shipping routes and it was too far from their planned route to make a rescue likely. Although the island had fresh water and an ample supply of seals and penguins for food and fuel, the savage Antarctic winter was fast approaching. The men only had a narrow shingle beach to call home and this was constantly blasted by gales and blizzards. One tent had already been destroyed and others flattened. Many of the men were mentally and physically exhausted. Somehow, they had to get help.

Shackleton decided to undertake one of the most daring sea voyages in history. They would sail the best of the lifeboats to the whaling stations of South Georgia. The problem was that this island lay some 800 nautical miles (1,500 km; 920 miles) across the Southern Ocean, one of the fiercest stretches of water in the world.

The open-boat journey

Shackleton's boat party would be venturing into a storm-lashed world where constant gales powered heaving waves – the feared Cape Horn Rollers – that frequently topped 18 m (60 ft) from trough to crest.

> **We felt our boat lifted and flung forward like a cork in breaking surf.**

They took the sturdiest of the three lifeboats, the *James Caird* (named after one of the expedition's sponsors) and got the ship's carpenter to further strengthen it. He raised the sides of the 6.9 m (22½ ft) long boat and added a makeshift deck of wood and canvas. He also fitted a mainmast and a mizzenmast with lugsails and a jib, sealed the craft with oil paints, lamp wick, and seal blood. Finally a ton (1,016 kg) of ballast was added to reduce the risk of capsizing.

Their target was ridiculously small and there was every chance that they would miss the island.

The navigation skills of the *Endurance's* captain, Frank Worsley, would be vital if they were to reach South Georgia. Worsley was a New Zealander who had honed his navigation skills as a sailor among the tiny, remote islands of the South Pacific.

On 24 April 1916, Shackleton, Worsley and four other men pushed the *James Caird* out into the hard grey waters that pummelled Elephant Island. They had food for one month, two 70 litre (18 gallon) casks of water (one of which was damaged during the loading and let in sea water), two Primus stoves, paraffin, oil, candles, sleeping bags and 'a few spare socks'.

The wind was a moderate southwesterly, but Shackleton ordered Worsley to set course due north, to get clear of the menacing ice-fields. As they progressed, the swell rose. By dawn, they were 45 nautical miles (83 km; 52 miles) from Elephant Island, sailing in heavy seas and Force 9 winds.

They worked in two three-man watches, with one man at the helm, another at the sails, and the third on bailing duty. It was hard going from the start: the men's clothing had been designed for the dry cold of Antarctic sledging, and wasn't waterproof. Icy seawater rubbed their skin raw. The only way to rest was huddled together in the tiny covered space in the bows.

Worsley's job was difficult to the point of impossibility. To navigate accurately with his sextant he needed to make sightings of the sun. But this was very rarely visible, and when it was the high pitch and roll of the boat made it very hard to be accurate.

After two days, Worsley put them at 128 nautical miles (237 km; 147 miles) north of Elephant Island. They were clear of the dangers of floating ice but were now in the treacherous Drake Passage, a band of ocean where huge rolling waves sweep round the globe, unimpeded by any land. Shackleton now set a course directly for South Georgia.

Launching the *James Caird* from the shore of Elephant Island, 24 April 1916. The incredibly cramped living quarters for six men for the next seventeen days at sea.

CHILE

Punta
Arenas

Falkland
Islands

South
Georgia

Cape Horn Elephant
Is. South
Sandwich
Group

South
Shetland Is. South
Orkney Is.

Antarctic
Peninsula

WEDDELL SEA

ANTARCTICA

1000 KM

600 MILES

KILOMETRES 0   200   400

MILES 0   100   200

SOUTHERN OCEAN

Stromness

South
Georgia

South
Sandwich
Group

1 DECEMBER 1914–
FEBRUARY 1915
The *Endurance* leaves
South Georgia and sails
to the Weddell Sea.

4 APRIL–MAY 1916
Shackleton and five other men then sail
a lifeboat 800 nautical miles (1,500 km;
920 miles) to South Georgia in an
astonishing feat of navigation skills and
human endurance. Once there they still
have to walk for thirty-six hours across
the uncharted island to reach the safety
of the whaling station.

Drake
Passage

South Orkney
Islands

5 SEPTEMBER 1916
Three months later, the entire crew
of the *Endurance* is rescued from
Elephant Island and taken to Chile.

Elephant Island

3 NOVEMBER 1915–APRIL 1916
The ship is finally crushed by the ice and
sinks. Shackleton and his men drift on an
ice floe then sail and row in lifeboats to
Elephant Island.

W E D D E L L

S E A

Sea
Ba

Riiser-
Larsen
Ice Shelf

Lyddan
Island

Brunt
Ice
Shelf

Caird
Coast

Coats La

Luitpold
Coast

South Shetland
Islands

Bransfield Strait

Graham Land

2 FEBRUARY–OCTOBER 1915
The *Endurance* is trapped in the ice and
drifts for eight months.

Larsen
Ice Shelf

A n t a r c t i c   P e n i n s u l a

Alexander
Island

Palmer
Land

Ronne Ice Shelf

Filchner
Ice Shelf

Berkner
Island

After five days' sailing they had travelled 238 nautical miles (441 km; 274 miles), but now the weather turned really bad. Heavy seas threatened to swamp the boat, and only continuous bailing kept it afloat. It became so cold that spray began to freeze on the boat and the added weight threatened to capsize them. The men had to take turns to crawl onto the pitching deck to chip the ice off the deck and rigging with an axe.

For two whole days the wind was too high for them to raise the sail. But they kept going and by 6 May they were only 115 nautical miles (213 km; 132 miles) from South Georgia. But the two weeks of constant toil in atrocious conditions had worn them down. Two men were particularly weak, while a third had collapsed and was unable to perform any duties.

Memorial cross for Sir Ernest Shackleton, Hope Point, Cumberland East Bay, South Georgia.

> **‘ The bright moments were those when we each received our one mug of hot milk during the long, bitter watches of the night. ’**

The next day, Worsley thought they were close to their goal but he advised Shackleton that he could be a few miles out. If they were too far north, they could be pushed right past the island by the fierce southwesterly winds. But they soon spotted seaweed and birds including land-loving cormorants, and just after noon on 8 May they saw land. Worsley was dead on and he had accomplished one of the most incredible feats of navigation in maritime history.

But, despite being so close to their journey's end, the heavy seas made immediate landing impossible. For twenty-four agonizing hours they were forced to wait offshore in 'one of the worst hurricanes any of us had ever experienced'. The vicious waves threatened to drive them onto the rocky South Georgia shore or the equally dangerous Annenkov Island, 8 km (5 miles) from the coast.

Finally, on 10 May, Shackleton knew that the weaker members of his crew would not last another day in the boat. They had to land, no matter how dangerous the conditions. They found as sheltered an area as they could, Cave Cove near the entrance to King Haakon Bay and, after several near-fatal attempts, landed the *James Caird*.

They were on the uninhabited southwest coast. The whaling stations were still 150 nautical miles (280 km; 170 miles) round the coast. Shackleton's plan had been to sail round, hugging the shore. But he knew that the boat wouldn't make such a voyage; nor would two of the exhausted men. After a few days' recuperation, he decided to traverse the island on foot and get help at Stromness. But no one had ever crossed the interior of South Georgia before.

Where no man had gone before

Early on 18 May Shackleton, Worsley and seaman Tom Crean left their three colleagues sheltering on a shingle beach under the upturned *James Caird* and started walking.

Because they had no map they had to improvise a route across mountain ranges and over glaciers. They had no camping equipment so they simply didn't stop. They walked continuously for thirty-six hours before reaching the whaling station at Stromness.

By now they were at the edge of total exhaustion, their faces savaged by exposure and wind, their fingers and toes numb with frostbite. The Norwegian seamen must have been staggered to see, as Worsley wrote, 'a terrible trio of scarecrows', walking into their bunkhouse.

Later that same day, 19 May, the whalers sent a motor-vessel to King Haakon Bay to pick up the three other men from the *James Caird*. But the Antarctic winter had now set in, and it was more than three months before Shackleton could retrieve the twenty-two men they had left on Elephant Island. Finally, on 3 September 1916, every single man who had sailed on the *Endurance* reached the safe haven of Punta Arenas in Chile.

> **‘ the voyage of the *James Caird*... ranked as one of the greatest boat journeys ever accomplished. ’**

Two years later Shackleton headed back to Antarctica on another expedition. On 5 January 1922, he died suddenly of a heart attack in South Georgia.

The *James Caird* was brought back from South Georgia to England in 1919. It is on permanent display at Shackleton's old school, Dulwich College.

1,700 Miles of Ocean

When the British cargo steamer *Trevessa* sank in the Indian Ocean in June 1923, the forty-four-man crew were cast adrift in two open lifeboats. The men set out to sail and row 2,700 km (1,700 miles) to reach land and twenty-six days later thirty-five survivors landed in the Mauritius Islands.

DATE:
1923

SITUATION:
Shipwreck

CONDITION OF CONFINEMENT:
In open boats under the tropical sun

DURATION OF CONFINEMENT:
23 and 26 days

MEANS OF ESCAPE:
Sailing, occasional rowing

NO. OF ESCAPEES:
34

DANGERS:
Drowning, starvation, dehydration, exposure

EQUIPMENT:
Rations for a few days, oars

ABOVE RIGHT
The beautiful landscape of Mauritius in the Indian Ocean.

The great storm

The forty-four men on the merchant freighter *Trevessa* were experienced sailors. They had crossed and re-crossed the great oceans of the world many times. Several of them had seen naval action in the Great War, which had ended just five years earlier. But the storm that engulfed the ship in the Indian Ocean on 3 June 1923 was like nothing any of them had ever seen before.

A heavy metal cargo

The vessel had taken on a cargo of zinc concentrates in Fremantle, Australia and was on its way to Durban before heading on to Europe. It had travelled 2,150 km (1,340 miles) and was in the middle of the southern Indian Ocean when the storm struck. Huge seas washed over the boat, pounding the decks and flooding the hold.

The waters that penetrated the hold soon inundated the cargo. The zinc concentrates had the consistency of wet cement and the bilge pumps weren't able to clear the flooding water. Although engineers worked furiously to clear the hold they were fighting a losing battle.

The *Trevessa* began to go down by the head, and quickly.

A leader among men

The Captain, Cecil Foster, was the kind of man you would want to be in charge in a situation like this. He had been on a boat that was torpedoed and sunk in the War, so he had experienced a similar situation before. He was also naturally cool and commanding under pressure; although his ship was visibly sinking beneath him, he was able to make some brave and bold decisions that would ultimately save the lives of his men.

Foster's wartime exploits had shown him the value of tinned milk, which he had seen save many castaways. In the hectic minutes before the *Trevessa* sank he ordered his steward to pack condensed milk rather than tinned meat into the lifeboats.

The 5,000-ton steamer went down in less than three hours. At 2.15 a.m. on 4 June 1923, the forty-four crew were adrift in the Indian Ocean. The speed of the sinking meant they had had very little time to grab anything useful. Many had hardly any clothes on, after being dragged from their beds and hauled on deck.

Adrift in open boats

The two clinker-built lifeboats were 8 m (26 ft) along with a beam of 2.4 m (8 ft) and a single mast with lugsail. Captain Foster took charge of one boat with twenty men in it.

The mate led the twenty-four men in the other boat.

Foster had managed to send a distress message by radio, but he knew they could not rely on being picked up. They should strike out for land.

The Captain's wise choice was to aim for Mauritius. The winds, rain for drinking water, and temperatures would be more favourable, and the chance of seeing other boats was increased.

They only had 3.3 litres (7 pints) of water per man, 550 biscuits and two cases of condensed milk. They had cigarettes, tobacco, charts and sextants but no radio or working compass. Latitude was observed with the sextants, and they steered by the sun and stars.

So there was no time to be wasted. Captain Foster ordered the men to start sailing west right away and he immediately put everyone on strict rations.

Ships that part in the night

The captain and the mate tried to keep the two boats sailing together, but the captain's boat had a much bigger sail so was therefore faster, and after six days in rough seas, the mate's boat began to lag behind.

Soon each boat was alone on its circle of endless ocean.

At first the men's spirits were remarkably high: all hands had survived the sinking and they had a modest store of rations. But as the days turned into weeks and the food and water ran low, the men were forced to endure constant suffering.

The ship had sunk in the horse latitudes and the men endured the extremes of weather for which that region is famous. Heavy seas threatened to swamp the boat completely. They were also often suddenly becalmed and were forced to row in the burning tropical heat. The men suffered from severe sunburn and agonizing salt-water sores which the rowing made worse. They started to die.

The brutal sun, the salt spray and the elements were all taking their toll and by the seventeenth day two men in the captain's boat had died.

The second boat

The mate's boat endured even more tragedy. A violent storm threw the engineer overboard and they were unable to find him.

Four men became so delirious with dehydration that they ignored the warnings of the others and took to drinking seawater. Studies have shown that sipping small quantities of salt water can sometimes be beneficial in a survival situation. But it seems that the four men consumed too much and they quickly died.

Over the reef to safety

Despite the sufferings that the men endured, Captain Foster maintained a rigid discipline that undoubtedly saved many of the men's lives. On 26 June, twenty-three days after sinking, the captain spotted land. Here fate made one final play for the men's lives: a dangerous coral reef lay between them and the sands of Rodrigues Island.

But help came with the aid of some fishermen who piloted a safe course through the coral to the blessed beach.

The men on the mate's boat would have to suffer for three more days before landing at Bel-Ombre, Mauritius. These men were at the very limits of endurance: one crewman died just two hours before land was sighted and the others were so exhausted they had to be carried ashore. Another sailor died soon after their arrival.

But of the forty-four men who took to the boats, thirty-four had survived. They had travelled 2,700 km (1,700 miles) and lasted more than three weeks in open boats under the burning tropical sun.

The return home

When the survivors reached Gravesend in August 1923 they enjoyed a heroes' welcome. Captain Foster and the mate received the Lloyd's Silver Medal for their seamanship and courage and were received by the King and Queen at Buckingham Palace.

Following the enquiry into the loss of the *Trevessa*, every British lifeboat carried a pound of condensed milk for each passenger. Lifeboats on certain categories of ship were also fitted with emergency radios.

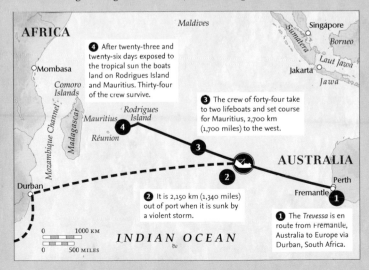

AFRICA

Maldives

Singapore

Sumatera

Borneo

Mombasa

4 After twenty-three and twenty-six days exposed to the tropical sun the boats land on Rodrigues Island and Mauritius. Thirty-four of the crew survive.

Laut Jawn

Jakarta

Comoro Islands

Jawa

3 The crew of forty-four take to two lifeboats and set course for Mauritius, 2,700 km (1,700 miles) to the west.

Rodrigues Island

Mauritius

4

Réunion

3

Madagascar

Mozambique Channel

AUSTRALIA

Durban

2

Perth

2 It is 2,150 km (1,340 miles) out of port when it is sunk by a violent storm.

Fremantle

1

1 The *Trevessa* is en route from Fremantle, Australia to Europe via Durban, South Africa.

0   1000 KM

0   500 MILES

INDIAN OCEAN

The Two who were Spared

TORPEDOED BY A GERMAN WARSHIP, ONLY SEVEN OUT OF THE ANGLO
SAXON'S FORTY-ONE CREW MADE IT INTO A LIFEBOAT. FIVE MORE MEN
WOULD DIE, LEAVING JUST TWO SOULS CLINGING ONTO LIFE AS THEY
DRIFTED 4,345 KM (2,700 MILES) ACROSS THE ATLANTIC TO COMPLETE
ONE OF THE LONGEST EVER OPEN BOAT VOYAGES.

DATE:
1940

SITUATION:
TORPEDOED BY A
GERMAN WARSHIP

**CONDITION OF
CONFINEMENT:**
CAST ADRIFT IN A LIFEBOAT

**DURATION OF
CONFINEMENT:**
70 DAYS

MEANS OF ESCAPE:
DRIFTING IN A LIFEBOAT,
EATING SEA CREATURES

NO. OF ESCAPEES:
2

DANGERS:
DROWNING, STARVATION,
DEHYDRATION, SUNBURN,
INSANITY

EQUIPMENT:
SOME SUPPLIES AT FIRST;
LATER, NOTHING

ABOVE RIGHT
Caribbean island of Eleuthera, Bahamas.

Torpedoed and left to die

It was summer 1940 and the Battle of the Atlantic was in full sway. British and German warships and submarines vied for control of vital international waterways. Merchant vessels were fair game and late in the evening of 21 August the British tramp steamer *Anglo Saxon* had the misfortune to stray into the sights of the German raider *Widder*. It was the end of the British vessel's voyage, but just the start of an amazing journey of survival for two of her crew. They would drift for more than 4,345 km (2,700 miles) and spend seventy days afloat as their fellow crewmen died beside them.

Cast adrift

The British tramp steamer *Anglo Saxon*, of 5,595 tons, and crewed by forty-one men, had a full cargo of Welsh coal and was making good time on her way to Argentina.

But when she was off the west coast of Africa on 21 August 1940 she was sighted by the German Armed Merchant Raider *Widder*. Captain Ruchteschell, commander of the *Widder* knew he could blow the *Anglo Saxon* out of the water, but he decided to wait till darkness fell before attacking, to maximise his advantage surprise.

At 8.08 p.m., just a few minutes before the moon was due to rise, Captain Ruchteschell ordered his men into action. He steered his ship on a course to intercept the unsuspecting British vessel and when they were 2,300 m (2,500 yards) away Ruchteschell gave the order to fire. The *Widder's* large calibre shells immediately took out the tramp's deck gun and set fire to its ammunition. She then steamed to within 550 m (600 yards) and raked the decks with incendiary machine gun bullets, killing several sailors. Ruchteschell decided to dispatch the crippled vessel quickly and fired a torpedo. This struck home and the *Anglo Saxon* was soon under the grey waves of the Atlantic.

Two large lifeboats and a smaller one were launched. The *Widder* fired on the men in the large lifeboats, killing them. The smaller boat drifted away unseen by the Germans.

Seven men in a boat

The small boat had seven of the original forty-one crew on board. Some of the sailors had sustained injuries in the attack, and one man soon died of his wounds on 1 September. Another injured man weakened and slipped overboard a few days later.

The remaining five men's only rations were some canned water and hard ship's biscuits.

Rations on the lifeboat were only enough to last them a few days, even with strict rationing.

But they saw no ships and the current drifted them away from the Canaries, the nearest point of land. They were being taken across the Atlantic.

Madness takes over

As days turned into weeks for the men in the boat, their bodies and minds began to deteriorate. The rations ran out. Still they saw neither ships nor land. Their choice now was whether they would die of thirst or go mad from drinking seawater. Two of the men chose instead to jump overboard.

> ❛ **Two men could bear the strain no longer and stepped over the side in a suicide pact.** ❜

The last man to die went insane and was also lost overboard.

By 24 September only Robert Tapscott and Roy Widdicombe were still alive. They would continue to cling to life despite the most arduous trials for a further month.

They had something that their fellows did not: unshakeable optimism. As they wrote in the log:

> ❛ **All water and biscuits gone, but still hoping to make land.** ❜

Nature's rations

Now all the pair had to eat and drink was the little rainwater they could collect, drifting seaweed and a few small sea creatures that they scooped into the boat. This would be their only sustenance for the next thirty-seven days.

As they got weaker they argued viciously. At one point, they also contemplated suicide. They were also struck by a savage hurricane that lasted for a full three days.

But on Wednesday, 30 October a farmer named Martin was working in his fields on the island of Eleuthera in the Bahamas when he glanced over at the nearby beach. To his astonishment he saw a ship's boat and, utterly exhausted on the sand beside it, two men.

He ran for help and soon the men were ferried to the hospital in Nassau by plane. Although they had lost a worrying percentage of their bodyweight and were nearly delirious with thirst and hunger, the men made a swift recovery.

Clear across the ocean

Of the seven original survivors from the *Anglo Saxon*, only Robert Tapscott and Roy Widdicombe lived to reach the Bahamas. They had battled the elements to survive in a small open boat over seventy days, making one of the longest ever lifeboat journeys in maritime history covering some 4,345 km (2,700 miles).

Tragic aftermath

Roy Widdicombe was returning home three months later on the SS *Siamese Prince* when it was torpedoed by German submarine *U-69*. All the crew were lost. Robert Tapscott became the sole survivor of the sinking of the *Anglo Saxon*.

A poor sort of justice

After the war Captain Ruchteschell was put on trial, the only Armed Raider captain to face a court. Robert Tapscott was there to give evidence that the *Widder* opened fire on the lifeboats as they left the sinking *Anglo Saxon*.

Ruchteschell was sentenced to ten years in jail and he died in custody.

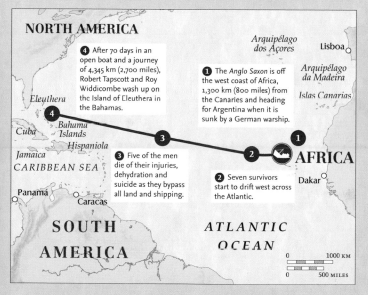

NORTH AMERICA

❹ After 70 days in an open boat and a journey of 4,345 km (2,700 miles), Robert Tapscott and Roy Widdicombe wash up on the Island of Eleuthera in the Bahamas.

Arquipélago dos Açores   Lisboa

Arquipélago da Madeira

❶ The *Anglo Saxon* is off the west coast of Africa, 1,300 km (800 miles) from the Canaries and heading for Argentina when it is sunk by a German warship.

Islas Canarias

Eleuthera

❹

Bahama Islands

Cuba

Jamaica   *Hispaniola*

CARIBBEAN SEA

❸

❸ Five of the men die of their injuries, dehydration and suicide as they bypass all land and shipping.

❷

❷ Seven survivors start to drift west across the Atlantic.

❶

AFRICA

Dakar

Panama   Caracas

SOUTH AMERICA

ATLANTIC OCEAN

0   1000 KM
0   500 MILES

The Longest Journey

When Poon Lim's ship was torpedoed by a Nazi U-boat, he ended up alone in an open life raft on the South Atlantic Ocean. He drifted for more than four months, eating seagulls and drinking shark blood to survive. His journey is the longest survival on a raft at sea.

DATE:

1942–3

SITUATION:

Shipwreck

CONDITION OF CONFINEMENT:

Cast away alone on a life raft

DURATION OF CONFINEMENT:

133 days

MEANS OF ESCAPE:

Catching fish and birds, drifting across the Atlantic

NO. OF ESCAPEES:

1

DANGERS:

Drowning, starvation, dehydration, being shot by the Germans

EQUIPMENT:

Some rations, a life raft

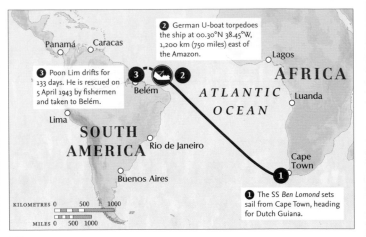

2 German U-boat torpedoes the ship at 00.30°N 38.45°W, 1,200 km (750 miles) east of the Amazon.

3 Poon Lim drifts for 133 days. He is rescued on 5 April 1943 by fishermen and taken to Belém.

1 The SS *Ben Lomond* sets sail from Cape Town, heading for Dutch Guiana.

The castaway

It was 23 November 1942 and the South Atlantic was a hazardous place to be. German U-boats ranged through these waters, picking off lone and undefended Allied shipping. For Poon Lim, a 24-year-old Chinese steward on board a British merchant vessel, one of these encounters would throw him into a survival situation of unparalleled intensity.

The SS *Ben Lomond* was on its way from Cape Town to Dutch Guiana with a crew of fifty-five. The ship was armed but slow and was sailing alone, rather than as part of a convoy. When German submarine *U-172* spotted it 1,200 km (750 miles) east of the Amazon it must have looked just like a sitting duck. The U-boat torpedoed the ship.

Most of the crew were killed instantly. The few survivors scrabbled to save themselves. Poon Lim grabbed a life jacket and jumped overboard just before the ship's boilers exploded. The ship immediately began its final journey to the bottom of the Atlantic.

Poon Lim trod water, desperately keeping his head above the waves. He knew he had to find a life raft soon. One raft bobbed into view, and his heart lifted when he saw it had some of his shipmates clinging to it. But the craft was caught by a current and drifted away.

> Of the SS *Ben Lomond's* fifty-five crew, eleven men survived the sinking. Ten were picked up; Poon drifted away alone.

After two hours of paddling, Poon finally saw another raft a few hundred feet away. He swam to it and climbed aboard.

A home in the middle of the ocean

The wooden life raft was 2.4 m (8 ft) square. It was stocked with a few tins of biscuits, a 40 litre (11 gallon) jug of water, some chocolate, a bag of sugar lumps, some flares, two smoke pots and an electric torch. Poon estimated that by rationing himself to just a few swallows of water and two biscuits in the morning and in the evening, he would be able to stay alive for a month.

Over the next few weeks, as Christmas came and went and 1942 became 1943, Poon kept himself alive by nibbling and sipping his rations.

Down but not out

With his food and water running low, Poon knew he needed a new plan for survival. He took the canvas covering off his life jacket and used it as a receptacle to catch rainwater.

Then he set about constructing fishing equipment. Dismantling the electric torch he found a wire that might serve as a fishhook. For days he shaped the tiny piece of metal, using the water jug as a hammer. His supplies were tied to the raft with a piece of rope; this could be unravelled and used as a fishing line. He pried out a nail from the raft's planking and used it to take the ration tin apart. Using his shoe as a hammer he fashioned a piece of the metal into a rudimentary knife.

Bait would be pieces of his precious biscuits. But Poon didn't have many left. And if the fish didn't bite relatively soon, his bait would turn to mush in the water and be wasted.

It took many attempts, but finally a fish snatched at his lure and he flipped it into the raft. Then he gutted it using his biscuit-tin knife and ate its flesh. The guts became bait for his next meal.

Poon knew he would have to stay in shape physically if he was also to keep his mind together. So when the sea was quiet he began a regime of swimming twice a day to stretch his cramped muscles. He wasn't a confident swimmer and it demanded real nerve to leave his sanctuary and take to the deeps, eyes scanning the water intently for sharks.

A balanced diet

Poon became fairly adept at catching fish. He would let the fillets bake in the sun to improve their taste. But around the end of January he spotted sea gulls and decided to vary his menu a little.

He gathered seaweed that had clung to the bottom of the raft and formed it into the shape of a bird's nest. Then he laid out some of his more pungent pieces of baked fish to attract the gulls. Finally, one of the gulls began coming closer. Poon lay absolutely still in the raft. The gull landed and began tucking in. Poon grabbed the bird by its neck. The bird put up a vicious fight, but eventually Poon dispatched the creature. He quartered the bird, drank its blood, and ate its flesh and organs.

A large storm hit and spoiled his fish and fouled his water. Poon became exhausted and severely dehydrated. He needed to catch something big. His next quarry would be one of the sharks that frequently circled his raft. He used the remains of his last seagull as bait. For a while the sharks circled warily. Then one gulped the bait. It was several feet long and it snapped and flipped furiously when Poon hauled it into the raft. Eventually he bludgeoned the fish to death with his water jug.

Poon drank the shark's blood. He also sliced open the fins and let them dry in the sun, a delicacy he had often enjoyed back home.

Ships that pass

He twice came agonizingly close to rescue. A freighter passed, and to Poon's delight he saw that the crew had spotted him. But they sailed on.

A patrol of United States Navy planes also saw him, and one dropped a buoy in the water. With cruel luck, however, a storm blew up and flung him far from the marker.

He had another more sinister encounter. A U-boat passed by, its gunners enjoying target practice at the expense of some seagulls.

Poon thought the Germans might practice on him too, but the crew chose to leave him to his fate.

So Poon drifted on, counting days with notches on the side of the raft.

Across the Atlantic

At the start of April, Poon noticed that the colour of the water had changed. It was no longer the blue-black of the deep ocean but lighter and greener. More birds flew overhead and seaweed floated by. Then, on 5 April 1943, after 133 days in the life raft, Poon Lim saw a small sail on the horizon. He had no flares left, so he frantically stripped off his shirt and waved it, jumping up and down so violently he nearly capsized the raft.

The sail began to head towards him. It was a tiny Brazilian fishing boat. The three astonished crew gave Poon water and dried beans. They then fired up their motors and turned for land. Three days later they docked at Belém at the mouth of the Amazon River in Brazil.

❛ I hope no one will ever have to break that record. ❜

No one has survived for longer than Poon Lim on a raft at sea.

Returning a hero

Poon had lost 9 kg (20 lb) during his ordeal, but he was able to walk unaided. After a few weeks' recuperation in hospital in Brazil he returned to Britain via Miami and New York.

King George VI presented him with the British Empire Medal, the highest civilian award. The Royal Navy incorporated his survival techniques into the manuals they put in their vessels' life rafts. His employers gave him a gold watch.

After the war, Poon Lim emigrated to the United States, eventually gaining citizenship and settling in Brooklyn, where he died on 4 January 1991.

Five Days in a Deadly Sea

The USS *Indianapolis* left San Francisco on 16 July 1945 with a deadly cargo: enriched uranium for the atomic bomb that would be dropped on Hiroshima. But after delivering its payload the ship was sunk by a Japanese submarine and 880 men were cast into shark-infested water. Rescue would not reach them for five days.

DATE:
1945

SITUATION:
Ship sunk by torpedoes

CONDITION OF CONFINEMENT:
Floating in the open ocean

DURATION OF CONFINEMENT:
4½ days

MEANS OF ESCAPE:
Rescue

NO. OF ESCAPEES:
316 out of 880

DANGERS:
Exposure, dehydration and shark attacks

EQUIPMENT:
Life vests, some lifeboats

ABOVE RIGHT
The paradise island of Guam, the largest and southernmost of the Mariana Islands.

The deadliest mission

The cruiser USS *Indianapolis* reached the US air base at Tinian in the Northern Mariana Islands on 26 July 1945. It was from here that the atomic attacks on Hiroshima and Nagasaki would be launched on 6 and 9 August, and the *Indianapolis* delivered enriched uranium and other vital parts for *Little Boy*, the first bomb to be dropped.

Death from below

Having delivered its historic payload, *Indianapolis* was then sent to Guam, 200 km (124 miles) away. Many of its crew had just completed a tour of duty and here they were replaced by other sailors. They were very fortunate. Then on 28 July, she was directed to join the battleship USS *Idaho* at Leyte Gulf in the Philippines to prepare for the invasion of Japan. The *Indianapolis*, unescorted, departed Guam on a course of 262 degrees making about 17 knots (31 km/h; 20 mph).

The 2,125 km (1,320 mile) voyage was scheduled to take three days. But at 12.14 a.m. on 30 July, she was half way to her destination when she was spotted by the Japanese submarine *I-58*. The American ship had no effective submarine detection equipment and was caught completely unaware. The submarine launched six torpedoes, two of which hit the ship. The first blew away the bow and the second struck half way along the starboard side, igniting a fuel tank and a powder magazine. The huge explosion split the ship to the keel and knocked out all electric power.

> ❛ I started to walk forward to see what I could see and what I seen was about sixty-foot of the bow chopped off, completely gone. ❜

The damage was catastrophic and *Indianapolis* went down rapidly by the bow, rolling to starboard. Just twelve minutes later the 190 m (623 ft),

9,800 ton cruiser was beneath the waters of the Pacific.

Afloat on a burning sea

There were 1,196 men on board and over 300 went down with the ship. The rest of the crew, 880 men, found themselves adrift amid the flaming wreckage in the middle of the night. The surprise and speed of the sinking meant that only a handful of lifeboats had been launched and many men were without lifejackets.

> **Well this isn't too bad, we thought, we'll be picked up today.**

They could do nothing but cling to anything that floated and wait to be rescued. What they couldn't have imagined was that help was five days away.

Five days with the sharks

It was brutally cold in the water at night. With dawn came a little welcome warmth, but it also brought something dreadful: sharks. The oceanic whitetip shark is a notorious hazard for survivors in warm water and the attacks would continue until the men were rescued five days later.

Three-quarter port bow view of the USS *Indianapolis* at sea.

One survivor, Woody James, wrote: 'The day wore on and the sharks were around, hundreds of them. You'd hear guys scream, especially late in the afternoon. Seemed like the sharks were the worst late in the afternoon than they were during the day. Then they fed at night too. Everything would be quiet and then you'd hear somebody scream and you knew a shark had got him.'

Although some men found rations, including Spam and crackers, amongst the debris, most had nothing to eat and no fresh water. During the day the temperature reached 27°C and the men were exposed to the full might of the tropical sun. At night they faced the prospect of hypothermia as the temperature plummeted.

Some men suffered from severe peeling of the skin, and there were many sailors who had been badly injured in the torpedo attack. Their wounds made them weak and the blood in the water attracted sharks.

> **Day 3... Some of the guys been drinkin' salt water by now, and they were goin' berzerk.**

They developed sores in their mouths and throats, which were exacerbated by the salt water. As they became dehydrated and took in seawater, the levels of sodium in the men's bodies increased, which led to weakness, oedema, seizures, dementia and death. Some of the men killed themselves or one another as the hallucinations and madness took control.

Sharks were a notorious hazard for the survivors in the warm waters of the ocean.

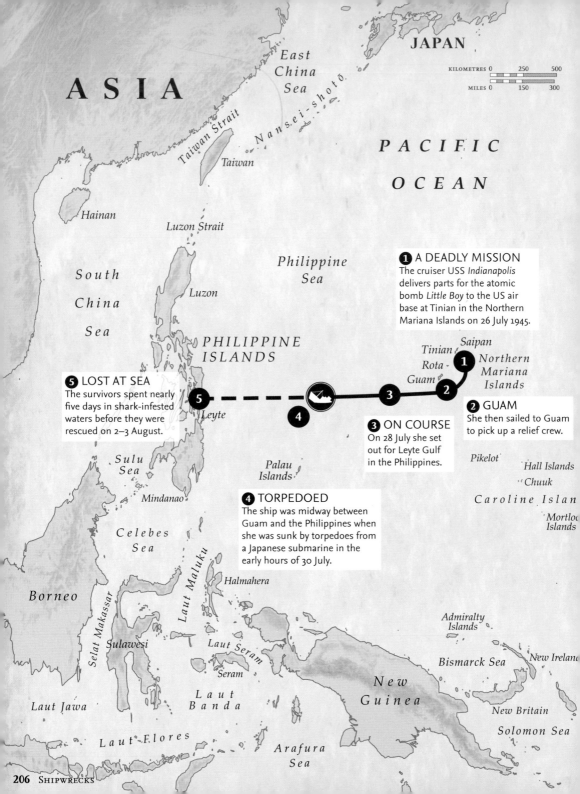

ASIA

East China Sea

JAPAN

KILOMETRES 0 250 500
MILES 0 150 300

Taiwan Strait

Nansei-shotō

Taiwan

PACIFIC

OCEAN

Hainan

Luzon Strait

Philippine Sea

South China Sea

Luzon

PHILIPPINE ISLANDS

1 A DEADLY MISSION
The cruiser USS *Indianapolis* delivers parts for the atomic bomb *Little Boy* to the US air base at Tinian in the Northern Mariana Islands on 26 July 1945.

Tinian · Saipan
Rota
Guam

1

Northern Mariana Islands

2

5 LOST AT SEA
The survivors spent nearly five days in shark-infested waters before they were rescued on 2–3 August.

5

4

3

Leyte

3 ON COURSE
On 28 July she set out for Leyte Gulf in the Philippines.

2 GUAM
She then sailed to Guam to pick up a relief crew.

Sulu Sea

Palau Islands

Pikelot

Hall Islands

Chuuk

Mindanao

4 TORPEDOED
The ship was midway between Guam and the Philippines when she was sunk by torpedoes from a Japanese submarine in the early hours of 30 July.

Caroline Islan

Mortlo Islands

Celebes Sea

Laut Maluku

Halmahera

Admiralty Islands

Borneo

Selat Makassar

Laut Seram

New Ireland

Sulawesi

Seram

New Guinea

Bismarck Sea

Laut Banda

New Britain

Laut Jawa

Solomon Sea

Laut Flores

Arafura Sea

Lost at sea

Although it sank in just twelve minutes, radio operators on the *Indianapolis* did manage to send distress calls, and three separate stations picked them up. But tragically for the men in the water, no one acted on the call. One station commander was drunk and another had ordered his men not to disturb him. The third commander thought the call was a Japanese prank.

The *Indianapolis* was not required to make regular reports; the Navy generally assumed that ships of its size would reach their destinations on time unless reported otherwise. This meant that the *Indianapolis* was not missed until 31 July, a day and a half after it sank, when it should have arrived at Leyte. Even then, the Operations Officer in Leyte noticed its absence but did not immediately investigate the matter or report it to his superiors.

The men would be in the water with the sharks for two more days.

A heroic rescue

It wasn't until 11 a.m. on 2 August, the fourth day after the sinking, that the survivors were discovered, and then they were only spotted by accident. Wilbur C. Gwinn was piloting his PV-1 Ventura Bomber on a routine antisubmarine patrol when he radioed his base at Peleiu in Palau and reported 'many men in the water'. He dropped a life raft and a radio transmitter but could do no more.

Thankfully, his report was now acted on. All air and surface units capable of rescue operations were dispatched to the scene at once.

Two men now made bold decisions that saved lives. Lieutenant R. Adrian Marks was piloting a PBY Catalina seaplane when he got the call to lend assistance. His crew began dropping rubber rafts and supplies, but Marks could see men being attacked by sharks and knew he could do more. Standard procedure forbade him

Lieutenant Marks was piloting a PBY Catalina seaplane when he received a call to assist in the rescue of the men. Marks and his crew saved the lives of fifty-six men.

from landing on the water in such a situation, but Marks disobeyed this directive. He landed on the open sea and immediately began picking up the stragglers and lone swimmers who were at the greatest risk of shark attack.

When his plane was full of men he tied survivors to the wings with parachute cord. This damaged the wings so badly that the plane would never fly again and later had to be sunk, but Marks and his crew saved the lives of fifty-six men.

En route to the scene, Marks had overflown the destroyer escort *Cecil J. Doyle* and alerted her captain, W. Graham Claytor, of the emergency. On his own authority, Claytor decided to divert to the scene. The *Doyle* arrived during the night and, disregarding the safety of his own vessel, Captain Claytor pointed his largest searchlight into the night sky to serve as a beacon for other rescue vessels.

For the men in the water, this was the first sign that help had at last arrived. But for most of the men of the *Indianapolis* it was too late.

After nearly five days of starvation, dehydration, exposure and constant shark attacks, of the 880 men who went into the water, only 321 came out alive. Five more perished of their injuries leaving 316 ultimate survivors.

Indianapolis was the last major US Navy ship sunk by enemy action in the Second World War. It was the greatest single loss of life at sea in the history of the US Navy.

Nailed to the mast

The ship's captain, Charles Butler McVay III, was one of the survivors. He faced a court-martial in November 1945 and was convicted of 'hazarding his ship by failing to zigzag'. More than 350 US Navy warships were lost in the Second World War, but McVay was the only captain to be court-martialled. His sentence was later remitted, but the guilt weighed heavily on McVay and in 1968 he committed suicide.

In October 2000 the US Congress passed a resolution that finally completely exonerated Captain McVay.

The Widowmaker

Deep in the Atlantic Ocean the Soviet submarine *K-19* suffered an accident that nearly caused a meltdown in its nuclear core. Several crew members walked in to certain death in the severely radioactive area to fix the leak. Their brave self-sacrifice saved most of the crew and managed to avert a nuclear disaster at the height of the Cold War.

DATE:
1961

SITUATION:
RADIATION LEAK

CONDITION OF CONFINEMENT:
IN A SUBMARINE FLOODED WITH RADIATION

DURATION OF CONFINEMENT:
12 HOURS FOR SOME, SEVERAL DAYS FOR OTHERS

MEANS OF ESCAPE:
SELF-SACRIFICE OF FELLOW CREW

NO. OF ESCAPEES:
117

DANGERS:
RADIATION POISONING, EXPLOSION, DROWNING

EQUIPMENT:
IMPROVISED REPAIRS, BOLD DECISION-MAKING, BRAVERY

ABOVE RIGHT
Coastline of the volcanic island of Jan Mayen, Norway.

A baptism of fire

When *K-19* first entered active service on 18 June 1961, Cold War tensions were rising. In 1958, Intermediate Range Ballistic Missiles had been deployed in the UK, and more were sited in Italy and Turkey in 1961, putting over 100 US nuclear missiles within striking distance of Moscow. In autumn 1962 the tensions would flare up into the Cuban Missile Crisis, the closest the world has ever come to a nuclear war.

Its inaugural mission was a month-long wargame to simulate a missile strike on Russia from the Barents Sea. For *K-19*'s 34-year-old captain, Nikolai Zateyev, and the 138 other crewmen and observers on board, these external factors must have multiplied the normal pressures of life inside the cramped submersible craft.

But after two weeks at sea all was well. Dives and missile systems tests had been successful. The crew had even celebrated Captain Zateyev's

35th birthday with homemade ice cream and a double ration of wine. The submarine turned for home.

But in the early hours of 4 July, *K-19* was cruising 100 m (328 ft) below the surface of the North Atlantic, when the wail of an alarm shattered the morning routine.

The pumps in the starboard nuclear reactor's cooling system had stopped. The needles on the system pressure gauge flickered and fell. There was a rupture in the piping that circulated cooling water through the reactor. With no coolant, the reactor core would catastrophically overheat and a nuclear explosion was likely to follow. Worse still, in the race to get the submarine built and launched, the Soviet navy had not fitted the recommended backup cooling system.

The situation could hardly be more serious. Somehow the reactor must be cooled – and quickly. But the submarine was 2,400 km (1,500 miles) from home.

Fixing a hole

First, the captain gave the order to surface and radio for help. But with a sickening sense of timing, the sub's antenna failed: they wouldn't be able to contact Moscow.

Now their only hope was to somehow improvise a new cooling system and get water into the reactor pressure vessel to cool the core. Unfortunately this meant that a team of crewmen would have to work within the shielded reactor area, which was flooded with a lethal radioactive cloud. Incredibly, the ship carried chemical suits, rather than radiation suits. There would be no way to protect the men from contamination. If they stepped into the core they would be stepping towards certain death. But if no one did the job, then everyone on board would die, either from radiation poisoning or from an explosion.

At 6.30 a.m., an eight-man repair team stepped into the contaminated Compartment 6 of the starboard nuclear reactor to fix up a new cooling system. The captain later wrote in his memoirs:

> 6 They walked into that compartment without hesitation, ready for hard work. I saw the same calm, the same self-possession in Ryzhikov, Kashenkov, Penkov, Kharitonov, Savkin and Starkov. 9

The air around the men in the reactor was lit by the pale violet of ionized hydrogen, which ignited with a pale blue flame around their welding torches. Retaining their concentration amid the intense heat and increasingly debilitating radiation poisoning must have required a superhuman effort.

They cut an air-vent valve from the reactor and welded a water pipe onto the valve stub. This allowed cooling water to flow into the stricken reactor. The temperature dropped from 800°C – close to the melting point of the rods – and began to stabilize.

But the patch job had taken over an hour. Simply opening the shielded reactor area had caused deadly radioactive steam to spread through the sub's ventilation system. More radioactive steam escaped as water cooled the reactor. Radiation also seeped from drain piping in Compartments 3 through 8.

Human exposure to radiation is measured in rems, which stands for 'röntgen equivalent in man'. Exposure to 100 rems will cause radiation sickness. A measure of 450 rems causes death in around 50 per cent of cases. The eight K-19 sailors who did most work on the leaking nuclear reactor sustained doses of 5,000–6,000 rems.

It was not until the repair team came out of the reactor that the full horror of what the crew was facing became apparent. The men ripped their gas masks off revealing horrifically blistered and swollen faces. They vomited yellow and white foam uncontrollably.

Worse was to come. Valves began to fail in Compartment 6 and the jury-rigged piping sprang a leak. Another team would have to go in to the core. The first men must have been fairly sure they were going to die. The second team could have been in no doubt.

Nevertheless, they stepped up. The ship's executive officer Vladimir Yenin was one of the first men to volunteer for the job.

Heading south

Meanwhile Captain Zateyev had a hard decision to make. He knew that the men in Compartment 6 would die horrible deaths. But he also knew that everyone else on board would similarly perish if they tried to sail the 2,400 km (1,500 miles) home – that would take them a week.

Two officers suggested that they set course for the NATO base on nearby Jan Mayen island. Perhaps scared that doing so would put his country's latest weapons in the hands of the enemy, Zateyev refused. Fearing a mutiny, he then ordered all small arms thrown overboard except for five pistols, which he gave to his most trusted officers.

Instead he made a bold and risky decision. He had remembered a chart he had accidentally glimpsed in the briefing room back home. It had shown that several Soviet diesel subs would be in waters south of K-19. This was in the opposite direction to home. But that's the course that K-19 took.

The next thing the captain did was issue everyone on board with a large ration of vodka. He later claimed this would lessen the effects of radiation poisoning; he had seen an intoxicated operator at an accident in a nuclear power plant emerge unscathed. But it may just have given the crew a dose of liquid courage.

American warships nearby had also heard the transmission and offered to help, a rare event during the Cold War, but Zateyev, afraid of giving away Soviet military secrets to the West, refused and sailed to meet the S-270.

K-19 sailed south for eight hours with no reply to their short-range distress calls. Zateyez was on the point of abandoning his plan when they finally received a response from a diesel submarine, S-270. After rendezvousing and disembarking the sickest men, K-19 was towed home.

The price of survival

Almost all the submarine, including its ballistic missiles, was severely contaminated. When it finally docked at Polyarnyy, near Murmansk, on July 9 it poisoned everything within 700 m (2,300 ft).

In less than a week, the eight men from the repair team had died of

GREENLAND

Greenland Sea

Svalbard
Spitsbergen

Barents Sea

① MISSION
K-19 heads for the North Atlantic for a month-long 'war game'.

③ CATASTROPHE
After turning for home, it is in the Norwegian Sea near the island of Jan Mayen when the cooling system on its starboard reactor ruptures.

Jan Mayen

Polyarnyy
Murma

Tromsø

③

④

Norwegian Sea

①

Reykjavík

ICELAND

④ CONTAMINATION
Highly contaminated with radiation, it surfaces and heads south looking for compatriot diesel submarines.

⑤

Gulf of Bothnia

EUROPE

⑤ RESCUE
It makes contact and is towed back to Russia.

②

② TESTING
The new submarine tests its dive capabilities and missile systems near Greenland.

Bergen

Baltic Sea

ATLANTIC OCEAN

North Sea

British Isles

KILOMETRES 0   200   400   600
MILES 0   100   200   300

radiation poisoning. Another fourteen crew members died in the next two years. Although the remaining 117 men survived, they all suffered from some radiation-related illness. Captain Zateyev died of cancer in 1998, aged 62.

K-19 was decontaminated, repaired, and returned to service in 1964. During its two-year refit many shipyard workers fell ill. Its new crew nicknamed it 'Hiroshima'.

Unlucky or just badly built?

K-19 was considered an unlucky vessel even before it took to sea. It was laid down at the naval yard in Severodvinsk on 17 October 1958 and was a first generation Soviet nuclear submarine. It was equipped with nuclear ballistic missiles. In 1959 a fire broke out while its ballast tanks were being constructed, killing three workmen. Tradition was broken at its launching ceremony on 11 October, when a man rather than a woman was chosen to smash the champagne bottle against the vessel. The bottle bounced off the rubber-coated hull without breaking. To sailors and submariners this is an extremely bad omen.

The official explanation of the disaster is that a drop from a welding electrode had fallen on a cooling circuit during the initial construction. However, this was perhaps a symptom, rather than a cause, of the problem. Soviet leaders had been so desperate to build a nuclear submarine fleet rivalling that of the US that they rushed designs through production without proper testing. Many naval officers, including Captain Zateyev, had lobbied for extra safety features such as emergency backup cooling systems but had been ignored.

Captain Zateyev and his crew were exonerated in an enquiry. But because the accident was a state secret, they were also sworn to secrecy. It wasn't until after the collapse of the Soviet Union that they were allowed to tell their story.

The Russian Hotel class nuclear submarine K-19, pictured in the Atlantic during its journey back to Russia, 1 March 1972. It was crippled by a fire off Newfoundland and had to be towed home.

Their extraordinary bravery was not fully recognized in their home country until March 2006, when Mikhail Gorbachev nominated Captain Zateyev and his surviving crewmembers for the Nobel Peace Prize.

Another near disaster

Five years after resuming active service, K-19 was involved in another serious accident. On 15 November 1969 the submarine was cruising in the Barents Sea at a depth of 60 m (200 ft) when it smashed into the American attack submarine USS Gato. The collision caused catastrophic damage to K19's bow sonar systems and its forward torpedo tube cover. But by blowing its emergency main ballast the captain was able to bring the sub to the surface and limp it home to port. After lengthy repairs, K-19 returned to the fleet.

A third tragedy

On 24 February 1972, K-19 was at a depth of 120 m (390 ft), some 700 nautical miles (1,300 km; 810 miles) from Newfoundland when hydraulic fluid leaked onto a hot filter causing a vicious, uncontrollable fire. Twenty-eight sailors died, but K-19 was once again repaired and returned to action.

K-19 never lived down its reputation as 'Hiroshima' and was finally decommissioned in 1991. The ceremony also served as a reunion for Captain Zateyev and the remaining survivors of K-19. The submarine languished in a shipyard until it was scrapped in 2002.

Together Alone

MAURICE AND MARALYN BAILEY WERE LIVING THEIR DREAM – SAILING THEIR YACHT FROM ENGLAND TO NEW ZEALAND WHEN IT WAS STRUCK BY A WHALE AND SUNK. FOR THE NEXT FOUR MONTHS THEY DRIFTED ACROSS THE PACIFIC IN A TINY RAFT, EATING TURTLES AND DRINKING STORMWATER TO SURVIVE.

DATE:
1973

SITUATION:
SHIPWRECK

CONDITION OF CONFINEMENT:
FLOATING ON THE PACIFIC IN A LIFE RAFT

DURATION OF CONFINEMENT:
117 DAYS

MEANS OF ESCAPE:
RESCUE

NO. OF ESCAPEES:
2

DANGERS:
STARVATION, DEHYDRATION, DROWNING

EQUIPMENT:
LIFE RAFT, SOME RATIONS, SOME EMERGENCY EQUIPMENT

LEFT
A sperm whale dives into the ocean.

ABOVE RIGHT
Maurice and Maralyn Bailey with the sextant and life raft which helped them to survive four months afloat. They told their incredible story in the book *117 Days Adrift*.

The dream

Escaping suburbia and exploring the wide world together, that was their dream. And while many people never achieve their ambitions, Maurice and Maralyn Bailey were the kind of people who put their plans into action.

They sold their house in Derby and moved to the south coast of England to oversee the construction of their dream – a beautiful yacht of 9.5 m (31 ft) with twin keels. They intended to fit her out, live on her and ultimately sail her to New Zealand.

They called her *Auralyn*, a combination of their names.

In June 1972 they set out from Southampton. They sailed via Spain, Portugal, Madeira, and the Canary Islands before crossing the Atlantic to the West Indies. They enjoyed the freedom of life on the ocean and the closeness to nature. They made friends in the ports they visited. The stresses of shore life were far, far behind them.

By early February 1973 they were in Panamá where they had *Auralyn* overhauled, repainted and restocked with provisions to last nine months. They were ready to cross the Pacific.

On 27 February 1973 they left Panamá on a course to the Galapagos Islands, ten days' sailing to the southwest. The ocean was blue and peaceful, and they had everything they wanted.

Six days into their Pacific adventure, they were having breakfast one morning when there was a noise like a small explosion on the port side. A 12 m (40 ft) sperm whale was thrashing wildly off their stern. Its blood frothed in the water. Their first concern was for the injured mammal; then they found the hole.

It was 45 cm (18 inches) long and 30 cm (12 inches) high, below the waterline on the port side. They tried to cover it with a sail then stuff it with blankets. It was no good. *Auralyn* was going down. Maurice and Maralyn launched their life raft and small inflatable dinghy. They grabbed as much essential gear as they could and abandoned their beloved boat. Fifty minutes after the whale had struck they watched their dream slip below the Pacific waves. It would be four months before they set foot on another boat.

The long float

Their life raft was roughly circular and 1.4 m (4½ ft) across. Not big enough for them to lie down, nor could they stand and move about. With the kit stowed around its rubber tube walls they had just enough room to stretch out their legs when sitting down. Unable to both lie down together, they would take turns sleeping for a few hours at a time. The raft also lost air slowly, so the person on watch had to keep it pumped up.

The raft had a rubberized dome cover which would keep off rain and direct sunlight but not heat. The dinghy, which was roped to the raft, was about 2.7 m (9 ft) long with a seat and oars.

As far as provisions went, they had enough tins of food and water for twenty days with careful rationing.

Also on board were two plastic bowls and a bucket, a kit bag of clothes, compass, oilskins, an emergency pack, a torch, logbook, an almanac, charts, sextant and diary. Maralyn had also salvaged some books.

The couple discussed the possibility of a rescue. No one in England was expecting them to call for months. There had been vague plans to meet other yachtsmen at the Galapagos Islands, but nothing concrete. And even if their friends did report them missing, where would authorities start the search?

They might drift into a shipping lane. But this was the Pacific, not the English Channel. The ocean is vast. Months might pass between ships. Even then, their little craft could barely be seen above the swell. To them the horizon was only 5 km (3 miles) away: their little world was tiny indeed.

The first few days

Their first breakfast on the raft was biscuits smeared with margarine; a luxury compared with what they would later eat. Lunch was a handful of peanuts. They rationed themselves to a pint of water each a day.

Maurice reckoned they were 480 km (300 miles) east of the Galapagos. The current they were in would take them northwest, past the islands. Could they row south using the dinghy's oars to the same latitude as the Galapagos? The drift would then bring them to land. It would mean rowing 16 km (10 miles) every day while towing the raft.

It was too hot to row during the day, so they worked at night, taking turns. Towing the raft made it painfully slow going and after eight hours they were exhausted, had blistered hands and, even on double water rations, were excruciatingly thirsty.

Their first night's efforts had taken them 6 km (4 miles) south, but they had drifted 48 km (30 miles) west. However fast they rowed, the current would take them past the Galapagos before they got far enough south. After two more hard nights trying they let the ocean take them.

They soon discovered that 15 litres (4 gallons) of their precious water had been contaminated by sea water. They needed to collect rain if they were to survive. But for four days the sun roasted them from a cloudless sky. They tried to keep cool during the broiling heat of the day by soaking their clothes in sea water. Lightning came but no rain. They were literally in the Doldrums, the area either side of the equator where ships were often becalmed for days or weeks at a time.

But they weren't totally alone. Maurice and Maralyn were surprised to sea that turtles came right up to the boat. Many bumped into it. Worried that barnacles on the creatures' shells would damage the raft, they pushed them away with the oar. They still had food, so it wasn't necessary to think about eating one. Yet.

March

The first week had passed quickly; they had kept busy with their routines and it was easy to be optimistic.

A Green Turtle, the species the Bailey's managed to catch and eat to stay alive.

Then on 12 March, eight days after *Auralyn* sank, they saw a ship – a small fishing boat or yacht. It was just 3 km (2 miles) away and closing. They quickly dug out their emergency flares.

The first one was a dud. Maurice threw it into the sea in frustration. Then he sent up two more. The ship was only 1.5 km (1 mile) away. But it hadn't seen them. Their craft was so small and low and the sea so big that the odds of being spotted were not on their side. A boat would practically have to be on top of them to see them. And the chances of that happening in the Pacific were very low.

Their spirits were equally subdued. They wanted to kill a turtle and use its meat to fish with, only they hadn't repacked the fish hooks into their emergency pack at Panama.

The turtles were so docile and unafraid that they bumped the boat as if in greeting. It wasn't that hard to grab one and haul it into the boat. Killing it, however, was a little trickier. They stunned the beast with the raft's paddle, only for it to come flapping back to life as they cut its throat. Eventually they dispatched it and collected its rich blood. But they were more nauseated than hungry and they threw it overboard. The fish had no such scruples and they sucked greedily at the congealing blood. They did, however butcher the turtle and keep four steaks of its white meat.

Maralyn had the idea of turning safety pins from their first-aid pack into hooks. They watched with joy as fish immediately went for the dangling turtle flesh. They soon landed several purple-grey trigger fish, each 15–23 cm (6–9 inches) long – ample for their breakfast.

Fish were easy to catch and fillet and soon they ate little else. The white-meat steaks were palatable, as were the hearts and eyeballs, which contained a thirst-quenching liquid.

Their days became occupied with the business of catching and gutting fish. They also read their books to each other a page at a time, played word games and improvised dominoes and playing cards from the logbook's blank pages.

At one point a huge sperm whale surfaced right beside them, close enough for the spray from its blowhole to fall like raindrops on the canopy. It slashed around them for what seemed like an age, apparently making advances towards the raft. There was nothing they could do but sit perfectly still, admire its majesty and hope it didn't push its suit further. One flick of its tail and they would be capsized in an instant. They would lose their gear and worse: Maralyn couldn't swim. Eventually, its love unrequited, the whale dived beneath the waves.

I would rather serve a prison sentence; at least there would be a known date of release! Here every day becomes more of a nightmare.

From *117 Days Adrift* by Maurice & Maralyn Bailey.

At last a new day brought rain. Maralyn placed a bucket beneath the lookout opening in the raft's cover to collect water. To their dismay this was undrinkable: it was contaminated with the waterproof rubber coating washed from the canopy. Gradually, the taste improved as this coating washed off.

They caught and ate another turtle, eating its white meat and green fat with half a tin of Bolognese sauce. Then they drank its blood and ate its heart. Rainstorms came more frequently, allowing them to top up their containers with clean water. But they also had to spend hours mopping up the floor to avoid being swamped.

Towards the end of March they saw another ship, a tanker. They only had two flares left. The first was another dud. The last flare fired, but the ship didn't see them. They were close enough for them to see the warm light of the cabins through the portholes.

April

Although they were both getting thinner by the day and their hair was becoming long and straggly, some squalls in early April brought them plentiful water. There were also many turtles around the raft. They tied a rope round the rear flippers of a big one to see if it could tow them. It promptly set off towards the Galapagos. Delighted, they attached a line to another one, but it set off in the opposite direction.

Another ship passed only 0.8 km (½ mile) away. Maurice had made a smoke flare from scraps of cloth doused in kerosene and set in a cake tin. Again, no one on the vessel saw them. Two more boats missed them. Then began several days of really rough weather. They were now drifting 32 km (20 miles) a day northeast.

Maurice was fishing one day when his catch pulled away, the hook flew back and punctured the dinghy. They patched it, but as they did so, a whole container of water fell overboard. The raft was also punctured by spines of a fish. They stayed sane by drawing up detailed plans for their next boat.

The patches in their emergency pack didn't work. The floor of the raft now sagged and pinched their flesh. They were unable to get comfortable for more than five minutes at a time and had to pump air into the raft every half an hour.

What's more, by now the raft's canopy was no longer waterproof. Every shower soaked them and they had to bale out the boat almost constantly.

May

The new month brought more bad weather. The cotton seam between the two rings of the raft was also rotting. If it got much worse the raft would fall apart. Further bad luck dogged them: they got sick at this time from water that had turned green from too much algae.

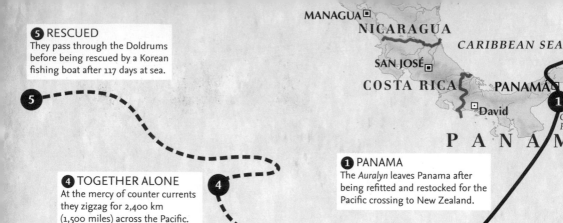

⑤ RESCUED
They pass through the Doldrums before being rescued by a Korean fishing boat after 117 days at sea.

① PANAMA
The *Auralyn* leaves Panama after being refitted and restocked for the Pacific crossing to New Zealand.

④ TOGETHER ALONE
At the mercy of counter currents they zigzag for 2,400 km (1,500 miles) across the Pacific.

③ DINGHY AFLOAT
Maurice and Maralyn take to the dinghy. They attempt to row south, but the Humboldt Current pushes them northwest.

② AURALYN SINKS
The yacht is six days into its first leg to the Galapagos when it is struck and sunk by a whale.

PACIFIC OCEAN

ISLAS GALÁPAGOS
(Galapagos Islands)

I. Isabela
(Albemarle I.)

KILOMETRES 0 100 200 300 400

MILES 0 50 100 150 200

KILOMETRES 0 1000

MILES 0 500

The sixth and seventh ships came and went.

For the next six weeks they saw no ships at all, and came to realize the true vastness of the ocean. They were continually busy fishing or gutting and preparing their meal.

They talked endlessly of food, anything that wasn't fish gills, heads, livers or eyes. By the end of May, Maurice was very ill. A hacking cough brought up blood. His ulcerated sores were agonizing in the salt water. Sharks bashed into the underside of the raft, making them yell with pain and leaving bruises.

They did have one piece of good fortune: a female turtle provided them with dozens of protein-rich eggs.

June

With another new month, the couple tried a new tactic of preserving their food. Sometimes the sea was bountiful: they occasionally caught over one hundred trigger fish a day. But storms could also make fishing impossible.

They tried drying fish to see if they would keep only for a downpour of unbelievable ferocity to turn their larder to mush.

On 5 June they hit a new low. Continual storms were tossing them around the ocean like a cork. Waves frequently overwhelmed the raft forcing them to bale furiously. They were continually hip-deep in water and their sores had become raw wounds.

They were managing only minutes of sleep at a time. Maurice went fishing in the dinghy only for a massive wave to swamp him, sending their bait and fishing gear under.

On 21 June a school of sharks started circling. Maralyn reached over the side and caught the tail of a small one, and soon had it wrapped in a towel in the boat. They caught and ate three.

Amid the scrabbling for survival they had odd moments of calm and an almost spiritual closeness to

Maurice and Maralyn Bailey relive their ordeal at the London Boat Show, January 1974.

nature. The incredible display of stars on a clear night brought Maurice peace and a feeling of understanding towards his fellow man. They enjoyed a visit from a whale shark, the largest fish in the world and one of nature's most elusive characters.

They also captured two baby turtles, which they kept as pets in the dinghy.

30 June, day 118

It was the first time he had slept longer than an hour for weeks and Maurice was dreaming there was someone else in the raft with them when Maralyn said: 'Get out to the dinghy. A ship is coming.'

There was a small, rusty fishing boat 0.8 km (½ mile) away. It was the first ship they had seen for forty-three days. As it went past Maralyn was waving so hard she nearly tipped them over. But, like the seven other boats before, it kept on sailing.

Then they stared at each other in disbelief. It was coming back.

It really was going to pick them up. Just then they realized they were naked. They struggled into their

soaking tennis shorts and rotting shirts and let their pet turtles swim free in the ocean.

Suddenly the hard hull of the boat was right beside them. Lines were thrown down. Foreign voices chattered excitedly above. Then one man said:

'Can you speak English?'

'We are English,' Maurice replied.

Going home

Maurice and Maralyn had drifted 2,400 km (1,500 miles). They had each lost around a quarter of their bodyweight. Their legs were barely able to support their emaciated frames.

On 13 July, the *Weolmi*, the Korean fishing boat that picked them up, reached Honolulu. The Baileys stepped onto dry land amid a swarm of reporters. Their story had made them world famous. They enjoyed a few days of luxury as guests of the manager at the Sheraton Waikiki, then they returned to England.

The following year, they were back on the ocean in their new yacht, the *Auralyn II*.

Condensation of *117 Days Adrift* by Maurice and Maralyn Bailey, published by Adlard Coles Nautical. Reproduced with permission.

The Life Raft

AFTER FORTY-THREE DAYS OF DRIFTING IN HIS TINY LIFE RAFT, STEVEN CALLAHAN WAS EXCITED: HE HAD SPEARED A FISH. BUT THE CREATURE JERKED AND THE BROKEN SPEAR PUNCTURED HIS RAFT. SOMEHOW HE HAD TO MAKE A REPAIR, KEEP THE WATER OUT AND STAY SANE. IT WOULD BE ANOTHER THIRTY-THREE DAYS BEFORE HE WAS RESCUED.

DATE:
1982

SITUATION:
SHIPWRECK

CONDITION OF CONFINEMENT:
ADRIFT IN A LIFE RAFT

DURATION OF CONFINEMENT:
76 DAYS

MEANS OF ESCAPE:
SELF-DISCIPLINE, HUNTING FISH, CATCHING RAINWATER

NO. OF ESCAPEES:
1

DANGERS:
DROWNING, DEHYDRATION, STARVATION

EQUIPMENT:
SOME RATIONS AND HIS BOAT'S EMERGENCY EQUIPMENT

ABOVE RIGHT
Yacht at high speed.

One man against an ocean

Steven Callahan was self-reliant even by the standards of solo yachtsmen: he had been sailing since he was 12, had helped build a 12 m (40 ft) yacht before he was out of high school and by the time he was 22 he was a professional boat-builder.

But on this voyage he would push the boundaries of what a man can do on his own at sea.

The dream

Ever since he had devoured the books about famous ocean voyages as a teenager, Callahan had dreamed of having a great adventure of his own. In 1980, aged 29, he decided what that voyage would be: the Mini Transat 6.50, a prestigious solo transatlantic race where the yachts are limited to 6.5 metres (21 ft) in length. The race went from Penzance, England to Antigua, West Indies with a stopover in the Canary Islands.

First, he had to get a suitable boat. Callahan sold his old trimaran and scraped together all the money he could to build a new vessel, the *Napoleon Solo*, a 6.5 m cruiser. He designed, built and fitted-out this craft himself.

Then he needed to qualify for the race, by sailing 966 km (600 miles) single handed in *Solo*. In June 1981 Callahan sailed out of Newport, Rhode Island to do just that. His destination was Bermuda and he made the demanding 635 nautical mile (1,000 km; 730 mile) voyage successfully. He then picked up his friend Chris Latchem and they made an exhilarating Atlantic crossing to Cornwall, England for the start of the race.

The race

There were bad omens from the start. In September severe gales in the English Channel damaged many yachts before the race had even started. One French sailor was killed when his boat was wrecked on the Lizard.

At the start of the race the yachtsmen faced 3 m (10 ft) waves and high winds. On the first leg to Spain five out of the twenty-five starters sank. Luckily all the sailors were rescued.

Callahan arrived safely in La Coruña, but his hull had been dented by debris. The race was over for him. However, he still dreamed of making the solo Atlantic crossing and he managed to repair his boat before continuing down the coast of Spain and Portugal, then out to Madeira and the Canaries.

Calm before the storm

On the night of 29 January 1982, Callahan set sail from El Hierro, the most southerly island of the Canaries. For six days the going was fair. He made good time; enjoyed the subtly changing face of the sea; relaxed in the sun with a novel. Then the storm hit him.

> ❛ Each ten foot wave that sweeps by contains more tons of water than I care to imagine. ❜
> Steven Callahan in *Adrift*

After lashing down everything that needed to be secured, he went down below to get some rest as the night seas roared around him. Around midnight he was shaken in his bunk by a colossal crash, and Callahan jumped up to see a torrent of water flooding over the boat. He had been hit by something large, probably a whale. He was going to have to abandon ship.

> ❛ BANG! A deafening explosion blankets the subtler sounds of torn wood fiber and the rush of sea. ❜
> Steven Callahan in *Adrift*.

But Callahan had designed his cruiser well, and the watertight compartments he had built

prevented the vessel from sinking immediately. Callahan was able to retrieve a sleeping bag, a cushion, some food, charts, a short spear gun, flares, torch, solar stills for producing rainwater and a survival manual.

Then he climbed into a circular life raft 1.7 m (5½ ft) in diameter and watched his dream go under. Just before dawn, a huge wave broke the rope linking the life raft to the boat and Callahan drifted away.

Alone and unheard

Callahan knew he couldn't count on being rescued. He had an EPIRB (Emergency Position Indicating Radio Beacon) but this was not monitored by satellites at the time, and the ocean he was drifting across was too empty

for him to be heard by aircraft. He was not in a shipping lane.

Agonizingly, in his time adrift he saw nine ships but none of them noticed his emergency flares.

The South Equatorial Current and the trade winds were taking the raft west. But he was around 3,000 km (1,864 miles) from the most easterly of the Caribbean islands. He was going to have to rely upon himself for as long as possible if he were to survive his ordeal.

The right attitude

Callahan knew that mental discipline would be the key to his

A yacht in choppy waters off the coast of Gran Canaria, Canary Islands.

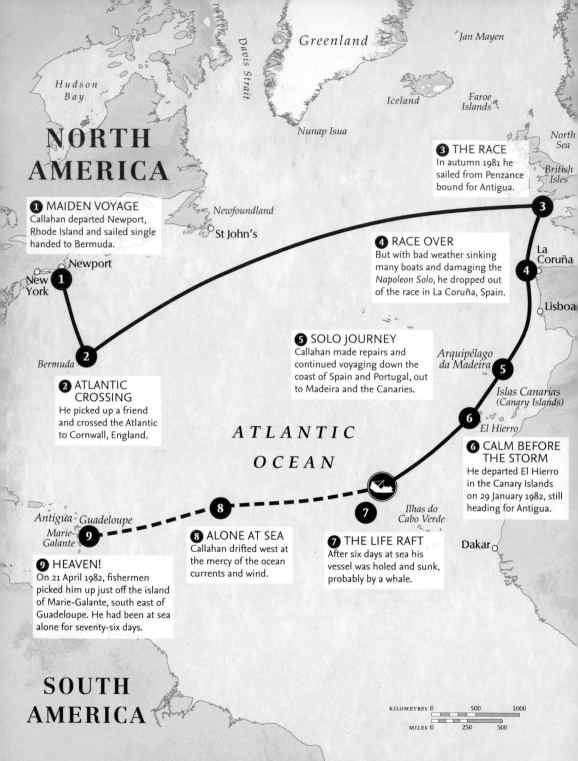

Greenland

Jan Mayen

Davis Strait

Hudson Bay

Iceland

Faroe Islands

Nunap Isua

NORTH AMERICA

North Sea

❸ **THE RACE**
In autumn 1981 he sailed from Penzance bound for Antigua.

British Isles

Newfoundland

3

❶ **MAIDEN VOYAGE**
Callahan departed Newport, Rhode Island and sailed single handed to Bermuda.

St John's

❹ **RACE OVER**
But with bad weather sinking many boats and damaging the *Napoleon Solo*, he dropped out of the race in La Coruña, Spain.

La Coruña

New York

Newport

1

4

Lisboa

❺ **SOLO JOURNEY**
Callahan made repairs and continued voyaging down the coast of Spain and Portugal, out to Madeira and the Canaries.

Arquipélago da Madeira

Bermuda

2

5

❷ **ATLANTIC CROSSING**
He picked up a friend and crossed the Atlantic to Cornwall, England.

Islas Canarias (Canary Islands)

ATLANTIC OCEAN

6

El Hierro

❻ **CALM BEFORE THE STORM**
He departed El Hierro in the Canary Islands on 29 January 1982, still heading for Antigua.

8

7

Ilhas do Cabo Verde

Antigua *Guadeloupe*

Marie-Galante

9

❽ **ALONE AT SEA**
Callahan drifted west at the mercy of the ocean currents and wind.

❼ **THE LIFE RAFT**
After six days at sea his vessel was holed and sunk, probably by a whale.

Dakar

❾ **HEAVEN!**
On 21 April 1982, fishermen picked him up just off the island of Marie-Galante, south east of Guadeloupe. He had been at sea alone for seventy-six days.

SOUTH AMERICA

KILOMETRES 0   500   1000

MILES 0   250   500

Triggerfish became part of Callahan's diet whilst drifting across the Atlantic Ocean.

physical survival. He routinely exercised, navigated and made repairs. He gave himself tasks to perform and set targets. He rationed what little food he had, but this didn't last long and he soon looked around for new sources of nutrition.

He noticed that dorados (dolphin fish) had started to swim near his raft, so he made a makeshift spear. After many frustrating attempts at killing one, he noticed that when he pressed his knees in the centre of the raft's floor the fish would cluster round and hit the protrusion this made. This brought them closer for longer and he was able to successfully make a catch.

Callahan also caught triggerfish, flying fish and birds, which were attracted by the fish. His little raft soon developed its own little ecosystem including barnacles on the underside, which he harvested. Callahan used two solar stills and other improvised devices to collect an average of 0.5 litre (1 pint) of water a day. He scraped rust from peanut

and coffee cans, and added the flecks to his dwindling supply of drinking water, hoping this would add iron to his weakening body. When his hunting was successful he stored his food and water for emergencies.

On the forty-third day alone on the ocean, a dorado he had speared squirmed loose and rammed the broken spear into one of the raft's inflated tubes, leaving a gaping hole. Callahan patched the raft but his repair often came loose and for the remainder of his ordeal he struggled constantly to keep water out of the boat.

> **Dorados were the main fish that kept Callahan alive, but the same species nearly killed him.**

But, metre by metre, he drifted across the Atlantic.

Spotted

On 20 April 1982, he saw heaven: lights on the island of Marie-Galante, south east of Guadeloupe. The next day some fishermen spotted the birds that hovered above his raft and sailed to investigate. They were astonished to be greeted by a skinny man with a long beard who looked ill but was nevertheless smiling broadly.

Steven Callahan had lost a third of his bodyweight and was covered with scores of saltwater sores. He had travelled 1,800 nautical miles (3,300 km; 2,050 miles) across the ocean and spent seventy-six days alone. But he was alive.

After a brief visit in a local hospital, he spent a few weeks recovering on the island. Then he continued his journey, hitchhiking on boats up through the West Indies.

If anything the experience further cemented Callahan's love of the ocean. He went on to make many more epic voyages, many of them alone. He also used his experiences to help others: he designed an improved life raft with a better canopy, a fibreglass bottom and, most importantly, a sail so that survivors don't have to just drift.

Islands of Les Saintes, Guadeloupe.

The Last Friend

WHEN NOVICE SAILOR RICHARD CHARRINGTON JOINED FOUR FRIENDS ON A CATAMARAN IN THE MEDITERRANEAN, HE WAS EXPECTING A FUN VOYAGE OF GOOD CONVERSATION AND FINE WINE. THEN A FREAK STORM CAPSIZED THE BOAT AND HE CLUNG DESPERATELY TO LIFE AS ONE BY ONE HIS FRIENDS SLIPPED INTO THE TOWERING WAVES.

DATE:
1995

SITUATION:
SHIPWRECK

CONDITION OF CONFINEMENT:
CLINGING TO A CAPSIZED CATAMARAN

DURATION OF CONFINEMENT:
16 HOURS

MEANS OF ESCAPE:
RESCUE

NO. OF ESCAPEES:
1

DANGERS:
DROWNING

EQUIPMENT:
LIFE JACKET

LEFT
A catamaran anchored in the Mediterranean.

ABOVE RIGHT
Sea view from the island of Porquerolles in the South of France.

The victory voyage

It was a cool autumn evening in the South of France and the five friends were winding down on the deck of their catamaran. The trip was a celebration; the men were in business together and their latest venture had gone well. On board were four Frenchmen: brothers Jean-Claude and Philippe, Hervé, Pascal and Englishman Richard Charrington. Their catamaran, *Bayete*, was a new Catana 44 packed with the latest electronics and safety equipment. Richard and Philippe were novice sailors; the other three were very experienced.

Tomorrow they'd have work to do; they'd be sailing for the Balearics on the first leg of an epic journey. They would then pass through the Strait of Gibraltar and on to Casablanca where they'd join 100 other craft in the 1995 Transat des Passionnés regatta to the Canary Islands and then across the Atlantic to the Caribbean.

A nasty little storm had blown up earlier in the day, forcing them to shelter in the protected harbour at the island of Porquerolles. But it seemed to have passed them by, and now they could afford to kick off their deck shoes and enjoy their meal of lamb with herbs and sip a glass or two of fine burgundy.

The quiet storm

At 8 a.m. the next morning the sun was beating down from a cloudless blue sky. It was so calm that their largest sail, a spinnaker, couldn't catch enough wind and they had to start the engines. They didn't have an official forecast as the French meteorological office was on strike, but the barometer was rising, and other weather forecasters indicated that the storm had passed.

The boat headed out into the Golfe du Lion. Here the mistral wind often causes sudden storms between Corsica and the Balearics, making it the most dangerous area of the

Mediterranean. On this day it would also combine with Arctic winds from the northwest into a freak storm of eighty knot winds and wave troughs as deep as 10 m (33 ft).

> **❛ The Mediterranean was brewing its own little perfect storm. ❜**

But the onslaught started subtly. Around noon the boat ran into some slow rollers. These made the greenhorns, Richard and Philippe, seasick, but didn't unduly worry the others. By 2 p.m., though, the wind had picked up markedly and everyone on board was being violently ill.

It was also starting to make them uneasy in their minds; the wind was now preventing them from steering the *Bayete* on their desired course. The Balearics were to the southwest on a heading of 210 degrees, but the best they could manage was 180 degrees, straight south.

An hour later, Richard's hand-held barometer sounded an alarm; the pressure was falling at an alarming rate. He showed it to Jean-Claude and together they laughed at what they took to be an erratic reading from a cheap piece of kit. Unfortunately for the friends, it was a warning that they ought to have heeded.

Speeding up

Still the wind and waves rose. Around 4 p.m. Jean-Claude decided to unfurl a few feet of the jib and run before the storm.

For almost an hour the crew had a wild ride, doing 12 knots (22 km/h; 14 mph) and almost surfing the rising waves. They shot up huge, steep faces and over spraying crests then crashed down hard into the face of the next wave. As the bows plunged several metres into solid water it seemed like the boat was ramming a wall, time and time again.

To Richard it was utterly terrifying.

Slowing down

Around 5 p.m., the wind gauge was tipping 80 knots (148 km/h; 92 mph) – hurricane speed – and it felt much colder. Even Jean-Claude knew that they were in danger. There was no point in them continuing so far and fast off course. He decided to furl the sail and use the engines to turn into the wind. They would then deploy the sea anchor. This acts almost as an underwater parachute, slowing the boat as it is blown by extreme winds.

But as they tried to secure the sea anchor to the bows, it was snatched from their grasp and blown into the water before the lines could be tied to the bows.

They fought the wind for more than half an hour to get one line secured. But their hands were too cold to grip properly and the other line still flicked free. Finally, Jean-Claude was forced to attach it to the wire between the bows that held the mast. This seemed to temporarily solve the problem but, crucially, the sea anchor was now at an angle to the boat, which had tragic repercussions later.

At the time though, they felt victorious. All they had to do was sit out the storm. They went below, stripped out of their heavy gear and tried to get some sleep.

Richard didn't sleep at first. He sat up in the salon, jerking backwards and forwards to the sharp pitch of the boat and feeling that he was way, way out of his depth.

Yachts in Porquerolles harbour.

High waves during a storm in the Mediterranean Sea.

Richard found himself looking at Jean-Claude and Hervé's survival suits and wishing he had one too. Then Hervé disappeared.

A wave simply knocked him out of the hatch. He skidded down the convex hull, scrabbling for a piece of rope. Jean-Claude dived out and tried to pull him back in.

But the bulky suits with their thick fingers make gripping difficult. Hervé kept sliding. Another wave struck and he was gone forever. Then Jean-Claude was sliding down after him. He caught Richard's eyes and the terrible truth was clear to both of them.

> ‘ He knew it, I knew it, and he was gone. I was the last to look him in the eye as he was swept away. ’

One by one

With two men gone, Richard could fit both of his legs in the hatch now. He felt safer, but also guilty: two of his friends had died to give him that extra grip.

Philippe began to get rapidly worse. Already nearly rigid with cold, he had just watched his brother get swept away to his fate. He decided to get his body down into the hatch, out of reach of the waves.

But the water in the hatch quickly chilled his body. Some time around midnight, three hours after the boat flipped, he lost consciousness. Soon Philippe was dead.

Now Pascal wanted to go below. He thought he might be able to find an airspace where they could wait out the storm. They pushed Philippe's dead body down out of the way and Pascal dropped into the water. It wasn't long before he was back with bad news: the boat was too flooded for him to find any sanctuary. He climbed out, but the dip had dangerously lowered his temperature.

Not long after he climbed back, Richard was astonished to hear Pascal start complaining of being

Once he did finally turn in, he had only been asleep for two hours when he was thrown back to consciousness by the boat slowly flipping over.

He rolled out of his bunk onto the ceiling and his gear crashed down on top of him. He pulled on a tracksuit top and bottoms, then a waterproof padded jacket and a life jacket.

Jean-Claude then appeared: he yelled at them to get out through the escape hatch. With the boat now upside down he was worried that it was going to sink, in which case they needed to get into the life raft.

Climbing up to hell

The way out was through a hatch in the floor, which was now above their heads. They stood on the underside of the salon table and crawled out onto the bottom of the boat.

As soon as the hatch opened, waves smashed into them and water flooded into the boat. The wind and waves were so loud that the men couldn't hear each other even though they were within touching distance.

Although Philippe brought the Emergency Position-Indicating Radio Beacon (EPIRB), it was ripped away as soon as they were outside. Now they

knew that any rescue attempt would be decoyed to the wrong place.

The life raft should have automatically deployed. It hadn't. Hervé tried to find the line that would launch it. But this was deep underwater, hidden away across a sloping smooth fibreglass surface with no handholds. With the boat pitching sharply and the water so cold, trying to swim to the line would be suicide.

Help wasn't coming. They could not escape. The storm seemed never-ending. They could only hold on.

Hanging in the hatch

The five men sat, each with one leg in the open hatch, clinging onto stray ropes and each other – anything to stop them sliding into the ferocious ocean. Meanwhile the waves tried to strip them from their perch, pounding and pulling them relentlessly.

Richard's tracksuit bottoms had been torn from his body, leaving him naked from the waist down. The sharp edge of the hatch opening had begun to tear the skin from the back of his bare leg. Every tilt of the boat, every thump of a wave and the pain got worse.

F R A N C E

Marseille Toulon

GOLFE DU LION Île de
Porquerolles Îles
d'Hyères

SPAIN

Barcelona

❶ THE VICTORY VOYAGE
3 November 1995: the catamaran
Bayete is en route from Porquerolles
to the Balearics on the first stage of
a journey that would pass through
the Strait of Gibraltar and on to
Casablanca.

❷ SPEEDING UP
The boat is caught by a violent
storm just a few hours after
leaving port. They run with the
gale for a while before hurricane-
force winds blow them off course.

❸ SLOWING DOWN
After dropping the sea anchor
to slow their progress they try
to wait out the storm.

❹ *BAYETE* CAPSIZES
But huge seas capsize the
catamaran in the night,
150 km (93 miles) off the
coast of Marseille.

❺ HANGING ON
The crew climb onto the hull.
The emergency beacon is
torn from their grasp and
drifts away, pointing potential
rescuers to a false position.

❻ SOLE SURVIVOR
The five friends cling to the
upturned boat in a battle
for survival. Only one man
is still alive when rescuers
arrive the next day.

MEDITERRANEAN

SEA

Menorca
(Minorca)

Mallorca
(Majorca)

ISLAS BALEARES
(BALEARIC ISLANDS)

Illa de Cabrera

KILOMETRES 0   50   100

MILES 0   25   50

too hot. Terrified, he watched his friend tear off his jacket and throw it into the sea.

Hypothermia and exhaustion had made Pascal delirious. The heat he felt was an illusion. It wasn't long before his exposed body succumbed to the cold. His hands loosened their grip on the rope; his legs dangled loose.

And Richard was alone.

Hanging on... and on

Dawn brought Richard no solace, only the terror of being able to see the enormity of the waves that smashed into him every twenty or thirty seconds. He could also see his dead friends, now pale and stiff.

His eyes were almost swollen shut with the constant saltwater dousing. When he did manage to look at his legs he could see the flesh was either black with frostbite or red with blood. Richard knew he was going to die. The only question was when and of what – drowning or hypothermia?

> **⁶ I didn't have any hope I'd be rescued. No hope at all. ⁹**

At one point he was thrown off balance by a wave and one leg came out of the hatch. As he toppled over his watch caught on a small eye ring. His wrist was badly gouged, but the watch saved him.

Thereafter he settled into a hellish routine. A wave would hit, submerging him. He would clench his muscles and keep hanging on. Once the water fell he would breathe. He would just have time to feel the pain from more torn skin or cracked bone and then the next wave would come.

He knew he had no hope of ultimate survival, but he held on because he was furious. He had told his family this would be a fun trip – wine, cigars and the celebration of years of hard work. Now, because he didn't face up to the real risks, he would never see them again.

Well, the storm wouldn't have it all its own way.

He clung on.

Hoisted back to life

Richard's legs had been numb for hours. Shivers wracked his body continuously. Hypothermia had him in its grip. So when he saw the helicopter with a diver dangling from a line beneath it, he thought it was a near-death hallucination.

But then the diver was beside him on the hull. He was shouting words in his ear, though they were lost in the still-raging storm. Then he was flying.

The pain of recovery

Although he was off the boat, Richard wasn't out of danger. He had so much internal bruising that when he arrived at hospital in Toulon, his urine was black. The doctor told him he would probably die from kidney failure.

He also suffered agony as his wounds were treated. The entire backs of his legs and his buttocks were one mass of red, raw flesh. The grafts to repair his skin needed more than 250 staples.

The once-in-a-lifetime storm

Since the race was first run in 1981, more than 5,000 sailors had entered the Transat des Passionnés and none had suffered any serious misfortune. The 1995 storm generated hurricane force winds of 170 km/h (106 mph) and raged for several days. Three further boats were wrecked or sunk. Six men were lost from the yacht *Parsifal*. And despite an extensive rescue operation, none of Richard's friends made it.

The *Bayete* did not completely sink. Catamarans are very buoyant and there was a chance that they could have ridden out the storm had they stayed below. But in the terrifying tumult of the storm, that wasn't obvious. Jean-Claude was an expert sailor and he did what he thought was right.

With cruel irony, Richard may have survived because he *wasn't* a lean and hardy sailor. He had more body fat than his friends, which may have helped him stay warmer longer in the cold.

Or it may simply have been luck. Low on fuel, the helicopter pilot had turned back to base when, from the very corner of his eye, he had spotted the tiny orange flash of Richard's life jacket against the white bottom of the boat.

A man being hoisted to safety after a helicopter rescue at sea.

HOSTAGES

Six Years in Beirut

JOURNALIST TERRY ANDERSON WAS PLAYING TENNIS IN BEIRUT IN 1985
WHEN HE WAS SNATCHED BY GUNMEN. HE WOULD SPEND THE NEXT SIX
YEARS IN BRUTAL CONDITIONS, CHAINED TO A BED AND KEPT IN SOLITARY
CONFINEMENT FOR MONTHS ON END. SOMEHOW HE FOUND THE COURAGE
TO STAND UP TO HIS CAPTORS AND RETAIN HIS SANITY.

DATE:
1985–91

SITUATION:
KIDNAPPING

**CONDITION OF
CONFINEMENT:**
CHAINED TO A BED, USUALLY
IN SOLITARY CONFINEMENT

**DURATION OF
CONFINEMENT:**
6 YEARS, 9 MONTHS

MEANS OF ESCAPE:
RELEASE

NO. OF ESCAPEES:
1

DANGERS:
MURDER, TORTURE,
STARVATION

EQUIPMENT:
NONE

ABOVE RIGHT
**An aerial view across the city of
Beirut, Lebanon.**

A quiet sort of courage

Some survivors display incredible physical bravery to overcome their ordeals. For others, the courage they show is mental or spiritual, but their triumph is no less impressive. Terry Anderson displayed more of that resilience than any other hostage.

A land tearing itself apart

In 1985, civil war had been a part of daily life in Lebanon for ten years. Car bombs, abductions and bloody gunfights between Christian and Muslim militias were almost commonplace in Beirut.

In 1982 Israel had invaded Lebanon and the Palestine Liberation Organization had withdrawn. An international peacekeeping force was then stationed in Beirut. In October 1983, two huge truck bombs killed 299 American and French servicemen. An Iranian-supported group known as Islamic Jihad (a precursor to Hezbollah) claimed responsibility.

When the peacekeeping force subsequently withdrew, Islamic Jihad turned its attention on Westerners living in Lebanon. It snatched several hostages, either in retaliation for American support for Israel or to use as bargaining chips in the release of their own prisoners. Beirut became a very dangerous place to be.

Game, set and match

Terry Anderson was a prominent journalist in Beirut – he was chief of the city's Associated Press (AP) bureau and was widely known. He had a Lebanese partner, Madeleine Bassil, who was seven months pregnant.

> ❛ I had seen the car passing by twice at the courts. It had a sinister look, but I didn't think much of it at the time. You get used to seeing things like this in Beirut. ❜

On Saturday 16 March 1985, he and Don Mell, an AP photographer, played tennis. Anderson was dropping Mell off at his apartment afterwards when a green Mercedes screeched to a halt in front of them.

Three bearded gunmen jumped out. They approached slowly at first, then like cats going for the kill. The first gunman levelled his 9mm pistol at Mell's forehead. The photographer froze in terror. The two other men raced up to Anderson's car and dragged him out into the street. Grappling him in a bear hug, the gunmen pushed Anderson into the Mercedes.

For a split second the friends' eyes met. Anderson shot Mell a silent appeal, but the black pistol still pointed at his head made help impossible.

Next moment the engine was revving throatily and the car was speeding towards the green line, the division between East and West Beirut. For Terry Anderson it was a high speed journey into hell.

The start

'Get in. I will shoot,' the man hissed at Anderson, and crammed him into the space between the front and back seats. Another man threw an old blanket over Anderson and the journalist could feel the cold muzzle of a gun barrel against his neck. 'Get down. Get down.'

As the car veered madly up a hill and shot round a corner, the front-seat passenger leaned over the back of his seat. 'Don't worry. It's political,' he said calmly.

If this comment was meant to reassure Anderson, it didn't succeed. He thought of all the other Americans who had been kidnapped in Beirut for political reasons: Father Lawrence Martin Jenco had been missing two months; the Reverend Benjamin Weir, ten months; William Buckley, a year. No one knew if they were dead or alive. Anderson knew he was in deep, deep trouble.

Soon he was locked in a darkened underground room. Alone and lost to the world he had been a part of.

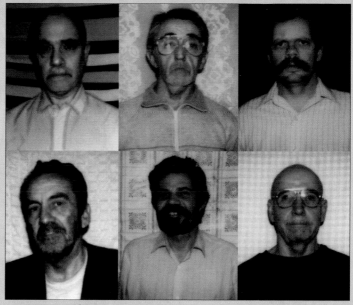

A picture composed from six Polaroid images released to the press on 15 May 1985 in Beirut by the Islamic Jihad Organization, showing six Western hostages kidnapped by the Jihad. *From left to right*: Father Lawrence Jenco (USA), William Buckley (USA), journalist Terry Anderson (USA), two French diplomats Marcel Carton and Marcel Fontaine and Reverend Benjamin Weir (USA).

Alone in the darkness

Anderson's initial emotion was disbelief: journalists weren't supposed to be kidnapped. They were usually off limits – it was they who told the story of groups like Islamic Jihad to the world. But eventually the reality of his situation sunk in and he knew he would have to take an active approach to his confinement if he was to remain sane.

He was kept on his own for years at a time and he learned to counter the profound loneliness of utter solitude by living his life hour by hour, not regretting what was in the past or dreaming about the future. He called this mentality 'doing time' and it kept him focused and positive.

The conditions of Anderson's captivity were brutal. Much of the time he was blindfolded and chained by the wrists and ankles to a bed. His captors often used him as a punchbag, beating him, jumping on him, jabbing him in the ribs and ears with their rifle barrels.

When they weren't physically hurting Anderson they would terrorise him psychologically, threatening him with more savage treatment and denying him any facet of normality. During one three-year stretch he only saw the sun once.

'I'm not an animal'

One day, after receiving some particularly brutal treatment from his captors, something flipped inside Anderson. An unstoppable feeling rose from deep within him and, taking form in his tired vocal chords, expressed a simple truth. He told the guards: 'You can't do this to me. I'm not an animal'. The comment stunned his kidnappers; in their surprise they asked Anderson what he wanted.

'A Bible,' he replied. Soon after he was given a 'brand new, revised, standard American Bible'. It was the start of a loosening of his shackles, literally and metaphorically.

For nearly seven years, Terry Anderson was moved from cell to cell around the war-torn city of Beirut, Lebanon.

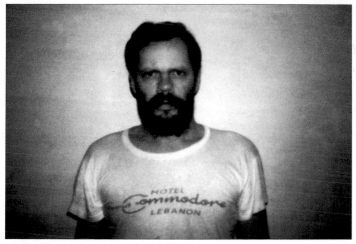
A picture of hostage Terry Anderson issued by his kidnappers.

between 1982 and 1991 to be released and he was the longest held.

Return to the Lion's Den

Remarkably, Anderson has no feeling of vengefulness toward his captors. In 1996, he returned to Lebanon and met the secretary-general of Hezbollah, the current name of the organization blamed for his kidnapping.

❛ People call me a victim of Lebanon, say I lost seven years of my life. I didn't lose them—I lived them. ❜

In 2002 he was awarded a multi-million dollar settlement from frozen Iranian assets, in compensation for his captivity. He used the money to start charitable organizations, including his Vietnam Children's Fund which has built over 40 schools in Vietnam, providing an education for more than 20,000 students.

Conditions began to get marginally better. He was moved to a bigger cell. Then his captors gave him a radio. By the final year of his imprisonment they were regularly giving him magazines: Time, Newsweek, Businessweek, The Economist and, surreally, Fortune magazine.

The end of the nightmare

Terry Anderson's ordeal ended as suddenly as it began. On 4 December 1991, the 2,454 day of his ordeal, two of his guards came in and told him he was being released. They gave him a shirt, a pair of trousers and shoes, then left.

He had a few hours to gather his thoughts and listen to the news of his own imminent release on the radio. Then, as he was about to embark on his final ride to freedom one of his captors handed him a bouquet of half a dozen carnations. 'Give this to your wife,' the man said, 'and tell her we're sorry.'

Within minutes he was free. He was soon back in the arms of Madeleine and was saying hello to the six-year-old daughter he had never met.

Anderson's release may have been due to Saddam Hussein's invasion of Kuwait in August 1990. Fifteen members of Islamic Jihad who were being held in a Kuwait prison were

released following the invasion. Since they had achieved their goal, Anderson's captors no longer needed him as a bargaining chip.

Anderson was the last of the dozen American hostages held in Lebanon

Former hostage Terry Anderson meets with Associated Press colleagues in New York upon his release from captivity in December 1991.

The Girl from the Secret Cellar

Natascha Kampusch was just 10 years old when she was snatched on her way to school by Wolfgang Priklopil. Her captor kept her as a slave in a tiny, soundproofed underground cell. But Natascha survived her ordeal and after eight years of imprisonment she made a courageous bid for freedom.

DATE:
1998–2006

SITUATION:
Kidnap

CONDITION OF CONFINEMENT:
Locked in a cellar

DURATION OF CONFINEMENT:
8 years

MEANS OF ESCAPE:
Running away

NO. OF ESCAPEES:
1

DANGERS:
Abuse, torture, starvation

EQUIPMENT:
None

Snatched on the way to school

Natascha was born on 17 February 1988 and grew up in Vienna. Her parents separated when she was just a few years old and Natascha divided her time between them. On 1 March 1998, she returned to her mother's home in Vienna's Donaustadt district from a holiday in Hungary with her father.

The next morning she got up, packed her bag and set off for school as usual. Her family would not see her again for eight years. She was 10 years old.

The police start searching

A 12-year-old witness reported seeing Natascha being dragged into a white minibus. Police launched a massive manhunt, focusing on this key lead. They searched 776 minivans including that of Wolfgang Priklopil, a former engineer who lived about half an hour from where Natascha lived.

Priklopil had no alibi for the time of the abduction. He admitted owning a minibus, but claimed he needed it to transport rubble from work he was doing to his home. Police accepted his explanation.

Since Natascha was still carrying her passport (having been on a trip to Hungary with her father), police extended the search abroad. But with no more leads, the trail eventually went cold.

Her family dealt with the loss and uncertainty as best they could. And for eight years the rest of the world forgot about Natascha Kampusch.

Eight years underground

Priklopil imprisoned Natascha in a windowless, soundproofed cellar underneath his garage. It measured just 5 m² (54 ft²) and had a thick concrete door reinforced with steel. This entrance was concealed behind a safe.

> **❛You're no longer Natascha. Now you belong to me.❜**

This tiny cell was her entire world for the next six months. Later on, Priklopil allowed her periods of time upstairs in his house, but always sent her back to the chamber to sleep, and while he was at work. He told her that the doors and windows of the house were rigged with high explosives. He also claimed to always carry a gun and threatened to kill her if she attempted to escape.

Her life became one of extreme submission to her captor. Priklopil forced her to walk round the house exactly 1 m (3 ft) behind him. He regularly beat her, sometimes so badly she could hardly walk, and

ABOVE RIGHT
A video-screen image shows Natascha Kampusch during her first interview after escape in 2006.

234 Hostages

manacled her to him while she slept. She was forced to shave her hair and work around the house as a slave.

Priklopil tried to crush all hope from the girl, telling her that her family had refused to pay a ransom for her and were 'happy to be rid' of her. By the time she was 16, she weighed less than 38 kg (6 stone); Priklopil was keeping her constantly hungry to make her too weak to escape.

As well as the physical and mental abuse, Natascha was tormented by loneliness. This hurt her so much she even yearned for the company of her captor, playing games to keep him with her longer.

'...when the kidnapper came back later, I asked him to put me to bed properly and tell me a goodnight story. I even asked him for a goodnight kiss. Anything to preserve the illusion of normality.'

Survivor's spirit

But despite her youth and vulnerability there was something in Natascha that refused to give in. She attempted to attract passers by during her early years of captivity by throwing bottles of water against the walls. When she realized escape was impossible she tried to make the best of her situation and educated herself.

The hidden room and hiding place of kidnapped Natascha Kampusch.

She innately felt that she was missing something and did everything she could to fill that gap. She devoured the few books and newspapers that Priklopil brought her and kept her radio tuned to Ö1, a station that features educational programmes and classical music.

'I tried to educate myself, to teach myself skills. I have learned to knit for example.'

Escape

After her eighteenth birthday, Priklopil let her leave the house but only if she stayed right by his side. He threatened to shoot her if she made any noise.

> ❛ Then he'd grab me by the throat, drag me to the sink, push my head underwater and squeeze my windpipe until I almost lost consciousness. ❜

On 23 August 2006 Natascha was cleaning her kidnapper's BMW 850i in the garden. At 12.53 p.m., Priklopil's mobile phone rang and he moved away from the noise of the vacuum cleaner to take the call. Natascha saw an opportunity. She placed the vacuum cleaner on the ground, leaving it running, and took off.

Priklopil didn't see her go – the caller later said he completed the phone conversation calmly. This gave Natascha a vital head start. Her legs had not moved this fast for years, but she found the speed she needed. She ran for 200 m (200 yards) through suburban gardens, jumping fences and begging passers-by to call the police. At first it seemed no one would take her seriously. After five minutes of flight she stopped at a house and desperately knocked on the window. The 71-year-old woman who lived there was astonished to see a pale, bedraggled young woman staring in at her. 'I am Natascha Kampusch,' the girl said.

The woman called the police, who arrived just a few minutes later and

The house where kidnapped Natascha Kampusch was found after eight years captivity.

took Natascha to the police station in Deutsch Wagram. Natascha was formally identified by a scar on her body and DNA tests. Police also later found her 1998 passport still in the cell she had occupied.

Natascha's health was generally good, although she weighed only 48 kg (106 lb), only 3 kg (6½ lb) more than when she disappeared. She had grown only 15 cm (6 in).

When Priklopil found that the police were after him, he jumped in front of a train near Wien Nord station in Vienna. Years earlier he had told Natascha that authorities 'would not catch him alive'.

A new life

Throughout her ordeal something kept Natascha going. Police were astonished by her intelligence and vocabulary, considering what she had been through.

Natascha managed to sympathize with her captor, calling him 'a poor soul', despite his abuses, and she cried when told he was dead.

Overall, Natascha seemed to adapt remarkably well to her new life. In 2008 she bought the house in which she suffered so much, and occasionally visited it.

On 1 June 2008, Natascha started to host her own talk show on the Austrian TV station PULS 4.

Ten Years as a Secret Slave

A YOUNG SCOTTISH WOMAN WAS VISITING RELATIVES IN PAKISTAN WHEN SHE WAS KIDNAPPED IN BROAD DAYLIGHT AT ISLAMABAD AIRPORT. FOR THE NEXT TEN YEARS SHE WOULD SUFFER BEATINGS, STARVATION AND DISEASE AS SHE LIVED THE LIFE OF A SLAVE IN A NOTORIOUS TRIBAL KIDNAP CAMP.

DATE:
2000–10

SITUATION:
KIDNAP

CONDITION OF CONFINEMENT:
HELD HOSTAGE IN A FORCED LABOUR CAMP IN PAKISTAN

DURATION OF CONFINEMENT:
10 YEARS

MEANS OF ESCAPE:
ARMY INTERVENTION; RELEASE; WALKING TO SAFETY

NO. OF ESCAPEES:
1

DANGERS:
TORTURE, EXECUTION, EXHAUSTION, STARVATION, DISEASE

EQUIPMENT:
NONE

ABOVE RIGHT
A Sikh temple in Lahore, Punjab, Pakistan.

Going home alone

Naheeda Bi was 28 but had never travelled alone before. It was April 2000 and she was standing in the check-in line at Islamabad Airport. Three months before she had set out from her home in Glasgow with her mother Rabia and gone to visit her grandmother in the Punjab. Her grandmother had recently become ill, so Rabia had sent her daughter home. The family dropped her off at the airport and now she was about to board the plane that would take her to Manchester on the first leg of her journey back to Scotland.

So she was lonely without her mum, and a little unnerved by the bustle of the terminal, but she had no reason to suspect anything serious might happen to her.

Then, from nowhere, two men in uniform approached.

'Your flight has been cancelled'

They roughly pulled her aside and told her she was in the wrong place and that her plane had been delayed.

The men took her into a side room and told her to wait while they checked for her. Naheeda sat alone for several hours before the men returned and told her that she had missed her flight.

Now a little panicky, Naheeda phoned her dad back in the UK. He told her to call her family in Pakistan, who said they would send Uncle Masood, her mother's brother, to get her.

Relieved, Naheeda settled down to wait for Masood to arrive. As she sat in the stuffy airport office, the uniformed men offered her a glass of water. Naheeda sipped it and the next thing she knew she was waking up alone in a dark, windowless room.

The first two months

Naheeda was lying on a rough concrete floor. The room was almost completely dark, but she could just make out that there was no furniture,

only dirt and debris. She wouldn't leave this dim cell for at least two months.

Two men came in and yelled at her in a language she didn't understand. (She would later discover this was Pushto, a language spoken primarily in Afghanistan and western Pakistan.)

When Naheeda didn't respond the men began kicking and punching her. Finally they shaved her head and injected a sedative into her feet.

> **❛ I felt like dying. I thought that if there was a way I could kill myself I would do it. ❜**

After a few days, the kidnappers brought in a mobile phone and gave it to Naheeda. A man on the other end of the line spoke Punjabi and Naheeda could understand him. He said that her parents were also in Pakistan and that she would be fine as long as her father paid them £500,000. Naheeda's father was a successful businessman; she was sure he could get the money.

But after a few more conversations with this man, Naheeda heard nothing more. Instead she became subject to a brutal daily routine of beatings, sedation and intimidation. Her rations were just a little water and a tiny amount of rice each day. She was not allowed to leave the room and had to use a hole in the corner as a toilet.

The gun girls

One day, without warning, Naheeda's kidnappers blindfolded her, threw her in the back of a truck and drove for several hours to a group of buildings in desert scrubland.

Here she was delighted to see her Uncle Masood. But he was not here to free her; he had been taken hostage at the airport too.

Almost as soon as they were reunited, Naheeda and Masood were split up and she was put in a room with about twenty other women and girls. Here they were forced to work making munitions.

Living conditions were filthy and the food barely enough to survive on. Illness became the norm, with all the women suffering from frequent vomiting and diarrhoea.

Her kidnappers subjected them to random brutality. Women would be dragged from room to room by their hair, verbally abused and beaten. Sometimes new people would arrive, sometimes others would leave.

> **❛ Sometimes people would be taken away and we would never see them again. Some people were killed. ❜**

There was no more contact from the man who had called for ransom and no news of her parents. Occasionally they would be moved to a new location and she might catch a glimpse of her uncle, but the routine would be the same: munitions work, beatings, sickness and disappearances.

For the next ten years, this would be her whole life.

Salvation from nowhere

Naheeda didn't know it, but it was now May 2010 and she was 38. A man entered the dim room, marched across to Naheeda and interrupted her work to hand her a mobile phone. Naheeda held it to her ear. Someone on the other end of the

The landscape of the Swat River valley in Pakistan.

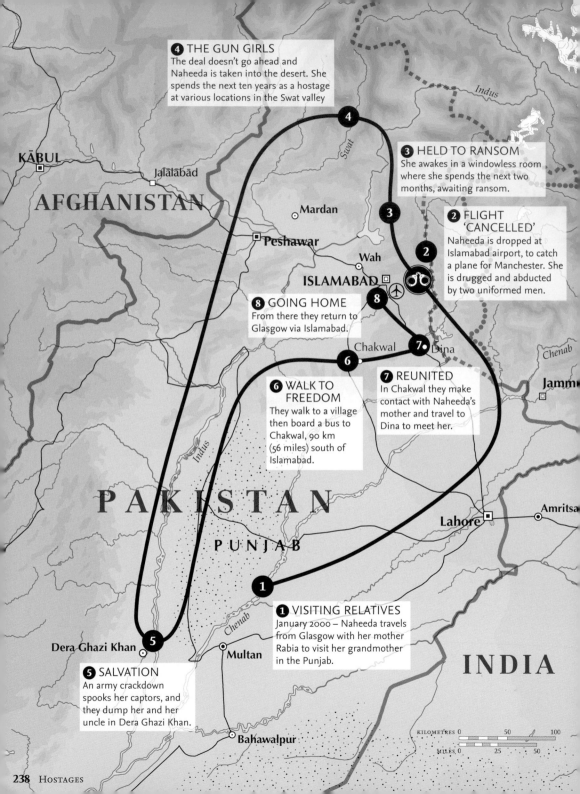

4 THE GUN GIRLS
The deal doesn't go ahead and Naheeda is taken into the desert. She spends the next ten years as a hostage at various locations in the Swat valley

3 HELD TO RANSOM
She awakes in a windowless room where she spends the next two months, awaiting ransom.

2 FLIGHT 'CANCELLED'
Naheeda is dropped at Islamabad airport, to catch a plane for Manchester. She is drugged and abducted by two uniformed men.

8 GOING HOME
From there they return to Glasgow via Islamabad.

6 WALK TO FREEDOM
They walk to a village then board a bus to Chakwal, 90 km (56 miles) south of Islamabad.

7 REUNITED
In Chakwal they make contact with Naheeda's mother and travel to Dina to meet her.

1 VISITING RELATIVES
January 2000 – Naheeda travels from Glasgow with her mother Rabia to visit her grandmother in the Punjab.

5 SALVATION
An army crackdown spooks her captors, and they dump her and her uncle in Dera Ghazi Khan.

KĀBUL
Jalālābād
AFGHANISTAN
Mardan
Peshawar
Wah
ISLAMABAD
Chakwal
Dina
PAKISTAN
Chenab
Jamm
PUNJAB
Lahore
Amritsa
Indus
Swat
Dera Ghazi Khan
Multan
Chenab
INDIA
Bahawalpur

KILOMETRES 0   50   100
MILES 0   25   50

Naheeda Bi with her father Akram Hussain and mother Rabia Bi at the family home in Glasgow, Scotland, on 6 June 2010.

linc said, 'Hello, who is speaking?' The voice was strange, but Naheeda recognised it instantly: it was her mother. Too emotional to speak herself, she dissolved into tears.

A few days later, Naheeda and her Uncle Masood were blindfolded and loaded onto a truck with some other hostages.

They were driven for a day through remote countryside. Then the truck stopped and the two of them were literally thrown into the road. The truck drove off.

They later discovered they were dropped in Dera Ghazi Khan in the Punjab, a dangerous tribal area rife with outlaws and criminal gangs.

Alone on the dusty road, Naheeda and Masood started walking. Several hours later they reached a tiny settlement where they persuaded two farmers to give them a lift on their tractor.

Reaching a larger village they managed to scrounge some money for a bus. This rattled for a day and a night through the winding Punjab roads before reaching Chakwal, a city 90 km (56 miles) south of Islamabad.

In Chakwal, they called Naheeda's mother. She gave them the incredible news that she had already made her way to Pakistan, and was at that moment in hotel in a town called Dina, with Naheeda's father and brother, waiting for further word from the kidnappers.

Torn by hope of escape and fear that they might at any moment be retaken, Naheeda and Masood hurried the 96 km (60 miles) to Dina. They ran into the hotel and there, with open arms and tears in her eyes, was Naheeda's mother.

> **We got to the hotel and my mother was waiting. I thought I was dreaming.**

Amid shrieks of delight and relief, her father and brother ran from their room to join them. Within a few days they would all be back in Scotland.

Naheeda's kidnap is one of the longest ever endured by a Briton.

She was held for almost twice as long as journalist John McCarthy, who was a prisoner for five-and-a-half years in Beirut.

> **I still cannot believe my hell is over. When I wake up, I look around the room twice. Just to make sure that I am really here.**

Reason for release

Pakistan is one of the most dangerous countries in the world for kidnap and ransom. It's likely that Naheeda was being held in the infamous Swat valley in the North Western Frontier Province (NWFP) of Pakistan. This tribal region borders Afghanistan and is rife with outlaws and criminal gangs. The Pakistani army had launched a crackdown in the region in the weeks before Naheeda's release.

The kidnappers may have started dumping their hostages when they heard that the army was closing in on them.

Kidnapped by the FARC

Íngrid Betancourt Pulecio was a presidential candidate in the 2002 Colombian elections when she was kidnapped by the Revolutionary Armed Forces of Colombia (FARC). Imprisoned in a brutal jungle camp she was starved and tortured for six and a half years until her dramatic rescue by Colombian security forces.

DATE:
2002–8

SITUATION:
Held hostage

CONDITION OF CONFINEMENT:
Hidden in a rebel camp deep in the Colombian jungle

DURATION OF CONFINEMENT:
6½ years

MEANS OF ESCAPE:
Military rescue mission

NO. OF ESCAPEES:
15

DANGERS:
Execution, starvation, torture

EQUIPMENT:
None

LEFT
In 2008 a helicopter marked with the International Red Cross logo, takes off in San José del Guaviare, to pick up Colombian politicians Clara Rojas and Consuelo Gonzalez held for years in secret jungle camps by FARC rebels.

ABOVE RIGHT
A checkpoint held by young guerrillas from FARC on the road where Íngrid Betancourt was kidnapped.

Ideals worth dying for

Although Íngrid Betancourt was driving deep into rebel territory, she didn't feel scared. Yes, the FARC felt threatened by her strident anti-drug and violence presidential platform. It was true, too, that the recent peace talks between the government and the rebels had reached an impasse after more than three years of negotiations. The FARC had also increased their activities in the Demilitarized Zone (DMZ) and political hostage taking was a thriving business for them. But Betancourt had been part of the peace negotiations and had met many of the FARC leaders. She was someone with whom they could work in the future – surely she would be more valuable to them as a free woman.

Besides, you need to take some risks if you're going to be President of Colombia, and the hugely positive publicity her trip could generate would be worth any dangers.

They stopped at a FARC checkpoint near the town of San Vicente del Caguán. Armed men approached the vehicle. Betancourt smiled and asked for permission to pass. The men did not smile back.

Within minutes Betancourt was a hostage. For the next six and a half years she would live in a harsh jungle camp, aware that at any moment she might outgrow her usefulness and get a bullet in her head.

FARC

The Revolutionary Armed Forces of Colombia (*Fuerzas Armadas Revolucionarias de Colombia* in Spanish), also known as FARC, is a Marxist-Leninist revolutionary guerrilla organization. The largest and oldest insurgent group in the Americas, FARC was established as a military wing of the Colombian Communist Party in 1964.

It claims to represent the rural poor in a struggle against Colombia's wealthier classes. FARC also opposes United States influence in Colombia and what it sees as the theft of

Colombia's natural resources by multinational corporations. It mainly funds its activities through hostage taking and taxation of the cocaine trade.

Estimates of its strength vary from 9,000 to 18,000 guerrillas. It controls between 30 and 40 per cent of the territory in Colombia, much of it in mountain regions and dense jungle.

The fearless candidate

Íngrid Betancourt Pulecio was born in 1961 into a wealthy French-Colombian family. She enjoyed a privileged upbringing in Paris and England and was once profiled in Vanity Fair. Her father had been a Colombian government minister and she followed him into politics as a staunch opponent of drugs and corruption. On 20 May 2001 she announced her intention to run for President. Her campaign reflected her bold, irreverent personality: she handed out free Viagra samples, promising to 'invigorate' Colombians in the fight against corruption.

She was on a campaign bus trip around the country when she was kidnapped along with her running mate, Clara Rojas.

The danger of rescue

The presidential election was eventually won by Álvaro Uribe. Perhaps wanting to demonstrate its strength, his new administration refused to negotiate with FARC for Betancourt's release unless the rebels agreed to a ceasefire. FARC ruled this out. They were willing to free their twenty-three 'political hostages', but only in exchange for the release of all their jailed guerrillas, of which there were 500. Uribe would never agree to such a bargain.

With negotiations stalling, the other possibility was a risky rescue operation. But Betancourt's relatives pleaded with the government not to try this tactic. The governor of the Antioquia region, Guillermo Gaviria, along with his peace advisor and several soldiers, were kidnapped by

the FARC during a peace march in 2003. They were shot when the FARC got wind of an army rescue mission.

Political pinball

So began a long, slow game of negotiation and political posturing. Betancourt was a hostage in distress, but she was also a pawn in a very complex game.

She had ransom value to the FARC while a successful rescue would be a coup for President Uribe. Ms Betancourt also held French citizenship and was widely respected in that country. When Nicolas Sarkozy took over the French presidency from Jacques Chirac, he involved himself personally in negotiations for her release.

A further complication was that Betancourt was probably being held in the deep jungles of neighbouring Venezuela. The left-wing president of Venezuela, Hugo Chávez shared certain sensibilities with FARC and he had also fallen out with the government of France when Chirac had refused to sell him weapons. Politically, it was a mess.

In July 2003 the French government tried to launch a secret rescue mission from Brazil. But it failed to liberate Betancourt and caused a scandal for President Chirac.

In August 2004, Uribe's government announced that it had given the FARC a formal proposal in which it offered to free around fifty jailed rebels in exchange for the political and military hostages held by the FARC group, including Íngrid Betancourt. This did not come to fruition until 4 June 2007, when the government released thirty FARC prisoners. But the FARC decided to keep their captive.

On the road to Florencia, where Íngrid Betancourt was kidnapped with her campaign advisor Clara Rojas by members of FARC. The bus blocking the road is full of explosives and the graffiti spells out, 'Watch out, landmine, Viva FARC!'.

> ❛[Betancourt] is doing well, within the environment she finds herself in. It's not easy when one is deprived of freedom. ❜

Betancourt in ill health in 2007 whilst being held hostage in a secret jungle camp.

news station quoted several sources as saying that she had stopped taking her medication and stopped eating. Apparently she was in desperate need of a blood transfusion.

A few days later her son, Lorenzo Delloye, pleaded with the FARC and President Uribe. He believed his mother was very close to death and he urged both sides to cooperate and get her released before it was too late.

An audacious endgame

Sometime in the summer of 2007, Colombian military intelligence had set the wheels of a bold plan in motion when they managed to get an undercover officer accepted into the command structure of the FARC.

This agent went to work gathering information and gaining the trust of key FARC leaders. It took months for him to make the contacts he needed, but slowly his diligence began to pay off.

Within eight months he knew where the hostages were being held. Thanks to his information, Colombian forces were able to observe five of the captives bathing in the Apaporis River. They installed motion-sensors and video cameras in the jungle at the edge of the water to keep tabs on the location. At one point a FARC guerrilla who had walked into the jungle to relieve himself accidentally kicked one of the devices; but he didn't investigate further and the surveillance operation's cover remained intact.

Over the next few months, more intelligence officers infiltrated local FARC squads and even the leadership council of FARC.

In June 2008, General Freddy Padilla de León went to the defence minister with an audacious rescue idea. Their agents on the inside were now in the position to be able to trick the FARC into regrouping the hostages. Another team of agents would pose as members of a fictitious non-government organisation and

While the politicians horse-traded behind the scenes, Betancourt and others were living a harsh life in captivity deep in the jungle.

Harsh life as a hostage

An early FARC video of Betancourt showed that she was still lively and passionate. She called on the Colombian security forces to rescue her.

But six years of captivity would take a terrible toll on her. The last video of Ms Betancourt, taken in 2007, showed her sitting on a chair staring blankly at the ground. Her face was pale and haggard and her straggly hair grew past her waist.

> **❛ I feel like my children's life is on standby, waiting for me to be free, and their daily suffering makes death seem like a sweet option. ❜**

Many prisoners were kept in cages in the jungle, let out only to wash in the river or to get a beating.

Betancourt stated she was often tortured during her captivity.

In May 2007, a hostage called John Frank Pinchao escaped from the FARC camp. He reported that he had been detained with Betancourt and she was still alive. However, he said that many of the hostages in the camp were ill or injured. Betancourt had attempted to escape several times and had been recaptured and 'severely punished'.

He reported that Clara Rojas was also in the camp and she had given birth to a son (Emmanuel) in captivity.

> **❛ [she is] exhausted physically and in her morale. [...] Íngrid is mistreated very badly, they have vented their anger on her, they have her chained up in inhumane conditions. ❜**

Pressure mounts

In 2008, fears began to mount for Betancourt's health. On 31 March, a

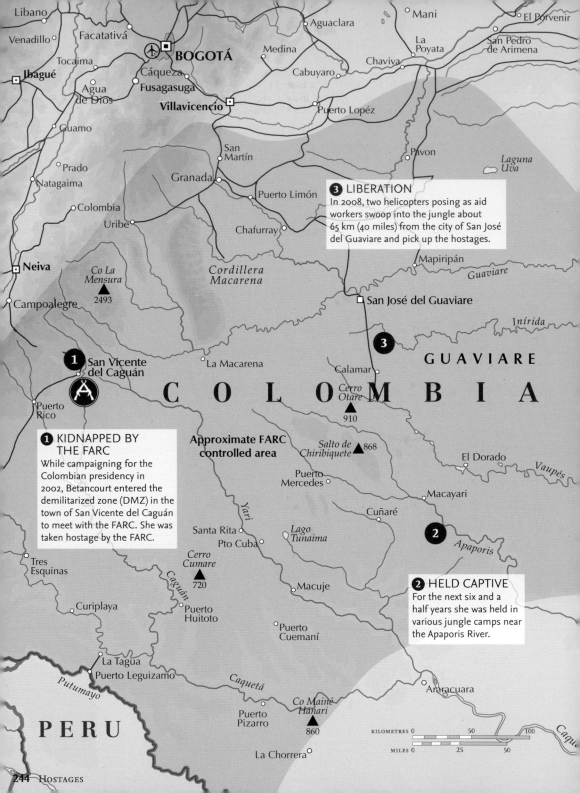

Libano
Venadillo
Facatativá
Mani
El Porvenir
Tocaima
BOGOTÁ
Aguaclara
La
Poyata
San Pedro
de Arimena
Cáqueza
Medina
Chaviva
Ibagué
Fusagasuga
Cabuyaro
Agua
de Dios
Villavicencio
Puerto Lopéz
Guamo
San
Martín
Pavon
*Laguna
Uva*
Prado
Granada
Natagaima
Puerto Limón
Colombia
Uribe
Chafurray
Mapiripán
Guaviare
Neiva
*Co La
Mensura*
*Cordillera
Macarena*
Inírida
Campoalegre
▲
2493
□ San José del Guaviare

3 LIBERATION
In 2008, two helicopters posing as aid
workers swoop into the jungle about
65 km (40 miles) from the city of San José
del Guaviare and pick up the hostages.

GUAVIARE

**1 San Vicente
del Caguán**
La Macarena
Calamar
C   O   L   O   M   B   I   A
*Cerro
Otare*
▲
910
Puerto
Rico

**1 KIDNAPPED BY
THE FARC**
While campaigning for the
Colombian presidency in
2002, Betancourt entered the
demilitarized zone (DMZ) in the
town of San Vicente del Caguán
to meet with the FARC. She was
taken hostage by the FARC.

**Approximate FARC
controlled area**
*Salto de
Chiribiquete* ▲ 868
El Dorado
Vaupés
Puerto
Mercedes
Macayari
Yari
Cuñaré
Santa Rita
Pto Cuba
*Lago
Tunaima*
2
*Cerro
Cumare*
▲
720
Macuje
Apaporis

2 HELD CAPTIVE
For the next six and a
half years she was held in
various jungle camps near
the Apaporis River.

Tres
Esquinas
Caguán
Puerto
Huitoto
Puerto
Cuemaní
Curiplaya
La Tagua
Puerto Leguizamo
Caquetá
Araracuara
Putumayo

PERU
*Co Mainé
Hañari*
▲
860
Puerto
Pizarro
Caqu

KILOMETRES 0   50   100
MILES 0   25   50

La Chorrera

fly in by helicopter, supposedly to fly the captives to a different camp to meet rebel leader Alfonso Cano.

The team on the helicopter would consist of two soldiers impersonating a TV cameraman and journalist, another two posing as FARC guerrillas, while four men would dress as neutral aid workers. The soldiers would prepare for their roles with acting classes.

President Uribe approved the plan and *Operation Jaque* (from the Spanish term for checkmate in chess) was launched.

Bait and switch

In late June, the undercover FARC agents ordered the movement of hostages from three different locations to a central area. From here, the hostages, agents, and about sixty real FARC members made a 145 km (90 mile) march through dense jungle to a landing zone. The agents told the FARC members that an 'international mission' was coming to check on the hostages and take them to see Cano.

Early on the morning of 2 July, the FARC rebels, hostages and agents gathered in a clearing as two unmarked white Mi-17 helicopters came clattering over the treetops and one of the aircraft set down.

Two Colombian security agents posing as FARC members jumped out of the chopper, ducking low as they walked under the rotor downdraft. As they stood up again, the rebels could see their T-shirts were emblazoned with the famous image of Che Guevara. The men explained that they had come for the hostages.

It took twenty-two minutes to organise the hostages, handcuffing them and loading them aboard the helicopter. The agents used pre-agreed code words to let the pilot and co-pilot know how the operation was progressing.

Two real FARC rebels got on the aircraft with the hostages and undercover agents. Then the rebels on the ground watched as the helicopter swept up and over the jungle canopy.

As soon as the helicopter was in the air, the agents put guns to the guerrillas' heads and told them to get on their knees.

Betancourt was bewildered. The men who had imprisoned her for six long years were now naked and blindfolded on the floor of the helicopter and a man in a Che Guevara T-shirt was undoing her handcuffs.

> 6 A soldier said: "We are the Colombian National Army. You are free." The helicopter nearly fell out of the sky with all the celebrations. 9

Fourteen other hostages were also freed, including eleven Colombian military and police officers and three American military contractors: Marc Gonsalves, Thomas Howes, and Keith Stansell. Two FARC members were arrested.

Liberation

The French government flew Betancourt's children, Melanie and Lorenzo Delloye, her former husband Fabrice Delloye and her sister Astrid to Colombia to meet her.

> 6 Nirvana, paradise – that must be very similar to what I feel at this moment. 9

Melanie and Lorenzo had been 16 and 13 when she was kidnapped. Now they were young adults.

Betancourt was waiting for them on the airport tarmac. As the plane door opened, she ran up the stairs and embraced them. Fighting back tears, she grabbed her family and bundled them back inside the plane to continue their reunion in private.

Betancourt *(centre)* talks with her children Melanie *(left)* and Lorenzo Delloye *(right)* after being rescued by the Colombian army in the jungle of the eastern department of Guaviare.

Buried Alive

WHEN ARMED GUNMEN KICKED DOWN HIS OFFICE DOOR IN BAGHDAD, ROY HALLUMS FACED EVERY US CONTRACTOR'S WORST NIGHTMARE – CAPTURE BY TERRORISTS. FOR THE NEXT 311 DAYS HE WAS KEPT BOUND AND GAGGED IN TOTAL DARKNESS AND UNDER THE CONSTANT THREAT OF A BLOODY DEATH BEFORE BEING FREED BY US SPECIAL FORCES.

DATE:
2004–5

SITUATION:
TAKEN HOSTAGE BY IRAQI TERRORISTS

CONDITION OF CONFINEMENT:
BURIED IN A CONCRETE BASEMENT

DURATION OF CONFINEMENT:
10 MONTHS, 7 DAYS

MEANS OF ESCAPE:
RESCUE

NO. OF ESCAPEES:
1

DANGERS:
MURDER, TORTURE, STARVATION

EQUIPMENT:
NONE

ABOVE RIGHT
The skyline of Baghdad.

Business as usual

It was 1 November 2004 and another ordinary day in the office for Roy Hallums. He worked for a Saudi Arabian company that organized food for the Iraqi army. Like all contractors, he knew that Baghdad was a dangerous place to work, but his office was in a relatively safe part of the city, and he had the protection of full-time armed guards.

It's true that kidnappings happened, but the chances of it being you that was taken hostage were slim. About a dozen Americans had been snatched in the last year, but that was out of a population of 39,000 US contractors who worked in the country.

> **❝ Come with us or we'll kill you. ❞**

So morbid thoughts were far from Hallums' mind as he sat at his desk, staring at his computer screen and planning out his day. Then his door

smashed opened and four armed men wearing ski masks stormed in.

And the nightmare that lurked at the back of every contractor's imagination became a sudden, violent reality for him.

The greatest fear

Hallums knew the trouble he was in. The terrorist Abu Musab al-Zarqawi had recently intensified his onslaught against Americans, abducting and beheading several westerners: Nicholas Berg in May 2004, Eugene Armstrong and Jack Hensley in September; and in October, just weeks before Roy's abduction, British engineer Ken Bigley. With a sickening lurch in his stomach, he realised there was a good chance that he was now being abducted by al-Zarqawi.

His hands were tied behind his back and he was dragged from the building as a gun battle erupted all around him. Then the clatter of automatic weapon fire faded as he was flung into a car and driven off at high speed.

Entombed

After a short time being moved from house to house around Baghdad, Hallums was taken south out of the city. He was taken into an unkempt farm building and dumped into a concrete cell dug out beneath one of the rooms. This black, airless pit was just 1.4 m (4½ ft) high and it would be his home for the next ten months.

He was blindfolded and tied up.

Roy Hallums' hands and feet were bound so tightly with nylon straps that he was rendered virtually immobile.

He listened as the kidnappers dropped the trapdoor back down over his head. They poured a square of fresh concrete over the hatch and laid a carpet on top. Over that, they placed a refrigerator. Hallums could have been a mile beneath the surface of the earth. No one would find him here. His fate was sealed.

Surviving in his mind

His food was as little as it took to keep him alive: a little rice, crumbs of cheese, a few sardines, some rotten fruit.

Occasionally he had company. At first he was held beside Roberto Tarongoy of the Philippines, Inus Dewari of Nepal and three Iraqis. At one point there were nine hostages in the tiny room. But the men couldn't see each other because they were blindfolded and they were often gagged so conversation was impossible.

Although Hallums was unable to move physically, he could travel in his mind. He began planning trips in his head, putting together long and detailed itineraries that would sometimes keep him occupied for days at a time. It was a mental discipline that helped him stay sane.

Hallums never saw his captors, but as time passed he built up a picture of their lives. He could hear that they had a television which they spent a lot of time watching. But because they were strict Sunni Muslims, they couldn't watch any programme that featured women with uncovered hair. That reduced the scope of their entertainment options; they almost exclusively watched Tom and Jerry cartoons.

The hostage business

Hallums also worked out that his captors weren't part of al-Zarqawi's group after all. It was more likely that this was just a 'family business', albeit a nasty one. This group had seen that there was money to be made kidnapping foreigners and they decided to get a piece of the action.

Like any businessmen, it was vital that the kidnappers made a good sales pitch. Theirs was in the form of a video of their captives. The kidnappers would prepare the captives for the camera by giving them scripts to memorize and then beating them.

❛ We want lots of crying and to help you cry, we're going to beat you. ❜

When Hallums' video was released on 25 January 2005, three months

A view across the suburbs of Baghdad.

US Army Apache helicopters fly on patrol over Baghdad's Green Zone.

after his abduction, it was the first and last time his family had evidence that he was alive. The film showed Hallums with a long beard and a gun to his head, pleading for his life.

The agony of waiting

As the months wore on, Hallums could see that the venture was paying off for the kidnapping ring. One by one the hostages who shared his dungeon were being released as their ransoms were paid. Although this gave him hope, it was also hard to bear. He could do nothing but wait in the darkness as the days turned into weeks and the weeks into months.

It also led his captors to increase the psychological pressure on him. They demanded his daughters' phone numbers, but there was no way that Hallums was going to let them threaten his loved ones too. When he refused, one of the men put the muzzle of a 9mm pistol in his mouth and said:

> **❛ If you don't tell me those phone numbers right now, I'm going to kill you. ❜**

Hallums kept his face blank and told him that he simply did not know the numbers. The man bought his bluff, pocketing his gun and returning back upstairs.

Delta force

Roberto Tarongoy was freed on 23 June 2005. He told American forces that he believed Hallums was still alive, but still nothing more was heard of him.

Meanwhile Susan Hallums, his ex-wife and still his close friend, was doing everything she could think of to win his freedom. She raised $40,000 for his release and even managed to contact the kidnappers through an intermediary to broker a deal. The kidnappers refused; they wanted $12 million.

Hallums' family was devastated – and partly angry that the government

US citizen Roy Hallums (*centre*) is seen shaking hands with Air Force Brigadier General Frank Gorenc before boarding a flight home from Iraq.

didn't seem to be doing much to help. What they couldn't know was that a special rescue unit had been searching for him the whole time.

This team's perseverance paid off. They got a tip-off from an Iraqi detainee and a unit from the US Army's elite Delta Force was dispatched to a farmhouse 24 km (15 miles) south of Baghdad.

When coalition troops arrived, the kidnappers had fled. On their first foray into the building they saw no sign of Hallums. The opening had been so neatly cemented over, that without detailed, specific information the troops would never have known where to look.

Below ground, Hallums heard movement but little suspected what was happening above his head. Then the hatch popped open and

somebody jumped down beside him. An American voice asked: 'Are you Roy?'

Hallums tore off his mask to see a US soldier standing in front of him. 'Yes,' he managed. 'Come on,' the soldier said, 'we're getting you out of here.' Hallums hugged him.

Going home

Roy Hallums had spent ten months and seven days in utter darkness. For most of that time he was also bound and gagged. He lost 16 kg (35 lb) during his months in captivity. His muscles had been unused for so long that it was physically hard for him to talk and impossible to walk immediately after his release.

But when he heard his daughter's voice on the phone just after his release, he managed to find his voice. 'This is Dad,' he said simply.

Christmas Day Heroics

It was Christmas Day 2009 and the 290 people aboard Flight 253 were just twenty minutes from landing in Detroit. Then 23-year-old Umar Farouk Abdulmutallab detonated the plastic explosives concealed in his clothing and chaos broke out. A Dutch passenger, Jasper Schuringa, heroically tackled the bomber, handcuffing him and enabling the pilot to safely land the plane.

DATE:
2009

SITUATION:
Attempted bombing

CONDITION OF CONFINEMENT:
On board a plane in flight

DURATION OF CONFINEMENT:
20 minutes

MEANS OF ESCAPE:
Passenger intervention

NO. OF ESCAPEES:
290

DANGERS:
Explosion, fire, falling to death

EQUIPMENT:
None

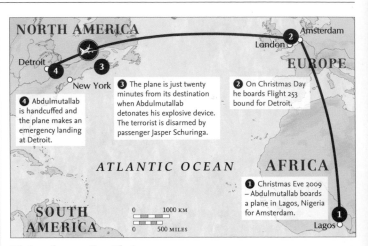

4 Abdulmutallab is handcuffed and the plane makes an emergency landing at Detroit.

3 The plane is just twenty minutes from its destination when Abdulmutallab detonates his explosive device. The terrorist is disarmed by passenger Jasper Schuringa.

2 On Christmas Day he boards Flight 253 bound for Detroit.

1 Christmas Eve 2009 – Abdulmutallab boards a plane in Lagos, Nigeria for Amsterdam.

Flying home for Christmas

It was 11.20 a.m. on 25 December 2009 and the passengers on Northwest Airlines Flight 253 were dreaming of Christmas. The Airbus A330-323E had left Amsterdam at 8.45 a.m. that morning with 279 passengers, eight flight attendants, and three pilots aboard. The flight had been routine but had felt long. Now, though, their excitement outweighed their tiredness. In less than an hour they'd be collecting their present-stuffed luggage from the carousel and heading for the taxi rank. If the traffic wasn't too bad they'd make it to their destinations in time for Christmas dinner.

Then Umar Farouk Abdulmutallab detonated a bomb and their Christmas fantasies went up in flames.

The underpants assassin

On Christmas Eve, Umar Farouk Abdulmutallab, a 23-year-old Nigerian, had arrived at Murtala Muhammed Airport in Lagos, Nigeria. He boarded KLM Flight 588 and at 11.00 p.m. took off for Schiphol Airport in Amsterdam. The next day he checked in for Northwest Airlines Flight 253 to Detroit with only carry-on luggage.

Abdulmutallab spent the flight in window seat 19A, which is near the wing fuel tanks and up against the plane's fuselage. For eight hours he barely moved, but as the plane approached Detroit he went to the lavatory. Twenty minutes later he returned to his seat.

The plane was now on its final descent. As Abdulmutallab slumped into his seat he murmured something about having an upset stomach. He then pulled a blanket over himself.

But there was nothing wrong with his stomach: beneath the blanket Abdulmutallab was preparing an explosive device. Sewn into his underwear was a plastic container packed with 80 grams (2½ oz) of plastic explosive powder. Under cover of the blanket he removed a small syringe of acid and stabbed its needle into the explosive and slammed home the plunger.

The chemical reaction was instantaneous. An explosion echoed through the cabin, yanking the passengers out of their peaceful Christmas dreams and back to a terrifying reality.

Our plane is on fire

For a moment it was too surreal to take in. It sounded like firecrackers had gone off and there was a strange smell in the air. Then the passengers saw that the suspect's clothing and the wall of the plane were on fire. Flames leapt up the sidewall of the plane and hungrily devoured the plastic interior.

> ❛ There was smoke and screaming and flames. It was scary. ❜

The quickest to react was Jasper Schuringa, a Dutchman who was seated at the far side of the same row as Abdulmutallab. Schuringa looked over and saw that the suspect's trousers were open, and that something was burning between his legs.

Schuringa leapt across the cabin and tried to pat out the flames. But the chemical reaction was too strong and Schuringa suffered burns to his hands. By now the flight attendants had grabbed a fire extinguisher, which they used to douse the flames on the suspect and the wall. Another passenger seized the partially melted and still-smoking syringe from Abdulmutallab's hand.

> ❛ I pulled the object from him and tried to extinguish the fire with my hands and threw it away. ❜

Schuringa now grabbed the suspect and hauled him out of his seat and forward into the business class area at the front of the plane. Despite the agonizing burns to his hands, Schuringa tore off the suspect's clothes to check for further explosives. A crew member arrived with a pair of plastic handcuffs and the two of them shackled Abdulmutallab.

Passengers broke into spontaneous applause as Schuringa walked back down the aisle to his seat.

The bomb that failed

Abdulmutallab had tried to detonate around 80 grams (2½ oz) of pentaerythritol tetranitrate (PETN), a crystalline powder from the same

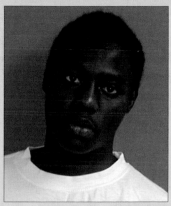

Umar Farouk Abdulmutallab, shown in this booking photograph released by the US Marshals Service on 28 December 2009.

chemical family as nitroglycerin and one of the most powerful of explosives. He had apparently brought the PETN onto the plane in a condom attached to his underwear.

The device on Flight 253 failed to detonate properly but if it had, the cabin depressurization that followed would have been catastrophic, and the stress on the fuselage may have torn the plane apart. Tests have shown that 50 grams (1½ oz) of PETN can blow a hole in the side of an airliner. The bomb that destroyed the Pan Am plane over Lockerbie in 1988 killing 270 people contained PETN.

Into custody

The suspect was kept cuffed and isolated in the forward section as the pilot brought the plane for an emergency landing at Detroit Metropolitan Wayne County Airport. Flight 253 touched down just before 1.00 p.m. local time and Abdulmutallab was instantly arrested. He was then taken to hospital.

Three days later, Al-Qaeda in the Arabian Peninsula (AQAP) claimed responsibility for the attempted bombing. On 6 January 2010, Abdulmutallab was indicted on six criminal charges by a federal grand jury, including attempted use of a weapon of mass destruction and attempted murder.

Jasper Schuringa (left) receives a special medal from Amsterdam deputy mayor Lodewijk Asscher (right) on 21 May 2010.

The Hostages who Fought Back

WHEN THE FREIGHTER *MAERSK ALABAMA* WAS ATTACKED BY HEAVILY
ARMED SOMALI PIRATES, THE CREW SURPRISED THE BANDITS BY FIGHTING
BACK AND GAINING THEIR FREEDOM. THE CAPTAIN WAS HELD HOSTAGE
FOR THREE TENSE DAYS AND MADE A BRAVE ESCAPE ATTEMPT BEFORE A
CLINICAL NAVY SEAL OPERATION KILLED THE PIRATES AND SAVED HIS LIFE.

DATE:
2009

SITUATION:
KIDNAPPED BY PIRATES

**CONDITION OF
CONFINEMENT:**
HELD AT GUNPOINT
ON A SHIP

**DURATION OF
CONFINEMENT:**
4 DAYS

MEANS OF ESCAPE:
CREW RETALIATION;
RESCUE BY NAVY SEALS

NO. OF ESCAPEES:
20

DANGERS:
MURDER, FRIENDLY FIRE

EQUIPMENT:
SHIP'S EQUIPMENT;
SNIPERS' WEAPONS

ABOVE RIGHT
The US *Maersk Alabama* container ship, docked
at the Kenyan coastal sea port of Mombasa.

Lawless waters

Piracy in the Gulf of Aden has been a major threat to international shipping since the late 1990s. Around 30,000 merchant vessels pass through the area, offering rich pickings for bold hijackers. Pirates often use captured vessels as 'mother ships' from which they launch swift assaults using small, high-powered craft. In 2008, there were 111 attacks, including forty-two successful hijackings. As of 11 December 2010, Somali pirates were holding at least thirty-five ships with more than 650 hostages.

Piracy is big business. Ransoms are usually paid, and the money offers pirates a lavish lifestyle otherwise unavailable in one of the poorest countries in the world where the average person earns less than $2 a day.

For merchant sailors it makes the waters of the Gulf of Aden the most dangerous on earth.

The hijacking

On 8 April 2009, the US-registered

Maersk Alabama was halfway through her 3,400 km (2,110 mile) journey from Djibouti to Kenya. Laden with 17,000 metric tons of cargo, of which 5,000 metric tons were relief supplies bound for Somalia, Uganda, and Kenya, the *Alabama* was 240 nautical miles (440 km; 273 miles) southeast of the Somali port of Eyl.

Pirates had already attacked five vessels that week, but the *Alabama* would soon be out of the most dangerous waters. The crew of twenty men could start to look forward to some well-earned time off when they got to Mombasa.

Then their worst nightmare came true. The FV *Win Far 161*, a Taiwanese fishing boat, came into view. Pirates had captured this vessel two days earlier near the Seychelles and the crew of the *Alabama* watched in horror as four heavily armed Somali pirates climbed from the fishing boat into a skiff and started speeding towards them.

The crew fired flares at the pirates, but that didn't scare them off. The bandits quickly boarded the ship. This looked like being a good payday.

Little did the pirates know that this crew was ready to fight back.

Ready for action

The *Alabama's* twenty crew had recently received extensive anti-piracy training: they had practised with small arms and learnt anti-terror tactics, basic safety, first aid and other life-saving measures. They had also run a piracy drill just the day before the incident.

As the four pirates left their skiff and climbed on board the *Alabama*, Chief Engineer Mike Perry and 1st A/E Matt Fisher reacted first, continuously swinging the ship's rudder. This threw up a swell of water, which swamped the pirate skiff and sunk it.

Engineers turn action heroes

Perry sounded the pirate alarm and ushered fourteen crew members into a secure space in the engine room, which the engineers had fortified for just such an occasion. They then used their technical knowledge to bypass the bridge instruments from down

below. Chief Perry took main engine control away from the bridge and Matt Fisher took control of the steering gear. Although the pirates were now on the bridge and had captured Captain Richard Phillips and two other crew members, they couldn't control the ship.

Chief Perry now cut the power to the ship's systems and the entire vessel 'went black'. The pirates were taken by surprise. Their leader, Abduhl Wal-i-Musi, set out to locate the other crew members and force them to hand over control of the vessel. He descended to the engine room. But with the vessel blacked out, he didn't see Chief Perry who was lurking outside the secure room, knife in hand, ready for just such a visit.

Perry pounced and after a dramatic cat and mouse chase in the darkened engine room, he turned the tables on their would-be captor, taking him hostage.

The hostages take control

Frustrated, the three other pirates decided to cut their losses and leave the *Alabama* with Captain Phillips as

a hostage. But since their speedboat had been sunk they were forced to use one of the *Alabama's* lifeboats.

For the next twelve hours the two sides faced each other down. Each had a hostage; an exchange was the logical outcome. The crew duly released their captive but the pirates refused to keep up their end of the bargain. They fled in the lifeboat with Captain Phillips.

Here come the big boys

Meanwhile the US Navy had heard about the incident and was launching a response. The destroyer USS *Bainbridge* and the frigate USS *Halyburton* were dispatched to the Gulf of Aden and reached the *Alabama* early on 9 April.

A guard of eighteen armed men then boarded the *Alabama* and escorted it to its original destination of Mombasa, Kenya. The crew safely disembarked on Saturday 11 April.

Stand off

Now the battle was between the USS *Bainbridge* and the pirates in the lifeboat.

For the next three days, the warship shadowed the lifeboat from a distance of several hundred metres, out of the pirates' range of fire.

Meanwhile the pirates set about extricating themselves from their sticky situation. The tiny 8.5 m (28 ft) lifeboat was covered but it gave them no protection. Captain Phillips was all they had to stop the Americans from blowing them out of the water.

The pirates started negotiating with the captain of the *Bainbridge* by satellite phone, asking for a ransom and also trying to buy time. They were also calling some of their comrades in other seized ships to come and help them get Phillips to Somalia. That would make it tricky for the Americans and would strengthen the bandits' hand.

On 10 April Captain Phillips made a gutsy attempt to escape from the lifeboat. He was only recaptured

The USS *Bainbridge* tows the lifeboat from the *Maersk Alabama* to the USS *Boxer* (in background) to be processed for evidence after the successful rescue of Captain Richard Phillips.

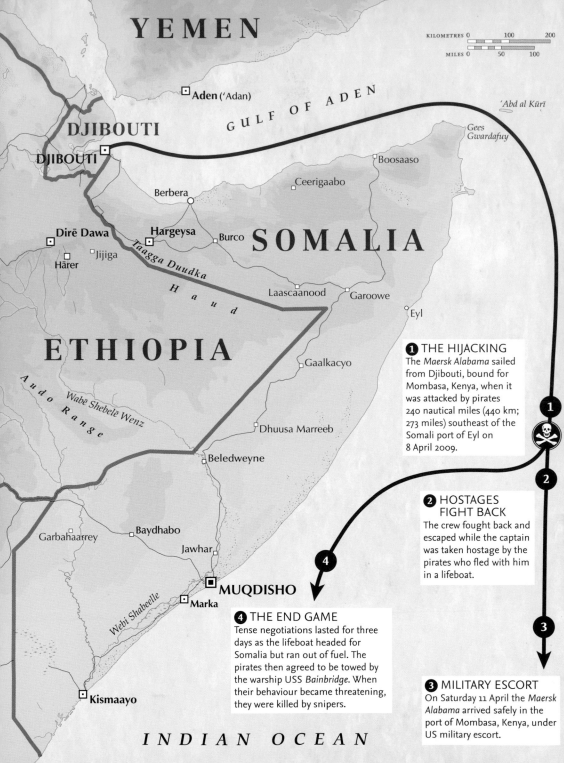

YEMEN

Aden ('Adan)

GULF OF ADEN

'Abd al Kūrī

Gees
Gwardafuy

DJIBOUTI

DJIBOUTI

Berbera

Boosaaso

Ceerigaabo

Dirē Dawa

Hargeysa

Burco

SOMALIA

Jijiga

Hārer

Taagga Duudka

Haud

Laascaanood

Garoowe

Eyl

ETHIOPIA

Audo Range

Wabē Shebelē Wenz

Gaalkacyo

1 THE HIJACKING
The *Maersk Alabama* sailed
from Djibouti, bound for
Mombasa, Kenya, when it
was attacked by pirates
240 nautical miles (440 km;
273 miles) southeast of the
Somali port of Eyl on
8 April 2009.

Dhuusa Marreeb

Beledweyne

1

2

2 HOSTAGES
FIGHT BACK
The crew fought back and
escaped while the captain
was taken hostage by the
pirates who fled with him
in a lifeboat.

4

Garbahaarrey

Baydhabo

Jawhar

MUQDISHO

Marka

4 THE END GAME
Tense negotiations lasted for three
days as the lifeboat headed for
Somalia but ran out of fuel. The
pirates then agreed to be towed by
the warship USS *Bainbridge*. When
their behaviour became threatening,
they were killed by snipers.

3

Webi Shabeelle

3 MILITARY ESCORT
On Saturday 11 April the *Maersk
Alabama* arrived safely in the
port of Mombasa, Kenya, under
US military escort.

Kismaayo

INDIAN OCEAN

when his captors fired shots over his head. This ratcheted up the tension in the lifeboat and just after dawn on Saturday one of the pirates fired on the USS *Halyburton*. No one was hurt but it marked a turning point in the drama.

> ❢ We are safe and we are not afraid of the Americans. We will defend ourselves if attacked. ❢
> **The pirate leader**

Hard bargaining

The pirates continued to demand a $2 million ransom for Phillips but now the Americans started playing hardball: they refused point blank to even discuss the demand. The pirates' situation grew increasingly desperate. They had used a satellite phone to call fellow pirates on other captured ships in the area to come and rescue them. But the sight of the US warship had scared these bandits off. The four men were on their own in the lifeboat.

The pirates then dropped their demand for money; they would release Phillips in return for their own freedom. The Americans refused that too.

One of the pirates, Abduhl Wal-i-Musi, had had enough. When the Americans sent a small craft to deliver food to the lifeboat, he deserted his comrades and jumped into the other boat as it came alongside.

As the harsh equatorial sun burnt down the lifeboat ran out of fuel and started drifting. The sea began to get choppy.

The commander of the *Bainbridge* offered the pirates a tow. They had no option but to accept. They secured the 60 m (200 ft) line thrown out by sailors on the *Bainbridge* to the lifeboat. Perhaps they could hold out a little longer and persuade their comrades to come in and rescue them.

What they didn't know was that US President Obama had authorised the use of force to free Phillips if his

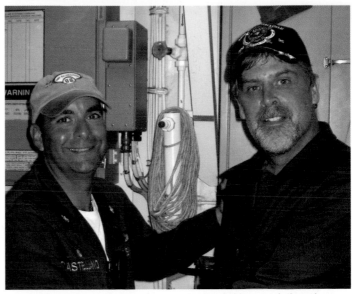

Captain Richard Phillips *(right)* master of the cargo ship *Maersk Alabama*, stands alongside US Navy Commander Frank Castellano *(left)*, commanding officer of the USS *Bainbridge*, after being rescued by US Naval Forces off the coast of Somalia.

life was in danger. A team of Navy SEAL snipers had been parachuted into the water nearby on Friday night and secretly brought on board the *Bainbridge*. Now they were ready to take action.

Endgame

The pirates were getting increasingly jumpy. As night fell on Sunday 12 April one of them loosed a tracer round toward the US warship. Another hijacker could be seen holding his Kalashnikov close to Phillips's chest. The commander of the *Bainbridge* thought he looked ready to use the weapon. He gave the kill order.

There were three snipers hidden on the stern of the warship, each one of whom trained his weapon on a separate pirate. Using night sights, they were waiting until all three of them had a clear shot. The *Bainbridge* was relatively stable but the tiny lifeboat was bobbing around. Inch by inch, the tow-rope connecting the two vessels was shortened. The lifeboat was now less than 40 m

(131 ft) from the stern of the warship. The snipers kept waiting for their opportunity. At last, two of the pirates could be seen in the door of the covered lifeboat and the third could be seen through a window guarding the bound hostage – the sharpshooters opened fire simultaneously.

The three pirates were killed instantly with clean headshots.

The SEALs then hauled themselves along the tow-rope to the lifeboat to rescue Phillips, who was unharmed.

The last pirate

Abduhl Wal-i-Musi was taken to New York to face trial. He pleaded guilty and on 16 February 2011 was sentenced to 33 years, 9 months in prison.

> ❢ I share the country's admiration for the bravery of Captain Phillips and his selfless concern for his crew. His courage is a model for all Americans. ❢
> **US President Barack Obama**

INDEX

BIBLIOGRAPHY

The Jungle Is Neutral	**F. Spencer Chapman**	The Reprint Society, 1950
117 Days Adrift	**Maurice and Maralyn Bailey**	Adlard Coles Nautical, 1992
Touching The Void	**Joe Simpson**	Pan Books, 1989
Papillon	**Henri Charrière**	Harper Perennial, 2005
Incredible Journeys	**Thomas Cussans**	Collins & Brown, 2007
Great Escapes	**Ian Crofton**	Quercus, 2009
Skeletons on the Zahara	**Dean King**	Arrow Books, 2005
Seven Years in Tibet	**Heinrich Harrer**	Harper Perennial, 2005
Alive: The Story of the Andes Survivors	**Piers Paul Read**	J.B. Lippincott Company, 1974
Adrift: 76 Days Lost At Sea	**Steven Callahan**	Houghton Mifflin Company, 1986
The Edge of the Sword	**Anthony Farrar-Hockley**	Frederick Muller, 1954

CREDITS

182 Shutterstock © turtleman
183 Shutterstock © Vladimir Melnik
184 Shutterstock © Daniel Gilbey Photography
186 Shutterstock © patrimonio designs limited **symbol**
188 Shutterstock © Eric Isselée
189 Corbis © Wolfgang Kaehler/CORBIS
190 Shutterstock © patrimonio designs limited **symbol**
191 Corbis © Bettmann/CORBIS
192 © Brodie Collection, La Trobe Picture Collection, State Library of Victoria.
193 Shutterstock © sabri deniz kizil **symbol**
194 Corbis © Bettmann/CORBIS
195 Corbis © CORBIS
196 Shutterstock / © Bojanovic **symbol**
197 Alamy © John Warburton-Lee Photography / Alamy
198 Shutterstock © BlueOrange Studio
199 Shutterstock / © patrimonio designs limited **symbol**
200 Shutterstock © Leonux
201 Shutterstock © patrimonio designs limited **symbol**
202 Shutterstock © patrimonio designs limited **symbol**
204 Shutterstock © vladoskan
205 Corbis © Bettmann/CORBIS
205 Shutterstock © James A Dawson
206 Shutterstock © patrimonio designs limited **symbol**
207 Shutterstock © Martin Spurny
208 Shutterstock © Alessandro Vigano'
210 Shutterstock © valkos **symbol**
211 Getty © Keystone/Hulton Archive/Getty Images
212 Shutterstock © bpatt81
213 Getty © Graham Wood/Evening Standard/Getty Images
214 Shutterstock © SecondShot
216 Shutterstock © patrimonio designs limited **symbol**
217 Getty © Les Lee/Express/Getty Images
218 Shutterstock © jefras
219 Shutterstock © maigi
220 Shutterstock © patrimonio designs limited **symbol**
221 Shutterstock © stephan kerkhofs
221 Shutterstock © Pack-Shot
222 Shutterstock © holbox
223 Shutterstock © Darius Daubaras
224 Alamy © niceartphoto / Alamy
225 Shutterstock © Iakov Filimonov
226 Shutterstock © patrimonio designs limited **symbol**
227 Shutterstock © John Clark
228 Shutterstock © Bobkeenan Photography
230 Shutterstock © diak
231 Getty © AFP/Getty Images
232 Getty © AFP/Getty Images
233 Corbis © Corbis/Corbis
233 Corbis © Najlah Feanny/CORBIS SABA
234 Getty © AFP/Getty Images
235 Corbis © Stamberg/epa/Corbis
235 Getty © Getty Images
236 Shutterstock © Naiyyer

237 Alamy © Robert Harding Picture Library Ltd / Alamy
238 Shutterstock © Christos Georghiou **symbol**
239 Getty © Barcroft Media via Getty Images
240 Corbis © DANIEL MUNOZ/Reuters/Corbis
241 Corbis © Pascale Mariani/Romeo Langlois/Corbis
242 Corbis © Pascale Mariani/Romeo Langlois/Corbis
243 Corbis © HO/Reuters/Corbis
244 Shutterstock © okicoki **symbol**
245 Corbis © Carlos Ortega/epa/Corbis
246 Wikipedia © Robert Smith **personal**
247 Shutterstock © sydcinema
248 Corbis © BOB STRONG/Reuters/Corbis
249 Getty © Getty Images
250 Shutterstock © Maksym Dragunov
251 Corbis © EVERT ELZINGA/epa/Corbis
251 Corbis © HO/Reuters/Corbis
252 Corbis © Antony Njuguna/Reuters/Corbis
253 Corbis © Ho/Reuters/Corbis
254 Shutterstock © megastocker **symbol**
255 Corbis © U.S. Navy/Handout/CNP/Corbis

Maps © Collins Bartholomew Ltd 2011

All mapping in this publication is generated from Collins Bartholomew digital databases.
Collins Bartholomew, the UK's leading independent geographical information supplier, can provide a digital, custom, and premium mapping service to a variety of markets.
For further information:
Tel: +44 (0) 141 306 3606
e-mail: **collinsbartholomew@harpercollins.co.uk**
or visit our website at: **www.collinsbartholomew.com**

If you would like to comment on any aspect of this book, please write to:
Collins Maps, HarperCollins Publishers, Westerhill Road, Bishopbriggs, Glasgow G64 2QT
e-mail: **collinsmaps@harpercollins.co.uk**
or visit our website at: **www.collinsmaps.com**
twitter.com/CollinsMaps